Debates, Differences, and Divisions

THE 25 ISSUES THAT SHAPE AMERICAN POLITICS

Michael Kryzanek
Bridgewater State College

Routledge
Taylor & Francis Group

LONDON AND NEW YORK

First published 2011 by Pearson Education, Inc.

Published 2016 by Routledge
2 Park Square, Milton Park, Abingdon, Oxon OX14 4RN
711 Third Avenue, New York, NY 10017, USA

Routledge is an imprint of the Taylor & Francis Group, an informa business

Credits and acknowledgments borrowed from other sources and reproduced, with permission, in this textbook appear on the appropriate page within the text.

ISBN : 9780205617647 (pbk)

Cover Designer: Bruce Kenselaar
Cover Image: iStock © aklionka

Library of Congress Cataloging-in-Publication Data

Kryzanek, Michael.
Debates, differences, and divisions : the 25 issues that shape American politics / Michael Kryanek.—1st ed.
     p. cm.
  Includes bibliographical references and index.
  ISBN-13: 978-0-205-61764-7
  ISBN-10: 0-205-61764-6
  1. Political planning—United States. 2. United States—Politics and government. I. Title.
  JK468.P64K78 2011
  320.60973—dc22

                                                                2010014169

To Grace Irene Sabo

from

Your Dziadziu

CONTENTS

Preface vii

About the Author ix

Introduction 1

Chapter 1 **Homeland Security** 15

Chapter 2 **The Terrorists** 31

Chapter 3 **Global Warming and Climate Change** 45

Chapter 4 **Health Care and Health Care Reform** 59

Chapter 5 **Illegal Immigration** 74

Chapter 6 **Taxing and Spending** 88

Chapter 7 **Social Security and Medicare** 103

Chapter 8 **Race Relations and Civil Rights** 116

Chapter 9 **Reforming Education** 129

Chapter 10 **Abortion Rights** 142

Chapter 11 **Gun Rights** 155

Chapter 12 **Gay Rights** 168

Chapter 13 **Capital Punishment** 180

Chapter 14 **Money and Politics** 192

Chapter 15 **Religion and Politics** 205

Chapter 16 **Science and Politics** 218

Chapter 17 **The Drug War** 231

Chapter 18 **Energy Use and Energy Conservation** 244

Chapter 19 **Poverty and Social Welfare** 258

Chapter 20 **National Defense** 271

Chapter 21   **Iraq and Afghanistan   284**

Chapter 22   **Iran   297**

Chapter 23   **China   310**

Chapter 24   **Israel and Palestine   323**

Chapter 25   **Globalization   336**

The Great Recession   348
Index   361

PREFACE

There are various ways to study American politics. There is the traditional institutional approach, in which the Constitution and the three branches of government are explained and analyzed in order to better understand the foundation upon which American democracy has been built. Then there is the policy or process approach, which accents the way the political system works from the initial inputs or demands of the citizenry all the way through the final outputs or policies. There have also been approaches to the study of American politics that stress the importance of examining the role of elites, groups and key players who influence the final outcomes of government policy making. All of these approaches are excellent explanatory methods for making what is arguably one of the most complex and complicated political systems in place in the world today.

However, there is also another approach to understanding American politics that serves as the basis for this book. American politics is driven and shaped in large part by a wealth of issues that reflect the ideas, the principles, the concerns, the fears, the morals and the hopes of the American people. Issues in many respects are the heart and soul of the American political system; the institutions of government respond to the issues; the process of policy making is a response to the issues and the elites, groups and players all seek to influence the manner in which the issues are addressed and resolved. There would be no American politics without issues, and without issues there would be nothing for the American people to complain about and demand that their elected representatives do something about.

Because the issue universe in American politics is so pervasive and critical to the functioning of American democracy, it is natural that there will be arguments over how best to deal with these matters. Many of the issues that make their way to the front burner of American politics are entangled in controversy and filled with pro and con positions. The fact that they are political issues means that they stimulate intense partisan pressures. As a result, it is accurate to state that the political issues in American politics foster debate, differences and divisions and that these issues often shape the agenda, the policy process and the political fortunes of politicians and political parties. Moreover, because many of these issues percolate from the American public through polls, organized campaigns or direct contact with public officials, they also foster debate, differences and divisions within the country at large.

This book, *Debates, Differences, and Divisions: The 25 Issues That Shape American Politics*, is thus designed to describe not just the key issues currently at the center of the national political arena, but to present the positions of both sides; the pros and cons that form the arguments and serve as the basis for the disagreements that drive the political system to action. Each of these issues is what political pundits often describe as hot button, which means they are important to the life and future of the country and they create ongoing ideological and partisan discussion. Each of the issues is presented in a similar format, with a section on background, a description of the issue from the various sides of the debate and the sources of the differences and the divisions that have been caused by those differences. Each issue also has key quotes from those leaders associated with the debate, along with important data and information that further illustrate the debates, the differences and the divisions. Finally, each chapter concludes with a debate topic, some critical thinking questions, key Internet sites to visit and helpful books to read.

Debates, Differences, and Divisions: The 25 Issues That Shape American Politics has been a joy to write and in many respects is the result of over thirty years of teaching American Politics to college undergraduates. Their questions, their concerns and their arguments have shown me that presenting American politics from the issue perspective is an excellent learning tool. This book is also the result of regular conversations with my colleagues in the political science department at Bridgewater State College. Whether in the hallways or over coffee or during colloquia, my colleagues have unknowingly stimulated my interest in the issues that shape American politics. Just like my students, I owe my colleagues a debt of gratitude. Of course working on a book requires enormous time away from family, and I am grateful to my wife Carol for her patience and support. I am also thankful for our three daughters, Laura, Kathy and Ann, and one son-in-law, Jim, who always would ask, "How's the book coming?" reminding me that I had a cheering section on my side. Keeping it all in the family, this book is dedicated to our first granddaughter, Grace Irene Sabo from her Dziadziu, which is Polish for grandfather. I also want to recognize Eric Stano at Longman for his enthusiastic support for this book and his faith that it had potential and also the anonymous reviewers who were enormously helpful with their suggestions. A debt of gratitude goes out to Aparna Yellai for her superb editing and production skills. Finally, I want to thank you the reader for picking up the book and hopefully benefiting from my research and analysis of these important issues. I hope I have been a help.

Michael Kryzanek
Summer 2010
Whitman, Massachusetts

ABOUT THE AUTHOR

Michael Kryzanek is Professor of Political Science and Executive Director of the Center for International Engagement at Bridgewater State College in Massachusetts. He is the author of several books on American politics, U.S. foreign policy and Latin American politics. Dr. Kryzanek is the founding editor of *Bridgewater Review*, the faculty research journal of Bridgewater State. He has been the recipient of numerous awards while at Bridgewater, including the DiNardo Award for Excellence in Teaching and the Lifetime Achievement Award. Dr. Kryzanek resides in Whitman, Massachusetts with his wife Carol and is the father of three daughters.

INTRODUCTION

Alexis de Tocqueville, the famous observer of American life during his journeys in the United States in the 1830s, said the following about the way Americans as a people approach politics:

> The political activity that pervades the United States must be seen in order to be understood. No sooner do you set foot upon American ground than you are stunned by a kind of tumult. . . . It is impossible to spend more effort in the pursuit of happiness.[1]

Tumult is indeed an appropriate word to describe the political environment in the United States as Americans express their opinions, advance their causes and seek to bring change. The issue arena in the American political system is expansive and dynamic, with a range of highly charged concerns that often reflect a public that has firm beliefs and passionate resolve. It is not an exaggeration to claim that the United States as a nation is in a constant state of political debate as Americans air their differences and accent their divisions with stunning regularity.

Throughout U.S. political history, Americans have taken great pride in the fact that despite differences over critical and emotional issues, compromise and consensus prevail and partisan and ideological disagreements fade as all the parties to a policy dispute come together and support the agreed-upon solution. However, in recent years compromise and consensus have been overshadowed by unbending intransigence among issue proponents and policy gridlock in the halls of Congress. Not only has the issue arena become overheated with more and more areas of concern and citizen demands making their way into the governing arena, but politics has become a relentless campaign to push and pull government toward specific policy goals. In many cases there is little room for compromise and consensus, but rather two rival camps poised for complete victory rather than "half a loaf." When a law is passed, executive order issued or a judicial decision rendered, there is often little sense of finality as both issue camps dig in their heels and continue their campaigns for total victory.

Much has been made of the issue tensions and confrontations that mark contemporary American politics. The operative phrase today is that America is a *divided nation*–Democrats versus Republicans, red states versus blue states, conservatives versus liberals, evangelicals versus seculars. At the core of the divisions stirring up the political pot are the issues, which serve as the focus of partisan debates and define electoral differences. In the era of the Internet, mass media and sophisticated marketing strategies, Americans are bombarded with partisan blogs, competing talk radio shows, 24/7 cable news programs and direct mail campaigns, all designed to inform but also to infuriate as they seek to build a case for a particular issue perspective. Although the vast majority of Americans stay on the fringes of these issue divisions, those who do take an interest have plenty of ammunition to solidify their positions and advance their causes.[2]

It is important to state that the view of a "divided America" is not without its skeptics and detractors. On many issues, polling data point to a broad public consensus, or at least an apathetic reluctance to be drawn into a debate about differences. American politics may not be so much divided, so the argument goes, as held captive by partisan ideologues and issue proponents who have effectively captured the national consciousness while the vast silent majority remains on the side lines. For example, in recent years, especially during the Obama administration, there has been a disturbing unwillingness of Democrats and Republicans to find common ground. American party politics has traditionally been defined by a fundamental sameness with policy differences relatively minor and national debates offering few significant electoral alternatives. Even today, despite the posturing and intransigence of the two parties, the politics of the center and moderation still have relevance in American politics, despite the passion that can surround a particular issue. The claim is made that all this talk of constant debates, irreparable differences and deep divisions is the stuff of ideologues controlling the political dialogue in the United States and the media pumping up the political noise, all in an effort to gain attention.[3]

The key to understanding the current political landscape of American politics and the impact of critical issues on the governing process and decision making is to develop a picture of the American people. What are the characteristics of national life that best defines them? What do they stand for or believe in? Are there any generalizations about American national life that can be made with a degree of certainty? This is of course an enormously broad series of questions that are not easily answered. However, some measures of American national life can help us better understand the American public and thereby give us some clues about the issue environment that is created from these characteristics, beliefs and generalizations.

One approach is to develop a demographic profile of the American people, basically a data-driven snapshot that describes who they are. In 2006 the Congressional Research Service of the Library of Congress issued a study entitled "The Changing Demographic Profile of the United States." The study showed that the United States is a nation of approximately 298.6 million people, making it the third-largest population globally with about 4.6% of the world's population (the population of the United States in 2009 was estimated to be 310 million). Population growth in the United States has increased by

85% since 1950, a considerable increase compared to other industrial countries such as Germany and Italy, which have experienced meager population growth. Although fertility and mortality rates have remained fairly constant over time, the impact of immigration has had a profound effect on population increases in the United States, and immigration is projected to be the key to population growth well into the remainder of this century.[4]

However, more than the overall population numbers, the study concluded that besides becoming bigger, Americans are also becoming older. The study found that since the 1950s the United States has been involved in a "profound demographic change: rapid population aging." In 1950 the population of the United States was represented by a pyramid with the wide base composed of young people and the tip the older Americans, whereas by 2050 the pyramid is predicted to become a rectangle as more and more seniors, who are part of the baby-boomer generation, live longer. By 2050 it is estimated that one in every five people in the United States will be sixty-five or older.

The other key finding of the Congressional Research Service study was that America is becoming racially and ethnically diverse. As a result of immigration and higher fertility rates among non-whites, American society is changing and will continue to change in terms of its racial and ethnic makeup. Currently 81% of Americans responded in U.S. Census questionnaires that they are white, followed by 12.6% African-American and 3.7% Asian American. The important conclusion of the study was that the percentages of African-Americans and Asian Americans are expected to increase significantly in the coming decades and Hispanic Americans will likely be viewed as a unique racial/ethnic group. The 81% white-American figure, for example, does not reflect the Hispanic population, which the U.S. Census Bureau does not currently recognize as a separate racial category. Americans of Hispanic origin are thus grouped with the white population. However, when separated out from the white category, Census data show that 36 million people can be identified as Hispanic or about 12.6% of the population. In real terms African-Americans, Hispanic Americans and Asian Americans make up almost a third of the current population in the United States. Census projections point to white Americans becoming a minority around the year 2042.

This demographic picture of the American people has profound implications for issue formation and policy development in the coming years. Because of an expanding, aging and diverse population, concerns over Social Security, health care policy, intergenerational distribution of governmental resources, immigration and racial and ethnic integration are certain to rise to the top levels of the national issue agenda. Government will face enormous pressure from these groups and the general public over how to address the challenges that will emanate from the changing demographic profile of American society. Because many of these issues will require the setting of budget priorities and dealing with highly sensitive race, ethnic and class relationships, the changing character of America's population is a critical ingredient in shaping national politics.

Another means of better understanding the political landscape of American politics and the link to important policy issues is to examine the national electorate. How Americans vote and the reasons behind their votes give powerful clues to defining public opinion. To get a better understanding of the political landscape and issue formation in American politics, the results of the 2008 presidential election are quite informative and helpful. Exit polls of American voters were compiled by CNN after the 2008 electoral victory of Barack Obama over John McCain. The exit poll results were broken down into a number of categories that sought to define the American electorate. Some of these categories provide clues to the core elements of the political landscape and the driving forces behind current issues.[5]

One of the important categories of the exit polls was the ideological definition of the American voter. In the CNN poll 22% of the respondents defined themselves as Liberals, 34% said they were Conservatives and 44% placed themselves in the middle of political spectrum as Moderates. Although Liberal, Conservative and Moderate are political labels that have imprecise meanings, it is safe to state that Liberals are in general supportive of government action to solve national problems and value personal freedom and privacy rights. Conservatives have generally been associated with smaller government and government deregulation of business, less taxation and a strong defense posture in the world. Moderates, as the word suggests, are somewhere in between Liberals and Conservatives, meaning that they may see some benefit from government action and regulation, support some but not all personal freedom and privacy issues and are cautious about but not rigidly opposed to government taxation and spending.

Clearly from the exit poll results on the ideological positions of the American voter, the Moderates are the dominant force in the political arena, balancing off the Liberal left and the Conservative right. The fact that the Liberals come in third in the exit poll and represent only about a quarter of the electorate suggests that support for big government solutions to national problems and the extension of personal freedom and privacy to ever-widening segments of American society is not fully in the mainstream of American thinking. Conservatives, although still behind the Moderates, represent a third of the electorate and provide a more substantial voice to their views on the limited role of government and the need to keep taxes low and protect the corporate and defense sectors of American national life. However, the Moderates, those Americans in the center of the political life in the United States, define the national electorate. Some would say that the Moderates are indecisive and uncommitted, whereas others will accent the fact that the Moderates are merely in the great traditions of compromise and consensus as they seek a middle road. However, the influence the Moderates have in American electoral politics means that political candidates must shape their positions on a range of national issues that use to the center of the ideological spectrum.[6]

The CNN exit poll also provided a list of the American electorate's concerns during the 2004 election. The list of issue concerns often provides another clue about what is going on among the electorate in terms of their policy positions, their values and their vision. In the CNN poll the five most important issue concerns in rank order were moral values with a 22%

response, the economy and jobs with a 20% response, terrorism with 19%, the war in Iraq with 15% and health care with 8%. *Moral values* was not defined, but it did suggest that Americans at that time were concerned over matters such as the character, integrity and honesty of government leaders and wanted government policy to have a moral base. The economy and jobs, which are traditionally at or near the top of the issue priority list, reflected the voters' ingrained concern that the elected president will have a significant impact on the status and direction of the national economy. The war in Iraq and terrorism reveal the changing nature of the issue landscape in America since 9/11 and the invasion of Iraq in 2003. Americans are now more focused on matters of national security and homeland defense and war, which is natural, considering the threats that terrorists continue to make against the United States and the concerns over the war in Iraq. Finally, the domestic agenda issue of health care showed that a critical problem in American society was on the minds of voters. In fact, health care outdistanced education and taxes, the perennial top-tier issue concerns in past presidential elections.[7]

Four years later in 2008 the American public was thinking differently about what mattered to them on the national issue agenda. In a CBS/*New York Times* poll in summer 2008 the list of top issues were the economy and jobs, gas and heating oil costs, the war in Iraq, the environment and health care. When compared to similar polls in 2007 and 2006 the war in Iraq moved down the list of key issues to be replaced with economic issues and concerns such as health care. It is important to note that by the time the election was held in November, the American people, facing the prospect of a economic meltdown, were thoroughly focused on the faltering economy and thinking almost exclusively about pocketbook issues and financial security.

It is also important to point out that examining issue politics through demographic data, ideological positions or polling priorities provides the popular side of the American political landscape. What is just as important, if not crucial, to understanding the way issues drive politics and government in the United States is the professional side of issue politics, namely the influence that special interest groups play in setting the policy agenda and shaping the final outcome of public decision making.

The process of American politics is increasingly driven by the interest group sector, which is not only large and ever-expanding, but also enormously powerful with a range of influence tools at its disposal to sway government. From campaign funds to small armies of expert staff members and lobbyists to sophisticated public relations and marketing strategies, today's interest group is a formidable participant in the governing process. Many of the issues discussed in this book are championed by huge interest group organizations that have the capacity to inundate Congress and the Executive Branch with email, mobilize grassroots demonstrations and spend money lavishly on Internet, television, newspaper and radio advertising and commercials. The old adage about one person fighting city hall and single-handedly bringing about change is rarely achieved in the United States; the politics of change is now the domain of a well-financed interest group that fights city hall or Congress or the president, and many times wins.

Special interests that act to advance specific issues or issue agendas come in many shapes and sizes. Economic groups such as the U.S. Chamber of Commerce (representing the business sector) and the AFL-CIO (the American Federation of Labor–Congress of Industrial Organization, the major labor organization) are concerned with a broad range of issues. The Chamber may concentrate on tax, trade and regulation issues, but may also weigh in on issues such as immigration reform and affirmative action in hiring. The AFL-CIO not only would concentrate on labor rights and safety issues, but also be involved on issues such as the impact of globalization on job security and energy independence. Professional groups such as the American Medical Association, which represents doctors, concentrate their efforts on health care reform and stem cell research, whereas the National Education Association, which is the primary group lobbying for teachers, speaks for its membership on education issues such as testing and teacher standards related to the No Child Left Behind Act. Also important are social groups, such as the American Association of Retired Persons (AARP), the largest interest group operating in the political arena, which naturally is concerned with Social Security and Medicare as well as pocketbook issues such as the cost of energy.

Despite the reputation of Americans as a nation that does not vote with great frequency (the United States is at the bottom of the list of voter participation, usually just ahead of Switzerland), Americans are joiners of groups, advocates of causes, avid volunteers and generous givers to charities. Much of this participation is at the local level and usually involves issues or concerns that are not national in scope or controversial in nature. However, when it comes to political issues that galvanize public opinion and energize the American people, there is an ever-growing and highly competitive interest-group sector with as many as 30,000 registered organizations and millions of dues-paying members seeking to influence the government and shape public opinion. These interest groups are part of what has come to be called a pluralistic society, as competing groups representing critical issues seek to change the political landscape of American society. This competition was viewed by the early founders such as James Madison as a check on the likely excesses of the majority, but in contemporary times the explosion of interest groups advocating for particular issues or causes has fostered a political climate best described as a series of constant debates with passionate differences and often causing deep divisions.

On the Record

James Madison, outlining his political philosophy and the impact of factions (groups) on the American system in Federalist #10, said the following:

> The latent causes of faction are thus sown in the nature of man; and we see them everywhere brought into different degrees of activity,

according to the different circumstances of civil society. A zeal for different opinions concerning religion, concerning government, and many other points, as well as of speculation as of practice; an attachment to different leaders ambitiously contending for preeminence and power; or to persons of other descriptions whose fortunes have been interesting to the human passions, have, in turn, divided mankind into parties, inflamed them with mutual animosity and rendered them much more disposed to vex and oppress each other, than to cooperate for the common good.

These so-called umbrella groups that address a wide range of national issues are also joined by single issue groups that, as defined, direct their energies and resources toward achieving a specific issue objective. The National Rifle Association has for years been one of the most effective groups active in national government as it zealously protects Second Amendment rights against any legislation that would limit gun ownership. The highly contentious abortion issue has fostered a number of active groups such as Planned Parenthood, a strong supporter of abortion rights, and National Right to Life Committee the primary anti-abortion organization. Racial and ethnic groups have also formed to champion issues critical to their constituencies. African-Americans are represented by the National Association of Colored People (NAACP) as they seek government programs to address poverty and welfare reform, whereas the Hispanic community is led by League of United Latin American Citizens (LULAC), which has been in the forefront of the challenges to immigration reform and discrimination against legal and illegal migrants. Finally, numerous groups have been formed in recent years that advocate on behalf of conservation and environmental preservation. Groups such as the Sierra Club and the National Resources Defense Council are active in the areas of global warming, pollution and energy independence.

FYI

In 2002 *Fortune* magazine listed the top twenty-five most influential interests groups in the United States. The list, in order of influence, is given here:

1. National Rifle Association
2. American Association of Retired People
3. National Federation of Independent Business
4. American Israel Foreign Affairs Committee (now American Israel Public Affairs Committee)
5. Association of Trial Lawyers of America
6. AFL-CIO

(continued)

FYI   (continued)

7. Chamber of Commerce of the United States
8. National Beer Wholesalers of America
9. National Association of Realtors
10. National Association of Manufacturers
11. National Association of Homebuilders of the United States
12. American Medical Association
13. American Hospital Association
14. National Education Association of the United States
15. American Farm Bureau Federation
16. Motion Picture Association of America
17. National Association of Broadcasters
18. National Right to Life Committee
19. Health Insurance Association of America
20. National Restaurant Association
21. National Governors' Association
22. Recording Industry Association of America
23. American Bankers Association
24. Pharmaceutical Research and Manufacturers of America
25. International Brotherhood of Teamsters

Source: Fortune

American politics is dominated by the twenty-five issues that make up this book, and government is often embroiled in policy debates over these key issues. However, just about every facet of national life has an organization advocating for a particular cause or objective. From the Tobacco Institute and the National Whiskey Distillers Council to the Gay and Lesbian Alliance and the National Organization for Women, the issue arena is highly specialized and ever-changing. It is thus no wonder that the American political system suffers from issue overload as it is bombarded by public opinion, lobbyists and well-organized campaigns all designed to get the attention of governmental leaders, all passionate about advancing their particular issue through the maze of national decision making.[8]

The connection between the issues that dominate American politics and the maze of government is an essential part of the policy process in the United States. The Founding Fathers purposely did not make it easy for a specific issue concern to be transformed into public policy. Not only is government divided into three competing and powerful governing bodies, but within those governing bodies there are numerous institutional checks and balances, partisan roadblocks, state and federal turf wars and bureaucratic wrangling. Taking an issue through this maze often takes years, suffers many setbacks and delays and endures inevitable compromises that are the result of fierce bargaining and political deal making. Foreign observers of the American political system often wonder how anything gets done within this maze. In fact James Bryce, a British observer, wrote in 1888 that "there is in the American government . . . a want of unity. The Sailors, the helmsman, the engineer, do not seem to have one purpose or obey one will so that instead of making steady way the vessel may pursue a devious or zigzag course, and sometime merely turn round and round in the water."[9]

The sailing analogy Bryce used that suggests that the American political system is often adrift, or at least moving in different directions, accurately depicts the challenges faced by proponents of a particular issue. Unlike parliamentary systems in which government is based on party majority and disciplined voting, the American presidential system with its separation of powers cannot guarantee that a political promise made to a specific issue constituency can be translated into a public policy. The American political system is a captive of a contentious confluence of party, group, public opinion, money and media, all contributing to what Bryce called "a want of unity" and leading to that zigzagging and frequent turning "round and round in the water." As we will see, issues such as immigration reform, gun legislation, global warming and energy initiatives have suffered the fate of endless delay and legislative death because the American political system is not designed to be efficient, speedy and effective.

Political scientists have attempted to make sense of the American political system and the issues and their proponents and opponents who seek to zigzag through the troubled waters of the policy process. Although the core steps in the traditional policy process model of American politics may vary a bit and have different titles, there is general consensus about the following stages in the way the American political system transforms problems into possible solutions:

Setting the political policy stage

Identifying the problem

Getting the problem on the national political agenda

Developing a policy prescription

Making the policy into law

Implementing the policy

Evaluating the policy

Data Bank

There are twenty-three separate ways to delay or kill a bill in the U.S. legislative process.

Before the policy process even begins, it is essential to recognize the values, the beliefs, the behavior patterns, the prejudices and the fears that exist within the character of the American public and the American institutions that will shape the manner in which national issues and national problems are handled. When the American public expresses its views on a particular issue directly to government officials or in a larger public opinion forum, that expression is often influenced by the dominant public culture in the United States at the time. For example, the political culture of the United States has often been described as fundamentally based on personal freedom, individualism and inalienable rights. Therefore an issue such as abortion would likely be framed by the American people in terms of this culture of freedom, individualism and rights – the rights of a woman to control her body versus the right of the fetus that is in her body.

The American political culture, however, is not just about freedom, individualism and rights; there are other aspects at work in the political environment that can shape the feedback of the people. The American political culture is also one that is guided by principles associated with equality, fairness, tolerance and community spirit. Therefore matters related to race relations are profoundly influenced by these values and beliefs as proponents of policies such as affirmative action and gay rights, which are designed to protect or enhance racial and gender fairness, accent this aspect of American national political culture.

For the policy process to begin in earnest and move toward some action, the American people have to show that they are concerned or angry about what they see around them and make a demand on government. This can be in the form of a letter or email to an elected representative, conversational links on Internet sites related to the issue, interest group pressure or demonstrations that seek to bring further attention to the issue. Government institutions and the political leaders who run those institutions do not respond to mere talk or random complaining, but if they see that a particular issue has wide interest and that there is a growing demand for action, they are forced to pay attention. Politicians read public opinion polls regularly and many of their actions related to pressing national issues are the result of listening to the people, or more likely influential lobbyists.

No list of issue demands, however, gets anywhere in the American political system without key elites becoming involved. Political party leaders and activists, think-tank experts, congressional committee staffers and interest group lobbyists are the keys to taking the public demand forward. An issue needs institutional or organizational representation to provide it with the lift necessary to carry it through and around the obstacle course, that is the complicated American governing process. Political parties and their connection to elections and control of the governing institutions of the Congress and the presidency are critical supports. Party leaders and activists can make a particular issue a priority and champion a cause as a way of winning votes and expanding power. Think tanks provide the brain power to assist decision makers in seeing the costs and benefits and the strengths and weaknesses of a proposed policy. Congressional committee staffs know the ins and outs of the legislative process and are key advisors to their bosses, who will eventually cast a vote on the proposed policy. And finally, interest groups and their professional lobbyists are vital players in the process because as professional advocates they can provide the organizational tools necessary to carry the issue through the process.

Called by some the black box of decision making (better known as government), it is where national issues become captive to the complexities of the American policy-making system. As stated earlier, nothing runs smoothly in American government, and more than likely issues will end up zigging and zagging their way through extended Congressional hearings, bitter partisan battles, frequent presidential disagreements and endless bureaucratic second-guessing. The issue will be in the hands of experienced legislative leaders, executive branch representatives and lobbyists, but that does not mean that the process will be any easier. There will be equally influential individuals and groups opposed to the issue who are just as adamant about using the system to clog up the machinery of government as the proponents are to make the machinery work smoothly. The black box of decision-making is appropriately named because it is difficult to see what is really going on, even though hearings, debates and votes are public. What is going on behind the scenes among legislators, executive branch representatives, party leaders and lobbyists oftentimes makes the difference as to whether an issue stays alive to move forward or is a victim of the system. When success is achieved it is often because deals are struck, compromises are made, middle ground is occupied and key players are satisfied about the eventual shape and direction of the issue legislation.

If the issue makes it through the black box it becomes an output of government, a public policy designed to address a need, solve a problem, expand a right, prohibit a practice or change a direction. This is often a proud moment of government as a president backed by smiling legislators signs a bill into law and hands out complimentary pens that were used in the ceremony. Speeches are given, credit is distributed and promises are made about the positive impact that the policy will have on the country. The long road of a public demand has been traversed as one group won and the other lost in the high stakes game of issue politics in American government.

The public policy is made law, but that does not end the process, as the bureaucracy is charged with implementing the legislation, which often gives these non-elected officials considerable influence in determining exactly how the policy solution will be put into place. Specific rules and regulations will need to be drafted, budgets will need to be drawn up, new tasks will likely have to be given to government employees and perhaps an organizational structure will need to be created to ensure that the general wishes of the decision makers are carried out. Once the bureaucrats have had their turn at the process, the policy is implemented, but the process does not end there, as all those people at the beginning of this long chain of events will be watching to see if indeed the new legislation is working and whether the decision made in the black box of government has lived up to its promises. The long journey to a policy may be over, but along the way it has likely exhausted the participants, taken years to accomplish and may look a lot different from what was proposed at the start.

The Founding Fathers coined the term E Pluribus Unum, "from many, one," to emphasize that their goal was to create a country in which the many units, in this case the individual states, would work together for the national good and remain united. E Pluribus Unum can also be used to describe the challenge that comes from the tumult of issue voices and causes as described by de Tocqueville and Bryce's zigzagging that occurs in American politics as issues enter the decision-making black box. The United States is indeed a nation of many voices, many concerns, many advocates and many visions. However, it is also a nation that can easily become immobilized and direction-less as its political system becomes overwhelmed with contentious issues and unbending issue groups. The First Amendment clearly gives each and every American the right to peaceably assemble and petition the government for a redress of grievances. However, the question that must be asked is at what point do all the debates, all the differences and all the divisions that accom-pany issue formation and issue advocacy compromise the need for "Unum"—unity. James Madison applauded the rise of factions that represented diverse interests, issues and causes, but there is also the common good, the national interest and the general will that the Founding Fathers were seeking when they dreamed of a nation of E Pluribus Unum. As we explore more deeply the twenty-five issues that shape American politics, it will be important to remember the alternatives—tumult and zigzagging or "From Many, One."

The Great Debate

The American political system seems rooted in vigorous debate, clear pol-icy differences and contentious political and social divisions. A spirited discussion that addresses this climate of conflict could serve as the basis for a debate.

Debate Topic

The American political system, which accents debate, differences and divisions is a constructive means of developing and implementing public policy or a dangerous and destructive flaw in the way Americans do politics?

Critical Thinking Questions

1. Is it possible to solve complex, national problems in a diverse, pluralistic, interest group–dominated political system as currently exists in the United States?
2. What recommendations do you have to help bring more speed and efficiency to the American policy-making process?
3. Does the American political system work for the benefit of the nation or for special interests?
4. How can American citizens ensure that the common good is being addressed rather than narrow interests?
5. Would the United States be better off with a parliamentary form of government rather than the current presidential system?

Connections

The Public Interest Research Group (PIRG) is organized around the country and on many college campuses. Check its website for information related to interest group activity and interest group contacts. http://www.pirg.org/

Local organizing is increasing and having an impact on both local politics and bringing issues to the national policy scene. See the website of Meetup: Organizing Local Interest Groups, http://www.meetup.com. A more recent example of grassroots organization is the Tea Party Movement and its efforts to lessen the power of the federal government. See Tea Party Patriots, http://www.teapartypatriots.org

One of the more active groups seeking to make the American political system work and be open to the public is the Center for Responsive Politics. Their website is http://www.opensecrets.org

Check out the websites of the key public policy players in American government–the House of Representatives, http://www.house.gov; the Senate, http://www.senate.gov; the White House, http://www.whitehouse.gov; and the bureaucracy, http://www.firstgov.gov/Agencies/Federal/Executive.shtml

Common Cause, a political reform group, which has as its mission statement, "Holding Government Accountable," is one of the leading advocates of political reform; it can be reached at http://www.commoncause.org

Some Books to Read

Cigler, Allan, J., and Burdett Loomis, *Interest Group Politics*, 7th edition (Washington, D.C.: CQ Press, 2007).

De Tocqueville, Alexis, *Democracy in America*, 2 vols. (1835).

Hamilton, Alexander, James Madison and John Jay, *The Federalist Papers*; ed. Clinton Rossiter (New York: New American Library, 1961).

Putnam, Robert D., *Bowling Alone: The Collapse and Revival of American Community* (New York: Simon & Schuster, 2000).

Theodoulou, Stella Z., and Chris Kofinis, *The Art of the Game: Understanding American Public Policy Making* (Belmont, CA: Wadsworth, 2004).

Notes

1. Tocqueville, *Democracy in America* (Harvey Mansfield and Delba Winthrop, trans., ed.; Chicago: University of Chicago Press, 2000)
2. The divisions in American society are the subject of the book by Bill Bishop and Robert G. Cushing, *The Big Sort: Why the Clustering of Like-Minded America is Tearing Us Apart* (Boston: Houghton Mifflin, 2008). Bishop and Cushing contend that growing isolation of Americans is creating extreme and divisive policy positions.

3. See my discussion of sameness and center politics in Michael Kryzanek, *Angry, Bored and Confused, A Citizen Guide to American Politics* (Boulder, CO: Westview Press, 1999).

4. "The Changing Demographic Profile of the United States," *Congressional Research Service (CRS) Report for Congress,* June 7, 2006.

5. See http://www.cnn.com/ELECTION/2008/

6. For a more detailed discussion of American values and beliefs see "State of American Political Ideology, 2009: A National Study of Values and Beliefs," Center for American Progress, http://www.americanprogress.org/issues/2009/03/political_ideology.html

7. This poll can be accessed at http://pollingreport.com/prioriti.htm

8. HBO presented a highly acclaimed program on the power and influence of interest groups in American politics. See "K Street 2003," HBO. See also Scott Ainsworth, *Analyzing Interest Groups: Group Influence and Policies* (New York: Norton, 2002).

9. James Bryce, *The American Commonwealth,* New Edition, (New York: The MacMillan Company, 1919).

1

HOMELAND SECURITY

Issue Focus

No function of government is more important than the protection of the homeland from invasion or threats to national security. The attack on America on 9/11 underscored the importance of homeland security and the need to develop the institutions, policies and procedures that will heighten national security and the safety of the homeland. To meet the challenges the nation faces from external and domestic terrorist threats, the Department of Homeland Security was formed in 2001. The department is a huge and expensive bureaucracy that is often under intense scrutiny. When there are failures in the system of homeland security and sectors of our economy and infrastructure are inadequately protected, questions are raised about whether our homeland is indeed secure.

Chapter Objectives
This issue chapter will seek to:
1. Examine the government institutions that are charged with protecting the country from threats – domestic and foreign terrorist attacks as well as natural disasters and pandemics.
2. Discuss the policies put in place by the government to address the threats and protect the American people and American assets.
3. Present the debates, differences and divisions that have arisen in the United States over the most appropriate, effective and legal approaches to protecting the homeland.

SOME BACKGROUND

As President George Bush stated in the aftermath of the terrorist attacks on the United States, "9/11 changed everything." Although change occurred at all levels of American society, from heightened public anxiety about the prospect of new attacks to an aggressive foreign and military policy in the Middle East, perhaps the most significant change was in the area of homeland security wherein the government took numerous steps to ensure that an attack on the United States would never happen again. Strengthening homeland security occurred on a number of levels, some organizational and bureaucratic, others more intrusive and controversial. The Bush administration quickly went about creating a new cabinet level Department of Homeland Security, which sought to streamline the disparate sectors of intelligence gathering and protection of vital resources and

22 Agencies

installations. The new department combined bureaucratic entities from twenty-two individual agencies, including the Coast Guard, the Federal Emergency Management Agency (FEMA), the Secret Service and Immigration and Immigration and Customs Enforcement. The secretary of Homeland Security (initially former Pennsylvania Governor Tom Ridge) was given extraordinary access to the president and wide powers to put in place government assets that would be capable of meeting the growing global terrorist threat.[1]

As constituted, the Department of Homeland Security has a number of responsibilities and mission objectives. At its core, the mission of the department is "protecting the territory of the United States from terrorists attacks and responding to natural disasters." From this mission statement the department is required to perform a wide range of functions including internal evaluations of the state of homeland security, protection of national assets, response to attacks and disasters, and cooperation with federal, state and local agencies and private entities to assure that the nation has in place the means necessary to prepare for and respond to terrorist attacks and natural disasters. To accomplish this task, Homeland Security has developed various programs, networks and advisory systems designed to provide a broad range of assessments on the current state of national preparedness and the vulnerabilities that exist, along with action initiatives designed to ensure that the nation, its citizens, its infrastructure and its economic structure are secure.[2]

protecting

The next step in the process of ensuring national preparedness is prevention and protection. To achieve these goals, the department has put in place two critical programs that address key targets that are likely on the terrorists' list. The Container Security Initiative (CSI) is directed by the U.S. Customs and Border Protection (CBP) and is charged with developing measures that will protect the ports of the United States and in particular monitor the container traffic that enters the ports on a daily basis. Many terrorist experts have said that the national ports and the containerized cargo that enters these ports provide an enormous opportunity for terrorists to bring in weapons of mass destruction, chemical and biological agents and other means that could be used to attack major U.S. cities. In addition Homeland Security has established the National Infrastructure Protection Plan (NIPP) that works with state and local authorities to devise plans that will ensure that bridges, roads, tunnels, water treatment plans, nuclear power and electric generating facilities and water reservoirs are properly secured and monitored. Since 9/11 government officials have been concerned that terrorists might seek to attack the United States by destroying its critical infrastructure and thereby creating economic havoc.[3]

prevention & protection

In the wake of the devastation of 9/11 and the terrorist attacks in such foreign capitals as London and Madrid, the Department of Homeland Security has also established a preparedness and response component to its overall mission. In particular, the department has initiated a First Responders program that is designed to train and equip fire, police and emergency medical personnel who would be the first on the scene of a terrorist attack. Homeland Security has developed a national grant program that allows states and local communities to purchase the equipment for the first responders and

preparation & response

provide the training essential for them to deal with a catastrophic event. Homeland Security has also developed a website, www.ready.gov, which provides valuable information on the type of emergencies citizens will face and the steps they can take to deal with those emergencies.[4]

Research Dev.

In addition, Homeland Security has placed extensive budgetary resources into research and development of technologies, which will assist the country in combating the terrorist threat. The Homeland Security Advanced Research Projects Agency (HSARPA) was established as the main conduit to work with private industry, academia, government and other research entities to develop a new wave of technologies that can be used to protect Americans and their property and respond to chemical, biological and computer-based threats from terrorist organizations. As a companion program to HSARPA, Homeland Security has also funded numerous "Centers of Excellence" on college and university campuses to enhance research efforts in a wide range of areas from agriculture to bio-defense to behavioral aspects of terrorism. The accent in both of these initiatives is to use the brainpower of Americans to foil terrorist attacks irrespective of their shape or form.[5]

Immigration & Border Security

The most comprehensive and active sector of Homeland Security is in the area of immigration and border security. The Coast Guard, the Customs Services, the Border Patrol and the Transportation Security Agency (the 50,000 ubiquitous airport screeners) are but some of the most visible government organizations that are at the front lines, ensuring that terrorist agents or materials that could be used in an attack do not enter the United States. In many respects, the whole area of immigration control and border security is the most difficult challenge the Department of Homeland Security faces as thousands of people from foreign countries enter the United States legally and illegally every day and millions of travelers yearly use domestic and international airlines.[6]

Today the Department of Homeland Security is the backbone of our domestic anti-terror strategy. However, because defending the homeland can come in conflict with personal freedom and other constitutional protections, and actions taken by various government agencies in the name of homeland security can raise citizen concerns, there have been numerous court challenges and ongoing political disputes. These challenges and disputes form the basis for the following discussion of the impact of homeland security on American rights and policy making.

DEBATES, DIFFERENCES AND DIVISIONS

Creating a brand new cabinet level department that brings together numerous agencies in response to a terrorist attack has not been easy and has not evolved smoothly. The formation of the Department of Homeland Security created the largest government reorganization since the formation of the Department of Defense over fifty years ago. With 208,000 employees and a budget of $43 billion in 2010 it was not unexpected that the enormous responsibility of protecting the homeland would encounter difficulties. Early on the department was taken to task for its now famous color-coded Homeland Security Advisory

System that alerted citizens to threat levels from Low through Severe. Critics viewed the five-stage risk designation system as a public relations gimmick that did little to protect the country and only heightened the anxiety level of American citizens. Numerous complaints also arose about lax searches at airports (on numerous occasions undercover agents were able to board airplanes with explosives and weapons on their carry-on luggage) and the wasting of million dollars of taxpayer money because of poor administration and accounting procedures. Clark Kent Ervin, who served as the Department's inspector general, described the internal management of Homeland Security as "chaotic and disorganized." When President Bush accepted the resignation of Secretary Ridge, he also recognized the problems at Homeland Security saying, "There hasn't been the management expertise and experience needed to integrate and effectively organize a huge bureaucratic challenge. Ideally, you need someone who's got corporate experience."[7]

On the Record

At the signing ceremony creating the Department of Homeland Security, President George W. Bush said the following:

> Today we are taking historic action to defend the United States and protect our citizens against the dangers of a new era. With my signature, this act of Congress will create a new Department of Homeland Security, ensuring our efforts to defend this country are comprehensive and united. . . . With a vast nation to defend, we can neither predict nor prevent every conceivable attack in a free and open society. No department of government can completely guarantee our safety against ruthless killers, who move and plot in shadows, yet our government will take every possible measure to safeguard . . . our people.

More serious criticism of Homeland Security came as a result of the response by FEMA to Hurricane Katrina on the Gulf Coast and in particular in the city of New Orleans in 2005. Although it was not a terrorist incident, the Bush administration and the FEMA administrator Michael Brown were vilified for their failure to respond quickly and effectively to the huge human tragedy that was left in the wake of Katrina. With primary emphasis being placed on dealing with a terrorist attack, the Department of Homeland Security was seen as woefully underprepared to handle a natural disaster. The disaster also laid bare the laxity with which FEMA hired key officials. Before he was named FEMA director, Brown was a lawyer for the International Arabian Horse Association, but a donor to Republican campaigns and well connected among Republican activists.

The failures of FEMA in New Orleans and the Gulf Coast were largely ones due to poor interagency coordination and emergency response time, both signs that Homeland Security had yet to put in place a network that could deal with a catastrophic event. Michael Brown was eventually replaced with a more experienced disaster manager, and FEMA underwent an extensive internal review of its response policies, but the confidence of the American public was shattered as they saw day after day televised news reports of thousands of people left homeless, without food, water and medical attention and with only minimal federal evacuation measures. Even today New Orleans is still reeling from Hurricane Katrina as large sections of the predominately African-American Ninth Ward remain a wasteland, and FEMA continues to be criticized for its inadequate response to the disaster.[8]

During the early days of the Obama administration the domestic challenge faced by the Department was not a hurricane, but the outbreak of a deadly strain of swine flu, which the Center for Disease Control in Atlanta calls by the letters H1N1. The flu virus was traced to Mexico but spread quickly to the United States. Homeland Security moved quickly to respond to the virus with a media and Internet blitz that sought both to inform the American people to the proper safety measures and updates on the current movement of the virus in the country. Unlike the Katrina debacle, Homeland Security was largely praised for its quick response and distribution of information.

In the area of preparedness and protection against a terrorist attack, Homeland Security faced mounting criticism, largely in the area of funding and its distribution. Congressional critics, primarily Democrats, charged that the department and its new secretary Michael Chertoff were failing to provide sufficient funds to major cities for the first responders or were distributing those funds in inefficient ways. Officials in such major cities as New York, Boston and Los Angeles complained about not receiving the funds they requested, whereas numerous smaller cities in the Midwest and West received significant grants, even though the threat levels to these communities were seen as minimal. Extensive criticism also arose of the department's failures in providing sufficient

FYI

The Department of Homeland Security, through its citizen website www.ready.gov, provides Americans with a range of security tips should this nation face a major terrorist threat or natural disaster. Under the title "Instant Answers" some of the references provided by Homeland Security are listed as follows:

1. When You Need to Know Where the Wind Is Blowing – U.S. Radar by Intellicast
2. When the Ground Is Shaking – Incident.com
3. When You Are on the Run – 600 Campsites
4. When You Want Alternative Accommodations – How to Build a Log Cabin
5. When You Want to Store Food – Government Food Safety Guide
6. What About Pet Safety?

Source: Department of Homeland Security

funding to protect America's railroads and seaports and in particular to provide closer inspection of the containerized cargo ships. But Homeland Security officials responded that many states and localities had not spent the money allocated to them, leaving millions of dollars sitting in Washington.[9]

Much of the criticism of the Department of Homeland Security has been generated by state and local officials who feel that their needs and opinions have been ignored by the Washington bureaucrats. At the root of the problem was the National Response Plan, which was designed to provide the guidelines for cooperation among federal, state, local, private and non-profit groups during an emergency. The plan has been attacked as convoluted, legalistic and complicated with no clear directives or lines of responsibility. Those outside the Washington bureaucracy of Homeland Security have for years been disappointed by the lack of collaboration among these groups and the failure of the federal government to share information and provide essential funding for emergencies. Criticism has also been generated at the state and local levels that Homeland Security is more focused on a terrorist attack than on natural disasters. Oklahoma's emergency management head stated in 2007 that he has never experienced "a more polarized environment between state and federal government" and that since Katrina, "the federal legacy is one of minimizing exposure for the next event and ensuring future focus is centered on state and local preparedness."[10]

With the onset of the Obama administration, the new secretary of Homeland Security, former Arizona Governor Janet Napolitano, criticized the 2007 national emergency preparedness exercise involving over 23,000 federal, state and local officials and costing $25 million. The exercise was designed to test the capability of governments at all levels to respond to a terrorist attack. Napolitano and other officials complained about the cost of the exercise, numerous examples of bureaucratic inefficiency and the poor post-exercise assessment of the ability of the United States to respond to a terrorist attack.[11] Napolitano, in her new job as secretary of Homeland Security, took a controversial position that the country was still not properly prepared for a terrorist attack.

Napolitano further generated controversy when she spoke about a government study which claimed that over 900 right-wing domestic hate and potential terrorist groups were active in the country. Napolitano suggested in the news conference that these groups were actively seeking to recruit members of the armed forces returning from Iraq and Afghanistan as potential members of their groups. Immediately veterans groups expressed their anger that the secretary would single out returning veterans as recruits for these groups. The secretary quickly softened her comments on the connection between hate groups and returning veterans from Iraq and Afghanistan, but it was clear that even mentioning the prospect of military veterans joining these groups opened a deep fissure between the department and veterans groups.

The department and Secretary Napolitano faced a major crisis on Christmas Day, 2009, when a young Nigerian boarded a plane destined for Detroit and in flight tried to blow up the aircraft with explosives hidden in his underwear. Critics of Homeland Security immediately lashed out at Napolitano and the intelligence community for not stopping the terrorist from boarding the plane, especially because he had a one-way ticket and no baggage. Secretary

Napolitano at first sought to assure the American public that the system worked, but it became clear after an internal review that the system had failed to recognize that the Nigerian had traveled to terrorist training camps in Yemen and that his father, a prominent banker, had warned the government of his son's involvement in terrorism. This incident spurred the department to step up its efforts at airport security, but many Americans and critics of Homeland Security kept up their criticism as further evidence that the government has not established an effective anti-terrorist system.

It is important to point out, however, that there have been some positive and encouraging developments at Homeland Security. Michael Chertoff has been lauded for tightening up the management and the surveillance arms of Homeland Security. There is now more cooperation and openness of information between the FBI and Homeland Security, which in the past was a major source of tension and was often viewed as a key failing of post-9/11 intelligence system. In 2006 the Department also worked closely with British officials to stop a terrorist plot that was designed to use transcontinental airplanes as attack weapons against buildings in the United States. Homeland Security officials responded quickly to the planned attack and instituted checkpoint measures in record time. Although some continue to see Homeland Security as too reactionary and lax in addressing the port and rail security, Chertoff and his deputies have been viewed as much more open and forthright in their assessments of terrorist threats and they have addressed many of the internal embarrassments that characterized the Department in its early days.

But while important for national security purposes, the growing pains in the Department of Homeland Security were overshadowed by the steps the White House took to introduce measures designed to investigate and monitor those individuals in the United States who were deemed potential or real terrorist threats. Within weeks of 9/11 the Congress overwhelmingly passed and President Bush signed the USA Patriot Act, which provided the government with wide powers to search the personal records, cell phone conversations, Internet communications and other information of those who were viewed as "enemy combatants." By defining these individuals as enemy combatants the Patriot Act established a new and controversial level of extra-constitutional powers, as the FBI was given expanded legal discretion to engage in these searches. At the same time Congress also created the Foreign Intelligence Surveillance Court, which was authorized to approve the searches. As constituted, the federal judges on the court meet in secret and legitimize the actions taken by the government under the Patriot Act. In 2006 the Patriot Act was reauthorized despite civil-liberties objections of many Democrats in the Senate. President Bush pressed hard to assure its extension for another five years although some questioned whether the Patriot Act violated the civil liberties of Americans.[12]

Right from the outset the Patriot Act was the target of civil libertarians, lawyers groups and a number of institutions such as libraries and colleges. Critics of the act stated that there was little debate over the legislation and little consideration given to the impact of the Patriot Act on constitutionally protected rights. In total, twelve existing laws were amended with significant changes, which greatly expanded the powers of government to interfere in areas that in the past were deemed private. In particular, so-called "sneak-and-peak" provisions of the new law allow law enforcement officials surreptitious searches and seizures using a new standard of "reasonable necessity" and permit authorities the option of not notifying the target of the searches that a search and seizure action has been taken. Both of these investigatory powers were changes from established Federal Rules of Criminal Procedures, but were deemed necessary to gather information of suspected terrorists. Criticism was also aimed at the expanded power given the government to search and seize library and bookstore records. National library groups protested the so-called library provision of the legislation as a violation of patrons' rights, whereas government officials defended it as necessary to track down suspected terrorists who were known to use computers in public libraries to email information and receive instructions from terrorist leaders.[13]

Initially public opinion was solidly in favor of the legislation as many Americans wanted the government to take aggressive action to protect the homeland from a terrorist threat, even if it meant a lessening of individual liberties. A Gallup poll taken in August 2003 showed that only a small number of the respondents believed that the Patriot Act went too far. But after four years of the Patriot Act and numerous public critiques of the dangers of expanded government investigatory power, support for the Patriot Act waned. By 2005 the number of supporters of the Patriot Act was about equal to the number of Americans who believed that the powers given to the government went too far.[14] There is an ongoing dispute over the impact of the USA Patriot Act on homeland security in terms of the number of arrests made, charges filed and successful convictions of suspected terrorists. Bush administration officials state that the public records of criminal action do not show the value of the new investigatory powers on targeting potential threats and developing new leads that assist law enforcement agencies elsewhere in the world in protecting their citizens from attack.

However, although the debate about the benefits and drawbacks of the Patriot Act swirled around the country, there is no doubt that the legislation offered the Bush administration a means of expanding presidential power in the war on terror. Much of the controversy surrounded the move by the Bush administration in 2005 to use the National Security Agency (NSA) to wiretap international phone calls and emails without the authorization of the special court set up by the Patriot Act and in violation of the Foreign Intelligence Surveillance Act (FISA). The Bush administration rejected the charges that it had broken the law and sidestepped proper judicial procedure stating that as commander in chief, the president has the inherent authority under the Patriot Act and FISA to take such action, especially in light of the ongoing terrorist threat to the country.

The action of the Bush administration regarding the use of the NSA spilled over into the extension of the Patriot Act in 2006. Democrats in Congress were determined to rewrite the bill or at least to change it significantly to limit the power of the president. After a series of delays over reauthorization, Congress did approve the extension of the Patriot Act but placed time limits on so-called roving surveillance and the authority to demand business records of suspected terrorists. President Bush, however, followed his signing of the Patriot Act extension with so-called signing statements, which said that he would not comply with the Congressional restrictions if they were in conflict with other laws. The electoral victory of the Democrats in the 2006 Congressional elections placed increased pressure on President Bush to limit his use of surveillance powers. In 2007 the president agreed to seek judicial approval for wiretaps and email monitoring and promised that he would abide by established procedures.

In August 2007 the Democratic-controlled Congress called a "Warrantless Surrender" as it passed the Protect America Act, which civil libertarians viewed as expanding the government's power to engage in eavesdropping on international calls and emails. In effect, the Protect America Act rewrote the FISA and in the process severely limited the ability of Americans to challenge the authority of law enforcement agencies to search and seize their personal electronic conversations. Those familiar with the legislation said that it would give the government the power to demand that private communications companies establish "permanent spying outposts," while in return providing them with immunity from any liability should they face civil suits. The Bush administration and those from both parties in Congress were convinced that government intelligence agencies needed to collect information from so-called "foreign to foreign" communications from terrorists who travel through the United States. The controversy over the legislation lies in the fact that the law allows surveillance of any communications, even from Americans who reside overseas, that involve "foreign intelligence," a term that is not only broad but also ambiguous. Also the court established to monitor this surveillance activity was pushed aside in favor of control by the attorney general and the director of national intelligence.[15]

Although the Protect America Act was designed to bring federal statutes in line with Bush policies and required the government to obtain a warrant if it was focusing its attention on an American citizen or organization inside the United States, in 2010 a federal judge, ruling on a case from 2004, stated that the NSA's surveillance program that monitored international phone calls and email messages was illegal, violating a 1978 statute that required court approval for such surveillance. The judge in the case said the NSA at the direction of the Bush administration subjected an Islamic charity in "Oregon" to an unlawful surveillance. The ruling cast doubt on current surveillance practices conducted by the Obama administration, which often follow the past practices of the Bush administration.[16]

Despite the controversy over the constitutionality of surveillance programs aimed at alleged terrorists, these spying activities are viewed as essential weapons in the war on terror. Furthermore, supporters of these programs state that the president should not be handcuffed in his effort to use modern electronic technology to monitor the phone calls and emails of suspected terrorists. But because advocates of civil liberties and opponents of government power in the area of privacy rights view the Protect America Act as a capitulation to presidential power and a climate of fear, the debate over setting the proper balance between the government's responsibility to protect its citizens and the constitutional protections against warrantless search and seizure will likely continue for some time to come.[17]

With the Obama administration taking office in January 2009, former Bush administration officials, including Vice-President Dick Cheney, criticized the Democratic president for the closing of Camp Delta in Guantánamo, Cuba, where many of the al Qaeda terrorists were detained. Cheney in particular said on numerous occasions that President Obama was jeopardizing the security of the United States by closing the base and sending the wrong signal to the terrorists that this country and this administration were not going to be as tough on terrorists or as vigilant as the previous administration.[18] As the debate over the closing of Camp Delta continued, President Obama changed course and decided to postpone taking any action on the terrorist base or on his proposal to house many of the terrorists in an unused prison in Illinois. Obama's efforts to transfer most of the terrorists to sites in the United States raised objections from many local, state and national leaders who charged that such a placement of these radical jihadists would endanger the residents who live close to the prisons. The Obama administration responded that many hardened criminals are already serving jail sentences in prisons throughout the country and that the addition of these terrorists would not pose any additional threat.

Whether it is the Department of Homeland Security providing the bureaucratic structure for national security or the USA Patriot Act or the Protect America Act creating procedures for tracking down terrorist threats, the issue of protecting the United States from a terrorist attack can be judged by the number of attacks or attempted attacks in the United States since 9/11 and also in terms of how secure the American public feels. As to terrorist attacks on the homeland, no group or individual has been able to successfully implement a plot aimed at bringing death and destruction to this country. There have been a handful of arrests of individuals and small cells that had as their objective targeting military installations and other infrastructure assets, but these plots were nipped in the bud either through effective government surveillance or as a result of citizen watchdogs who called police when they spotted something or someone that appeared suspicious. The planned attack on Ft. Dix in New Jersey in 2007, for example, was foiled as a result of a citizen who became concerned over the comings and goings of Middle Eastern men working at a local pizza parlor. As cell phone and other records showed, the men were in the early planning stages of entering Ft. Dix and killing as many soldiers as possible before they were captured or killed. Later in 2009 a would-be terrorist from Colorado was arrested with bomb making equipment that he planned to use to explode on a New York subway. And in 2010 a newly naturalized American citizen from Pakistan failed in an effort to explode a car bomb in Times Square, New York. He was captured moments before he was about to take off for Dubai and later Pakistan. These plots support the view of many experts that terrorism directed at the homeland are being developed by "lone wolf" homegrown terrorists with either no international ties to al Qaeda or rudimentary training by Middle East terrorist organizations.

The general success of the security system of the government is reflected in public opinion polls, although most of the opinion surveys continue to show a level of anxiety and concern about the future attacks. A CNN/Opinion Research Corporation Poll taken in January 2007 asked a sampling of Americans:

How likely it is that there will be further acts of terrorism in the United States over the next several weeks?

Very Likely	9%
Somewhat Likely	29%
Not too Likely	41%
Not Likely at All	18%
Unsure	3%

But a Fox News/Opinion Dynamics Poll taken in July 2007 asked a similar but different worded question to a sample group and received a more disturbing result.

How likely do you think it is that another terrorist attack causing large numbers of American lives to be lost will happen in the near future?

Very Likely	43%
Somewhat Likely	38%
Not too Likely	11%
Not Likely at All	3%
Unsure	4%

As can be seen from a comparison of the responses, when the threat of terrorism is made more general in scope and extended forward without time limits, a significant majority of Americans are convinced that the United States will be attacked by terrorists. The attack may not occur tomorrow or the next week, but it will occur sometime in the future.

What also is a cause for concern is the view of the American people on the ability of the government to reduce the threat of a terrorist attack. The Pew Research Center for the People & the Press conducted a regular poll of citizens from fall 2001 to winter 2007 and asked them how well they thought the U.S. government was doing in reducing the threat of terrorism. A sampling of their responses over time follows:

	Very Well	Fairly Well	Not too Well	Not at All Well	Unsure
11/01	35%	48%	8%	5%	4%
7/03	19%	56%	16%	8%	4%
2/06	16%	52%	20%	10%	2%
1/07	17%	37%	27%	17%	2%

As can be seen, the level of confidence the American people have in their government in reducing the threat of terrorism declines considerably from 2001 to 2007. No explanatory factors for the decline in confidence were addressed in the Pew survey.

For those concerned with the widening of search and seizure powers and surveillance measures adopted by the government in the post-9/11 period, the response of the American people points to a growing fear that individual liberties and personal privacy may be in jeopardy and should be limited. The same Pew survey asked Americans in September 2006 and January 2007 the following question, "In order to curb terrorism in this country, do you think it will be necessary for the average person to give up some civil liberties, or not?"

	Is Necessary	Is Not Necessary	Unsure
September, 2006	43%	50%	7%
January, 2007	40%	54%	6%

Although the time comparison is narrow and therefore may not be viewed as a thorough assessment of American attitudes toward civil liberties and anti-terrorism measures adopted by the government, the survey nevertheless reflects concern over perceived losses in individual rights and expanded government power.

Data Bank

In 2002 intelligence estimates stated that 5,000 al Qaeda and al Qaeda supporters lived in the United States. But in a secret FBI report in 2005 not one single al Qaeda cell could be identified.

From John Mueller, *Foreign Affairs*, September/October, 2006.

The American governing system has often been based on the principle of balance, ensuring that public policies and indeed the entire political life of the country would not fall prey to extremism or excesses in freedom or government power. Protecting the homeland from terrorist attacks after 9/11 has been a challenge for the government, civil libertarians and the American people. There is no doubt that al Qaeda and other groups aligned with radical Islamism are constantly plotting for ways to strike again at the United States and inflict horrendous destruction. The question that arises in this anti-terrorist environment is to what extent personal freedoms should be limited and government agencies should be provided with more intrusive powers to prevent terrorist attacks and protect American lives and property.

The Bush administration consistently asserted the necessity of establishing a vigorous wall of prevention and protection from terrorist attacks and has not apologized for expanding presidential powers, building an ever-expanding Homeland Security Department or seeking surveillance powers that some say are unconstitutional. The view of government leaders is that we are in a war against international terrorism and that it is absolutely essential that measures be taken to ensure that a 9/11 attack never happens again. Moreover, President Bush took the position on the importance of extending presidential powers as part of his sworn constitutional responsibility as commander in chief during time of war. However, some question the extent that the government has exerted its national security responsibility and bypassed legal precedents, ignored congressional input and violated constitutional principles. Some have even suggested that the measures taken by the Bush administration were based on fearmongering rather than clear threats from foreign or homegrown terrorists. The Obama administration, on the other hand, has sought to assure the American public that it has kept the protection of the homeland as its highest priority, although it has used extra-constitutional measures to achieve a solid wall of domestic security.[19]

However, although the advocates of personal freedom versus governmental power argue over how best to deal with the terrorist threat while upholding constitutional principles and practices, there has also been a more nuts-and-bolts debate over how best to secure the homeland. Questions are regularly raised as to whether the government is spending too much on airline security while ignoring railroads and ports, whether our borders are too porous allowing terrorists to walk right into the country and whether the government talks about national security but does not allocate enough budget resources to ensure that large cities and small towns are protected not just from terrorist attacks but from natural disasters. There has also been a growing discussion over whether the United States has prepared adequately for a cyber attack, which has prompted the Obama administration to significantly increase budget allocations for protecting the homeland from cyber terrorism. There is also increasing skepticism about whether the Department of Homeland Security has been a colossal waste of taxpayer money, as it turns into a bloated bureaucracy with huge gaps in fulfilling its mission.[20] These and other concerns continue to drive the debate over national security as do differences over the proper legal measures that should be supported to protect the homeland.

Protecting the United States from another 9/11 style attack or from small-scale violence remains the top priority of the government. But as has been shown, protecting the homeland is a complex task as the means available to terrorists are many and their commitment to attack the United States remains solid. It is because the enemies of the United States are still at work and pledging to once again kill as many of our citizens as possible that the security of the homeland will be at the forefront of the issue agenda and also the subject of intense debate, partisan differences and a divided citizenry on how best to ensure the safety of the nation.

The Great Debate

At the heart of the debate about how best to secure the homeland is the issue of the proper balance between personal freedom and national security.

Debate Topic

Can we protect the country from a terrorist attack and still remain an open and free democracy?

Critical Thinking Questions

1. Has the government gone too far in restricting personal rights to protect the homeland from terrorist attacks?
2. What role, if any, should the American public play in protecting the homeland from a terrorist attack?
3. Many Muslim men and women have been outraged at what they view as racial profiling and harassment by police and other government authorities. Is such profiling and harassment necessary?
4. Do you believe that another major terrorist attack on the United States is inevitable?
5. Is it possible to protect all sectors of the American economy and national life from a terrorist attack? What needs to be done?

Connections

The first place to start to understand homeland security is at the Department's website http://www.homelandsecurity.gov

The Department of Homeland Security provides a guidebook to citizens seeking assistance so as to prepare for a terrorist attack. See http://www.ready.gov

One of the most respected independent sources of information on homeland security is the Homeland Security Studies and Analysis Institute. Visit its site at http://www.homelandsecurity.org

A helpful guide to the war on terror and homeland security issues is available through the Constitutional Rights Foundation. See http://www.crf-usa.org/terror/America

The Journal of Homeland Security and Emergency Management is a new useful guide to the latest research and opinion on domestic security issues. See http://www.bepress.com/jhsem

Some Books to Read

Chertoff, Michael and Lee H. Hamilton, *Homeland Security: Assessing the First Five Years* (Philadelphia: University of Pennsylvania Press, 2009).

Howard, Russell, James, J.F. Forest and Joanne Moore, *Homeland Security: Protecting America's Targets* (New York: McGraw-Hill, 2005).

Radvanovsky, Robert, *Critical Infrastructure: Homeland Security and Emergency Preparedness* (CRC Publishers, 2006).

Souter, Mark and James Carafano, *Homeland Security: An Introduction* (New York: McGraw-Hill, 2005).

White, Jonathan, *Terrorism and Homeland Security* (Los Angeles, CA: Wadsworth, 2005)

Notes

1. See the Department of Homeland Security website, http://www.dhs.gov
2. http://www.dhs.gov/files/programs/preparedness.shtm
3. http://www.dhs.gov/files/programs/critical-infrastructure.shtm
4. http://www.dhs.gov/files/gc_1251897643286.shtm
5. http://www.dhs.gov/files/committees/prepresprecovery.shtm. See also statement of Bradley I. Buswell, Undersecretary (Acting) Science and Technology Directorate Department of Homeland Security, U.S. House of Representatives, Committee on Appropriations, Sub-Committee on Homeland Security, March 26, 2009.
6. http://www.usatoday.com/news/washington/2004-12-27-homelandUSAT_x.htm
7. See Donald Kettl, *System Under Stress: Homeland Security and American Politics*, 2nd edition (Washington, D.C.: CQ Press, 2007). Also see "Ex-official tells of Homeland Security Failure," *Miami Herald*, September 7, 2003.
8. "Katrina Relief Effort Raises Concerns Over Excessive Spending, Waste," Pew Research Center, 2005, p. 1.
9. John Mintz, "Hobbled Giant," http://www.washingtonpost.com/ac2/wp-dyn/A36519-2003Sep6?language=printer. See also John D. Solomon, "Asleep at the Wheel," *The Washington Post National Weekly Edition*, May 26-June 1, 2008, p. 27.
10. Ann Gerhert, "Homeland Insecurity," *Washington Post National Weekly Edition*, April 4–10, 2005, pp. 6–7. Also Spencer S. Hsu, "Department of Crisis Management," *Washington Post National Weekly Edition*, March 10–16, 2008, p. 10.
11. Eric Schmitt, "Secretary Orders Re-Evaluation of National Security Response," *New York Times*, February 17, 2009, A20.
12. The reauthorization issue regarding the Patriot Act can be seen at http://www.reformthepatriotact.org. See also "Senate Committee Passes Patriot Act Reauthorization Bill," *American Civil Liberties Union*, October 8, 2009. The entire debate over the USA Patriot Act can be seen at a website from the Electronic Privacy Information Center, http://www.epic.org/privacy/terrorism/usapatriot
13. Charlie Savage, "Judge Rules Against FBI on Data Gathering," *Boston Globe*, September 7, 2007, A2.
14. Ibid.
15. Carol D. Leoning, "Secret Court's Judges Were Warned About NSA Spy Data," *Washington Post*, February 9, 2006, A01.

16. See Charlie Savage and James Risen," N.S.A Wiretaps Were Unlawful, U.S. Judge Rules," New York Times, April 1, 2010 A1.

17. See "Democrats Capitulate to President Bush as Congress Gives Government Broad New Powers to Conduct Warrantless Surveillance on American Citizens," http://www.democracynow.org/print.pl?sid=07/08/06/1340209

18. See Sheryl G. Stolberg, "Obama Would Move Some Detainees to U.S." *New York Times*, May 22, 2009, A1.

19. "Guarding the Guards," *The Economist*, June 28, 2008, p. 36.

20. James Fallows, "Civilize Homeland Security," *The Atlantic*, July/August, 2009, p. 61.

2 THE **TERRORISTS**

Issue Focus

There is a new term in the language of war: asymmetrical warfare. This term means that war today is not conducted as it was in the past, when two armies faced each other on the battlefield and fought over land and strategic outposts. Today warfare is fought by "invisible" armies—suicide bombers, civilian insurgents, small cells of terrorists bent on blowing up a building, convoy or innocent civilians. This new kind of warfare has forced the United States to readjust its tactics and the manner in which it deals with those who would do harm to American soldiers and innocent civilians. It has led to concerns that the U.S. is using methods, including torture, that are not within existing domestic law or international conventions.

Chapter Objectives
This issue chapter will seek to:
1. Determine the strategies and actions taken by the United States to hunt down, capture or kill and interrogate al Qaeda and other terrorists.
2. Examine the debates surrounding the use of detention and torture-related techniques against terrorists in the custody of the United States.
3. Explore the continuing threats posed by terrorists and terrorist organizations against U.S. citizens and U.S. assets.

SOME BACKGROUND

It is not an exaggeration to say that the Bush administration's strategies and actions in response to the 9/11 attack on the United States will be analyzed and critiqued for years, if not decades to come. Since the Vietnam War, no foreign policy and national security issue has generated such widespread national debate and caused such intense political differences and divisions than the decision to engage in a pre-emptive military intervention in Iraq as the foundation of its global anti-terrorist strategy. Although the Clinton administration engaged in anti-terrorist actions, specifically the bombing of suspected al Qaeda targets in Sudan and Afghanistan, the scope of these campaigns was limited to air strikes (one that nearly killed Osama bin Laden) and later to policies that froze the assets of known terrorist organizations and individuals who collaborated with terrorists in the United States and elsewhere.

But in the aftermath of the attacks on the World Trade Center and the Pentagon (and also the attack on the USS Cole earlier in Yemen), the new Bush administration entered a war mode and began formulating invasion strategies that would not only retaliate against the al Qaeda terrorists and their international network but also change the governing environment throughout the entire Middle East.

In the days and weeks of national sadness and anger over the attacks, Bush administration officials such as Vice-President Dick Cheney, Secretary of Defense Donald Rumsfeld, Secretary of State Colin Powell, National Security Adviser Condoleezza Rice and CIA Chief George Tenet met frequently to map out the new war on terror. In the initial stages of these discussions it was clear that the al Qaeda training camps and base of operations in Afghanistan would be an essential target of retaliation. The Taliban Islamic radicals that controlled Afghanistan had welcomed Osama bin Laden and his al Qaeda fighters and provided them with the protection they needed to engage in their war against the United States. Preparations for a military strike against al Qaeda and the Taliban moved quickly, and support from the American public was overwhelming for a retaliatory strike against Afghanistan.[1]

Within months of the 9/11 attacks, the United States launched a joint military and CIA attack on Afghanistan that achieved considerable success in driving the Taliban out of key areas of the country, including the capital Kabul, and destroying the al Qaeda base camps along the rugged, mountainous Afghanistan-Pakistan border. The key battle was in the Tora Bora region where the U.S. military under the command of General Tommie Franks along with pro-American Afghan fighters bombarded the al Qaeda fighters. Despite the firepower reined on the Taliban positions at Tora Bora, the U.S. forces were unable to capture the fleeing Osama bin Laden.

With the Taliban out of power and al Qaeda on the run, the Bush administration declared that it had taken the first step in winning the war on terror. A new Afghan government under Hamid Karzai was installed in Kabul, and a country that had been wracked by war and cruel Islamic radicalism began a long journey toward democratic governance. Most important, many al Qaeda fighters and key organizational leaders were either killed or captured in the Afghanistan operation. The U.S. forces also retrieved valuable papers and computer files that would become critical in the hunt for other terrorists around the world. Osama bin Laden, however, remained at large and continued to rally his terrorist organization with regular videos sent to news organizations in the Middle East.

The relative ease with which the United States dismantled the Taliban regime and destroyed al Qaeda's base of operations emboldened the Bush administration to move against Iraq and its leader Saddam Hussein. By November 2001 George Bush and his national security team were discussing the prospects of an invasion of Iraq and the removal of Saddam Hussein. The Iraqi leader had been a thorn in the side of the United States since his invasion of Kuwait in 1990 and his refusal to allow United Nation's inspectors to examine without restrictions the status of his weapons of mass destruction program in the areas of nuclear, chemical and biological agents. Because the Bush administration believed that Iraq could develop into a key ally to terrorist groups and provide them with the means to wage further attacks against the United States, the invasion was given the highest priority.[2]

On the Record

In an interview with a British journalist during a visit by Prime Minister Tony Blair, a staunch supporter of Bush administration policy toward Iraq, the President, as recorded by Bob Woodward in his book *Plan of Attack,* stated:

> the worst thing that could happen would be to allow a nation like Iraq, run by Saddam Hussein, to develop weapons of mass destruction, and then team up with terrorist organizations so they can blackmail the world. I'm not going to let that happen.

Plan of Attack, p. 120

The now famous lightning invasion of Iraq in April 2003 quickly tumbled Saddam Hussein from power and created within the Bush administration a heightened sense of euphoria as it envisioned the transformation of Iraq into a functioning democracy and a pro–United States stabilizing force in the Middle East. But as the United States turned from becoming a liberating force that was greeted with initial goodwill to an occupying force that gradually faced heavily armed insurgents and homegrown al Qaeda terrorists, the initial policy of a pre-emptive strike and invasion of Iraq became the source of unending debate in Washington and indeed throughout the United States.

Now with the decision of President Obama to increase troop levels in Afghanistan and expand the war on terror by employing the Bush strategy of a military surge, the debate over how to respond to international terrorism has dominated the foreign and defense policy arena. Although as will be shown, the approaches of President Bush and President Obama in conducting the war on terrorism are different, both presidents have faced harsh criticism for either being too aggressive or too conciliatory, too willing to rely on a military strategy or too fearful about the political fallout for beginning a phased withdrawal. In both the Iraq and Afghanistan wars, there has been little middle ground.

DEBATES, DIFFERENCES AND DIVISIONS

The troubles faced by the United States in building a new Iraq in the midst of a growing insurgency became even more complicated with the torture scandal in the Abu Ghraib prison complex in 2004. Pictures from the prison showed U.S. military personnel engaging in a range of threatening, humiliating and sexually explicit actions against prisoners in their custody. The photos immediately touched off a firestorm of controversy over U.S. policies toward captured terrorists and made the U.S. policies the object of international criticism. Although the military personnel involved in the scandal were either tried and convicted or removed from duty and President Bush was reportedly dissatisfied with the handling of the scandal by Secretary of Defense Donald Rumsfeld, the United States had suffered a huge public relations defeat and questions were raised as to whether the country had lost its moral compass in Iraq in its attempt to elicit information from terrorists.[3]

The issue of torture and the handling of terrorists also generated significant national debate in connection with Camp Delta, the prison set up at the Guantánamo Naval Base in Cuba after the invasion of Afghanistan. International human rights organizations and numerous civil liberties groups in the United States accused the U.S. military personnel at Camp Delta of using torture methods in violation of established international war standards. As information filtered out of Camp Delta and from various other locations (many in eastern European countries such as Romania, Bulgaria and Poland) that prisoners were being subjected to a form of interrogation called water boarding, the debate intensified in the United States and the halls of Congress over permissible means of finding out key information from detainees.[4]

Because water boarding involves simulating the drowning experience by continuously pouring water over the detainee's face until he or she submits to answering questions, many critics of this policy stated that it was a violation of international agreements and placed the United States in the company of torturers. Bush administration officials denied the statement that water boarding was torture and stressed the importance of gaining valuable information from detainees. When asked about water boarding, Vice-President Cheney stated, "We don't torture. That's not what we're involved in." Attorney General Michael Mukasey, who was less clear about water boarding, said, "There are some circumstances where the current law would appear clearly to prohibit water boarding, but other circumstances would present a closer question." As for President Bush, his position was clear, "We do not condone torture. I have never ordered torture. I will never order torture. The values of this country are such that torture is not a part of our soul and our being."[5]

Although in the 2006 Detainee Treatment Act Congress had already banned any military use of water boarding, the fact that the CIA was using the water boarding technique created the confrontation between the White House and the Democrat-controlled Congress. Supporters of the White House position stated that Congress should not apply a military standard to an intelligence gathering standard, especially in time of direct threats to the United States. Because the use of water boarding gained such attention and raised serious questions about whether the United States condoned torture, the Bush administration sought to downplay its use as limited to only a few cases and essential for gaining information that stopped terrorist attacks.[6]

The handling of terrorist detainees also created another constitutional and institutional confrontation between the White House, Congress and also the Supreme Court. This time the issue was the right of detainees to have access to legal representation and ultimately a trial. The position of the executive branch dating back to 2002 was that the detainees were "unlawful combatants" who were outside the jurisdiction of civilian courts. Lawyers for the detainees complained that any individual held in a facility of the United States was entitled to challenge their detention, often termed the right of habeus corpus. As the issue of detainee rights worked its way through the federal court system, eventually the U.S. Supreme Court issued a decision.

In *Rasul v. Bush* (2004), the Court in a 6-3 ruling stated that the terrorists had habeus corpus rights and further that detainees could file challenges in U.S. district courts concerning their status as detainees. Later in *Hamdan v. Rumsfeld* (2006) the Supreme Court in a 5-3 decision stated that the military commissions established by the Bush administration without Congressional approval were unconstitutional and that the procedures laid out in the Geneva Convention on the legal rights of detainees did apply to the "enemy combatants" held at Guantánamo. After years of legal jockeying, in 2008 the Supreme Court by a vote of 5-4 overturned a Court of Appeals decision upholding the Military Commissions Act that the guarantee of habeus corpus does not apply to those "without property or presence within the United States." The high court, however, stated that indeed detainees had the right to challenge their imprisonment before a federal civilian court, thus opening up the floodgates of petitions for trial by detainees and dealing the Bush administration a stunning defeat.[7] The controversial ruling (*Boumedienne v. Bush*) heightened legal activity as many of the detainees pressed the courts to hear their case and supporters of detainee rights rushed forward to advance the cases of those held without opportunity to have their case heard in court.[8] By 2008 hundreds of detainees still did not have opportunities to challenge their incarceration, although scores of cases were filed for review in U.S. district courts by attorneys representing the detainees.

The next issue related to the detainees involved the decision by President Obama's Attorney General Eric Holder, who announced that the mastermind of the 9/11 attacks, Khalid Sheikh Mohammed, would be tried in civilian court, likely in New York City. Holder took the position that Sheikh Mohammed should be tried as any other criminal and receive the same legal rights during the trial. The decision touched off a new controversy as conservatives condemned the civilian trial, saying that Sheik Mohammed should be tried as an enemy combatant with limited rights in a military court. After the public outcry the Obama administration stated that it would not try Sheik Mohammed in civilian court and would instead move the proceedings to a military base. Despite this change of position, conservatives continued to paint the president and his attorney general as soft on the detainees and willing to provide them with constitutional protections.[9]

FYI

The Geneva Convention and the Use of Torture

In 1948 the United Nations General Assembly adopted an advisory resolution called the Universal Declaration of Human Rights. The United States was a signatory of the document. In Article five the matter of torture is addressed in the following manner:

> "No one shall be subjected to torture or to cruel, inhuman or degrading treatment or punishment."

In 1949 the Geneva Conventions were promulgated and also signed by the United States. Convention Three Article Seventeen states:

> "No physical or mental torture, nor any other form of coercion, may be inflicted on prisoners of war to secure from them information of any kind whatever. Prisoners of war who refuse to answer may not be threatened, insulted or exposed to unpleasant or disadvantageous treatment of any kind."

But later in Convention Four Article Five there is an exemption to the above-mentioned protection from torture:

> "Where in the territory of a Party to the conflict, the latter is satisfied that an individual protected person is definitely suspected of or engaged in activities hostile to the security of the State, such individual shall not be entitled to claim such rights and privileges under the present Convention. . . . In each case, such person shall nevertheless be treated with humanity."

Besides the issues surrounding how to handle the terrorists held in U.S. custody, there was debate over how to properly conduct the war, in particular whether the accent should be on crushing the insurgents or working out a political deal that would satisfy the various religious and regional groupings and then concentrate on nation-building and democracy-enhancement strategies. In 2007 President Bush began to refocus the war in anti-terrorist terms rather than by accenting nation building and democratization. Increasingly the refrain heard from the President was that, "fighting and defeating the terrorists in Iraq would ensure that they would not follow us home and attack the United States." Other leading Republicans such as Senator John McCain predicted that a precipitous pullout from Iraq would lead to chaos in Iraq and growing instability in the Middle East. Radicals in Iran and other countries would dominate the region and weaken the influence of the United States. As the civil war and anti-American insurgency continued in Iraq, what had initially began as a war of liberation and protection against weapons of mass destruction gradually evolved from the

Republican perspective to a war on terrorism and an essential line in the sand against those radical Islamists who sought to drive the United States out of the Middle East and threaten the homeland.

However, a growing chorus of critics in Congress, both Democratic and Republican, began to question the prospects of winning and the value of fighting the war on terror in Iraq, rather than going after a rejuvenated al Qaeda in the mountainous border regions of Afghanistan and Pakistan. Democrats in Congress and those seeking the presidency such as Barack Obama emphasized that all our presence in Iraq did was help al Qaeda to recruit fighters, which actually increased the terrorist threat both in Iraq and elsewhere in the region. The U.S. military was increasingly seen as fighting in the middle of a civil war with both sides targeting American soldiers. But opponents of the Bush policy in Iraq treaded lightly on criticizing the war for fear of being perceived as weak on terrorism, especially in the wake of a resurgent Iran, which many experts felt would move quickly to exert considerable influence on Iraq should the United States leave or reduce its presence in the country.

Data Bank

Osama bin Laden remains number one on the FBI's Most Wanted List. The reward for his capture, dead or alive, or proof of his whereabouts was originally set at $25 million. But in 2005 the State Department sought to double the reward to $50 million, and Congress went along with the request.

Source: FBI and the U.S. State Department.

As U.S. forces remained in Iraq and soldiers continued to be targets of warring religious factions and al Qaeda fighters, a critical policy question emerged that formed the debate among Washington political leaders and the American public—what would the war on terror become if the United States left Iraq? President Bush presented what he called a "dark vision" of Iraq and indeed the region after a withdrawal. Speaking at the 2007 American Legion convention in Nevada, the president stated frankly, "the region would be dramatically transformed in a way that could imperil the civilized world." Bush predicted that without the United States as a stabilizing force and political chaos dominating Iraq, terrorist centers would form, energy supplies to the world would be placed in jeopardy and a regional arms race would begin with Iran taking the lead in the development of nuclear weapons. Bush went further when he stated that without the presence of the United States in Iraq, "extremists could blackmail and sabotage the global economy."[10]

The "dark vision" of President Bush was based on the premise that radical governments in Iran and state-sponsored terrorist regimes in Syria and elsewhere would take advantage of a U.S. military withdrawal to reshape the region by intimidating pro-American countries such as Saudi Arabia, Kuwait and the United Arab Emirates and financing terrorist groups such as Hezbollah in Lebanon and Hamas in Palestine so as to embolden them in their mission to destroy Israel. In the opinion of the Bush administration, the Middle East would become a region constantly destabilized and radicalized with few moderates in power and no semblance of democratic governance. Such a set of circumstances would, according to the president, create a huge Islamist terrorist haven that would threaten western interests and be used as a launching pad for worldwide terrorist activities, including attacks on the United States or U.S. assets abroad.

The president's vision of a post–U.S.-occupied Iraq was not shared by his opponents in Congress or his critics in the media. Democratic candidates for the presidency stated that the real terrorist threat was in Afghanistan, where by 2008 the Taliban had regrouped and repopulated its forces to become a potent military force that boldly challenged undermanned NATO forces. During the presidential campaign Senators Obama and McCain argued over where the terrorist threat was most intense and lasting, in Afghanistan with the Taliban or in Iraq with Iranian-supported al Qaeda fighters. The disagreement between Obama and McCain, and indeed between Democrats and Republicans, liberals and conservatives, was over how long the United States should stay in Iraq and Afghanistan. At one point in the campaign Senator McCain was criticized for stating that the United States might have to stay in Iraq "100 years" to establish stability and root out al Qaeda, whereas Obama stressed a phased but steady withdrawal with the accent on Afghanistan not Iraq.

With the victory of Barack Obama in the November election, there was much anticipation in Washington and indeed around the world about how the new president would deal with the terrorist threat, including the status of Camp Delta, the handling of al Qaeda detainees and the controversial issue of torture. Quickly after the inauguration Obama signed an executive order closing Camp Delta and pledged that the United States would not employ torture techniques such as water boarding against al Qaeda or other foreign terrorists. Obama's decision to close Guantánamo immediately created a deep political divide in Washington as Republican critics demanded to know what the president's plans were for the 245 detainees remaining at Camp Delta. There was concern among many in Washington that these detainees would be released to fight once again, although Obama and his Secretary of Defense Robert Gates pledged that they would be dispersed to federal prisons throughout the country or sent to prisons in foreign countries.[11] The partisan division over the detainees became so intense that Congress denied funds for the closing of Camp Delta, as Democrats joined Republicans in a huge setback for the Obama administration.[12] By 2010 the Obama administration took the position that delaying the closing of Camp Delta beyond the promised date of January was the best course of action. White House officials acknowledged that the process of closing down the facility was much too complex, in large part because of the difficulty of placing the detainees in prisons either abroad or at home.[13]

Also the pledge not to use torture techniques became embroiled in a debate over whether water boarding was indeed torture and whether the United States had the responsibility to use what Republicans termed "enhanced interrogation techniques" as a means of gathering crucial information from detainees about possible future terrorist attacks. Again former Vice-President Dick Cheney entered the political fray stating on numerous occasions that the use of water boarding (which he did not define as torture) was critical in the early days and months after 9/11 in gaining important information about al Qaeda and al Qaeda terrorist plans.[14] The Obama administration maintained its position that it would not condone torture and included water boarding as a form of torture. Moreover, the administration stated that the use of water boarding only weakened the reputation and standing of the United States in the world.[15]

Obama's terrorist policies became even more controversial when secret CIA memos were released by the Justice Department (in response to a court filing by the American Civil Liberties Union) that described a range of interrogation methods, including water boarding, were employed on al Qaeda Chief of Operations Abu Zubaydah and on Khalid Sheikh. Beginning in 2002 and lasting until 2005, the memos showed that the Bush administration approved the use of water boarding and other techniques such as sleep deprivation and placing insects into the cramped cells of the detainees to elicit information. In releasing the memos President Obama said that he was opposed to torture techniques such as water boarding because " . . . I am convinced that the best way to do that (interrogate terrorist prisoners) is to make sure we're not taking shortcuts that undermine who we are."[16]

The release of the CIA memos intensified the partisan division as Bush administration officials castigated the president for releasing the memos and for not releasing memos that showed Vice-President Cheney's justifications that the techniques worked in terms of providing valuable information that crucial to stopping further terrorist attacks.[17] Other critics pointed out that the memos gave terrorists an inside view of what interrogation techniques the United States has used, thus providing them with opportunities to prepare to respond to such techniques in the future. Democrats also criticized the Bush legal team for their support of expanded (and in the view of Bush critics, unconstitutional) presidential powers to use torture methods as a wartime necessity. These powers are often referred to as based in the concept of a "unitary executive", which justifies a president having wide latitude in conducting national security policy. The concept of a "unitary executive, however, was viewed by Democrats as a direct attack on the separation of powers and Congress" responsibility to check and balance presidential actions.[18] The Obama administration, however, stood its ground and said that the memos pointed to numerous violations of the Geneva Convention and harmed the image and reputation of the United States around the world. Numerous military interrogators with experience in questioning terrorists came to the defense of the president, stating that other methods of eliciting information from enemy combatants were much more effective than techniques such as water boarding.[19]

The torture issue continued to divide members of Congress as Democrats pushed for hearings that would bring Bush Justice Department officials to testify on their justification for the use of torture techniques such as water boarding. Assistant Attorney General (and later an Appeals Court Justice) Jay Bybee, White House Counsel John Yoo and CIA General Counsel John Rizzo among others were targeted by Democrats as the chief supporters of the use of "enhanced interrogation techniques." There was also talk of a so-called Truth Commission to determine the extent of the Bush administration's support for the interrogation techniques with the veiled threat of possible prosecution of key officials. President Obama showed little interest in these hearings and a Truth Commission, fearing that it would divide the country and focus Washington policy makers and indeed the country away from his economic and domestic agenda, but liberal Democrats pressed on seeking to bring the Bush administration to account for what the Democrats believed was a pattern of illegal and anti-American activity. Republicans and those in the conservative movement were outraged that such an attack on the Bush administration was being pressed by the majority party in Congress as they believed that during the years after 9/11 the Bush administration acted properly in using such interrogation techniques, legal or illegal, to save American lives and property.[20]

Although the partisan debate swirls around Washington over detainees and their torture, there remains the critical issue of the future direction that terrorist activity will take against the United States and around the world. Currently there is a major debate in academic and national security circles about how threatening al Qaeda is to the United States and its allies and how the future of anti-terror campaigns will look. Some such as Mark Sageman, a former CIA officer, are convinced that al Qaeda's days are over, in large part because its leaders (except Osama bin Laden) are dead or in hiding. Future attacks on U.S. domestic and international assets will come from loose cells of jihadists who may be easier to identity and contain. Others such as Bruce Hoffman of Georgetown University fear that al Qaeda has been reinvigorated and is an even larger threat. Hoffman believes that in the future the United States will face an al Qaeda terrorist organization that has spread to most of the developing world. There are no shortages of foot soldiers ready to carry out terrorist attacks, according to Hoffman, and as a result the war on terror will continue for years to come.[21]

Another avenue to view the current state of the war on terror is the annual survey of 100 national security and foreign policy experts conducted by the Center for American Progress and the Carnegie Endowment for International Peace. The bipartisan survey published in the September/October 2008 issue of *Foreign Policy* found that the experts polled viewed the war on terror in a more positive light compared to past years. In the 2007 survey, 91% said that the world was "growing more dangerous for Americans and the United States." But in the 2008 survey, 70% agreed with that assessment. Furthermore in 2007 when asked if the United States was "winning the war on terror," only 6% of the experts agreed, but in 2008, 21% stated that the United States was "making headway in fighting terrorism." Finally in a general assessment of the global war on terror, 55% of the experts saw the threat from terrorist networks as increasing, down from 83% in 2007.[22]

Although there is disagreement about how threatening al Qaeda is and how it will operate in the future and some cautious optimism about the overall trend in the war on terrorism, there is little disagreement that the war on terror as conducted by the Bush administration alienated many in the Middle East who viewed the United States with a mix of suspicion and disdain. Efforts by the Bush administration to develop programs of public diplomacy to win the hearts and minds of the people in the Middle East failed, and international polls during the Bush years pointed to a low level of support for the United States and its policies in the region.[23]

Once in office Barack Obama sought to mend relations with the Middle East and to weaken the argument of terrorists that the United States was intent on dominating the region and waging war on Islam. Obama spoke early in his presidency in an important speech at Cairo University in Egypt that the United States respected Islam and sought to cooperate with the countries in the region, even Iran, which has been a major financial and arms supporter of al Qaeda and other terrorist groups. Obama's conciliatory position and his rejection of torture along with the promised closing of Camp Delta gave al Qaeda terrorists fewer sources of anger to direct at the United States and emboldened moderates in the region to reject the terrorist alternative. It is important to point out that while in office President Obama has greatly increased the use of pilotless drones equipped with Hellfire missiles that have killed scores of top Taliban leaders and hundreds of fighters in Afghanistan. The president has also expanded the use of Special Forces troops to infiltrate Taliban outposts and other terrorist hideouts elsewhere in the world to send a message that the United States is going to keep up the pressure against terrorists wherever they are hiding and operating. However, it is also important to point out that despite the change in tone by the Obama administration and the expanded use of drone attacks against the Taliban, it is impossible to predict whether these steps will guarantee an end to al Qaeda terrorism or other homegrown anti-U.S. attacks. The United States will continue to face a fanatical army of terrorists bent on killing Americans.

Finally, it is important to mention that terrorist attacks against the United States are not only from al Qaeda or similar organizations. Currently over 900 right-wing hate groups are active in the United States, and their numbers are growing, especially since the election of Barack Obama. Americans remember the bombing of the federal office building in Oklahoma City by Timothy McVeigh in 1995. In 2009 and 2010 new evidence was found of the willingness of right-wing fanatics to use violent methods to send a message to law enforcement officials and the American people. A killing of an abortion doctor by a pro-life devotee in a Wichita, Kansas, church, the fatal shooting of a guard at the National Holocaust Museum in Washington by an anti-Semitic extremist and the arrest of a Michigan extremist group that was believed to be targeting police officials are stark reminders that terrorism comes in various forms, but with the same deadly results.

The concern over right-wing extremism sparking homegrown terrorism was the topic of a study by the Department of Homeland Security in 2009. One of the key findings of the study was that "Threats from white supremacists and violent anti-government groups during 2009 have been largely rhetorical and have not indicated plans to carry out violent acts. Nevertheless, the consequences of prolonged economic downturn . . . could create a fertile recruiting environment for right-wing extremists and even result in confrontation between such groups and authorities similar to those in the past." Law enforcement officials at the federal, state and local levels are keeping a close eye on these groups, including infiltrating their ranks and monitoring their Internet, cell phone and social networking communications.[24]

Dealing with terrorists in our rule of law/constitutional rights system is bound to be controversial, especially during a time of war. Bridging the divide between those who believe firmly in constitutional protections and those who are concerned that protecting the country from attack is paramount will always be difficult.

The Great Debate

President Obama and former Vice-President Cheney engaged in a major public discussion over torture (or as Cheney termed water boarding, "enhanced interrogation techniques"). The discussion was framed by Obama as a need to return to American values and constitutional principles by rejecting torture, whereas Cheney emphasized the importance in the war on terror of protecting the homeland from another terrorist strike, even if that meant using controversial interrogation techniques.

Debate Topic

Should the United States use every means available, including military intervention, detention without constitutional rights and torture techniques in its battle against terrorists?

Critical Thinking Questions

1. Do you believe that water boarding is torture? What interrogation techniques should be permissible?
2. Was the Obama administration correct in pledging to close Camp Delta at Guantánamo?
3. What rights should foreign terrorist detainees have under the U.S. Constitution?
4. Should the President have expanded, even extra-constitutional powers, to fight terrorism?
5. Do you believe that the terrorist threat will weaken or strengthen?

Connections

The FBI War on Terror site is quite helpful in understanding the U.S. approach to combating terrorism. See http://www.fbi.gov/terrorinfo/counterrorism/waronterror.htm

The Obama policy on the war on terror can be accessed at http://www.whitehouse.gov/nsc/nss.html

DHS.gov

The Defense Department website on national security and anti-terror policies is also valuable. See http://www.defenselink.mil

John Robb writes a popular blog on terrorism and technology. See http://www.globalguerrillas.typepad.com

The organization Physicians for Human Rights has been one of the most outspoken critics of Bush torture policies. See http://www.physiciansforhumanrights.org

Some Books to Read

Allison, Graham, *Nuclear Terrorism: The Ultimate Preventable Catastrophe* (New York: Times Books, 2004).

Danner, Mark, *Torture and Truth: America, Abu Ghraib, and the War on Terror* (New York: New York Review of Books, 2004).

Krueger, Alan, B. *What Makes a Terrorist: Economics and the Roots of Terrorism* (Princeton, N.J.: Princeton University Press, 2007).

National Commission on Terrorist Attacks on the United States: The 9/11 Commission Report (New York: W.W. Norton, 2004).

Berman, Eli, *Radical, Religious and Violent: The New Economics of Terrorism* (Cambridge: MIT Press, 2009).

Notes

1. For background on the run-up to the Afghanistan invasion see Bob Woodward, *Plan of Attack* (New York: Simon and Schuster, 2004).
2. For background on the preparations for the invasion of Iraq see Robert Draper, *Dead Certain: The Presidency of George W. Bush* (New York, Free Press, 2007).
3. For a timeline of the controversy see the *American Journalism Review*, http://www.ajr.org/article/asp?id=3730
4. For a discussion of the reform of Abu Ghraib prison see a study conducted by the Carnegie Endowment for Peace at http://www.carnegieendowment.org/arb/?fa=show&article=22772
5. These quotes were presented in the *Washington Post National Weekly Edition*, February 18-24, 2008, p. 9.
6. Scott Shane, "Waterboarding Used 266 Times on 2 Suspects," *New York Times*, April 20, 2009, A1.
7. *Hamdan v. Rumsfeld*, 126 S. Ct. 2749 (2004).
8. For a discussion of the court decision regarding detainee rights in civilian court see Ronald Dworkin, "Why It Was a Great Victory," *New York Review of Books*, August 14, 2008, pp. 18–21.
9. Barton Gellman, "Courtroom Drama: Mohammed's Trial in New York City Could Be a Parable of Right and Wrong," *Washington Post National Weekly Edition*, November 23–29, 2009, p. 6. See also Otis Stephens Jr. "Presidential Power, Judicial Deference and the Status of Detainees in an Age of Terrorism," in David Cohen and John W. Wells, eds., *American National Security and Civil Liberties in an Era of Terrorism* (New York: Palgrave MacMillan, 2004).

10. President Bush Addresses the 89th Annual National Convention of the American Legion, Council on Foreign Relations, Essential Documents, August 28, 2007.

11. Sheryl Gay Stolberg, "Obama Would Move Some Detainees to U.S.," *New York Times*, May 22, 2009, A1.

12. David Herzenhorn, "Funds to Close Guantanamo Denied," *New York Times*, May 21, 2009, A1.

13. Peter Baker and David Johnston, "Guantanamo Deadline May Be Missed," *New York Times*, September 20, 2009, A27.

14. For background on the issue of Bush administration debates over torture, see Mark Mazetti and Scott Shane, "Debate Over Interrogation Methods Sharply Divided the White House," *New York Times*, May 4, 2009, A13.

15. Herzenhorn, "Funds to Close Guantanamo Denied," *New York Times*, op. cit.

16. Mark Mazetti and Scott Shane, "Memos Spell Out Brutal CIA Modes of Interrogation," *New York Times*, April 17, 2009, A1. See also Jane Mayer, *The Dark Side: The Inside Story of How the War on Terror Turned into a War on American Ideals* (New York: Doubleday, 2008).

17. Former Vice-President Dick Cheney's criticism of the Obama position on dealing with terrorism is contained in a speech at the American Enterprise Institute. See "President Obama's Anti-Terrorism Policy: Endangering America," Speech delivered at the American Enterprise Institute, Washington, D.C., May 21, 2009.

18. See Christopher Berry and Joel Gersen, "The Unbridled Executive," University of Chicago Law Review, 2008.

19. The response to former Vice-President Dick Cheney's criticism of President Obama's anti-terrorism policy can be found in a speech delivered at the National Archives Museum. See "President Obama's Anti-Terrorism Policy: Protecting American Lives and Principles," Speech delivered at the National Archives Museum, Washington, D.C., May 21, 2009.

20. For background on this issue of the Bush torture policy see Investigation into the office of Legal Counsel's Memoranda Concerning Issues Relating to the Central Intelligence Agency's Use of "Enhanced Interrogation Techniques" on Suspected Terrorists, a report by the Office of Professional Responsibility, Department of Justice (February 19, 2010). For a discussion of this report see David Cole, "They Did Authorize Terror, But . . . ," *New York Review of Books*, April 8, 2010, pp. 42–43.

21. See this debate discussed in Peter Bergen, "Dead or Alive?" *Washington Post National Weekly Edition*, August 25–31, 2008, pp. 25–26.

22. See "The Terrorism Index," *Foreign Policy*, September/October, 2008, pp. 79–85.

23. See, for example, a World Public Opinion survey on Iraqi support for the United States withdrawal, http://www.worldpublicopinion.org/pipa/pdf/sep06/iraq_sep06_rpt.pdf

24. Department of Homeland Security, "Rightwing Extremism: Current Economic and Political Climate Fueling Resurgence in Radicalization and Recruitment," 2009.

3 GLOBAL WARMING AND CLIMATE CHANGE

Issue Focus

Issues are often categorized as domestic or foreign, but with the concern over global warming the issue range has expanded to the entire planet. Dealing with the effects of global warming has thus become a global issue with governments from around the world seeking ways to form policies and agreements that stem the advance of global warming and its impact on climate change, species protection, environmental degradation and perhaps most important economic security and prosperity. Despite strong scientific evidence concerning global warming, there is also skepticism in some circles about the data, policies and agreements that have been proposed to deal with this challenge to the planet.

Chapter Objectives
This issue chapter will seek to:
1. Define global warming and the range of its impacts on environmental and climate conditions.
2. Present the contentious debates over the sources of global warming and the effect that public policies may have on the national economy and consumer choices.
3. Discuss the short- and long-term potential of global warming to change the planet and the way humans live on it.

SOME BACKGROUND

In 2006 former Vice-President Al Gore helped to develop and narrated a documentary film entitled *An Inconvenient Truth* and followed up the book with a movie by the same title. Gore's *An Inconvenient Truth* was basically a sophisticated slide show on the impact of global warming on the planet. Gore took viewers on a tour of regions of the world that had been dramatically affected by the warming of the earth. Gore's slide presentation, for example, showed how many of the arctic glaciers had shrunk significantly within a relatively short period of time (twenty to thirty years), and a disturbing environmental trend that if allowed to continue without major changes in economic activity and consumer lifestyle would lead to devastating consequences for human and animal life, sea levels and climate change. The slide show was an immediate box office success (Gore along with his collaborators on the project eventually won an Academy Award), and he later won the Nobel Peace Prize for his work alerting the world to the dangers of global warming.[1]

As a result of *An Inconvenient Truth* combined with dire warnings from the scientific community, global warming has entered the daily lexicon of conversation. As commonly defined, global warming is the gradual increase in global temperatures caused by the emission of gases that trap the sun's heat in the earth's atmosphere (often termed the greenhouse effect). Gases that contribute to global warming include carbon dioxide, methane, nitrous oxides, chlorofluorocarbons (CFCs) and halocarbons (the replacements for CFCs). The carbon dioxide emissions are primarily caused by the use of fossil fuels for energy such as coal, oil and natural gas. It is important to point out that some level of greenhouse gas emission is essential, because their absence would cause the earth's temperature to be around 0 degrees Fahrenheit, instead of an average of 59 degrees Fahrenheit. But as the level of greenhouse gases has increased, so has its impact on temperature and the resulting in climate such as changes in rainfall patterns, a rise in sea level and impacts on plants, wildlife and humans. Over the last one hundred years the earth has warmed up by about .6 degrees centigrade, and in each of the last ten years the average temperature for the earth has been the highest ever recorded.[2]

To see what many in the scientific community view as the impact of global warming on the planet and the potential it has for radically changing our world, the following specific examples of climate change provide a cautionary note on where we may be headed:

- Scientists predict that in fifteen years all the glaciers in Glacier National Park in Montana will disappear.
- In the summer months of 2005 more than 200 cities in the western United States broke all-time heat records. On July 19, 2005, Las Vegas hit a high of 117 degrees, a record.
- In 2004 the all-time record for tornadoes was broken.
- In July 2005, one month before Hurricane Katrina hit New Orleans and the southern Mississippi coastline, a study by scientists at the Massachusetts Institute of Technology concluded that global warming was making hurricanes more powerful.
- Over 14 million acres of spruce trees in Alaska and neighboring British Columbia have either died or are at risk from bark beetles, which are now thriving in the much warmer regions of North America.[3]

FYI

The top five largest polluting states as measured in millions of metric tons of carbon equivalents are Texas, California, Ohio, Pennsylvania and Florida. Texas is by far the largest polluter in the country with 166.6 metric tons of carbon equivalent emissions as measured in 1999.

Source: National Environmental Trust, 2002.

Defining global warming has never been much in dispute, nor has there been any difficulty of finding an ever-growing list of examples of how warming has affected the planet. But what has caused a storm of controversy are the issues of whether human activity, particularly industrial and consumer activity, is the root cause of the warming trend and whether public policy measures should be taken to limit or curtail the human activity causing the warming trend. Passionate debates have dominated the economic, social and political arenas over how best to respond to global warming and whether global warming is a major threat to the planet that must be dealt with immediately or a natural occurrence that does not require changes in lifestyle, a restructuring of economic activity or massive governmental intervention. But because global warming may have the potential to radically change the planet and threaten humankind, the issues of how serious to take this warming trend and how best to deal with the impacts strike at the heart of how we live, how we develop as a nation and how we look at the future.

DEBATES, DIFFERENCES AND DIVISIONS

The scientific community is largely in agreement that global warming is the result of human activity. Many of the key scientific societies and leading scientific journals have come to a consensus on the causes of elevated greenhouse gases and the resulting presence of global warming. The prestigious United Nations Intergovernmental Panel on Climate Change, which brought together the leading scientists in the world working on global warming, issued a widely discussed report in 2007 that stated clearly and without reservation that global warming is man-made and that if significant corrective measures were not taken soon the planet would face devastating consequences.[4] The key findings of the U.N. Panel are as follows:

1. Warming of the climate system is unequivocal.
2. Most of the observed increase in globally averaged temperature since the mid-20th century is very likely due to the observed increase in human emission of greenhouse gases.
3. Global warming and sea level rise will continue for centuries, even if green house gases were to be stabilized.
4. The probability that this is caused by natural or climatic processes alone is less than 5%.
5. The world temperature could rise by between 2 and 11.5 degrees Fahrenheit during the 21st century.

In 2009 the warnings of the U.N. Panel were validated by a group of environmental scientists meeting in Copenhagen, Denmark. The conclusion of these experts was that sea levels appear to be rising nearly twice as previously predicted in the 2007 study. The Greenland and Antarctic ice caps are melting at an accelerating rate with sea levels rising to a level at which low-lying regions will face catastrophic flooding, and in the process devastate coastal cities such as New York, Miami and Boston by 2050 and beyond.[5]

But scientific consensus has not curtailed opposing views on the source of global warming and the measures that should be taken to save the planet. Critics of the prevalent view, who make up a minority of the scientific community, state that scientists who support mainline global warming are ignoring alternative theories on the sources of the buildup of greenhouse gases and the positive applications of global warming on the planet. Furthermore, the critics state that the scientific majority is blindly following the consensus in order to not be ostracized from their profession and shut out from research grants. At the heart of the opposing view on global warming are questions about the accuracy of temperature readings that include readings of urban areas where higher levels of heat are generated, variations in global temperature over time despite rising carbon dioxide levels and solar activity in which the sun's output has changed over the last sixty to seventy years thus contributing to the warming of the globe. Moreover, after nearly twenty years of steady temperature increases (1970–1998, with 1998 being the warmest year on record) in the last few years temperatures in the United States have either held steady or increased only slightly, prompting some critics to state that global warming may be a temporary phenomenon.[6]

Jerry Taylor, the director of natural resource studies at the libertarian Cato Institute, is representative of the skepticism of global warming when he states, "Everyone accepts the fact that the planet's surface has warmed by about a degree Fahrenheit over the last 100 years. But it turns out that the warming is quite a bit below what the computer models say should have occurred by now. What it means is that on a January evening in Yellowknife, Canada, instead of being 28 degrees below zero it might be 25 degrees below zero. It's very hard to spin disaster stories around that."[7] The position of skeptics such as Taylor received an unanticipated boost in 2009 when a series of emails from scientists in England revealed that data on global warming had been tampered with to validate findings of temperature increases, while contrary data was suppressed. The controversy called "climategate" embarrassed the scientific community and put many of those who were in leadership roles in the global warming movement on the defensive. Although scientists on the U.N. panel continued to stress that their data was accurate, the issue of global warming was now not without significant debate.[8] The new skeptics in the global warming debate have been successful in turning public opinion in the United States away from acceptance of global warming as reality to concern that the scientific community may have gotten it wrong. A 2009 poll conducted by the Pew Research Center for the People and the Press found that Americans are less inclined to believe that there is strong scientific evidence that the earth has gotten warmer. Only 36 percent of the respondents believed that human activities contributed to temperature increases, whereas 57 percent stated that they agreed with scientists that the earth has gotten warmer over the last decade, a 14 percent drop from 2008 to 2009.[9]

These disagreements over whether global warming is a reality have served as the basis for the ideological and partisan battles that fill the halls of Congress and the White House. Liberals and environmentalists who view global warming as a human-made calamity that requires swift and comprehensive controls on fossil fuels rely heavily on the scientific consensus and chide conservatives in and out of government for ignoring overwhelming evidence of the connection between greenhouse gases and human activities. Conservatives and the business community retort that there is sufficient question about the reliability of the scientific data to move with caution and that the lockstep movement of environmentalists to put a break on fossil fuels regardless of the economic results would lead to a meltdown of the American economy.

But despite the disagreements and the use by political and environmental groups of these disagreements to influence public policy, there is no question that the United States is a critical player in the global warming debate, and much of the differences of opinion and the partisan divisions surrounding greenhouse gases and the proper public response to the warming of the planet have been at the center of national politics and have spilled over into the international realm as well. With the United States using about 25% of the world's resources, primarily fossil fuels, and the average American sending about 15,000 pounds of carbon dioxide into the stratosphere each year, other industrialized countries and many less-developed nations have accused the United States of perpetuating a national culture of energy wastefulness, following national policies that accent economic development over conservation and moving slowly to embrace alternative fuel sources.[10]

Criticism in the United States and foreign countries was especially harsh toward the Bush administration, which was accused of moving too slowly to embrace the position of those in the scientific community that believe global warming is fast approaching a "tipping point," where opportunities to stave off the harmful effects of climate and nature change may diminish significantly, leading to enormous environmental dislocations. Predictions of rising sea tides that would bury many coastal cities, to a new ice age that would destroy life as we know it, are often cited as realities of the near future of global warming. In the face of such harsh warnings, the Bush administration held fast to the position that full-scale government intervention in the national economy to address the dangers of global warming would severely weaken the United States, particularly by curtailing industrial production and crippling the automotive industry.

To better understand the politics of global warming and the current tensions that exist in the United States over this controversial issue, it may be helpful to review the manner in which government has responded through public policies and executive actions. The United States took a major step toward reducing emissions of greenhouse gases during the presidency of George H.W. Bush. Pledging to be the "environmental president," Bush pressed for the passage of the Clean Air Act of 1990. Despite oppositions from members of Congress representing industrial states such as Michigan and Ohio, Bush was able to fulfill his promise on clean air. The Clean Air Act placed stronger controls on fuel use by automobiles. The legislation required automakers to install pollution devices on cars to reduce dangerous emissions. The act also addressed emissions from factories. Industrial plants that emitted above a certain level of gases were required to install devices (commonly called scrubbers) that would clean the air. Paying for what many in the business community called the costliest clean air program in history, the yearly $2.5 billion price tag associated with the intent of the Clean Air Act was seen as a necessary step to address the areas of environmental regulation that had been neglected by previous administrations. Although some business leaders complained about the new level of regulation, the Clean Air Act of 1990 was viewed as a watershed of vigorous environmental policy.[11]

The victory of the Bush administration in its domestic environmental agenda was not easily transferable to the international arena. The Earth Summit in Rio de Janeiro, Brazil, in 1992 brought into view the debate between the United States and the less developed world over who would make energy sacrifices to avoid the dangers from global warming. The United States reluctantly signed a treaty that would require the country to place a limit on emissions of greenhouse gases at 1990 levels by the year 2000. However, although many less-developed countries doubted whether the United States would ever meet the requirements of the treaty, the Clinton administration began taking policy steps to achieve emission controls that met the emerging international standards. In Clinton's first term, a broad-based energy tax was proposed as a way of meeting this goal. Republicans, however, opposed the measure, arguing that the administration really wanted the tax for the sake of deficit reduction rather than to prevent global warming. The tax went down to defeat.

In the second Clinton administration the debate over global warming and greenhouse emissions became more strident, as new pressure was placed on the United States by the less-developed world and European powers. In 1998, at another United Nations Conference on the environment held in Kyoto, Japan, the Clinton administration took a controversial stance supporting more vigorous emission controls as a way of responding to the threats from global warming. Vice-President Al Gore, representing the United States at the conference, linked the extreme weather conditions the world recently experienced and the beginning of polar icecap meltdown as signs that the world community of nations must take serious measures in limiting emissions. Business leaders responded quickly to the Gore position, arguing that the economic vitality of the nation depended upon the continued productivity of our industrial base and that emission controls would cripple what had become at the time the longest and most sustained period of economic growth in U.S. history. The lines between environmentalists and supporters of economic growth had been clearly drawn, with the government at the center of the debate. The Kyoto agreement, although supported by the Clinton administration, was never ratified by the U.S. Senate.[12]

On the Record

In his book *An Inconvenient Truth*, Al Gore said the following:

> I have learned that, beyond death and taxes, there is at least one absolutely indisputable fact: Not only does human-caused global warming exist, but it is also growing more and more dangerous, and at a pace that has now made it a planetary emergency.

Once George W. Bush entered the White House, the emphasis on responding to global warming shifted from mandatory emission controls to technological advances and voluntary compliance. As a sign that he was wary of the environmental policies of the Clinton administration, President Bush placed a hold on 175 regulations, of which many were designed to put greater controls on corporate practices that could heighten the release of greenhouse gases and other pollutants. Bush was acting out of concern that the Clinton administration had introduced far too many regulations that established unnecessary restrictions on the corporate sector. Critics, however, countered that Bush was seeking to gut much of the progress made by the Clinton administration in using the regulations to protect the environment from global warming.

More evidence about the changed policy position on greenhouse gases emerged as the incoming Bush administration did not support the Kyoto Protocol and would not send it forward to the Senate for ratification. President Bush did, however, undertake the Clear Skies Initiative in 2002, which targeted power plant emissions of dangerous chemicals such as sulfur dioxide and mercury and sought a 70% decrease in the emission of these pollutants. Critics were quick to challenge the president on the initiative because it failed to address carbon dioxide, the main source of greenhouse gases. The Bush administration countered the arguments against the Clear Skies Initiative by stressing that instead of mandatory emission controls, an alternative plan that sought an 18% reduction in the emission of greenhouse gases over ten years was being put in place. The alternative plan was tied to a formula linking the amount of carbon dioxide emitted to each dollar of gross domestic product. This formula was touted by the president as slowing the growth of greenhouse gases without endangering the economy. In a speech announcing the Clear Skies Initiative, President Bush predicted that his alternative proposal would take the equivalent of 70 million cars off the road. As he stated at the announcement, "This is a common sense way to measure progress. Our nation must have growth. Growth is what pays for investments in clean technologies, increased conservation and energy efficiency."[13]

Despite the president's reluctance to address the carbon dioxide emission issue with mandatory controls and his accent on a mix of voluntary compliance by businesses, gradual measures to address greenhouse gas buildup and technological advances to replace fossil fuels, Bush faced a growing body of evidence that greenhouse gases were accumulating at rapid rates in the atmosphere and contributing to heightened temperature increases. As early as June 2001 a White House Commission reported to him that "national policy decisions made now and in the longer-term will influence the extent of any damage suffered by vulnerable human populations and ecosystems later in this century." In 2002 the Environmental Protection Agency (EPA) issued a Climate Action Report that linked global warming with human activity. With such reports and other data from academic and research sources, the White House began to concede that scientific conclusions on the influence of human-made sources of global warming could not be ignored. Nevertheless, the president continued to stress the dangers of mandatory controls on the American economy as contained in the Kyoto Protocol and instead pushed for voluntary initiatives.[14]

The Bush administration's position on global warming was weakened by a series of media reports which showed that the oil and gas industry executives were closely involved in shaping government studies on global warming. Philip Cooney, a White House aide and former oil company executive, was accused by members of Congress and environmental groups of changing the language used in government studies to downplay the influence of human-made sources on global warming. Cooney and business groups such as the Global Climate Coalition were viewed as aggressively seeking to influence the final drafts of government research. Also troublesome for the Bush administration was the public statements of James Hansen, the Director of the National Aeronautics and Space Administration's Goddard Center, who charged that the White House was misleading the American public and raising doubts about what he viewed as sound scientific research on the causes of global warming. Hansen stated that the Bush administration wanted only public statements from government scientists that "fit predetermined, inflexible positions."[15]

Although President Bush did not embrace the scientific conclusions about the human-made sources of global warming, in his 2006 and 2007 State of the Union addresses he did speak about the importance of weaning America away from foreign oil and moving quickly to develop alternative sources of energy using the latest technology. By continuing to stress technology and alternative fuel sources, the president was staying true to his position that mandatory compliance or other suggestions such as a carbon tax or gasoline surcharge would only lead to serious economic consequences for the American economy. As the president said in his 2006 State of the Union address, "America is on the verge of technological breakthroughs that will enable us to live our lives less dependent on oil. And these technologies will help us be better stewards of the environment, and they will help us to confront the serious challenge of global climate change."[16]

But President Bush's lukewarm position toward the dangers of global warming and his staunch opposition to mandatory emission policies gradually gave way to a willingness to move toward more aggressive and comprehensive policies that would address what more and more Americans were seeing as looming threat to the planet. By June 2007 President Bush went on record at a European summit in support of reducing greenhouse emissions by 50% by 2050 (still voluntary, not mandatory) and agreed to work more closely with the United Nations to achieve that result. It seems that the president in this global warming debate had been "overtaken by events" as states such as California and cities such as New York began to implement strong measures to limit greenhouse gases. Governor Arnold Schwarzenegger of California signed a unique agreement with British Prime Minister Tony Blair that both would work to reduce greenhouse gases.[17] In New York City, Mayor Michael Bloomberg took the unprecedented steps of requiring taxi cabs to be hybrid autos and instituting a heavy tax on cars coming into the city. As of

2007, 522 mayors of American cities representing 65 million Americans pledged to support the Kyoto Protocol's goal of reducing greenhouse emissions by 7% below 1990 levels by 2012.[18]

The clearest evidence that the president had been "overtaken by events" in the global warming debate was the movement of many high-level and high-profile business leaders who began a push to move toward a resolution of the emissions deadlock and take the country forward as quickly as possible to energy independence and a greening of America using alternative fuels and new technology. Jeffrey Immelt, the CEO of General Electric (GE), for example, made numerous public statements about his intention to take GE into a new generation of green technology and the commitment of the firm to more energy-responsible product development. CEOs such as Immelt were not without their critics, especially from worried shareholders concerned about the uncertainty of future profits if the company pursued an aggressive greening strategy. Oil and gas industries that worried over the future growth of their products opposed a more comprehensive and substantive energy policy. Despite some opposition, the trend in the automotive industry was toward a new environment-friendly approach to car making. Automotive leaders were talking hybrid cars, and agricultural interests were touting the benefits of ethanol and other oil substitutes that derived from corn, sugar and other commodity staples.[19]

Data Bank

Home-cooking stoves used in the less-developed world are one of the top sources of carbon dioxide emissions. These stoves, which burn wood, dung or crop residue, produce black carbon, which is now considered as the source of 18% of carbon dioxide (with 40% from fossil fuel emissions from petroleum products). Although "fixing" the carbon dioxide emission from fossil fuels will be a long and complex process, scientists claim that replacing the cooking stoves with more modern and efficient stoves that do not produce black carbon would produce a measurable decline in emissions in a relatively short period of time.

Source: *New York Times*, April 16, 2009, A1

Once in the White House, Barack Obama shifted gears quickly on the global warming issue. During the presidential campaign Obama promised to make the global warming threat a high priority and to put in place measures that would begin to aggressively attack the problem. On the campaign trail Obama said, "Few challenges facing America and the world are more urgent than combating climate change. The science is beyond dispute and the facts are clear. Sea levels are rising. Coastlines are shrinking. We've seen record drought, spreading famine, and storms that are growing stronger with each passing hurricane season."

Within days of taking office, Obama issued two executive orders, one that ordered the U.S. Department of Transportation to increase automobile fuel economy standards and the other ordered the U.S. EPA to begin developing a feasibility study that would allow individual states to enforce their own greenhouse gas emissions. The EPA directive was the result of California's efforts (opposed by the Bush administration) to allow states to develop their own greenhouse gas policies. Finally, in April 2009 Secretary of State Hillary Clinton announced that the United States would take the lead in negotiating a global warming treaty, saying, "The United States is fully engaged and determined to lead and make up for lost time both at home and abroad . . . we are back in the game."[20]

President Obama echoed these renewed efforts to move quickly and comprehensively to deal with the impact of global warming at an international climate conference in Copenhagen, Denmark in 2009. President Obama warned that "the time we have to reverse this tide (of global warming) is running out," action by his administration has been unsuccessful in forming a comprehensive bill to deal with greenhouse gas emissions. Again disagreements over the impact of tough regulations on key areas such as coal-fired power plants and the automobile industry have stalled what has come to be called climate change legislation in the Senate.[21]

Joined with these debates over public policies is the fundamental issue of how much of a sacrifice the American people are willing to bear and what that sacrifice will mean in terms of their quality of life. In an analysis by the *Washington Post*, legislation and executive branch regulation that sought to reduce U.S. fuel emissions by 60% in the next twenty years would require enormous changes to the American consumer and corporate landscape. Auto makers would have to double gas mileage, builders would have to overhaul building codes to make for greener structures and utilities would have to raise electric bills by 25% or more just to initiate the development and implementation of new energy-saving technologies. The *Post* study concluded that as many as 1 million wind turbines would have to be built, 400 new power plants using advanced technology would need to be placed on line and solar panels covering half of the state of New Jersey would be required. The cost for all this revamping of the American energy system would cost in the trillions and necessitate significant tax and rate increases that would have a marked impact on the pocketbooks of Americans.[22]

Even if the United States started immediately on a comprehensive plan to revamp its energy system and energy use, it would take decades to put into place an effective response to the ever-expanding march of global warming. Much of the Congressional legislation that has been offered in recent years uses 2020 to 2040 as target dates for the implementation of a national response to the rise in greenhouse gases and the progression of global warming. Meanwhile the policy recommendations from the scientific community to face the dangers from global warming are not just vague futurist projections, but rather firm beliefs that significant impacts from temperature could be seen this century. There is a growing group of scientists who believe that the planet could experience major environmental repercussions in a matter of decades, and that some of the changes we are seeing presently such as wild weather, eroding beaches, high temperatures and the extinction of various plant and animal species are but the harbingers of immediate dislocations from global warming. In June 2009 the Obama administration released another study on global warming that reinforced earlier predictions that global warming was already having significant impacts on climate, sea levels, polar ice caps and animal life.[23]

But alongside these warnings there continue to be those who question the wisdom of dealing with global warming by drastic and expensive public policies. Global warming skeptics such as Danish Professor Bjorn Lomborg question the practicality of spending billions, if not trillions, of dollars on programs to reduce greenhouse gases, when in his view the threat is not only distant, but the economic impact on the world's economy would not be devastating. Lomborg's position is summed up in this quote: "The cost and benefits of the proposed measures against global warming is the worst way to spend our money. Climate change is a 100 year problem, we should not try to fix it in 10 years."[24]

The policy responses on how best to deal with the impact of global warming on the planet are thus coming from all directions. The debates, differences and divisions that marked this issue in the past are slowly but surely being replaced with a cautious national consensus that a comprehensive national energy plan of action must be taken now rather than piecemeal adjustments and the promise of new technological breakthroughs. Even though there remain legitimate concerns that stiff controls on emissions would lead to economic dislocations, those concerns are now in competition with a growing public realization that the effects of global warming may be much more serious to humankind than the prospect of a possible economic slowdown.[25] As a result, some form of balance between growth and conservation must be reached in the United States and indeed around the world, and efforts to develop and introduce new technologies that replace fossil fuels must be advanced with greater speed. There are still many unknowns about global warming and the growing levels of greenhouse gases in the stratosphere, but there is little doubt that humans have contributed to this crisis and that humans will have to take steps to respond effectively to the crisis and protect the planet we all share.[26]

Meanwhile researchers continue to alert the world to the dangers of global warming. In 2010 in the prestigious Proceedings of the National Academy of Sciences, climate experts reported that rising temperatures could reach levels by 2100 where humans would be unable to live. Although the research of the National Academy is a worst-case scenario, the UN Intergovernmental Panel on Climate Change verified the threat to human existence because of global warming. Its study came to the conclusion that by 2100 temperatures would rise 7 degrees, unless drastic measures were taken to control greenhouse gases. While the debate on global warming continues, the consensus in the scientific community looks more and more distressing.[27]

The Great Debate

Much of the debates, differences and divisions regarding global warming are associated with the short- and long-term sacrifices that may have to be made to respond to the effects of temperature increases caused by carbon dioxide emissions.

Debate Topic

Should the United States take drastic economic and consumer measures to offset the impact of global warming?

Critical Thinking Questions

1. Do you believe that the impact of global warming is an immediate threat to our planet's survival?
2. How do you respond to the conservative position that the answer to global warming is new technology rather than controlling carbon emissions?
3. Is it possible for the American public to change its energy use to lessen the dangers from global warming?
4. Why is global warming not higher on the priority list of critical national problems and challenges?
5. What would be your policy recommendations for dealing with global warming?

Connections

The EPA has a campaign called "Reduce, Reuse, Recycle," which is designed to assist in the fight against global warming. Find out more about it at http://www.epa .gov/msw/reduce.htm

A number of websites deal with climate change. http://www.environet.policy.net and http://www.climateark.org are two of the best.

Many interest groups are involved in responding to global warming. The Sierra Club is one of the leading groups. See http://www.sierraclub.org/globalwarming

Alternative energy sources may be the key to responding to global warming. The most helpful website is http://www.eere.energy.gov/consumer/renewable_energy

A website that accents global warming skeptics' views can be found at http://www .globalwarmingskeptics.org

Some Books to Read

Lomborg, Bjorn, *Cool It: A Skeptical Environmentalist's Guide to Global Warming* (New York: Knopf, 2007).

James Hansen, *Storms of My Grandchildren: The Truth About the Coming Climate Change Catastrophe and Our Last Chance for Survival* (New York: Bloomsbury USA, 2009)

McKibben, Bill, *Fight Global Warming Now: The Handbook for Taking Action in Your Community* (New York: Holt Paperbacks, 2007).

Romm, Joseph, *Hell and High Water: Global Warming–The Solutions and the Politics and What We Should Do* (New York, William Morrow, 2006).

Nordhaus, William, *A Question of Balance: Weighing the Options on Global Warming Policies* (New Haven: Yale University Press, 2008).

Notes

1. Gore, Al, *An Inconvenient Truth* (New York: Rodale, 2006).
2. Seth Borenstein, "Effects of Warming Have Worsened Since Kyoto," *Boston Globe*, November 23, 2009, A2. See also "No Hiding Place," *The Economist*, January 9, 2010, pp. 78–79.
3. *An Inconvenient Truth*, op.cit. pp. 42–68.
4. See Elisabeth Rosenthal, "UN Chief Challenges US, China on Climate Change," *Boston Globe*, November 18, 2007, A3.
5. "A Sinking Feeling," *Economist*, March 14, 2009, p. 82.
6. See Bob Carter's critique of global warming, particularly his view that the planet has not had an increase in temperature since 1998. Bob Carter, "There IS a Problem with Global Warming . . . it stopped in 1998" http://telegraph.co.uk/comment/personal-view/3624242/There-IS-a-problem-with-global-warming . . . it-stopped-in-1998-.html
7. As quoted in Dennis Behreandt, "Global Warming Skepticism," *The New American*, http://www.thenewamerican.com/index.php/tech-mainmenu-30/environment/311
8. John Broder, "Scientists Take Steps to Defend Climate Work," *New York Times*, March 3, 2010, A1. See also "Spin, Science and Climate Change," *The Economist*, March 20, 2010, p. 13.
9. Dina Cappiello, "Skepticism Over Global Warming on Rise, Poll Suggests," *Boston Globe*, October 23, 2009.
10. See Gregg Easterbrook, "Hot Prospects: Who Loses and Who Wins in a Warming World," *Atlantic*, April 2007, pp. 52–66.
11. See the Clean Air Act in its entirety on the EPA website, http://www.epa.gov/air/caa
12. See a critique of the Kyoto Accords in Clive Cook, "Sins of Emission," *Atlantic*, April 2008, pp. 32–33.
13. The Clear Skies Initiative is explained and evaluated at http://www.cbsnews.com/stories/2002/06/03/tech/main510920.shtml
14. For a discussion of the dissent and controversy in the Bush administration over global warming policy, see "A Global Warming-Denying Bush Official Burrows in at the NSF," http://climateprogress.org/2009/01/27/kathie-olsen-denier-burrows-nsf/. See also Andrew Revkin, "Under Pressure, White House Issues Climate Change Report," May 30, 2008, A1.
15. See http://www.msnbc.msn.com/id/7195164.
16. See http://www.c-span/executive/stateoftheunion.ASP
17. Anthony Faiola and Robin Shulman, "Urban Greening," *Washington Post National Weekly Edition*, June 18–24, 2007, p. 33.

18. Sheryl Gay Stolberg, "Bush Calls for U.S. to Halt Rise in Gas Emissions by 2025," *New York Times*, April 17, 2008.

19. Easterbrook, Hot Prospects, op.cit. pp. 62–63.

20. John Broder, "U.S. Ready to Lead on Climate Pact, Clinton Says," *New York Times*, April 28, 2009, A16.

21. See "President Obama Says Global Warming is Putting Our Safety in Jeopardy," ABC News, September 22, 2009, http://www.abcnews.com/politicalpunch/2009/09/president-obama-says-global-warming-is-putting-our-safety-in-jeopardy.html

22. "Internal Rifts Cloud Democrats Opportunity on Warming," *Washington Post*, January 23, 2007, A01.

23. See "White House Sounds Alarm on Climate Change," http://www.cbsnews.com/stories/2009/06/16/tech/main5092090.shtml

24. Bjorn Lomborg, "Chill Out," *Washington Post National Weekly Edition*, October 15–21, 2007, p. 26. See also, "Full of Sound and Fury," *Economist*, July 14, 2007, pp. 32–33.

25. David A. Fahrenthold, "Assuaging Guilt or Saving the Planet," *Washington Post National Weekly Edition*, February 4–10, 2008, p. 15.

26. Steven Mufson, "Turning Down the Heat," *Washington Post National Weekly Edition*, July 23–29, 2007, pp. 6–9.

27. See "Report: Climate Change Could Render Much of the World Uninhabitable," USA Today, May 10, 2010, http://content.usatoday.com/communities/sciencefair/pkost/2010/05/report-climate-change-could-render-much-of-world-uninhabitable.html

4

HEALTH CARE AND HEALTH CARE REFORM

Issue Focus

To most Americans, health is a high priority, if not their highest personal concern. Access to health care services, cost factors, quality of care and the knowledge that a serious medical condition will be addressed in a timely manner are at the core of the health care debate, which is currently at the forefront of national politics. Added to these concerns is the proper role of government in a nation's health system. Because this issue is so personal and involves the intervention of government, health care and health care reform are hot-button issues in American politics.

Chapter Objectives
This issue chapter will seek to:
1. Explain the challenges facing all sectors of the health care industry in the United States—patients, medical professionals, hospitals and insurance companies.
2. Discuss the various policy options designed to address the health care crisis.
3. Examine the disagreements over the extent that government should become involved in dealing with the health care crisis. As evidence of the intensity of the debates, differences and divisions over health care and health care reform, this issue has lingered unresolved on the nation's policy agenda since the Truman administration.

SOME BACKGROUND

Just about everyone has heard the words, "your health is everything." In American politics health care and health care reform is the "everything" on the domestic issue agenda. Health care has rocketed to the top of the policy concerns of the American people and has become an issue that is central to electoral politics and partisan competition. In many respects the health care issue is a perfect storm of challenges for the American political system and indeed for all the major players that make up the health care industry from hospitals to doctors to insurance companies to patients. Americans take great pride in their health care system, and many of them have come to expect that health care should be viewed as a basic right, even though its costs are sky-rocketing. But their pride in the health care system and their view that they should be entitled to quality care, no matter the cost, has run up against the realities of the marketplace and the fact that their system is not without its limitations and breakdowns. As we shall see, much needs to be done to fix the U.S. health care system, and major disagreements continue on how to fix it.

From a dollars and cents perspective, the U.S. health care system is the costliest in the world. The United States spends $2.2 trillion annually, approximately 17% of its national income on health care, which is more than many of the other industrialized nations; that 17% is the equivalent to $5,540 for each man, woman and child in the United States. It is estimated that health care costs will rise to $4 trillion by 2019, taking almost 21% of the gross domestic product (GDP). However, although the United States spends a substantial portion of its national wealth on health care, many Americans are without health benefits. Currently, it is estimated that 47 million Americans are without a health care plan, and one watchdog group, Families USA, which monitors the impact of health care on the middle class, stated that in 2002–2003 as many as 82 million Americans were without health care at some point.[1]

The health care debate often returns to the matter of costs and the effect on the economy. Because many of the Americans who have health care insurance receive it as a benefit from their employer (as of 2006, 161 million Americans were covered with some form of health insurance through their place of employment), the cost of health care has had a major impact on corporate earnings. In 2006 one estimate of the cost of coverage to American employers for a family of four was $14,500 and was steadily rising above the rate of inflation each year. As a result of these heavy health care coverage costs, many businesses are scaling back their benefits or denying them to their employees, thus further increasing the ranks of the uninsured. These cutbacks have often led to difficult contract negotiations with unions and retirees from unions who resist any reduction or elimination of existing health care coverage. But in a competitive, global economy U.S. business leaders have taken a strong position on the need to focus on the costs related to health care and its impact on the corporate bottom line. In 2004 G. Richard Wagoner Jr., then chairman of General Motors (GM), told the Detroit Free Press that rising health care costs were "crippling the competitiveness of U.S. business," and that "it is well beyond time for all of us to put partisan politics behind us and get together to address this health care crisis."[2] In 2006 GM spent $5.6 billion on health care for 1.1 million employees and retirees. GM executives say that health care costs add $1,500 to $2,000 to the cost of their cars.[3]

Rising health care costs have also had serious financial impacts on local governments and hospitals. Many local communities have been faced with rising premiums for their employees at a time when homeowners and businesses are enduring higher taxes for public services. Whereas in the past most of the issues of local government finances involved employee salaries, currently salary issues are joined with government officials cutting back on the community's share of health insurance coverage. With respect to hospitals, the issue is the use of the emergency room by the uninsured, which not only places enormous demands on the staff, but leads to prohibitive costs that many small-size hospitals have been unable to carry. Hundreds of small- and medium-size hospitals have either closed or have had to merge with larger hospitals to survive, in part because of the costs related to care of the uninsured.

But besides the issues of coverage and cost, there is also growing evidence that the health care system, despite its reputation for technological sophistication and a high level of expertise, has serious deficiencies. For example, the distribution of medical professionals is heavily weighed toward urban areas, leaving many in rural locations with inadequate or completely absent care. Furthermore, the endless and complicated paperwork that accompanies a visit to the doctor or the hospital has left patients both frustrated and angry. There is also the growing concern among health care professionals that the issues of coverage and costs have placed the challenges of dealing with chronic illnesses such as cancer, diabetes and obesity in the background. The Partnership to Fight Chronic Disease, a non-profit advocacy group, has stressed the importance of placing greater emphasis on disease control and eradication. Kenneth Thorpe, the founder of the Partnership, stated in 2007 that, "for too long, the national debate has been focused on access and who gets covered. But what we should be talking about is how we can drive costs down and provide better care."[4]

There is no doubt that health care policy and health care reform are "hot" issues and their importance as a critical national priority is growing. President Obama made health care reform a high-priority policy objective, despite the inevitable costs involved associated with the government playing a larger role in solving this problem. However, responding to the challenges of health care in America during the Obama presidency is certain to create an ongoing ideological and partisan standoff. Meanwhile the number of uninsured grows, and the numerous breakdowns in U.S. health care systems continues unabated. And, with Americans now living longer and therefore placing greater strains on health care providers, the push for the reform of the system is certain to remain a controversial issue for years to come.

DEBATES, DIFFERENCES AND DIVISIONS

Fixing the health care crisis in the United States is not a new issue. In the 1970s, after years of lying dormant in Congress, the late Senator Edward Kennedy of Massachusetts sought to implement a universal medical coverage system in the United States modeled after the systems in Europe, often called the single-payer system. His efforts were never able to gain Congressional support and were often criticized by health care interest groups who were opposed to what they viewed as a turn toward socialized medicine and big government intervention. For years the problems associated with health care costs and the lack of a national health care policy languished in the background of public policy with little interest by either presidents or Congress. But as the problems associated with health care continued to worsen, especially the number of uninsured, President Clinton established the Task Force on National Health Care Reform in 1992. The Task Force was charged with recommending legislation that would reform health care in the United States.

On the Record

At a health care summit early in his administration, President Obama highlighted the importance of health care reform, saying at a White House meeting:

We cannot delay this discussion any longer. Health care reform is no longer just a moral imperative, it is a fiscal imperative. If we want to create jobs, rebuild the economy, and get our federal budget under control, then we must address the crushing cost of health care this year.

Source: White House Press Office

The formation of the Task Force ran into immediate controversy as the First Lady, Hillary Rodham Clinton, was appointed to lead the group. After extensive study from experts in the area of health care and highly publicized tours around the country to gather first-hand information from Americans who had been negatively affected by the system, the Task Force presented a complex 1,000-page proposal that required employers to provide insurance coverage to their employees through health maintenance organizations (HMOs) that would be closely monitored and regulated by the government. Immediately the proposal, which came to be called the Health Security Act, faced a storm of opposition as many of the sectors affected by the plan complained that the bill was heavy on bureaucratic intervention and had limited patient choice. A massive campaign, funded by conservatives and opponents of a government-directed health care insurance system, was waged. In what is now a famous ad campaign launched to help scuttle the Clinton Health Security Act, a middle-class couple, named Harry and Louise, sat in front of the cameras and bemoaned the reform as too complex and bureaucratic. The ad was paid for by the Health Insurance Association of America.[5]

With key interests opposed to the bill and the Democratic majority in the Congress not enamored with the Clinton proposal, the Health Security Act was scuttled. Because the power of the hospital and insurance sectors was so great and the perception of the American people that big government was going to control their health care so widespread, the bill never made it through the legislative process. In 1994 the Republicans took power in the House and Senate, thus further destroying any hopes of bringing government-directed health care reform to a vote. Many critics blamed Hillary Clinton for the failure of the Health Security Act, especially her inability to work with Congress and respond effectively to the interest group and media attacks. But the key to the defeat of the Clinton health care reform was the fact that the proposals were complex, bureaucratic and relied too heavily on government involvement.

FYI

The Canadian Single-Payer Health System

The United States is the only industrialized nation that does not have a government-sponsored and government-supported health care system. The so-called single-payer system, which is in place in Canada, is often viewed as a model for the United States. Currently, Canada directs 9% of its GDP toward the national health care system. All Canadians are covered by the single-payer system and receive an identification card that they take to the hospital for verification. Because of the single-payer system Canadians do not pay directly for their health care, but provincial taxes are considerably higher in Canada than they are in the United States. Although Canadians take great pride in their health care system, problems such as long waits for operations, a low-tech style of medical care and considerably lower pay for doctors and nurses have caused a brain drain of medical personnel to the United States.

Source: Jill Quadrango, *One Nation Uninsured*

Health care issues stayed in the background through the remainder of the Clinton administration and well into the Bush years as the country turned toward managed-care plans, which included HMOs (provide care from a network of participating doctors for a set fee), point-of-service plans (HMOs that allow members to choose doctors from outside their plan) and preferred provider organizations (PPOs) (health care organizations that provide a wider network of physicians and hospitals to their clients). From 1993 through 1997 each of the health maintenance options grew significantly while the traditional fee-for-service plans declined in popularity. With HMOs and their various offshoots, the pooling of administrative resources, the developing of health professional resources and stable doctor and hospital fees (often called co-payments) created for a time an answer to the burgeoning health care demands of the American public and the ever-rising costs of hospital stays, medical technology, testing and doctor visits. These answers turned out to be incomplete; short-term solutions did little to deal with the ever-deepening health care crisis facing America.

Although the Clinton administration had failed in its effort to achieve major health care reform along the lines of the single-payer systems of Europe, it was able to make some headway with respect to health care reform. In 1996 President Clinton signed into law a measure that companies keep providing coverage to those who got sick while holding valid policies. Later that year, at the urging of the president and with enormous public pressure forcing the issue into the forefront of policy priorities, Congress passed legislation requiring that insurance companies provide at least two days of hospital care for mothers giving birth. An outcry over the practice known as "drive-through deliveries," which was supported by insurance companies and managed-care operators seeking to trim hospital costs, stimulated a change in policy. And in 1997 President Clinton's Advisory Commission on Consumer Protection and Quality in the Health Care Industry proposed a Patients' Bill of Rights, which was designed to provide Americans with some rules and expectations as they interacted with the health care system and managed-care operators. Despite bipartisan support in the Senate with Senators Edward Kennedy and John McCain leading the way, the Patients' Bill of Rights was never enacted into law; however, the bill of rights became a set of guidelines that individual states and some individual HMOs adopted.[6] As originally proposed by the president's Commission on Consumer Protection and Quality in the Health Care Industry, the Bill of Rights sought to guarantee the following:

Information Disclosure

Choice of Providers and Plans

Access to Emergency Services

Participation in Treatment Decisions

Respect and Nondiscrimination

Confidentiality of Health Information

Complaints and Appeals to Resolve Differences

Consumer Responsibilities Regarding Their Own Care

Data Bank

Some of the key health indicators for the United States are:

Life expectancy at birth (males)–75 years
Life expectancy at birth (females)–80 years
Probability of dying (per 1,000 of population) between 15 and 60–males–137
Probability of dying (per 1,000 of population) between 15 and 60–females–81
Total expenditure on health as percentage of GDP–15.4%

Source: United Nations

But as the country moved further and further into managed care, criticism of the system and its limitations increased significantly. Patients complained about the decrease in the amount of time that doctors spent with them, the difficulty getting referrals to specialists, the numerous instances of health plans refusing coverage for pre-existing medical conditions and the setting of spending caps for those with insurance who have serious medical problems. Health care in the United States became the target of patients and doctors who viewed the system as too focused on the bottom line, controlled by accountants and less and less interested in the quality of care for the patient. The HMO system had indeed kept the cost of health care down or at least controlled, but in the process it created new problems that struck at the heart of the doctor-patient relationship. Many patients complained that doctors were forced to engage in "assembly line" examinations, while the doctors bemoaned having to negotiate with insurance companies to gain approval for certain procedures. As Bill Gradison, the president of the Health Insurance Association of America, stated, "The public said to do something about health-care inflation, and we've been largely successful in doing that. Now, patients are saying, 'Hold on, we don't like the way you're doing it.' "[7]

With the HMOs under fire and the American public complaining about coverage and cost, it was inevitable that the health care system would enter the political arena. By 2007 as the campaign for the Presidency began to take shape and the number of uninsured continued to rise, talk of universal coverage for Americans once again percolated to the top of the domestic policy agenda. However, although health care reform was viewed as a national issue with intense disagreements and partisan gridlock that characterized the issue for so long, reform efforts began to take root at the state level. State governments started to deal with the gaps and the inequities in the current private sector system of insurance coverage and moved toward universal health care programs. In 2007 Massachusetts became the first state in the nation to mandate that each of its citizens have health care coverage. State officials in Massachusetts established a highly visible and aggressive public relations program to alert citizens to the new program and to warn them that failure to sign up for the program would lead to the loss of a tax deduction on the state income tax form. Although many Massachusetts residents without health care benefits hailed the program, critics pointed out that premiums, even for narrow preventive care, were still too high for many low-income workers ($7,000 annually for a family of three) and placed an undue burden on small businesses, which were required to provide coverage to their employees.[8]

The movement of Massachusetts to develop a universal health care program and the interest of other states such as California and Hawaii spurred political leaders running for the White House to present their own proposals that would be national in scope. Hillary Clinton, reprising her role from 1993, presented a health care insurance plan that would require all businesses to provide their employees with coverage. Employees would be required to purchase the insurance from their employer or through a program much like that used by federal employees. Those unable to purchase the coverage because of low incomes would be provided with tax credits. Businesses, especially small businesses that in the past feared the financial impact of providing health care to their employees, would also receive tax credits to ease the burden. To deal with the opposition from insurance companies, the Clinton proposal accented that millions of new clients would buy the health coverage, and because they would likely use the coverage in a preventive manner, not just for emergencies, Clinton was confident that the insurance companies would enjoy new found profits.[9]

Clinton promised that if elected she would use the power of government to keep health care costs down, but said that the level of regulation and intervention by the federal government would not be as expansive as the 1993 version of universal coverage. Clinton's plan stressed the importance of mandatory health care insurance much like the Massachusetts plan. Clinton added that under her plan there would not be any denial of insurance coverage for a pre-existing condition. To pay for the new health insurance, tax cuts established by the Bush administration for those Americans earning over $250,000 would be repealed. The cost of the Clinton health care plan was placed at $110 billion a year. Her Democratic opponent at the time, Barack Obama, diverged somewhat from her health care proposal by not placing primary emphasis on mandates but rather emphasizing child health care, barring private insurers from rejecting people because of pre-existing medical illnesses and forming risk pools to reduce premiums.[10]

On the Republican side, health care reform and universal coverage barely resonated among the presidential candidates and their supporters. Most of the candidates placed health care reform far down on their list of national priorities, and when they did talk about health care, their position was that market-based and tax-related solutions were the only answer, not government-directed programs. Mitt Romney on the campaign trail in 2007, for example, derided the Clinton health care plan saying, " 'Hillary Care' continues to be bad medicine . . . in her plan we get Washington-managed health care. Fundamentally she takes her inspiration from the bureaucracies." When the Republicans did talk from a policy perspective about health care they accented health care vouchers that Americans would be encouraged to purchase or the establishment of high-risk pools for the uninsurable to provide catastrophic care.[11] For his part President Bush in his 2007 State of the Union address did talk about ending the tax exemption on employer-based health insurance and stressed that, "free market, profit-driven health care" was the best way to deal with the health care demands of the country.[12]

Despite its opposition to government-directed national health insurance, the Bush administration directed its attention to a prescription drug program administered through the Medicare system. On January 1, 2006, the government launched its Medicare Part D initiative that aimed to subsidize the cost of prescription drugs for the 21 million eligible Medicare recipients. The prescription drug plan was designed to assist those seniors who were the poorest and most prone to illness with low-cost coverage for medications. The retirees in the Medicare system with higher incomes were given the option of purchasing prescription plans that required out of pocket premiums with deductibles and co-payments. The aim of Medicare Part D was simple enough to provide prescription drug coverage at a low cost. But getting the program off the ground became difficult as many seniors were confused as the coverage was channeled through a number of participating insurance companies who had their own eligibility rules and coverage regulations.

Although the Bush administration allocated over $400 million to introduce the plan to the American public, at the early stages of the program only a fraction of those eligible signed up for the subsidized program. Complaints arose about long waits for telephone assistance and poor communication between the Medicare administration and local pharmacies. Stories of many seniors going to pharmacies and finding out that they had exceeded their coverage and were now in the donut hole ran rampant and created frustration and anger among seniors. Eventually, however, after all the various communication and insurance problems were ironed out, many more seniors signed up for the reduced drug cost program and by 2007 the program was receiving positive reviews.[13]

The Bush prescription drug program was criticized by Democrats in Congress and senior advocates as too weighed in favor of the insurance, pharmaceutical companies and HMOs. Critics claimed that the legislation was drafted by insurance and pharmaceutical lobbyists working with key Republican representatives in the House such as former Louisiana Congressmen Bill Tauzin and then jammed through the Congress by the leadership in the dead of night without the opportunity for debate or amendments. Representative Tauzin eventually left Congress and took a job as the president and CEO of the Pharmaceutical Research and Manufacturers of America, one of the leading lobbying groups representing the drug industry. He received an annual salary of $2 million.

The Medicare Prescription Drug, Improvement and Modernization Act of 2003, which established the Medicare Part D program, was seen by critics as another example of the Bush administration's attempt to privatize health care in the country by encouraging seniors to sign up for private prescription plans. Initially the plan was touted as a cost-saving measure with the estimated bill at $400 billion over ten years, but within months of the passage of the bill the cost estimates jumped to $534 billion, and many opponents of the privatization initiative predicted that the costs would increase even higher, especially since drug costs were rising above the level of inflation. (The White House in 2005 raised the estimate of the program to $1.2 trillion over ten years.)

There were some clear corporate winners in the new prescription drug system. The profit returns to the pharmaceutical industry were estimated at $139 billion, with the insurance companies and HMOs also reaping huge gains. The legislation passed by the Republican-controlled Congress prohibited any group purchasing agreements and volume discounts with the drug companies as was the case with the Veterans Administration. The result of this prohibition is that the drug companies and their allies in the insurance industry and HMOs were protected from government-sponsored competitive pricing arrangements. So although Medicare recipients gained some new benefits and criticism died down as enrollments went up, it was the private sector that became the clear profit winners in this new prescription drug initiative.[14]

The different approaches to health care in the United States were made even more vivid during the 2007 Congressional debate over the State Children's Health Insurance Program (SCHIP). The program provides insurance coverage to 6.6 million children from families that are above the federally defined poverty level but do not have the money to purchase health benefits. A bipartisan Congress approved by wide margins a bill to increase the SCHIP funding by $35 billion over the next five years; this would add over 4 million new children to the program.[15] President Bush threatened a veto of the legislation and offered his own proposal that would increase SCHIP funding by $5 billion over five years. The president stated that he was opposed to the large increase presented by the Congress because it would place too many children into a government-based health insurance program. The increase funding of the SCHIP program was to be achieved through new federal taxes on cigarettes.[16]

Many observers of the Congressional debate and the president's threatened veto saw the battle over SCHIP funding as a prelude to an electoral battle over national health care that would likely be part of the 2008 campaign. As *Washington Post* columnist E.J. Dionne stated, "If a proposal with broad bipartisan support that is friendly to state governments and covers the most beloved group in society–children–can't avoid being gutted for ideological reasons, what hope is there for a larger health compromise."[17] Although President Bush was in no mood to compromise over the program, many members of Congress, both Democrats and Republicans, were reluctant to turn down a bill that was designed to improve the health of young children. Those in favor of the SCHIP program and its expansion vowed that they would continue to press for the health insurance for children. President Bush eventually vetoed the SCHIP legislation, and the House and Senate were not able to override the veto as Republicans stood by their president despite the anticipated criticism from voters in their home state and district. Two weeks into his Presidency, Barack Obama signed legislation that expanded publicly funded health insurance for children, thus overturning the Bush administration opposition to the SCHIP program. The cost was placed at nearly $33 billion over four years, but most of the cost would be born by an increase in the cigarette tax. As the president said at the signing ceremony, "The way I see it, providing coverage to 11 million children . . . is a down payment on my commitment to cover every single American."[18]

As the debate over health care reform continues and the differences and divisions become sharpened, there is no shortage of policy recommendations on how best to provide coverage to the uninsured, keep costs down and provide quality. In the early days of his administration President Obama called a health summit at the White House and brought together a wide range of health care professionals. At the summit and later in other public pronouncements, Obama signaled that he was seeking a truly bipartisan solution to the health care crisis. Although the core of the Obama health care reform was the so-called public option, a government program akin to Medicare that would compete with the private insurance industry and provide a low-cost health care package to those currently without medical insurance. Other aspects of the reform effort would address issues such as denial of insurance for pre-existing conditions, bureaucratic waste and the burgeoning cost of health care to employers, both large and small.

Republican leaders in the health care debate were staunchly opposed to the "public option" part of the Obama health care reform and offered their own solutions to the problem by offering solutions that accent personal responsibility for medical coverage. Some suggested that Americans should be offered the opportunity to purchase their own insurance in a way similar to buying life or car insurance. Favoring personal decisions rather than a big government program, Republicans argued, would create more market competition that would likely drive down prices of insurance and also serve as an incentive to individuals to take better care of themselves, because individuals would be footing the bill for their own health care. The key to the Republican plan was a system of tax credits and tax incentives offered to Americans as a way of footing the bill for the medical coverage.[19] The important point stressed by the Republicans was that a government-controlled and government-directed program to provide health care coverage to the uninsured would devastate the private insurance industry and add on another big government bureaucracy.

A variation of the personal responsibility model offered by the Republicans is the medical savings accounts. During the Clinton administration the Republican-controlled Congress approved an experiment to permit Americans to start medical savings accounts. After languishing for years with little Republican support, the Bush administration began to promote the accounts as a private-sector answer to medical coverage. The accounts work in a manner similar to retirement plans as citizens can contribute a sum of money ($2,600 for an individual and $5,150 for a family) to a tax-deductible account and use that money to pay for medical bills that were not part of any government-sponsored program. The objective of the medical savings accounts is to encourage Americans to provide for their own health care just like they provide for their own retirement. Critics of the savings accounts point out that many low-income Americans and those entering senior status might not be able to afford to place money aside for health care and that only those who are wealthy could take advantage of this opportunity.

By June 2009 the health care reform issue began to take shape. In a major address to the American Medical Association, President Obama laid out some of the key elements of his plan. Obama sought to link health care reform to the national economy as he stressed that if no changes are made to the manner in which medical care is delivered and paid for, both the business sector and the government would face costs that could easily keep the nation in a recession and further add to the national debt. Obama continued to stress the importance of the "public option" of his health reform package, but tried to gain support from doctors by accenting the importance of taking care of patients rather than dealing with insurance companies over approving tests and procedures and being reimbursed for their work. Obama also talked about his position on malpractice insurance (a sore spot for doctors, some of who booed the president) and the need to establish a national medical data base to bring greater efficiencies to a bureaucratically weighted down system of medical care. After the speech Republicans shot back that they would not accept any "public option" health care reform and stressed that the Obama plan would be cumbersome and would severely weaken the private sector insurance industry.[20]

The debate in Congress, the media and coffee shops on Main Street finally came to a vote in March 2010. Health care reform legislation was not only a fight between Democrats and Republicans, conservatives and liberals, but among an army of lobbyists representing the insurance industry, hospitals, pharmaceutical corporations, doctors and nurses associations, health care reform activists and the emerging Tea Party anti–big-government movement. It became clear early on in the debate that there would be differences on the bill between the House and the Senate and indeed among the Democratic members in both houses.[21]

Although the Republicans were united in their opposition to the public option and what they viewed as inevitable tax increases and government bureaucracy, the Democrats were faced with disagreement among their members over issues such as whether abortions would be covered in the new reform bill, whether insurance would become mandatory and whether businesses would be penalized for not providing health insurance to their employees.[22] To move the bill forward, the Obama administration eventually dropped the public option and concentrated their efforts on insurance industry reform in the area of extending coverage to children up to the age of 26, guaranteeing insurance to those with a pre-existing condition, requiring insurance companies to provide insurance to those who have lost their job or moved to a new job and doing away with caps on payments to the insured for expensive procedures.[23]

After weeks of partisan wrangling, a Senate version of the health care reform bill passed that served as the basis for a future agreement with the House. Republicans attacked the Senate bill as filled with secret deals that mollified conservative Democrats and much too expensive (estimated at the time at $1 trillion over a ten-year period). The Republicans' message did strike a chord with the American people as support for a major overhaul of the health care system waned, although most people liked many of the changes required of the insurance industry. On the Democratic side of the Congress, members in both houses were still at loggerheads over how to get the bill passed. President Obama, declaring that the time for debate was over, pushed the Democrats in Congress to find a compromise version of the Senate and House bills and move to a vote.[24]

On March 21, 2010, the House of Representatives by a margin of 216–212 votes passed a phased-in version of health care reform (the original Senate bill), with many of the popular insurance changes implemented almost immediately, while putting off till 2014 the more unpopular tax increases and mandates that caused concern among Americans and galvanized Republican opposition. Accompanying the vote was a smaller version of the bill (called a fix) that required the Democratically controlled Senate to pass a companion bill that met the objections of many members of the House. The Republicans in both houses were unanimous in their opposition. On March 23 President Obama signed the historic legislation and achieved what presidents since Harry Truman had failed to accomplish–comprehensive health care reform.[25]

Despite this victory, the opponents of health care reform vowed to repeal the bill and work to defeat those Democrats who voted for the bill. Many Americans remained skeptical about the bill and were unclear about how the bill might affect them. Serious concerns remain about the role of government in health care and the cost of nearly $1 trillion over ten years. The Obama administration praised the bill as not only morally right, in that it would cover an additional 32 million Americans and bring reform to the insurance industry, but that it would also help to bring down the federal deficit with reforms in the Medicare program. Saying that health care reform remains a hot-button issue is an understatement. The legislation has passed, but the debate continues.

Since the importance of good health in this country is an issue with a wide public consensus, the attainment of this goal in terms of establishing policies, programs and reforms breaks down the consensus, creating only debate, differences and divisions. The conflict associated with health care reform is one of those issues where fundamental agreements over the broad concerns do not lead to a consensus on the details.

The Great Debate

Health care reform has proven to be a difficult policy problem to resolve. Part of the problem is the basic issue of whether Americans are entitled to guaranteed health care, even though such guarantees would be costly and involve some form of government intervention.

Debate Topic

Is health care in the United States a basic right that should not be denied to Americans despite the cost?

Critical Thinking Questions

1. Why do you believe the United States the only industrialized country not providing universal health care?
2. Should the government take policy measures to limit the influence of the pharmaceutical companies and permit more competition through access to foreign markets, government-sponsored bidding contracts and an increase in generic drugs?
3. Some have said that Americans should solve their health care crisis using tax breaks and other private sector incentives. Do you agree?
4. Should health care benefits be part of an employment package or should the employee be responsible for his or her health care coverage?
5. Should Americans be forced, through mandated-care programs, to either buy their own health care coverage or have access to inexpensive but government-supported health plans?

Connections

A good place to start learning about national health care is the U.S. Health and Human Services website. Health and Human Services is responsible for all government programs related to social welfare and health. http://www.os.dhhs.gov

The trade organization representing the health insurance companies of the United States has a website that is worth viewing to gain a perspective on this critical sector of the U.S. health care system. See http://www.ahip.org/

The Consumers Union is a watchdog of the health industry in the United States. Check out its website http://www.consumereport.org

The American Medical Association is active in the debate on national health care and other health care policies. www.ama-assn.org

Massachusetts has the nation's first state-directed mandated health care program. The program called the Commonwealth Connector is explained at http://www.mahealthconnector.org/portal/site/connector

Some Books to Read

Behan, Pamela, *Solving the Health Care Problem: How Other Nations Have Succeeded and Why the United States Has Failed* (Albany, NY: State University Press of New York, 2006).

Cohn, Jonathan, *Sick: The Untold Story of America's Health Care Crisis* (New York: Harper Collins, 2007).

Emanuel, Ezekiel J., *Healthcare, Guaranteed: A Simple, Secure Solution for America* (New York: Public Affairs, 2009).

Longest, Beaufort, *Health Policymaking in the United States* (Washington, D.C.: Health Administration Press, 2005).

Quadagno, Jill, *One Nation, Uninsured: Why the United States Has No National Health Insurance* (New York: Oxford University Press, 2005).

Notes

1. Data on health care in America can be found at the Families USA website. See http://www.familiesusa.org
2. David Broder, "Our Broken Health Care System," *Washington Post*, July 15, 2004.
3. Lee Hudson Teslik, "Health Care Costs and U.S. Competitiveness," Council on Foreign Relations, March 4, 2009, http://www.cfr.org/publication/13325
4. David Broder, "An Urgent Case for Fixing Health Care," *Washington Post*, May 29, 2005.
5. See the discussion of the 1993 Health Security Act and the failed Clinton effort to reform health care on the PBS News Hour, http://www.pbs.org/newshour/forum/may96/background/health_debate_page2.html
6. See Patel, Kant and Rushefsky, Mark, *Politics, Power and Policy: The Case for Health Care Reform in the 1990s* (New York: M.E. Sharpe, 1997).
7. Interview with Bill Gradison, http://www.content.healthaffairs.org/cgi/reprint/4/4/41.pdf
8. "Study Praises Mass. Health-Care Program," *Washington Post*, June 4, 2008, A08.
9. "Clinton Calls for Universal Health Care" http://ABCnews.go.com/politics/wirestory?id=3610855
10. The various positions of the candidates running for the Presidency in 2008 can be found in an article by Perry Bacon Jr. and Anne Kornblut, "A Reformer, Reformed," *Washington Post National Weekly Edition*, September 24–30, 2007, p. 13.
11. Ibid. p. 13.

12. http://www.c-span/executive/stateoftheunion.asp
13. The Department of Health and Human Services website explains the drug prescription program. See http://cms.hhs.gov/prescriptiondrug
14. Ceci Connelly, "Millions Not Joining Medicare Drug Plan," *Washington Post*, February 21, 2006, A1.
15. Jacob Weisberg, "Drug Addled: Why Bush's Prescription Plan is Such a Fiasco," Slate, January 8, 2006. http://slate.com/id/2134456
16. Sasha Issenberg and Susan Milligan, "Bush Vetoes Children's Health Insurance Bill," *Boston Globe*, October 4, 2007, A2.
17. *Washington Post*, September 26, 2007, A19.
18. Noam Levy, "Obama Signs Children's Healthcare Bill," *Boston Globe*, February 5, 2009, A2.
19. See, for example, the Republican Party health care proposals at http://www.gop.com/2008Platform/HealthCare.htm
20. See Helene Cooper, "Obama Tries to Woo Doctors on Health Care," *New York Times*, June 16, 2009, A1.
21. See Arnold Relman, "The Health Care Reform We Need and Are Not Getting," *New York Review of Books*, July 2, 2009, pp. 38–40. See also Dan Balz and Jon Cohen, "Deep Divisions," *Washington Post National Weekly Edition*, November 23–29, 2009, p. 13 and the website of the *New England Journal of Medicine*, http://healthcarereform.nejm.org
22. Robert Pear and David M. Herzenhorn, "Haggling Over Abortion Compromise in Health Bill," *New York Times*, November 5, 2009, A19.
23. For a comparison of the House and Senate versions of the bill see "Health Reform: How the Bills Stack Up," *Washington Post National Weekly Edition*, November 23–29, 2009, p. 16. See also the website of the Kaiser Family Foundation, http://www.kff.org/healthreform/sidebyside.cfm
24. Carl Hulse, "White House Pushes Senate to Act Quickly on Health Care Bill," *New York Times*, November 9, 2009, A1.
25. Robert Pear and David M. Herszenhorn, "Obama Hails Vote on Health Care as Answering 'the Call of History,' " *New York Times*, March 21, 2009, A1.

5 ILLEGAL IMMIGRATION

Issue Focus

No issue presented in this book creates such strong opinions among the American people as how the United States should deal with its illegal immigrant population. One of the founding principles of American political culture is the importance of holding to the rule of law, yet the United States is a nation made up of immigrants from all over the world, who often contribute to the general economy and enrich its society. Those immigrants who come to the United States as undocumented aliens have touched off a furious debate as to how to properly match the American governing principle of the rule of law with the reality of millions of illegal immigrants who are part of the national economy.

Chapter Objectives
This issue chapter will seek to:
1. Explore the extent of illegal immigration into the United States and the reasons for the migration of undocumented workers.
2. Discuss the pros and cons of the policy responses of federal, state and local governments to illegal immigration.
3. Examine the benefits and drawbacks of illegal immigration on the American economy, federal, state and local services and the melting-pot culture, traditionally a key part of the U.S. immigrant tradition.

SOME BACKGROUND

There is perhaps no more passionately debated issue on the American political agenda than illegal immigration into the United States. Although the United States is a nation with millions of illegal immigrants and the Statue of Liberty calls out "give me your tired, your poor, your huddled masses longing to be free," when it comes to those from far away nations who enter the country illegally, the welcome sign becomes a point of contention. Public opinion polls consistently show that Americans remain open to foreigners who follow the immigration laws and enter the country through the established channels. But when it comes to migrants who climb a fence from Mexico into California, arrive by a broken-down fishing boat from Haiti or travel long distances from Central America, Brazil or

China, the common response by a majority of majority of Americans is direct–imprisonment or deportation.

The issue of illegal immigration into the United States, however, is not so cut and dried and the solutions not so direct. Up to 12 million illegal immigrants (this is the working estimate, but officials admit that they do not have any valid means to measure the number of illegal immigrants in the country) are currently residing in the United States, and they come to the country in search of work–work that is not that difficult to find–especially in low-wage jobs such as landscaper, roofer, meat packer and restaurant and hotel service worker. Some of these illegal immigrants eventually return home with sufficient money to start a business or build a new home, but many stay and blend into American society hoping that they will not be arrested by immigration officials and forced to go back to certain poverty in their country of origin.

The issue of the growing presence of these illegal immigrants in the United States has entered the political process as government officials from local town governments to the Congress and the president have weighed in on how the United States should respond to this influx of workers. There has been no shortage of solutions to illegal immigration, from securing the border with Mexico with cement and steel walls, using the U.S. military, Coast Guard and state national guards to beef up patrols, fining and arresting employers who knowingly hire the undocumented and staging massive roundups of illegal immigrants. Both President Bush and the Congress also presented legislative proposals designed to address the illegal immigration issue, but to date these proposals have been bogged down over controversial issues such as amnesty and creating a pathway to citizenship for those in the country without proper documentation.[1]

President George W. Bush took a number of steps to limit the flow of illegal immigrants into the United States. The $2 billion Secure Border Initiative (SBI) was presented as the "most technologically advanced border security initiative in American history." The SBI was a mix of video surveillance of border entry points, unmanned drones and heat-sensing devices designed to enhance the ability of the Border Patrol to spot the movement of illegal immigrants from Mexico. In 2006 the U.S. Immigration and Customs Enforcement Agency began a renewed effort to raid businesses that had hired undocumented workers. And finally, also, in 2006, the Congress passed the Secure Fence Act, which funded (at the cost of $2 billion) a 700-mile fence, fifteen feet high, with the critical section of the fence erected from Calexico, California, to Douglas, Arizona, the prime entry point for illegal immigrants.[2]

But with each step taken by the Bush administration and the Congress, controversy followed, usually associated with whether any of these initiatives will actually work or whether the United States must accept illegal immigrants as an essential part of its economy. Although clear differences and divisions exist over illegal immigration, the passion that Americans express about these 12 million workers seems to be one thing that is common to the debate. The debates surrounding these new arrivals to the United States have raised a range of questions and concerns about who Americans are as a people, how they will be able to maintain their diverse ethnic and racial identity and whether they remain committed to offering the American dream to a new generation of undocumented immigrants.

These questions and concerns exist within the economic and social context of the new rules of trade and production, often called globalization. Globalization not only has changed the movement of goods and services, but also has had a major impact on work and workers. Whereas in the past the movement of people to work in a foreign country was largely seasonal and limited to a few economic sectors, globalization has intensified the need for labor (usually cheap, unskilled labor) and created a huge army of international workers drawn by jobs to advanced, industrialized countries such as the United States. Unless globalization undergoes a radical transformation in the coming years or countries such as the United States shut down their borders, this international workforce will continue to travel in search of jobs and greater income, regardless of whether they possess proper documentation.

On the Record

The U.S. Border Patrol places signs along the paths taken by illegal entrants into the United States, who are usually led by unscrupulous guides called "coyotes." The coyotes collect thousands of dollars in fees and then often leave the illegals stranded in desolate desert areas; many die. One of the signs reads as follows:

FOR THE COYOTES YOUR NEEDS ARE ONLY A BUSINESS AND THEY DON'T CARE ABOUT YOUR SAFETY OR THE SAFETY OF YOUR FAMILY. DON'T PAY THEM OFF WITH YOUR LIVES

Source: *The Devil's Highway* by Luis Alberto Urrea

DEBATES, DIFFERENCES AND DIVISIONS

There is no more divisive and contentious aspect of the debate over illegal immigration in the United States than the economic consequences of having as many as 12 million undocumented aliens living and working in the country. Broadly speaking, the issue is whether the illegal immigrants are a drain on the national economy as they take jobs away from Americans, depress wage scales and heighten the costs of education, health care and crime or whether they are contributing members of the American economy as they pay taxes, spend on consumer goods and perform work functions that Americans have shown little interest to bear by advocates on either side of the debate.

Those who criticize illegal immigration and its impact on the national economy stress that undocumented workers siphon taxpayer dollars away from vital services. The Colorado Alliance for Immigration Reform, a vocal opponent of illegal immigration, cites data that "dozens of hospitals in Texas, New Mexico, Arizona and California have been forced to close or face bankruptcy because of federally-mandated programs requiring free emergency room services to illegal aliens."[3] For example, Cochise County, Arizona, spends annually about 30% of its $9 million budget on illegal immigrant care. Also at issue in terms of social welfare spending at the state and local levels are the so-called anchor babies, more than 300,000 babies born yearly to parents of illegal immigrants who add to the cost of hospital care and eventually to the educational systems of cities, towns and counties. Using data from the national census, the anti-immigration organization, the Center of Immigration Studies, found that the cost of illegal immigration in 2002 was over $10 billion as households of undocumented aliens received an estimated $2,700 more in services than they paid in taxes. The costs were in Medicaid payments (medical assistance for the poor), food assistance, the federal prison and local court systems and federal and local aid to school districts.[4] The debates over the cost of illegal immigration continues with new data, new inferences from the data, and new challenges to the data. For example, in 2004 a report from the federal government stated that illegal immigrants cost the United States $10 billion a year from securing the border to Medicaid payments.[5] The conservative Wall Street Journal in 2006 agreed with the federal assessment, but also stated that the economic benefits to the United States of illegal immigration may be as high as $13 billion a year.[6]

On the other side of the illegal immigration argument is the position that these workers make significant economic contributions to the American economy that go well beyond the costs that they may incur. In 2003 Thunderbird, the American Graduate School of International Management in Arizona, conducted a study of the economic impact of illegal immigrants in the state. The study did point out that illegal immigrants used over $250 million in social services and another $31 million in uncompensated health care, but at the same time these illegal entrants paid over $600 million in federal taxes and state sales taxes, for a net profit to Arizona of $319 million. The study also showed that illegal immigrants generated over $4 billion in purchases in the state, paid $1.5 billion in rents and mortgages and gave Arizona banks nearly $57 million in fees related to $486 million in remittances (money sent from workers in the United States to the country of their origin).[7] Another study done in 2010 by the University of California at Los Angeles found that legalizing undocumented immigrants would add an estimated $1.5 trillion to the U.S. GDP over a ten year period (GDP).[8]

Data Bank

The 698-mile border fence along portions of the nearly 2,000 mile U.S.-Mexican border is only partially complete (only about 643 miles of fence were erected as of May, 2010). As planned, five hundred eighty miles of the fence is designed to limit pedestrians and is made up of twelve-foot steel pilings. The remainder of the fence is designed to limit vehicle access to the United States. The fencing is found primarily around urban areas such as San Diego, California, and El Paso, Texas. Where there are gaps in the fence, the Border Patrol has developed so-called virtual fencing–electronic sensors and other night vision equipment. Already portions of the fence have been destroyed as illegal immigrants continue to seek entry into the U.S. by any means possible.

Source: U.S. Border Patrol

In the face of such intense passion and disagreement over illegal immigration, it would be natural that advocates on both sides of the issue would set their sites on the government and pressure officials to address this nagging and controversial problem. In his 2006 State of the Union address, President Bush called for a comprehensive immigration plan that would "address the problem of illegal immigration and deliver a system that is secure, productive, orderly and fair." Although the president accented the need to secure U.S. borders, he did propose a guest worker program and the opportunity for current illegal aliens to work toward gaining full citizenship status. President Bush's proposal sought to balance the pressure from his own party, which pushed for sealing the border with Mexico, and business interests, which wanted to continue the practice of hiring immigrant laborers. Because the president's plan for immigration reform was critical to the political debate that ensued throughout 2006 and 2007, it is instructive to present the core proposals that he presented to the Congress.

An increase in the numbers of Border Patrol agents along with National Guard units to heighten surveillance, install barriers and patrol access points.

A further expansion in the funding of the president's Secure Border Initiative and its accent on using high-tech methods of surveillance and detection.

An expansion of "expedited removal" allowing for captured illegal aliens to be sent back to the country of their origin more quickly.

An increase in the detention facilities, which will allow Border Patrol agents to incarcerate larger numbers of illegal aliens.

Training of 1,500 state and local police officials to work with federal officials to protect the border.

A tougher stance on workplace enforcement and stiffer fines for employers who knowingly hire illegal aliens.

Strengthening the ability of the Department of Health and Human Services to develop a more sophisticated database to determine whether illegal aliens have acquired Social Security cards.

The development of a tamperproof identity card for every legal foreign worker so that businesses can verify the legal status of their workers.

The creation of a Temporary Worker Program that allows employers to hire workers only for jobs that Americans have not taken, that is, limited in terms of time in the United States with the understanding that these workers will return home, and the issuance of the Temporary Worker status only when the economy warrants it.

A program that allows illegal immigrants the possibility of earning citizenship status by paying a penalty for their illegal entry, learning English, paying taxes, passing a background check and holding a job continuously for a set number of years. When these requirements are met the illegal alien would be considered for citizenship but must go to the "back of the line," meaning that all other immigrants who have followed the rules will be given priority status for citizenship. There will be no amnesty, but rather an emphasis on citizenship, loyalty to the United States and assimilation into American society.[9]

FYI

Ninety percent of the over 10,000 Border Patrol agents are stationed in various enforcement sections along the border with Mexico. In 2006 the Border Patrol apprehended 1.2 million illegal immigrants and returned them to their homelands. In recent years the number of arrests of illegal immigrants has dropped significantly, in large part due to the stepped up security along the border and a declining American economy. The Border Patrol has installed fixed cameras and sensors buried in the sand that detect human movement. Also the Border Patrol uses blimps, unmanned drones and helicopters to complement its standard SUVs in the search for illegal entrants to the United States.

Source: U.S. Border Patrol and the *New York Times*, May 14, 2009

President Bush's immigration reform package had something in it for everyone, from the "secure the border" group to the "let them stay" group. But the last proposal dealing with the possibility of earning citizenship caused the most fury and became the key focus of the political debate in Congress and indeed the country. Republicans in Congress, especially those from border states, were furious with the proposal citing that such a program would reward illegality and likely increase the prospect of immigration. Democrats, on the other hand, saw the proposal as a good step forward toward resolving this contentious issue by setting the bar high and requiring illegal immigrants to take certain steps toward citizenship, including going to the end of the line and waiting till the immigrants received proper documentation.

What appeared to some to be a reasonable compromise proposal by the president set off intense opposition from the Republicans in Congress. Representative James Sensenbrenner from Wisconsin introduced the Border Protection, Anti-Terrorism and Illegal Immigration Control Act, which was in stark disagreement with the president and rejected the guest worker and pathway to citizenship proposals. Besides strongly pushing for the border fence, Sensenbrenner went even further by advocating that illegal immigrants face felony, not misdemeanor, charges for crossing into the United States, requiring that they face mandatory detention after being apprehended and that employers face increased fines (up to $40,000) for hiring undocumented aliens. As Representative Sensenbrenner said of his bill, "With the border controls and the enforcement of employer sanctions, the jobs for illegal immigrants will dry up . . . and if you can't get a job because employer sanctions are enforced, my belief is that a lot of the illegal immigrants will simply go back home."[10]

The Sensenbrenner bill diverged significantly not only from the White House proposal, but also from work being done in the Senate, where a spirit of compromise existed among Democrats and Republicans. With Senators Kennedy of Massachusetts and McCain of Arizona taking the lead and bringing together a broad coalition of Democrats and Republicans, the Senate developed the Comprehensive Immigration Reform Act, which incorporated the guest worker program and the controversial pathway to citizenship. Because the Senate bill was viewed by many as a middle-of-the-road proposal, the essentials of the legislation are provided here:[11]

> A speeding up of the construction of the 700-mile border wall and the hiring of an additional 18,000 new Border Patrol agents.

> The creation of a database that will provide employers the opportunity to verify the status of job applicants.

> The formation of a "guest worker" program that would allow some 400,000 illegal immigrants currently without proper documentation to live and work in the United States for up to three two-year terms.

> The creation of a "Z" visa that would allow undocumented immigrants in the United States before January 1, 2007, and who identify themselves as legally eligible to enter a citizen track after paying a fine of $5,000, returning to their homeland for a period of time, undergoing a background check and having no criminal record. The Z visa would be valid for four years and renewable for another four years, while the immigrant applied for citizenship status.

> The development of a merit system for awarding permanent resident status (the green card) that would require proof of English proficiency and civics and education courses designed to improve work skills.

Those applying for and gaining the Z visa would be placed at the end of the line of all those considered for U.S. citizenship.

Only spouses and minors of illegal immigrants would be eligible to apply for the Z visa, not extended family members.

The bipartisan coalition of senators was convinced that they had presented a viable alternative to the stringent House position and the president's proposal, especially with the introduction of the Z visa and its demanding requirements for citizenship. However, opponents of the Senate version of immigration reform mounted a vigorous media and grassroots campaign using talk radio, mass mailings and Internet networks to place enormous pressure on the Senate and its compromise. The public pressure against the Senate version was so intense that the coalition broke apart and the bill died an early death. With the House refusing to endorse the Senate version and the Senate incapable of fighting back the wave of public opinion, comprehensive immigration reform was put aside in favor of piecemeal policies such as the border fence and more vigorous enforcement of employer hiring practices.

Into this presidential and Congressional mix over illegal immigration reform was the growing presence of the Latino community in the national debate. During the discussions in the House and the Senate, millions of Latinos throughout the United States protested in largely peaceful demonstrations in most major cities in the country. The demonstrations showed the enormous grassroots organizational power of the Latinos (fueled in part by Spanish language television and radio stations). In April 2006, in over 102 cities, crowds that varied from 100,000 to 500,000 protested the Sensenbrenner bill and endorsed the concept of a pathway to citizenship in the Senate bill. The demonstrations reached a high point on May 1 when the Latino protestors staged the "Great American Boycott" that was designed to remind Americans of the important economic impact of immigrants, legal and illegal, on the national economy.[12]

The boycott did not appear to have much of an effect as many immigrants went to work (some fearing retribution from their bosses), and most continued their normal buying habits. There was also a backlash from many Americans who were bothered by the fact that demonstrators carried Mexican flags and displayed signs with slogans such as "We are the Only Owners of the Continent." Nevertheless, despite the points of controversy surrounding the demonstrations, the message was loud and clear that Latino "power" in the American political system could not be ignored and that the Latino community throughout the country had the capacity to band together to make their voices heard on the illegal immigration issue.

With the immigration reform legislation battle in stalemate, the debate over illegal immigration did not come to an end, but was refocused in different directions, primarily at the state and local levels. Nineteen states passed various forms of employer sanction laws that penalized those who knowingly hired illegal immigrants. Some of the states with such legislation such as Nevada wrote the bills with language that was so general and expansive that prosecution of employers would be difficult, if not impossible. In Nevada a massive building boom until 2008 was aided by illegal immigrants who formed a sizeable portion of the workforce. The Nevada legislature and the business community thus created a bill that was unenforceable and would not limit the building boom.

In neighboring Arizona, however, the legislature passed a stiff employer-sanction bill called the Fair and Legal Employment Act. The legislation established the power of the state to suspend for ten days, and after numerous offenses, revoke business licenses of those firms who hired illegal immigrants without proper documentation. The purpose of the law was to create an anti-illegal immigration climate and force undocumented aliens to leave the state. Anti-illegal immigration groups pushed hard for the legislation as they claimed widespread support from small businesses, contractors and farmers. One state representative in Arizona summed up the position of the supporters of the legislation when he said, "Illegal immigrants have no business being here, none. Shut off the lights, and the crowd will go home. I hope they will self-deport." But before the bill was officially implemented in January 2008, immigration groups supportive of illegal aliens went to federal court to challenge the law as beyond the scope of state power. The argument was made that immigration is a federal matter and the states do not have the right to punish employers who hire illegal immigrants. David Selden, who represented a coalition of business interests, stated, "It's only the federal government that has the authority to decide who is an illegal alien." According to Selden, "state and local government can only take action against a business after the federal government has determined that a worker is in the country illegally."[13]

Arizona continued to press forward with legislation designed to secure the border. In 2010 Republican governor Jan Brewer signed into law a measure that allowed police to stop those individuals that they viewed as possible undocumented aliens. The legislation immediately was challenged by the Hispanic community in Arizona as a form of racial profiling and an unconstitutional intervention into federal responsibility to secure the border. The law caused a nation-wide debate and in some cases an economic boycott against Arizona businesses. Although the bill was immensely popular throughout the country, constitutional scholars agreed that immigration was a federal matter and only Congress could address the issue with legislation that dealt with the illegal immigration, something that Congress had heretofore refused to act on.[14]

Attempts have also been made at the local level to control illegal immigration. In Hazelton, Pennsylvania, Mayor Lou Barletta enforced the city's new Illegal Immigration Relief Act, which imposed fines on landlords who rented apartments and houses to illegal immigrants. The law also denied business permits to companies that hired undocumented workers. The law further required tenants to register with the city and pay for a housing permit, which would be granted contingent on compliance with the law. The Hazelton law was similar to over ninety such ordinances around the country that sought to limit illegal immigration into communities by controlling housing rentals and sanctioning landlords and businesses. Mayor Barletta pushed for the new law as a result of a crime wave in Hazelton that he attributed to the rising population of illegal immigrants. Although Hazelton is a city of only 30,000 it had become increasingly popular for immigrants leaving Philadelphia and New York City to find employment there.[15]

The Hazelton Illegal Immigration Relief Act was the subject of a lawsuit brought by Hispanic advocacy groups who contended that the city did not have the authority to restrict illegal immigration through housing and employment sanctions. Again, the argument forwarded by these groups was that the federal government has the sole power to regulate immigration and that the Hazelton law violated the due process and equal protection clauses of the Fourteenth Amendment. The suit against the Hazelton law reached federal district court and the presiding judge found that the Illegal Immigration Relief Act violated federal laws and was a usurpation of the government's exclusive control over matters related to immigration. Although the judge's ruling affected only Hazelton, it showed again that the failure of the Congress and the president to enact comprehensive immigration reform sparked efforts at the state and local levels to control illegal immigration, even though the authority to do so was not within the boundaries of the Constitution. The Hazelton ruling is now on appeal before a federal appeals court, but communities seeking to restrict illegal aliens by passing restrictive renting and hiring ordinances got a boost when a federal appeals court upheld a restrictive ordinance in Valley Park, Missouri, stating that communities are not barred from imposing employment regulations that go beyond federal regulations.

The increasing involvement of the states and localities to address the illegal immigration issue in the United States became even more complex and heated when the former governor of New York, Eliot Spitzer, took a position favoring issuing driver's licenses to illegal immigrants. Spitzer's position stemmed from his belief that providing the licenses would be a way of identifying illegal immigrants and developing a database on residents without proper documentation in the state of New York. The decision by Spitzer opened up a new debate as many in New York and around the country saw the move by the governor as accepting the illegal status of these immigrants and legitimizing their status. Even immigration advocates felt that the idea was flawed because most illegal immigrants wanted to remain unknown to the authorities or would purchase illegal driver's licenses for identification purposes. Heavy public opinion against the proposal forced Spitzer to withdraw the idea of driver's licenses for illegal immigrants, proving once again that in the absence of clear policy from Washington states and localities will take matters into their own hands, even if they face constitutional barriers or strong public opposition.[16]

The issue of illegal immigration into the United States with all its complexities and divisions touches the core of the American experience. The guiding principle of the United States is the assimilation of peoples from all over the world from the early Pilgrims to the migrants from Latin America and the Caribbean. The Pilgrims who arrived on the Mayflower would be considered illegal immigrants today. Others such as the huge wave of European immigrants during the period from 1880 to 1920 benefited from a national policy that officially welcomed a new workforce.

What differentiates these early arrivals from the immigrant arrivals of today is not just that over 12 million are undocumented and come here by crossing borders illegally, but that many Americans are concerned that the concept of the melting pot no longer has value. The so-called Mexicanization of some parts of California and the Southwest, where whole sections of cities and towns are enclaves of Mexican life with few signs of linkage to the United States, has caused a backlash among many resident Americans who are angry over bilingualism, protection of illegal immigration rights and open displays of Mexican nationalism. Thus the resulting fear among many Americans is that over time the Mexican immigrant population will form two nations with little common heritage and no concept of a national melting pot.[17]

Prominent thinkers and writers such as the late Harvard University Professor Samuel Huntington and television commentator Patrick Buchanan have each written books that raise disturbing questions about the latest wave of arrivals on American shores. Huntington in his book *Who Are We? The Challenge to America's Identity* states that the new arrivals from Mexico have not assimilated into American culture and have little loyalty to the United States. Huntington praises the Anglo-Protestant ethic that in his opinion is the foundation of American society and laments that these values of liberty, equality, the rule of law and individual rights have not been embraced by recent immigrants. He sees Mexican immigrants as seeking separation from resident Americans and showing little interest in the American way of life.[18] Buchanan in his book *State of Emergency* is much more threatening in his prediction about the impact of illegal Mexican immigration into the United States. As he says, "If we do not get control of our borders by 2050 Americans of European descent will be a minority in the nation their ancestors created and built. No nation has ever undergone so radical a demographic transformation and survived." Buchanan even goes so far as to suggest that some Mexicans in the United States dream of the day when they become the controlling majority in states such as California, Arizona, New Mexico and Nevada, which were taken by the United States after the Mexican-American War in 1848.[19]

With the economic meltdown taking center stage after the inauguration of Barack Obama, the issue of what to do about the presence of 12 million illegal immigrants into the United States began to fade into the background. There are still quasi-vigilante groups such as the Minutemen in Arizona who keep watch on illegal border crossings, national commentators such as former CNN commentator Lou Dobbs and Fox's Bill O'Reilly continue to push the issue into the spotlight. But with the Hispanic vote going to Barack Obama in the 2008 election, the Republican Party has been reluctant to push for a stringent immigration reform bill, feeling that their candidate in the 2012 presidential election could be hampered by a get-tough-on-illegal-immigrant policy.

As for President Obama, his position shifted once he was faced with the enormous challenges of the faltering economy. Rather than push early for immigration reform along the lines of the Kennedy-McCain model, he instead talked about the importance of border security (including $27 billion in the 2010 budget for stronger controls on illegal Mexicans entering the United States), preventing employers from hiring illegal immigrants and improving bureaucratic roadblocks to settling longstanding immigration issues of those applying for citizenship.[20] The Obama administration also directed the Department of Homeland Security to use Section 287(g) of the Immigration and Nationality

Act to train local police officials to enforce immigration laws. Although this decision pleased state and local officials who were now given the authority to work with federal officials to track down illegal immigrants, human rights and civil liberties groups have complained that many of the arrests are arbitrary and that too many immigrants who are in the country legally have been harassed.[21]

Despite the accent on border security and get-tough measures on illegal immigrants, the Obama administration pledged to work on the issue of immigration reform and lobby members of the Congress to smooth the legislative process. In the meantime as a way of mollifying the Hispanic community the Obama administration did establish a policy position that the raids on factories and other work places would be limited, if not abandoned, as a way of lessening the tensions between Hispanics and the government. With respect to the Arizona law and the backlash that followed, the President moved immigration reform forward in 2010, but the same issues that scuttled the reform effort during the Bush years–amnesty, pathway to citizenship and guest worker status- remained areas of deep political divisions.

Although comprehensive immigration reform is yet to be addressed, the divisive national debates continue and the juggernaut of globalization, with its requirement that work and labor be flexible and open, continues. Interestingly, the recession has forced many illegal immigrants to return to their home countries because they have been laid off or their wages have been cut.[22] Nevertheless, calls for militarizing the border, increasing deportations or creating a hostile environment for illegal immigrants continue to be popular among a vast majority of Americans. However, a counterweight to this opposition to reform is the reality of the growing influence of the Hispanic community. Politicians from both parties recognize that the Hispanic voting bloc is critical and policy actions that alienate Hispanics could translate into defeat at the polls.

After over a year in which immigration reform was a backburner issue, it now has gained new momentum. Ideally government, business, interest groups and the American people will arrive at some middle ground on this difficult issue. But meanwhile the passion that has driven the debate over this issue has not abated; it has only been placed on hole. And when the debates does begin the issue will again divide not just the political arena, but also American society.[23]

The Great Debate

What to do with the 12 million illegal immigrants already in the United States is the fundamental question of immigration reform. The pathway to citizenship is the most controversial issue of the policy proposals.

Debate Topic

Should illegal immigrants be granted a pathway to citizenship with stiff application requirements but no punishment for their original illegal entry into the United States?

Critical Thinking Questions

1. What are your recommendations for dealing with the estimated 12 million illegal immigrants in the United States?
2. Should immigrants who are here legally be required to learn English, and should the U.S. government make English its official language?
3. Do you believe that illegal immigrants are a drain on the United States and local economies, or are they an economic plus?
4. Many critics of illegal immigration are outraged over the so-called anchor babies, whose birth in the United States by illegal immigrants gives them automatic citizenship. Is this good government policy?
5. Do you think a twelve-foot steel fence along the southern border with Mexico makes the United States look like a walled-off nation akin to the Soviet Union that put up the Berlin Wall?

Connections

A valuable resource for understanding the border control problem is the website of the U.S. Border Patrol, http://www.cbp.gov/xp/cgov/about

One of the most respected sources of information on the immigration reform debate is the Federation for Immigration Reform. Visit their site at www.fairness.org

A support group for illegal immigrants is the Immigrant Solidarity Network; its website is at http://www.immigrantsolidarity.org

Immigration Watchdog is an organization that monitors the illegal immigration controversy. Visit its site at http://www.immigrationwatchdog.com

The Center for Comparative Immigration Studies at the University of California at San Diego is recognized as having a reputation for solid and non-partisan research on immigration. Its site is http://www.ccis-ucsd.org

Some Books to Read

Rivera, Geraldo, *His Panic: Why Americans Fear Hispanics in the U.S.* (New York: Celebra/Penguin, 2008).

Mills, Nicolous, *Arguing Immigration: The Debate over the Changing Face of America* (New York: Touchstone, 2007).

Haerens, Margaret *Illegal Immigration: Opposing Viewpoints* (New York: Greenhaven Press, 2006).

Romero, Fernando, *Hyperborder: The Contemporary U.S. Mexico Border and Its Future* (Princeton, NJ: Princeton Architectural Press, 2007).

Newton, Lina, *Illegal Alien or Immigrant: The Politics of Immigration Reform* (New York, NYU Press, 2005).

Notes

1. The issue of illegal immigration and national security is raised in a book by Terri Givens, *Immigration Policy and Security: U.S., European and Commonwealth Perspectives.* (New York: Routledge, 2007).

2. "Two Sides of the Border Fence," *Washington Post National Weekly Edition*, October 23–29, 2006, p. 30. Also see "Fighting the Fence," *Economist*, June 14, 2008, p. 43.
3. http://www.cairco.org/econ.html
4. http://cis.org/articles/2001/mexico/execsum.html
5. See Mary Fitzgerald, "Illegal Immigrants's Cost to Government Studied," Washington Post, August 26, 2004, A21.
6. See "Costs and Benefits of Illegal Immigration," Wall Street Journal, June 26, 2006. "The debate on the costs and benefits of illegal immigration thus goes on and is certain to continue."
7. "The Economic Impact of the Arizona-Mexico Relationship," The American School of International Management, 2003.
8. UCLA Study Says Legalizing Undocumented Immigrants Would Help The Economy, See http://immigrationclearinghouse.org/ucla-study-says-legalizing-undocumented-immigrants-would-help-the-economy.html
9. See "Bush Calls for Changes on Illegal Workers," CNN, January 8, 2004. http://www.cnn.com/2004/ALLPOLITICS/01/07/bush.immigration/index.html
10. Charles Buffington, "Immigration Issue Splits GOP," *Washington Post*, May 27, 2006.
11. The National Immigration Law Center reviews the Senate bill at http://www.nilc.org/immlawpolicy/CIR/index.htm
12. Teresa Watanabe and Hector Becera, "How DJs Put 500,000 Marchers in Motion," *Los Angeles Times*, March 28, 2006.
13. Mary Jo Pitzi, "Agreement Heard Against Employer Sanction Law," *Arizona Republic*, November 15, 2007.
14. "See Randall Archibold," Arizona Enacts Strengthened Law on Immigration," New York Times, April 24, 2010, A1.
15. "Judge Strikes Down Pennsylvania Illegal Immigration Law," http://www.foxnews.com/story/0,2933,290960,00.html
16. http://www.immigrationwatchdog.com/?p=4844
17. See Robert Pastor and Jorge Castenada, *Limits to Friendship: The United States and Mexico* (New York: Knopf, 1988).
18. Samuel Huntington, *Who Are We? The Challenge to America's Identity* (New York: Simon and Schuster, 2004).
19. Patrick Buchanan, *State of Emergency* (New York: Thomas Dunne, 2006). A debate over cultural assimilation of immigrants occurred at a Congressional hearing between John Fonte, Director of the Center for American Common Culture, and Gary Gerstle, the James Stahlman Professor of History at Vanderbilt University. See Testimony during hearings on "Comprehensive Immigration Reform: Becoming Americans–U.S. Immigrant Integration" before the U.S. House of Representatives, Committee on the Judiciary, Subcommittee on Immigration Citizenship, Refugees, Border Security and International Law, May 16, 2007.
20. For background on the illegal immigration issue as President Barack Obama began his presidency see Marc Lacey and Ginger Thompson, "Obama's Next Foreign Policy Crisis Could be Next Door," *New York Times*, March 25, 2009, A1.
21. See "The Continuing Crackdown," *The Economist*, September 19, 2009, p. 40.
22. Diane Solis and Stella Chavez, "Illegal Immigrants Returning Home in Large Numbers," *Dallas Morning News*, July 31, 2008, http://www.dallasnews.com/sharedcontent/dws/news/texassouthwest/stories/073008dnmetimmig.19ccbe64.html
23. See my discussion of the future of immigration policy in Michael Kryzanek, *United States-Latin American Relations*, 4th edition (Westport, CT: Praeger, 2008), pp. 237–238.

6 TAXING **AND** SPENDING

Issue Focus

The lifeblood of any government is revenue and what political leaders decide to do with that revenue. Collecting taxes and then spending those taxes on national priorities is one of the core functions of American government. As can be expected, when taxes are collected from the American people and American business, the result is often displeasure, if not anger, at having to hand over hard-earned earnings to the government. However, there is just as much displeasure and anger at the manner in which taxes dollars are spent as government decides where to channel revenue, especially if the government spends more money on policies and programs than it takes in from taxpayers. These issues of taxing, spending and debt have become contentious issues in contemporary American politics.

Chapter Objectives
This issue chapter will seek to:

1. Explore recent tax policies in the United States and the effect of these policies on the American taxpayer.
2. Examine government spending priorities and the impact of spending on deficits and the national debt.
3. Discuss the different approaches to tax and spending policies taken by Democrats and Republicans.

SOME BACKGROUND

The old adage that the only certainties in life are death and taxes points up the centrality of the issue of paying the government "its due" and the government establishing policies that determine what citizens and corporate entities will be required to transfer to the Treasury of the United States. Although setting tax rates and collecting taxes is a fundamental requirement of any government and paying taxes is one of the primary responsibilities of citizens, the relationship between the American people and their government becomes strained and contentious when taxes are the subject: there is an inevitable certainty that debates, differences and divisions will follow over who should pay and how much should be paid to the Treasury. The difficult relationship that exists between the government and the American people over taxes and tax policy is best shown in public opinion polls when respondents are asked to name their least favorite government agency. Their response is usually the Internal Revenue Service (IRS), which has as its primary function collecting corporate, personal income and other excise taxes. As in the Bible, tax collector remains even today one of the least respected occupations in our society.

The issue of taxation has its origin in the early days of the revolutionary era when the colonists resisted the British policy of extracting money from them through the Stamp Act and later the Townsend Act to pay for foreign debts. The rallying cry of "No taxation without representation" has become part of Americana and underscores the importance taxation has played in shaping American political culture. Later in the revolutionary period, Massachusetts farmers engaged in what came to be called Shay's Rebellion as they challenged the authorities over new taxes placed on their farms. Although the rebellion was put down (after the government had to raise private funds to pay its soldiers), popular resistance to unfair or imposed taxes continued.

Once independence was achieved and the new country sought to establish a fiscally sound government, problems remained in raising taxes, as the major sources of funding the national government were excise taxes on land ownership and trade transactions, highly speculative government-held bonds and lines of credit from foreign allies. The early Federalist Party disappeared from the political scene in large part because of scandals associated with bond speculation and excise taxes on western farmers. Constitutional issues also arose about the power of the national government to establish banks that would not be taxed by the states. In one of the most important Supreme Court decisions in U.S. history, *McCulloch v. Maryland*, Justice John Marshall took the side of the federal government and validated its right to establish a national bank in Maryland that would not face taxation from the state of Maryland. Marshall upheld the right of the federal government to tax and engage in other fiscal matters as part of its constitutional implied powers.

But the most serious and controversial development regarding taxation occurred during and after the Civil War as the country needed additional revenue and began turning to the income tax as the most direct manner of taxing citizens. In 1862 a law was passed requiring that Americans with incomes above $600 would pay a 3% tax, whereas those with incomes over $10,000 would pay a 5% tax. Although the law was abolished in 1872 and the courts argued for years over whether any income tax had to be apportioned among the states based on their census, pressure remained to use income tax as the primary means of raising revenue. Finally, in 1913 the Sixteenth Amendment was passed by the states establishing the income tax as the law of the land and allowing Congress the responsibility of setting and raising rates.[1]

As the United States developed into a world power and the government (especially during the New Deal era under President Franklin Delano Roosevelt) assumed greater domestic responsibilities to respond to the needs of poor, unemployed, aged and infirm citizens, the need for additional revenue increased. Raising taxes during wartime to pay for what was considered a national emergency was less controversial during the Depression and World War II era. But as government got bigger and budgets to run the country entered the billion- and later the trillion-dollar range, support for tax increases began to wane, and presidents and presidential candidates pledged to resist new taxes. Public opinion polls from the 1980s onward when anti-tax, less-government President Ronald Reagan took office showed that Americans were averse to tax increases and wanted their government to cut government spending rather than taking more money out of their pocketbooks.[2]

Although opposition to tax increases began to dominate the domestic policy scene, special interest politics entered the realm of fiscal affairs as the U.S. tax code became the target of constant lobbying to gain specific credits, exemptions, deductions or incentives that would diminish the tax burden or perhaps even eliminate it. In response to this pressure, Congress made regular additions and adjustments to the U.S. tax code and in the process contributed to the most complex tax laws in the world. The U.S. tax code spread to thousands of pages of arcane rules and regulations, and a growing professional industry of tax preparers and accountants responded to the need for interpreting the law and using it to legally avoid the tax bill. Taxation thus became not just a tool of fiscal management for the country, but also a political and ideological minefield as tax policy became embroiled in partisan struggles over not only how the tax burden would be distributed among the American people and American corporations, but also what areas of income, profit, property or stock would receive special benefits.

The combination of growing aversion to taxes and the scramble to gain tax benefits and advantages contributed to an increasing awareness of the fairness issue. Americans questioned with greater frequency who should pay the largest share of taxes. Middle-class taxpayers complained about carrying the largest burden of taxation at the expense of the wealthy and corporations, whereas the wealthy and corporations responded that they pay enormous tax bills and that heightened taxation only punishes wealth accumulation and restricts economic growth. Liberal Democrats in particular jumped on the tax fairness bandwagon as they regularly chastised conservatives and in particular Republicans in Congress for passing legislation that provided generous tax advantages to those at the highest income levels in the nation. Claims that taxes were responsible for growing income inequality and that a class war was being instigated by unfair tax policies were heard with greater frequency in Congress and on the campaign trails.[3]

It should come as no surprise that when government sets policies that are designed to remove money from people's pocketbooks or corporate ledgers, such policies would become a major issue area, and that debates, differences and divisions would follow. Most Americans would agree that government is a necessary evil and that many services of government are absolutely essential for the good of the country. However, paying for those essential services is where problems arise, and so taxation has become one of the most contentious issue areas of public policy. Every American would agree that he or she owes the government his or her due; the question though is how much that due is.

DEBATES, DIFFERENCES AND DIVISIONS

Our discussion of taxes and tax policy in the modern era is best begun with the election of Ronald Reagan in 1980. Reagan ran and won the presidency on a platform of lower taxes and less government. His plan, dubbed Reaganomics, was a decided shift away from the dominant model of economic policy that was in place since the New Deal days of Franklin Delano Roosevelt. Rather than accenting the role of big government and ever-expanding taxes, Reagan talked about the importance of stimulating the economy by huge tax cuts and sharp reductions in government spending, except for expenditures related to national defense. The theory supporting Reagan's position on taxes and spending as the key to economic growth was based on an economic theory called "supply-side economics." Supply-side economics stressed the importance of creating business and consumer demand by shrinking the tax burden. By providing Americans and American corporations with tax cuts, Reagan believed that the economy would grow faster, and by slashing government spending, the need for more borrowing to cover federal expenses would diminish, and thus the need to raise interest rates would be lessened.[4]

In 1981 Reagan won an early victory on tax cuts when Congress shared his position and passed a measure that reduced the average tax rate by 23%. In 1986 Reagan was able to push through a much more ambitious tax policy with the passage of the Tax Reform Act, which eliminated more than twelve tax brackets, replacing them with just two (15% and 28%). The Tax Reform Act also cut certain personal exemptions and standard deductions and removed millions of poor people from the tax rolls. Corporations also benefited by a reduction in the top rate from 46% to 34%, but lost out with the repeal of the investment tax credit and the closing of a number of favorable loopholes in the tax code. By the time Ronald Reagan left office, income tax rates, especially at the high end, dropped significantly as the top personal tax bracket was reduced by 42% in seven years. During the Reagan years, the tax cuts helped businesses to expand investment in new equipment and buildings, while creating a financial boon for investors in the stock market.[5]

However, there was a price to pay for supply-side economics as the loss of revenue coupled with continued government spending, particularly in national defense, created ever-growing federal deficits averaging between $150 billion and $250 billion each year. The ballooning deficits and the skewing of the tax breaks toward business and the wealthy spurred critics to describe supply-side economics as really "trickle down economics," having barely a trickle of tax relief for the majority of Americans and contributing to a growing trickle of national debt that future generations of Americans would have to deal with. As the Reagan administration left office in 1989, the debate over who benefited from supply-side economics and the downside of steep revenue losses began in earnest, with Democrats increasingly calling for middle-class tax cuts and a kind of "soak-the-rich" policy that reduced the tax benefits enjoyed by the wealthy and corporations.[6]

On the Record

In his State of the Union address on January 26, 1982, Ronald Reagan said the following:

> Raising taxes won't balance the budget, it will encourage more government spending and less private investment. Raising taxes will slow economic growth, reduce production, and destroy future jobs, making it more difficult for those without jobs to find them and more likely that those who now have jobs could lose them.
>
> So I will not ask you to balance the budget on the backs of American taxpayers. I will send no tax increases this year and I have no intention of retreating from our basic program of tax relief. I promise to bring the American people—to bring their tax rates down and to keep them down, to provide them with incentives to rebuild our economy, to save, to invest in America's future. I will stand by my word.

Ronald Reagan's successor, George H.W. Bush will always be remembered for his rallying cry of "Read my lips, no new taxes." Seeking to emulate Reagan's approach on tax policy, George H.W. Bush continued to emphasize the supply-side approach that changed the American political economy. But by 1990 Bush faced an ever-growing federal deficit and was openly critical of Reaganomics, even to the point of calling it "voodoo economics." As a result Bush recanted his promise of no new taxes and increased the income tax to the great displeasure of his conservative base and the American voting public. George H.W. Bush lost the 1992 presidential election to Bill Clinton for a number of reasons, including a downturn in the economy, but the failure of Bush to keep his famous promise of "Read my lips: no new taxes" weakened his traditional voting base and showed him to be trapped in the political culture of tax cuts created by his predecessor Ronald Reagan. It may have been economically sound to raise taxes to deal with out-of-control deficits, but the idea of tax cuts had caught on among conservatives and the business community, and Bush, to his regret, went against the conservative-business tide.[7]

The election of Bill Clinton in 1992 brought the first Democratic to the White House since Jimmy Carter in 1976. Clinton ran on a platform of strengthening the American economy by pushing for free trade agreements and budget restraint. But one of his most controversial economic positions was a tax increase on the wealthy. As a Democrat, Clinton believed that the Reagan-Bush years had concentrated too many tax breaks at the high end of the income scale and that it was time to give low- and middle-income Americans some tax relief. In 1993, despite overwhelming Republican opposition, Congress passed the Omnibus Budget Reconciliation Act, which raised taxes on the top 1.2% of the wealthiest Americans, while giving tax reductions to 15 million low-income people. The Clinton initiative also provided tax breaks to small business owners, who in the past had been overlooked as the Republicans concentrated many of their corporate cuts on large enterprises. Clinton also used the legislation to develop a series of budget goals designed to rein in government spending that was creating an ever-growing federal deficit. Clinton's goal was to reduce the federal deficit by 50% during his administration.[8]

In the last few years of his presidency, Bill Clinton was able to move the federal expenditure ledger from a deficit to a surplus, the first time that had occurred since the administration of Lyndon Johnson in the late 1960s. In 1998 the surplus was $69 billion, in 1999, $126 billion and in 2000, $236 billion (in a carryover from his administration there was a surplus during the first fiscal year of the George W. Bush administration as well). Clinton would tout his deficit reduction efforts (due in large part to the decrease in defense spending as a result of the end of the Cold War) along with the revenue received from his tax hike on the wealthy, but critics pointed out that Clinton merely benefited from a strong economy with low employment, a sizzling stock market and high consumer spending levels. However, whatever the reason, Clinton and the Democrats reminded the American people that it was possible to control government spending and not be burdened by huge government deficits as occurred during the Reagan and Bush presidencies.

Data Bank

Tax freedom day is the day each year when American taxpayers finish paying their federal tax obligations to the government and can work for themselves rather than pay the IRS. In 2009 Tax Freedom Day was April 13, eight days earlier than in 2008, because of the recession and Obama stimulus package, which included temporary tax cuts. In 2010 Tax Freedom Day was April 9th, again earlier because of tax cuts and the recession.

The return of the Republicans to power after the victory of George W. Bush in the 2000 election also meant a return to supply-side economic policies. Bush wasted no time in convincing the Republican Congress to pass his Economic and Tax Reconciliation Act of 2001. The centerpiece of the legislation was a one-time rebate to the American taxpayer (a "typical family of four" received around $1,600).[9] However although the president touted the tax rebate and his concern over helping the average American family deal with the financial demands of everyday life, his tax policy continued to accent a reduction in income tax rates, which in most cases benefited those in high-income brackets. A joint study from the Urban Institute and the Brookings Institution in 2006 found that the 2001 tax cuts gave on average $118,000 in tax benefits to .3% of the American households with incomes of $ 1 million or more, whereas households in the middle 20% of the income range received $740.[10]

The Bush tax bill not only reduced the tax rate but also linked the tax cuts with a significant drop in the capital gains tax, which is applied to the profits that individuals acquire as a result of the sale of stock and property. The capital gains tax was reduced from 28% to 15% and was further evidence of the Bush administration's position of using tax policy to benefit those who participate actively in the stock market. In 2003 Bush sought to move forward the timetable for the reduction of the capital gains tax more quickly because he was convinced that lessening the tax on stocks and property would further stimulate the economy. The Republican Congress supported the new timetable, along with tax reductions on dividend income. Finally, the tax legislation also repealed the estate or so-called death tax on inheritance income over $250,000, which Democrats roundly criticized as an unnecessary change in the tax code that benefited only a miniscule number of Americans at the highest income levels. Republicans, however, found the estate tax an infringement on the right of Americans to keep the wealth accumulated within a family and away from the revenue-seeking IRS. Liberal economist Paul Krugman summed up the argument of critics of the Bush tax approach and the skewed nature of the tax cuts:

> The reality is that core measures of both the 2001 and the 2003 tax cuts mainly benefit the very affluent. The centerpieces of the 2001 act were a reduction in the top income-tax rate and elimination of the estate tax–the first by definition, benefiting only people with high incomes; the second benefiting only heirs to large estates. The core of the 2003 tax cut was a reduction in the tax rate on dividend income. This benefit, too, is concentrated on very high-income families.[11]

After passage of the 2001 tax legislation the Bush administration sought to make the cuts and other measures permanent after the law's expiration in 2010. The extension of the legislation became a point of contention between Republicans and Democrats who fought over not just the impact of the cuts on the American economy, but also their long-term impact on the federal deficit. It was estimated that making the tax cuts permanent would cost the government $3.5 trillion over ten years and continue to contribute to the federal deficit, which from 2001 to 2006 increased by $2.3 trillion. President Bush pushed aside the criticism of the tax cuts and their impact on the federal deficit when he said in 2006, "You cut taxes and the tax revenues increase." This classic supply-side argument endeared President Bush to those who viewed his tax policies as stimulating growth, enriching Americans and eventually having a positive impact on the federal deficit as a strong economy created new jobs and new wealth and, with that, new sources of revenue.

However with the tax cuts implemented during the Bush presidency, the surplus achieved during the later years of the Clinton administration quickly faded away, and deficit spending returned. As a result of the Bush rebates, further tax cuts in later years, the prescription drug program and of course the wars in Afghanistan and Iraq, the surplus was transformed into a $3 trillion deficit. The disappearance of the surplus prompted Democrats in Congress, who worried about the fate of numerous social programs threatened by the decline in government in revenue, to claim that the Bush administration was purposely seeking to downsize the federal government and starve it of revenue so that new programs, such as a universal health care plan and additional money for education and social welfare, could not be introduced.

Despite the criticism of those in Congress who feared the long-term impact of budget deficits, President Bush held steady to his position that the tax cuts, coupled with strict cost-cutting measures of the federal budget, would turn government revenue collections from red to black. In a major address in July 2007 President Bush said that his tax policies had indeed achieved the desired impact on the budget deficit. The president stated that the deficit had been reduced by more than $200 billion since 2004 and had settled at $205 billion for the fiscal year 2007–2008. Moreover, Bush stated that the deficit was at 1.5% of the gross domestic product, the lowest in forty years. With a continuation of his tax-cutting policies and budget constraints, Bush promised that by 2012 the deficit would be wiped out with a surplus of $33 billion. Democrats immediately accused the president of using "accounting gimmicks" and understating the costs of the Iraq war, the rise in the costs of Social Security and Medicare and what they viewed as a weakening economy.[12]

FYI

The Office of Management and Budget, which is an agency under the direction of the White House, publishes a yearly breakdown of the federal budget dollar–where the revenue comes from and where it goes. The following is the breakdown for the 2011 budget:

Where Revenue Comes from
$1.12 trillion from individual income taxes
$935 billion from Social Security and Medicare taxes
$270 billion from corporate income taxes
$74 billion from excise taxes
$27 billion from customs duties
$25 billion from estate and gift taxes
$87 billion from other sources
$1.27 trillion deficit requiring borrowing

(continued)

FYI   (continued)

Where the Revenue Goes
$875 billion to national defense
$730 billion to Social Security
$520 billion–all other discretionary spending
$491 billion to Medicare
$297 billion to Medicaid
$648 billion to other spending
$251 billion to interest on the debt
$3 billion to disaster costs

Source: Office of Management and Budget

Discussing the debates surrounding tax policy in the United States and pointing out the differences and divisions is not a simple matter of Democrats versus Republicans, liberals versus conservatives. Today most public opinion polls will point to the fact that Americans are opposed to tax increases and support candidates for office who are not tax-and-spend proponents. Most politicians are afraid to use the "T" word when running for office and pledge that they will address the spending side of the federal ledger, not the revenue-generating side. However saying that, it is possible to show that liberal Democrats, who often represent Americans of the lower and middle classes, support tax policies that are progressive in nature, meaning that tax revenues should fall most heavily on the individuals who make more money. Tax increases, if any, should be shouldered by the wealthy. For example, in running for the presidency in 2008, Barack Obama stressed that if he would be victorious he would implement a tax policy that would decrease the tax burden of 95% of the American public, while increasing the tax burden on the top 5%. Although Republican John McCain accused Obama of "class warfare" by attacking the wealthy, Obama's message on tax cuts for most working class Americans struck a chord with the American people.

Once in office Obama also targeted American firms that established tax havens outside the United States to lessen their corporate tax burdens and in the process deprived the government of billions of revenue. Although business groups complained that any legislative effort to close the overseas tax havens would have a negative impact on the competitiveness of U.S. corporations, Obama was adamant that the tax code needed to be changed on the matter of fairness, job creation and patriotism. As he stated in prepared remarks in May 2009:

. . . many (corporations) are aided and abetted by a broken tax system, written by well-connected lobbyists on behalf of well-heeled interests and individuals. It's a tax code full of corporate loopholes that makes it perfectly legal for companies to avoid paying their fair share. It's a tax code that makes it all too easy for a number–a small number of individuals and companies to abuse overseas tax havens to avoid paying any taxes at all. And it's a tax code that says you should pay lower taxes if you create a job in Bangalore, India, than if you create one in Buffalo, New York.[13]

Even though Obama ran on a platform of tax cuts for 95% of Americans, once he pushed the stimulus and bailout plans, advanced the health care reform process and increased the military presence in Afghanistan, his opponents in the Republican Party and the growing Tea Party movement were constantly reminding Americans that tax increases were inevitable as deficit spending increased. The anti-tax drumbeat got louder as more Americans came to believe that they would have to foot the bill for government spending.

It is not possible to talk about tax policy in the United States without talking about spending policy, or simply the budget of the federal government. The federal government during the last year of the Bush administration spent $2.7 trillion. Such a large expenditure has a definite impact on the national economy. Much of what the government spends annually is classified in the category of non-discretionary funds, money that must be paid to Americans for various entitlement programs such as Social Security and Medicare. After the government pays interest on the money that it borrows, what revenues remain are targeted to national defense and other discretionary programs, from funding the Federal Bureau of Investigation to the NASA space program to the interstate highway system. It is the discretionary spending that becomes the core of the partisan debate over national priorities and budgetary decisions. Although the federal budget, which is over 1,200 pages and is contained in three huge books, is a mass of financial data and expenditure statements, it is in reality a blueprint of how the government defines what is important for the country and what scarce resources (the taxpayers' money) should be spent on.

The partisan and ideological differences and divides that occur over the federal budget are often concentrated in the areas of national defense spending and social welfare programs. Democrats are ever on the alert to determine whether the Defense Department is spending money lavishly and foolishly on new weapons systems. Cost overruns for new weapons are often at the center of the debates concerning national defense spending. Republicans, on the other hand, keep close watch over the expenditures of the Departments of Health and Human Services, Education and Housing and Urban Affairs. Each of these departments administers many of the social programs that Republicans see as bloated and foster a climate of dependence on government handouts rather than on personal responsibility.

The issue of government spending became the key argument Republicans made once President Obama took office. One of his most controversial early actions was the introduction and passage of a $3.8 trillion budget, considerably larger than the previous Bush budget proposal of $3.1 trillion and creating a huge deficit, estimated to be $1.3 trillion, that Republicans stressed would not only place the American economy in a weakened state but leave a huge unpaid legacy for future generations. Republicans further criticized the Obama administration because the non-partisan Congressional Budget Office projected that between 2011 and 2020 at the current rate of spending, which included the stimulus spending, the bank and corporate bailouts and the national health care reform, the deficit would rise an additional $6 trillion.[14] The Republican opposition in Congress made deficit spending and the projected deficits the foundation of their criticism of Obama's economic recovery policies and his social welfare programs. In fact, in the wake of growing deficits the Obama administration sought a three-year freeze on discretionary spending that would trim federal spending by $250 billion over ten years. Republicans immediately castigated the president for what they viewed as a minor spending freeze that would not address the projected deficit of over $6–9 trillion in the coming years.[15] Obama and the Democratic majority in Congress were not deterred by the enormity of the budget or the deficit and reminded their Republican critics that Bush era budgets were also huge and left yearly deficits, including the 2009 budget that had a deficit of over $1 trillion. The following is an overview by department of the proposed Obama fiscal 2010 budget:

**2010 Presidential Budget Requests
by Cabinet Department**

In billions of dollars	
Commerce	$13.8, up 48%
State	$51.7, up 9.5%
Veterans Affairs	$52.5, up 10%
Homeland Security	$42.7, up 1.2%
Defense	$533.7, up 4%
Energy	$26.3, up .4%
Treasury	$13.0, up 5%
Education	$46.7, up 12.8%
Housing/Urban Development	$47.5, up 18.5%
Health/Human Services	$821.7, up 7.5%
Interior	$10.6, up 6.2%
Environmental Protection	$10.5, up 34.6%
Agriculture	$26.0, up 8.8%
Labor	$13.3, up 4.7%
Justice	$23.9, up 6.3%
Transportation	$72.5, up 2.8%

Source: Office of Management and Budget

Because the federal budget, except for those few years during the Clinton administration, has been out of balance and building huge national debts, there have been frequent Congressional efforts to insert a requirement for a balanced budget into the system of spending decisions. Although the budget process in the United States includes a long and complex interaction between the White House Office of Management and Budget, the Congressional Budget Office and numerous Executive and Congressional committees and working groups, the final spending product is as much a political decision as a rational economic deliberation. To ensure that budgets were indeed balanced, political solutions have been attempted in the past that sought to build a budget document that kept spending in line with revenue. Efforts to create a Balanced Budget Amendment to the Constitution, the attempt by presidents to seek a specific line-item veto as a budget check and even the impoundment of approved spending measures by presidents have all met with failure. Budget decisions continued to be influenced by partisan policy positions, constituency pressure and ideological objectives.[16]

Spending decisions have been highly publicized in recent years. During the Bush administration, budgetary issues moved front and center as the issue of earmarking, a practice in which a member of Congress or a group of members identify a specific project as necessary for their home district and state and then proceeds to move that project through the legislative process without open debate and with little concern over its impact on the overall budget. In 1995 there were 1,439 such earmarks, costing the taxpayers $10 billion, but by 2005 the number of earmarks had risen to 13,997 with a cost of $27.3 billion. In 2006 the cost of earmarks was placed at $29 billion. Although many of these projects were worthy, as they funded research centers and medical facilities, others were laughable such as the $500,000 for the Teapot Museum in Sparta, North Carolina, and the so-called $233 million Bridge to Nowhere linking a sparsely populated island in Alaska to the mainland.

Billions of dollars in earmarked projects continue to move through the Congress despite the efforts by some members such as Senator Tom Coburn of Oklahoma and Representative Jeff Flake of Arizona. Both men have repeatedly scolded their colleagues for inserting earmarked projects into appropriations bills or even into bills with little, if any, connection to the project as a way of moving their pet projects forward without any sort of legislative oversight. The efforts of Coburn and Flake have had some impact on the earmarking process, and the Democrats who took over power in 2006 pledged to create legislative guidelines for the earmarking process and be more vigilant when such projects are pushed through without debate. In the end, however, it is just too tempting for a member of Congress to tell his or her constituents back home or a special interest that a pet project was funded, even though that project and hundreds of others were in effect budget busters.[17]

Taxes and spending issues, despite their complexity, have really been quite simple to define in terms of political issues. Taxes go either up or down, either the rich or the middle and lower classes benefit and the money citizens pay to the government is prioritized toward either national defense or social welfare. Much of the debate, differences and divisions have been over these relatively simple options. There are always discussions of tax reform such as simplifying the tax code with a flat tax (a set percentage of taxation without all the deductions), moving to a European value-added tax (a form of a sales tax where a particular good is taxed at every stage of its production and distribution) or establishing a national sales tax and ridding the country of the income tax. There have even been discussions about instituting a national lottery that would generate the money needed to run the government. However, these reform efforts fall by the wayside as too much has been invested in the current system and too many interests benefit from maintaining the status quo. What happens, thus, is that the president and the Congress tinker back and forth with the tax code and with spending priorities, making short-term decisions that benefit one group over the other or accent one priority over another. This kind of political tinkering with taxation and spending is unlikely to change.

The Great Debate

The debate over who should carry the heaviest burden of taxation in the United States remains a politically charged issue with Americans. Wealthy individuals or corporations fight increases in tax rates, whereas middle-class Americans grumble over the tax burden they carry.

Debate Topic

As a means of providing new revenues for social programs in health care, education, housing and veterans affairs in this country, should the government increase taxes on the wealthy?

Critical Thinking Questions

1. If you were asked to provide the president with a list of spending priorities for the United States, what would those priorities be?
2. Cutting taxes, the hallmark of Reaganomics, has led to regular budget deficits and a growing national debt. Where do you stand on the tax cut versus deficit/debt issue?
3. Do you think the United States should enact a balanced budget amendment as a means of ensuring that yearly deficits will not occur?
4. Earmarks are often designed to support special projects in a region or state and are pushed by members of Congress in response to citizen pressure. Is there anything wrong with this practice of bringing home the bacon?
5. What needs to be done to return the U.S. budget to a surplus?

Connections

To gain a more precise understanding of the U.S. budget, check out the website of the Office of Management and Budget. The site summarizes the yearly budget of the government. See http://www.whitehouse.gov/omb

To gain a congressional perspective on government spending and overall economic policy matters, visit the website of the Congressional Budget Office at http://www.cbo.org

The Concord Coalition is a non-partisan watchdog group that takes stands on matters of U.S. fiscal policy. See http://www.concordcoalition.org

Grover Norquist is the most visible opponent of taxes and tax increases. His group, Americans for Tax Reform, can be reached at http://www.atr.org

The American Tax Institute provides solid research on tax policy and its impact on the nation and its economy. See http://americantaxpolicyinstitute.org

Some Books to Read

Konisburg, Charles, *America's Priorities: How the U.S. Government Raises and Spends $3,000,000,000 (Trillion) Per Year* (New York: Author House, 2008).

Cataldo, Anthony, J. and Arline A. Savage, *U.S. Individual Federal Income Taxation: Historical, Contemporary and Prospective Policy Issues* (Oxford, UK: Elsevier Science, 2001).

Peterson, Peter, *Running on Empty: How the Democratic and Republican Parties Are Bankrupting Our Future and What Americans Can Do About It* (New York: Farrar, Straus and Giroux, 2005).

Reynolds, Alan, *Income and Wealth* (Westport, CT: Greenwood Press, 2006).

Steuerle, C. Eugene, *Contemporary U.S. Tax Policy* (New York: Urban Institute Press, 2004).

Notes

1. A short history of the U.S. tax system can be seen at the U.S. Treasury website. See http://www.ustreas.gov/education/fact-sheets/taxes/ustax.shtml
2. For a comprehensive presentation of Reagan tax policy and the position of President Reagan on taxes see http://www.presidentreagan.info
3. A debate between conservative commentator Dinesh D'Sousa and liberal journalist E.J. Dionne can be seen at http://www.slate.com/id/3665/entry/24002
4. Reaganomics is explained by conservative economist William A. Niskanen at http://www.econlib.org/library/Enc1/Reaganomics.html. Also see the Cato Institute's defense of Reaganomics in a paper entitled "Supply Tax Cuts and the Truth about the Reagan Economic Revival" http://www.cato.org/pubs/pas/pa-261.html

5. Bruce Bartlett, *Reaganomics: Supply-Side Economics* (Westport, CT: Arlington House, 1981).

6. Paul Krugman of Princeton and a *New York Times* columnist has been a long-time critic of Reaganomics. See his view on Reagan tax policy at http://www.pkarchive.org/economy/taxcutcon.html

7. The criticism of the tax increase by President George H.W. Bush is discussed in Jack Germond, *Mad As Hell: Revolt at the Ballot Box* (New York: Warner Books, 1993).

8. See "New Tax Cuts Primarily Benefiting Millionaires Slated to Take Effect in January," *Center for Budget Priorities*, September 19, 2005.

9. See "Assessing the Economic Growth and Tax Relief Reconciliation Act of 2001," Web Memo, the Heritage Foundation, http://heritage.org/research/taxes/taxcuttable.cfm

10. See http://tpcprod.urban.org/publications/url.cfm?ID=901006

11. See Elena Schor, "Democrats Criticize Bush Budget for Fudging Iraq Costs," *The Guardian*, February 4, 2008, http://www.guardian.co.uk/world/2008/feb/04/usa.elanaschor

12. See "Debate Over the Tax Cuts," *PBS Online News Hour*, http://www.pbs.org/newshour/bb/economy/jan-june03/taxes_5-14

13. Jackie Calmes and Edmund Andrews, "Obama Calls for Curbs on Offshore Tax Havens," *New York Times*, May 4, 2009, A1.

14. "Stemming the Tide," *The Economist*, November 21, 2009, pp. 26–28.

15. Jackie Calmes, "In $ 3.8 Trillion Budget, Obama Pivots to Trim Future Deficits," *New York Times*, February 1, 2010, A1.

16. Allen Schick, *The Federal Budget: Politics, Policy, Process* (Washington, D.C.: Brookings Institution Press, 2000).

17. "Earmarks–Congress Stealing Taxpayers Money," *Boston Globe*, June 29, 2006, and also "In Search of Presidential Earmarks," *Wall Street Journal*, February 21, 2006.

7 SOCIAL SECURITY AND MEDICARE

Issue Focus

Although many Americans are wary of government intervention in their lives, they welcome the two most popular public programs in the history of the United States—Social Security and Medicare. Designed to provide a level of income and medical security for seniors, both of these programs have mushroomed in cost in recent years as the baby-boomer generation reaches retirement age and as a result creates greater health care needs. The question of what the government will do to respond to the fiscal challenges of these programs is one of the greatest public policy challenges of this century.

Chapter Objectives
This issue chapter will seek to:
1. Explain the formation of Social Security and Medicare as key social welfare programs initiated by the U.S. government.
2. Discuss the serious financing challenges facing Social Security and Medicare, the two largest social insurance entitlement programs in the United States.
3. Describe the various proposals designed to address the future funding shortfalls in both Social Security and Medicare.

SOME BACKGROUND

In 1940 Ida Fuller of Brattleboro, Vermont, received her first Social Security check of $22.54. For the next thirty four years of her life, she continued to receive a monthly check for that amount, totaling nearly $21,000 in Social Security benefits. Although she had contributed only about $22 in payroll taxes and because the new program had started only four years before she retired, Ida Fuller became the first American to be able to count on the help of the government in her retirement. Social Security was one of the landmark New Deal programs developed during the administration of Franklin Delano Roosevelt and was designed to provide Americans with a safety net of benefits to make their lives more secure. For much of its history, Social Security was a fiscally sound program that had enormous support among the American people and is still considered the most successful social program initiated by the U.S. government.

Sixty eight years later, Kathleen Casey-Kirschling was the first baby boomer (those Americans born after 1946) eligible to receive her initial Social Security check. Because Casey-Kirschling was sixty-two and was retiring early, she received only 75% of what she would have received if she waited until she was sixty-seven, the full retirement age. Casey-Kirschling, a seventh-grade teacher from New Jersey, is part of what has come to be called the "silver tsunami," over 80 million Americans who will be eligible to receive Social Security benefits in the coming years. Casey-Kirschling is starting an entitlement trend that has the potential to create economic havoc. By 2017 the Social Security program will pay out more benefits than it receives in taxes, and by 2041 experts estimate that the money in the Social Security Trust Fund, which is the repository of the taxes paid to provide retirees with their benefits, will be depleted.[1]

The chief problem facing Social Security is the graying of America. In 1900, for example, one in twenty-five Americans was sixty-five years or older, but by 2040 the number will be one in four. Presently the baby-boomer generation is the fastest-growing segment of the American population. At the same time the U.S. workforce is shrinking. In 1970, 3.7 workers per beneficiary were paying taxes into the Social Security system, but by 2040, two workers per beneficiary will be paying taxes. The clear result will be that the Social Security system will generate less revenue just at the time the number of recipients is on the rise, a perfect storm of fiscal and social welfare challenges. Although Congress, starting with the Reagan administration, began to cut back on generous yearly cost-of-living adjustments indexed to the inflation rate and no cost-of-living increases were given to Social Security recipients in 2010, the fiscal challenges continued with little sign of relief. By the early 1990s it was becoming evident to

Population Growth (%) By Age Group (1995–2040)

Age	Growth
Under 20 years	5
20–64 years	24
65 and older	112

Number of Workers Per Social Security Beneficiary (1970–2070)

Year	No of workers
1970	3.7
1990	3.4
2010	3.0
2030	2.0
2070	1.8

Source: National Commission on Retirement Policy

Washington policy makers that population growth was driving the Social Security system and determining its destiny.[2]

Although the Social Security challenges are indeed considerable, an even greater challenge in health care is related to the silver tsunami. In 1964 the administration of Lyndon Johnson initiated a number of social programs designed to address poverty, health care and aging to attain what he termed a "Great Society." One of its most significant initiatives was the introduction of Medicare, a medical insurance program targeted to seniors (over age 65) and disabled youth, as a health companion to Social Security. Part A of Medicare covers hospital stays and is funded through payroll taxes. Part B is for doctor visits and is paid through a combination of general revenue and premiums paid by the recipients. Part C provides supplemental insurance coverage for expenses not covered by Parts A and B. In 2006 Part D, the prescription drug program that provides seniors with drugs at a reduced cost, was added.

Like Social Security, Medicare started with modest outlays of federal dollars but has mushroomed to the point where it is also in financial difficulty. By 2050 it is estimated that Medicare will account for between 8% and 9% of the entire U.S. federal budget. Although many experts believe that their projections about when the Social Security Trust Fund will be depleted have remained fairly constant at around 2040 (although for the first time since the 1980s Social Security will run deficits for 2010 and 2011, which will require dipping into accumulated surpluses), the projections of when Medicare becomes a full-blown fiscal crisis have continued to drop. In 2004 those who study Medicare financing dropped their projection about when the Medicare financing crisis would hit from 2026 to 2019. Those projections are now down to 2017. Every year the doomsday clock related to Medicare continues to wind down as health care costs skyrocket and the percentage of national gross domestic product (GDP) tied to Medicare continues to edge upward.[3]

The fiscal crisis associated with Social Security and Medicare is compounded by the fact that for the last twenty years surpluses in the Trust Fund have been used for regular governmental appropriations. In other words, the government has been covering part of its yearly deficits by borrowing from the Trust Fund. This borrowing has not been a problem to date because there has been enough money to cover the transfer of revenue from the Trust Fund to regular governmental appropriations. To cover the loss of revenue in the Trust Fund, the government has purchased Treasury bills (interest-bearing notes). But when the Trust Fund begins to go into deficit as the silver tsunami surges forward, the government will have to find the money to deal with the deficit.[4]

Today Social Security and Medicare are at the center of a national debate not just over how to deal with out-of-control costs and the possible bankruptcy of key social welfare programs, but also over the wisdom of huge government-sponsored and government-funded entitlement initiatives. With Roosevelt's New Deal and Johnson's Great Society, the federal government assumed the responsibility of providing for the retirement and health care of seniors. Before the Great Depression the United States responded to social welfare concerns on a more personal and local level. The family unit, the church or synagogue, the neighborhood and a network of charity organizations were the primary sources of assistance to those who needed a helping hand or a long-term safety net. During the heyday of Democratic dominance in Congress, especially in the 1960s and 1970s, the government continued the tradition as provider of last resort, which resulted in huge government outlays, new taxes and large bureaucracies.

But the election of Ronald Reagan and the realities of future population pressures forced government to think about alternatives to providing financial security to retirees and medical assistance to seniors. Social Security and Medicare remained the foundations of the U.S. entitlement system, but new ideas and proposals entered the political arena as talk of privatization of retirement savings, new forms of medical insurance and restrictions on eligibility for benefits became more commonplace. However, anytime two long-serving popular federal programs that provide a large dose of financial security face criticism or replacement with new options, political and popular tensions are sure to follow. These tensions and the debates, differences and divisions that feed them have fostered one of the most difficult policy challenges of our time.

DEBATES, DIFFERENCES AND DIVISIONS

When a public policy has the potential to wreak financial havoc on the U.S. Treasury and bring uncertainty to millions of Americans, it follows that political leaders will enter the fray and introduce their vision of how to fix what is broken or will break. In terms of Social Security and Medicare, an added component to this policy challenge is that the threat from these major programs is not just financial, but also generational. If the experts are right and some twenty or thirty years from now the two major programs designed to provide a financial safety net for America's seniors go under, then the burden of providing for those retirement pensions and medical insurance will likely fall on those who are still working. The only way out of this box is to advance controversial proposals that delay access to or drastically scale down benefits, both of which hit hard at seniors. The other more traditional options are more borrowing and higher taxes, both of which place a significant financial burden on the younger generation. In other words, the Social Security and Medicare funding dilemma is not only about how best to take care of grandma and grandpa in their senior years, but it is also about how much of the financial burden their grandchildren will have to bear to ensure that Social Security and Medicare remain solvent.

In some respects the challenge of Social Security, which is primarily a matter of funding is at present more manageable and less threatening than Medicare. Although the Social Security program may go into deficit down the road, it can be fixed with tax increases, more borrowing or maintaining a sustained and vibrant economy that would pump money into the government's coffers. Although new taxes or borrowing is not attractive and solid economic growth in the long run is uncertain, experts and political leaders are at present not supporting drastic measures such as extending the age when benefits can be received to seventy years of age or drastically reducing benefits such as eliminating regular cost-of-living increases. Both of these measures would likely meet with stiff opposition from seniors and groups representing them, such as the American Association of Retired Persons (AARP).[5] Nevertheless, something must be done and the sooner the better. Republican Senator Judd Gregg, an influential member of the Senate Budget Committee, stated in 2009 when it became clear that the Social Security Trust Fund was running out of money faster than expected, ". . . we better get to working on Social Security and stop burying our heads in the sand. . . . The Social Security Trust Fund, though technically in balance, is going to put huge pressures on taxpayers very soon."[6]

The key in the projected shortfall in Social Security is whether young workers would be willing to pay higher taxes, to keep the program going. There is general agreement that in the next twenty-five years the financing problem will be manageable and that payroll tax increases will not be necessary. However, further into the future, somewhere between 2050 and 2075, for example, the Trust Fund shortfall may rise to $20 trillion and could require tax increases of as much as 54% in payroll taxes along with serious cuts in benefits. This is obviously a long way off, but it does point out that Social Security is a ticking time bomb: when it does go off, it will have a devastating impact on young workers.[7]

On the Record

Social Security Commissioner Michael Astrue said the following in the continued debate over how to deal with the impending Social Security financing challenge:

We are already feeling enormous pressure from baby boomers being in their peak disability years and now we're preparing for so many of them to file for retirement. . . . There is no reason to have any immediate panic. I and most people who are familiar with the situation are confident that there will be some pain along the way, but we will get there and Social Security will be there for future generations.

Source: Press Release, Social Security Administration

Although the Social Security financial crisis may be a long way off and involves not just dollars and cents but also potential generational tensions, it does not mean that the political system is ignoring some short-term fixes. Much of the policy debate surrounding Social Security stems from Republicans in the Congress, who have waged a public relations campaign touting the benefits of privatizing the retirement system and creating individual savings accounts. With individual savings accounts, workers' retirement benefits would depend on how much they contributed to their own account over the lifetime of employment and more importantly how well the savings account performed as the contributions would be placed in various types of investment mechanisms such as mutual funds, annuities, bonds and the stock market. Under this system there would be no payroll taxes and the accent would be on personal responsibility, rather than a government-sponsored and government-administered program.[8]

Despite the accent on personal responsibility in preparing for retirement, the individual savings account proposal was not without its detractors. A bipartisan National Commission on Retirement Policy advocated for a go-slow approach, suggesting that only 2% of the payroll tax be shifted into the accounts with workers receiving a range of investment options.[9] But more conservative members of Congress advocated for a two-thirds shift in payroll taxes to the individual savings accounts. Supporters of the plan were convinced that the Social Security system was headed for a breakdown, and the only way to effectively provide for retirement benefits was to move quickly and comprehensively to privatization. The Republican position raised opposition from many economists and congressional budget analysts who agreed that there would be transition costs associated with a shift to individual savings accounts as money would have to be found to cover existing Social Security pensions during the time the system was moving toward partial privatization.[10]

FYI

Social Security, more formally known as the Old Age, Survivors and Disability Insurance (OASDI), is the program that provides old age, survivors and disability insurance to eligible Americans. The program is funded by contributions from workers and their employers through a payroll tax that is equivalent to 6.2% of covered wages. The Internal Revenue Service collects the taxes and deposits the contributions into the Trust Fund. The revenues in the Trust Fund pay for the benefits to eligible pensioners. As a result of a change in the law in 1983, a retiree must be sixty-seven years old to receive full benefits. The Trust Fund associated with Medicare is called the Hospital Insurance (HI) Fund. Like the Social Security Trust Fund, the HI Fund is also used to collect Medicare payroll taxes similar to Social Security. In 2004 the assets of the Social Security Trust Fund were $1.6 trillion, whereas those of the HI Fund were $183 billion. The significant difference between the Social Security Trust Fund and the HI Fund shows why Medicare is considered in more imminent danger of financial collapse.

Source: "Social Security and Medicare: The Impending Fiscal Challenge," Report from the Kansas City Federal Reserve Bank, 2006

But the real opposition to the individual savings accounts came from Democrats who viewed the proposal as financially risky, because workers would be asked to make investment decisions without the financial expertise and then hope that their return would not be threatened by a downturn in the stock market. Inherent in this position from the Democrats was that the government provides workers with a guaranteed stream of pension money without the hassles and fears that come with personal investment. The Democrats also stated that the individual savings accounts were merely a way of enhancing the business of Wall Street investment firms who would enjoy a substantial increase in their business as workers flocked to them to start their retirement accounts.[11] Needless to say, the Democratic position of cautioning against moving too quickly to privatization won the day as the economic meltdown experienced in 2008 and 2009 when millions of Americans lost huge portions of their personal savings in 401K accounts pointed to the dangers of relying on the stock market for retirement income.

Data Bank

Social Security and Medicare costs for 2008 were estimated to be $625 billion and $599 billion, respectively. Social Security beneficiaries and Medicare recipients now number nearly 50 million and 43 million Americans, respectively. The average Social Security monthly payment per worker is $1,007 (in 2008), whereas the net estimated lifetime benefits for Medicare recipients (benefits minus taxes paid) is for men, between $108,000 and $240,000, and for women, (who live longer), between $142,000 and $277,000. In 2008 Medicare premiums were increased to $96.40 a month for most recipients.

Source: Social Security Administration and the Urban Institute

Although the Republicans have backed off their push for privatization of Social Security, Democrats have launched their own short-term solution to deal with the future financial insolvency of the retirement program. At present all earnings of American workers up to $90,000 are taxed for Social Security purposes at 12.4%. But every dollar earned above $90,000 is exempt from taxation. By removing the cap, which affects only high-wage earners, the funding gap in Social Security would close over the next seventy-five years.[11] The earnings gap would in effect raise the payroll tax of the high-income earners by 1.9%, a small increase but with a major impact on Social Security solvency. In 2005 President Bush expressed an interest in raising the cap on income above the $90,000 mark, but wealthy seniors raised objections to the payroll tax increase. The payroll cap increase has remained on the back burner of Social Security reform.[12]

From a worker's point of view, however, the reforms proposed by Republicans and Democrats are not just about dollars and cents or public or private pension programs, but about a key issue of whether the retirement age will be boosted in the coming years as a way of further delaying the financial breakdown of the Social Security Trust Fund. More and more Americans are seeking to retire at an earlier age, as was the case with baby boomer Kathleen Casey-Kirschling. Should the age for receiving retirement benefits be increased beyond sixty-seven years old, there would likely be a public outcry. Currently, many Americans retire early, take a smaller percentage of their Social Security benefits and work part-time to supplement their income until they reach the age when they can receive full benefits. But any policy change that would increase the retirement age to seventy, as some political leaders have suggested, would force seniors to radically change their post-work plans.

Pushing the retirement age forward creates other problems. Studies from the General Accounting Office show that American workers who remain on the job beyond the time they are eligible to receive Social Security benefits are more susceptible to work-related injuries and require disability payments to cover the impact of the injuries. Many businesses, however, are increasingly supportive of raising the retirement age to receive Social Security benefits because they see an experienced and conscientious workforce among the seniors who can be tapped for part-time employment. Businesses have also supported an extension of the retirement age as a possible answer to the illegal immigration issue. Should the government crack down on the presence of illegal aliens in the workplace and diminish the number of these workers, the alternative would be to rely on those in their late 60s and perhaps early 70s as "replacement workers."[13]

Although numerous proposals are designed to address the long-term fiscal problems associated with Social Security, it is the Medicare program that is in immediate fiscal crisis mode and requires quick and comprehensive reform. As stated earlier, the Medicare trustees continue to push forward the year when the program goes in the red. With health care costs rising above the national inflation rate each year and the addition of the new prescription drug program, new fiscal pressures have increased significantly. There is no relief in sight from the reality of a gigantic deficit under the current structure of the program.[14] However, like Social Security, the looming crisis in Medicare is not on most Americans' radar screens, and politicians usually avoid the problems by admitting there is a fiscal challenge, but then making only vague promises to fix the inevitable shortfall. The problem with Medicare reform is that most Americans and certainly most politicians have a short-term outlook. Polling data on national priorities often find Medicare reform far down the list. Also, during the 2008 presidential campaign both party's candidates were asked during the debates what they would do to fix the out-of-control Medicare obligations. The candidates gave no specific plan on how to fix the problem, other than the need for fiscal reforms. Medicare is one of those programs that Americans depend on and politicians proudly point to as a success, but then when a crisis looms in the distance, reforms are put off for another day. President Obama at first shied away from the Social Security and Medicare debates, making general statements about the need to preserve Social Security and Medicare and to reject privatization schemes. However, in his health care reform law Medicare will be cut by $500 billion in 2014 through what the president says are cost savings such as reducing payments to hospitals and insurance companies and increasing payroll tax premiums on couples making more than $250,000.[15]

Medicare Costs as Percentage of GDP
2010 – 3.7
2020 – 4.5
2030 – 6.2
2040 – 8
2050 – 8.5
2060 – 10
2070 – 11

Source: Report of the Medicare Trustees

One of the key reasons Medicare stays in the background of public opinion and is avoided like the plague by politicians is that reform efforts will be much more controversial and include considerable changes in the manner in which health care for seniors is delivered and paid for. The options available to policy makers are generally fraught with sacrifice and if implemented would create a groundswell of citizen outrage. Of course, one of the obvious answers is to raise taxes (the Democrats target the wealthy) or to require larger premiums (which some Republicans have supported), but to do so would require hefty increases that are certain to create opposition.

But the other options are no more attractive. There have been proposals to reduce the services provided by Medicare, which usually pays for 80% of hospital and nursing home stays (within a set period) along with services such as ambulance transportation, diagnostic tests, laboratory services and emergency room visits. But a cutback in these services or a reduction in the percentage that the program would pay for would place an enormous financial burden on seniors. There have also been some doomsday scenarios regarding health care delivery as a result of the financial shortfalls in Medicare. Rationing of medical services has been raised as a possible outcome, with seniors either having to wait long periods for procedures or becoming part of a triage system in which doctors and nurses determine the order of care rather than respond quickly to a medical condition.[16]

Doctors and hospitals have also not been immune to the reform initiatives, as proposals have been presented to limit or reduce the reimbursements that Medicare provides hospitals and doctors for services provided. For years hospital executives have been complaining that the government has been shortchanging them in Medicare reimbursements. As a result hospital income has been reduced, forcing, according to hospital executives, the closing or the merging of hospitals. Doctors as well have complained that Medicare payments for medical services they render have been reduced, cutting into their incomes and making it less attractive to work in gerontology. In recent years some level of reimbursement adjustment has been found for hospitals and doctors, but down the road it is anticipated that the matter of Medicare reimbursements to hospitals and doctors will be central to the debate over how to save the senior health program.[17]

Perhaps one of the potentially divisive proposals to reform Medicare in the short run was presented by the Bush administration in 2007. The president, as part of his fiscal 2008 budget, proposed that seniors making more than $80,000 would pay higher premiums and deductibles for the prescription drug program. In effect, the proposal advocated for a means test that would be required for participation in the costly drug program. Republicans in the Senate championed the proposal, but it was defeated on its first try. The AARP worked vigorously against the change, saying that it would erode the incomes of seniors. Despite the defeat, the White House stressed that the change to a means test would save $10 billion over five years, but more importantly it would secure the concept of means testing as a new factor in providing Medicare benefits.[18]

In 2006 economists from the Federal Reserve Bank in Kansas City presented a lengthy study entitled "Social Security and Medicare: The Impending Fiscal Challenge." Their conclusion points to not only the enormity of the problem but also the urgency for remedial action. An excerpt from the conclusion of their study is given here:

The government's fiscal challenge is to insure the long-run viability of both programs. Under current law, the dedicated sources of revenue available to the government are woefully inadequate for financing the benefits promised to current and future beneficiaries. The present value of the government's future obligations over the next seventy-five years is estimated to be $35.6 trillion. As a result, the government would need to increase revenues, reduce spending, or increase borrowing by running larger budget deficits. However, the cumulative value of the larger budget deficits would need to be $35.6 trillion in present value terms, which is significantly larger than the nation's federal debt–the cumulative sum of past budget deficits of $7.4 trillion at the end of 2004.[19]

Former Illinois Senator Everett Dirksen once talked about federal expenditures and said, "a billion here, a billion there, but after a while it becomes real money." With Social Security and Medicare, it is not a "billion here and a billion there," rather it is $35.6 trillion in obligations over the next seventy-five years, and that would be on top of an already sizeable $9.4 trillion national debt. These numbers are truly mind-boggling and show clearly why reforming the financial structures of Social Security and Medicare are so important, even though the impact of impending bankruptcy and debt is years away. If the American people faced the prospect of such a huge financial liability in their own households, even if it were years away, they would most likely take some corrective action. But right now both the American people and their political leaders are in the traditional policy mode so common in the U.S. political system: putting off till tomorrow what needs to be dealt with today.[20]

Unlike the issues that have been presented so far, the problems and challenges of dealing with the fiscal woes of Social Security and Medicare are currently not creating intense debate, partisan differences and social divisions; they are only distant concerns that will be addressed in another decade. However, once the silver tsunami of Social Security and the mind-boggling cost increases associated with Medicare come into play, these two programs will rise to the top of the list of political issues facing the government and indeed the entire country. The best that can be hoped for is that true to the American political tradition, Americans will somehow muddle through and create a patchwork of fixes–public, private or both–that carry the programs forward. The unknowns about dealing with Social Security and Medicare are how intense the generational divide will be, whether the solutions presented to deal with these two vital programs will foster difficult debates and how serious differences over retirement and health benefits will divide the young and old. The future of Social Security and Medicare is in the hands of the young people who will be asked to make decisions about those years older than them, and those decisions may require major sacrifices and radical changes in the way the U.S. government operates.[21]

The Great Debate

In many respects fiscal reform of Social Security and Medicare is a generational matter with the prospect of younger Americans paying more in taxes in the future to cover the costs of these entitlement programs for the baby-boomer generation.

Debate Topic
To what extent should the younger generation pay for the pension and health care needs of seniors?

Critical Thinking Questions

1. Do you believe that Americans should be responsible for their own retirement benefits, or should we rely on the government taking care of the funding through programs such as Social Security?
2. As a way of lessening the costs of Medicare, some analysts have suggested limiting health care services for seniors, some sort of means testing or significant increases in premiums and deductibles. Do you agree or disagree?

3. If Social Security is the so-called third rail of American politics–immune from change or significant reform–how can the government resolve the future funding problems?
4. One of the most serious proposals for reforming Social Security is extending the age when retirement benefits can be collected to seventy years. Is this a wise recommendation?
5. Even though retirement is likely a long way off, how will you plan for it and the medical costs associated with it?

Connections

The major advocate for seniors in both the Social Security and Medicare policy debates is the American Association of Retired Persons. See http://www.aarp.org

The National Commission on Retirement Policy is one of the key sources of information and policy alternatives related to reforming Social Security and Medicare. The Commission is associated with the Center for Strategic and International Studies. See http://csis.org/

The Social Security Administration is a critical source of information on the program. See http://www.ssa.gov/

The Centers for Medicare & Medicaid Services (CMS) is the key source for information on the program. See http://www.cms.hhs.gov

The government website for Medicare is at http://www.medicare.gov

Some Books to Read

Clark, Robert, Marilyn Moon, Timothy M. Smeeding, Robert Louis Clark, eds. *Economics of an Aging Society* (New York: John Wiley & Sons, 2004).

Gale, William, John B. Shoven, Mark J. Warshawsky, eds. *Private Pensions and Public Policies.* (Washington, D.C.: Brookings Institutions Press, 2004).

Mackell, Thomas J. *When Good Pensions Go Away: Why America Needs a New Deal for Pensions and Healthcare Reform* (New York: John Wiley & Sons, 2008).

Shaviro, Daniel, *Who Should Pay for Medicare?* (Washington, D.C.: American Enterprise Institute for Public Policy, 2004).

Steuerle, C. Eugene, Eduward Gramlich, Hugh Heclo and Demetra Smith Nightingale, *The Government We Deserve: Responsive Democracy and Changing Expectations* (New York, Urban Institute Press, 1998).

Notes

1. "First U.S. Baby Boomer Applies for Social Security," http://www.reuters.com/article/idUSN15383509
2. Robert Pear, "Finances of Social Security and Medicare Deteriorates," *New York Times*, May 2, 2006, http://www.nytimes.com/2006/05/02/washington/02benefit.html

3. "The Impact of Social Security and Medicare on the Federal Budget," Congressional Budget Office, http://www.cbo.gov/ftpdoc.cfm?index=3982&type=0
4. Ibid.
5. See the position of the AARP on Social Security reform at its website, http://www.aarp.org/research/socialsecurity/reform
6. Lori Montgomery, "The Vanishing Surplus," *Washington Post National Weekly Edition*, April 6–12, 2009, pp. 23–24.
7. Robert Pear, "Social Security Underestimates Future Life Spans, Critics Say," http://www.nytimes.com/2004/12/31/politics/31benefit.html
8. See the Republican position of Social Security Reform at http://www.ontheissues.org/Social_Security.htm#RepublicanParty
9. See the report's findings at http://www.socsec.org/facts/Check_Lists/checklist3.pdf
10. Mike Allen, "Democrats Mobilizing on Social Security," *Washington Post*, February 15, 2005, A02. Also see the Democrat position on Social Security at http://www.democrats.org/a/national/secure-retirement
11. Jonathan Weisman, "Upper-Income Seniors: Pay More," *Washington Post National Weekly Edition*, December 15–21, 2007, p. 35.
12. "Social Security and Medicare: The Impending Fiscal Crisis," *Federal Reserve Bank of Kansas City–Economic Review*, First Quarter, 2006.
13. Jesse J. Halloral, "Raise Retirement Age to Save Social Security," *Business Week*, August 1, 2008.
14. See the problems associated with Medicare reform and public opinion at http://publicagenda.org/issues/pcc_detail.cfm?issue_type=medicare&list=1
15. See Lisa Wangsness, "Major Health Care Changes Won't Take Place Until 2014," *Boston Globe*, March 23, 2010, A12.
16. 2006 Annual Report of the Board of Trustees of the Federal Hospital Insurance and Federal Supplementary Medicaid Insurance Trust Fund, May 1, 2006 (pdf).
17. The issue of physician payment is discussed in "Medicare's Physician Payment Rules and The Sustainable Growth Rate,"http://www.cbo.gov/fpdocs/74xx/doc7425/07-25-SGR.pdf
18. Jonathan Weisman, "Means Test Sought for Medicare Drug Plan," *Washington Post*, October 5, 2007, A01.
19. Social Security and Medicare: The Impending Fiscal Challenge, op. cit. p. 30.
20. Mary Agnes Carey, "Reining in Medicare Costs," *Congressional Quarterly Weekly*, January 30, 2006, p. 417.
21. Laurence J. Kotlikoff and Scott Burns, *The Coming Generational Storm: What You Need to Know About America's Economic Future* (Cambridge, MA: MIT Press, 2005).

8

RACE **RELATIONS** AND CIVIL RIGHTS

Issue Focus

There is little doubt that the most divisive social issue in the United States has been race relations. From the days of the slave trade when Africans were forcibly brought to American shores to the deep national differences over slavery that led to the Civil War to the Civil Rights movement in the 1950s and 1960s, the United States has often been defined in terms of how it deals with racial discrimination and how it moves toward creating a nation that advances equality for all its people. The election of Barack Obama as the country's first African-American president signaled a turning point in race relations, but many in the African-American community continue to face racial bias and see the struggle for civil rights as an ongoing process of acceptance and social justice.

Chapter Objectives
This issue chapter will seek to:
1. Describe the struggle of African-Americans for civil rights and the evolution of the civil rights movement in the United States.
2. Examine the current debates over government policies designed to ensure racial equality, the differences in approaches to eradicating racial discrimination and the race-based divisions that still remain in American society.
3. Discuss the status of race relations in the United States as a result of the election of its first African-American president.

SOME BACKGROUND

America has often been called a nation of immigrants, but it is also a nation of former slaves and natives who were either brought to the country against their will or forcibly pushed out of their ancestral homelands to make way for the white man. The history of race relations in the United States, especially with respect to African-American slaves and Native Americans, is disturbing and sad. The slaves brought to the country from West Africa to work in the fields of the South were not only denied their basic civil and human rights, but they were treated as simple property easily bought and sold by landowners who were anxious for inexpensive labor. The natives who occupied the country before the white man landed were often treated as unwanted interlopers who could be moved from place to place to accommodate the white man's dream of extending the frontier westward. The slaves and the natives were expendable, and many endured the cruelest treatment.

Over time with the natives worn down from fruitless wars against the white man and relegated to reservations, the struggle for civil rights shifted to the millions of slaves who made up large segments of the population in southern states. The Civil War, which was fought in part over the issue of slavery, ended with a victory by the North and the promulgation of the Thirteenth Amendment abolishing slavery, the Fourteenth Amendment promising "equal protection of the laws" and the Fifteenth Amendment granting voting rights to former slaves. However, even after the war and the issuance of the Civil War Amendments, discrimination and segregation continued in the United States. In many of the southern states so-called Jim Crow laws were instituted, which effectively made former slaves second-class citizens and shut them out from any equal treatment in the white man's world. Blacks faced new roadblocks to full citizenship, and those who questioned the separate system were many times the victims of unfair justice and worse yet, physical intimidation, beatings and public lynching.

It was not until the post–World War II era that blacks made an organized and aggressive effort to change the face of race relations in the United States. Using the courts, economic boycotts, civil disobedience and public demonstrations, blacks began the civil rights movement in the United States. The National Association of Colored People (NAACP) (founded in 1909) became the primary voice of the movement representing the interests of black people in state capitals, in the halls of Congress and at the Supreme Court. Young lawyers such as Thurgood Marshall, who argued the key school desegregation case before the Supreme Court (*Brown v. Board of Education of Topeka Kansas*), religious leaders such as Dr. Martin Luther King, who led many marches for freedom throughout the South, and ordinary citizens such as Rosa Parks, who bravely refused to give up her seat to a white man and move to the back of the bus, stepped forward to rally American citizens to take action against discrimination and segregation.[1]

The push for equal treatment and the breakdown of the racial barriers that existed in the United States were not easy. Political leaders and governmental officials in southern states steadfastly refused to acknowledge the inherent injustices of discrimination and segregation and did everything in their power to stop the civil rights movement. Governor George Wallace of Alabama stood in the doorway of the University of Alabama to stop blacks from enrolling, and southern senators used filibuster techniques in the Congress to stop legislation that would end discrimination and segregation. Federal marshals had to be brought into Mississippi to ensure that local officials would not block blacks from registering to vote. Stiff resistance to civil rights activism in the South took the form of church burnings, assassinations of demonstrators and organizers and widespread police brutality. Dr. Martin Luther King, the leader of the civil rights movement and the inspirational voice of black America, was assassinated in Memphis, Tennessee, in 1968 as he prepared to demonstrate in favor of that city's garbage men who were on strike. King's assassination set off days of rioting in many of the major cities and made clear the anger and division that existed between white and black America over the issue of race relations and civil rights.[2]

Although the death of Dr. Martin Luther King pointed out the hatred that still lingered in the United States, the civil rights movement achieved some notable successes, including the passage of the Civil Rights Act of 1964, a landmark piece of legislation that placed the federal government as the guarantor of an open and equal society in key areas such as housing, transportation, employment and accommodations. In 1965 Congress passed the Voting Rights Act that tore down the barriers put in place in the South and elsewhere to deny blacks the right to vote and compete fairly for public office. Both of these bills were followed by other civil rights laws and bureaucratic regulations that moved the United States away from segregation and in effect ended the era of de jure (law-based) racial discrimination. Much needed to be done, however, to ensure that political and social rights were expanded to include economic opportunity and fair distribution of economic benefits for black America (ending de facto discrimination). By the beginning of the 1970s, the civil rights movement had become a force to be reckoned with and an accepted part of the process of moving America from two separate countries to one.[3]

On the Record

Now I say to you today my friends, even though we face the difficulties of today and tomorrow, I still have a dream. It is a dream deeply rooted in the American dream. I have a dream that one day this nation will rise up and live out the true meaning of the creed: "We hold these truths to be self-evident, that all men are created equal."

Dr. Martin Luther King Jr., Speech at Civil Rights March on Washington, August 28, 1963

In the years since the death of Dr. Martin Luther King, the civil rights movement has pushed forward with a wide agenda for change. Black leaders such as the Reverend Jesse Jackson and the Reverend Al Sharpton have followed in the footsteps of Dr. King, charging that America remains a nation where discrimination remains, though perhaps in a more subtle and less oppressive manner. They and other leaders from a new generation of African-Americans continue to point out that black people face daily challenges in finding jobs, purchasing homes, dealing with the police and enduring racist comments and attitudes. Many African-Americans believe the struggle for racial equality is by no means over, and the remedies for ensuring that African-Americans are treated equally has caused new debates and fostered new differences and divisions in the United States. This chapter discusses these debates and these new differences and divisions.

FYI

Some Important Dates in the Civil Rights Movement

1954–Supreme Court declared school segregation unconstitutional.

1955–Rosa Parks refused to move to the back of the bus in Montgomery, Alabama.

1957–Arkansas Governor Orval Falbus used National Guard to block nine black students from attending Little Rock High School. President Eisenhower sent federal troops to protect students and ensure integration of the school.

1960–Four black college students began sit-in at lunch counter in Greensboro, North Carolina.

1962–President Kennedy sent federal troops to the University of Mississippi to ensure that James Meredith, the school's first black student, could enroll and attend classes.

1963–Dr. Martin Luther King delivered "I Have a Dream" speech in Washington.

1963–Church bombing in Birmingham, Alabama, killed four black girls.

1964–Congress passed Civil Rights Act after seventy-five-day filibuster by southern senators.

1965–March was conducted from Selma to Montgomery, Alabama, to demand protection for voting rights.

1965–Malcolm X was assassinated.

1965–Riots broke out in the Watts section of Los Angeles.

1965–Voting Rights Act was signed into law.

1968–Martin Luther King was assassinated in Memphis, Tennessee.

1978–Supreme Court ruled in the *Bakke* decision that medical school admission policies that set aside positions based on race were unconstitutional.

1983–Martin Luther King federal holiday was signed into law.

1990–President George H.W. Bush vetoed civil rights bill that he viewed as imposing racial quotas on employers. A watered-down version of the bill eventually passed.

1996–The Supreme Court ruled that race could not be used in creating congressional districts.

2003–The Supreme Court found that an affirmative-action point system designed to enhance the chances of minorities getting into the University of Michigan was unconstitutional.

2006–Despite southern Republican opposition, the Voting Rights Act of 1965 was re-authorized.

2008–Barack Obama was elected the first African-American president of the United States.

DEBATES, DIFFERENCES AND DIVISIONS

Although de jure discrimination is now largely a memory in the United States, many disturbing examples of de facto discrimination remain as numerous gaps between white and black America reveal that much needs to be done to fulfill the dream of racial equality. For example, U.S. Census data point to a striking difference between blacks and whites in terms of income. In a study done in 2005, the Census Bureau found that the median household income of African-Americans was $29,689, whereas that of whites was $45,631. Furthermore, the percentage of African-Americans in poverty (again using U.S. Census data) in 2003 was 24%, whereas that of whites was 11%. Although a vibrant and expanding African-American middle class has indeed been evident, the percentage is quite small compared to the white middle class. In a study done in 1997, only 4% of U.S. businesses were owned by African-Americans, and the salaries of African-American professionals such as doctors, lawyers and business executives were considerably less than their white counterparts'.[4]

The economic disparities that exist today between blacks and whites in America have become the target of much of the action of the contemporary civil rights movement. To remedy the disparities, African-American leaders remain committed to the affirmative-action policies that were instituted during the administration of President Lyndon Baines Johnson. Affirmative-action policies basically seek to ensure that minorities and women are not discriminated against in hiring and promotion. And to ensure that such discrimination does not occur, federal regulations provide guidelines and requirements that businesses and other institutions must follow to create a fair hiring and promotion playing field and to guarantee that there will be a level of diversity in the workplace. However, although the goals of affirmative-action policies fall within the tradition of equal opportunity and anti-discrimination, the program to require businesses and institutions to abide by the federal regulations and foster a diverse workforce has come under intense scrutiny and passionate debate.

The opposition to affirmative action is based on the position that hiring, admission and promotion procedures should be guided by merit and achievement, not by a desire to right the wrongs of the past or to create a more diverse workforce. Supporters of merit-based procedures for hiring, admissions and promotions argue that affirmative action fosters a quota mentality as employers and institutions show preferential treatment toward minorities and women to validate their commitment to a diverse workplace. Since affirmative action was implemented, there has been an ongoing debate about whether the federal regulations foster "reverse discrimination" as white males are allegedly denied jobs, admissions and promotions to achieve a government-imposed directive. Proponents of the merit-based approach believe that minorities and women should not advance because of the assistance of the government, but rather should use their personal talents, skills and initiative to succeed. There is great faith among the merit-based proponents that the United States remains a nation of equal opportunity, if only the citizens, no matter their race, gender or disadvantaged state, work within the existing economic and social system.[5]

The supporters of affirmative action, particularly in the African-American community, take issue with the critics of the policy. They make the argument that both subtle and overt racism and discrimination continue in American society and that without the pressure from government, hiring, admissions and promotions in business and institutions would be skewed toward whites. Leaders in the African-American community continue to battle those in government who would gut affirmative action and replace it with merit-based procedures. Although affirmative-action guidelines continue to remain in place and are supplemented by state anti-discrimination policies, public opinion in support of the program has waned in recent years and Supreme Court decisions have chipped away at the use of race as a key factor.[6]

Affirmative-action policies have been challenged on a number of occasions, some making it all the way to the Supreme Court. Most of the significant decisions involved admission policies to colleges and universities and professional schools. The landmark *Bakke* case (*Regents of the University of California v. Bakke*) in 1978 struck down a point system that allowed minorities with lower test scores to enter the medical school. The Court saw the California system of allocating admission seats to minorities based on race was in effect an unconstitutional quota system. The Court, however, did uphold the principle of affirmative action, which aimed to create a diverse student body and compared the use of race as similar to choosing candidates for admission based on geographic considerations.[7] Since the *Bakke* decision, the Supreme Court has narrowed the circumstances in which preferential treatment of minorities is acceptable under the Constitution. For example, in 1995 the Court eliminated fixed quotas in the granting of government contracts, thereby reversing the decision in the *Fullilove* case in 1980 (*Fullilove v. Klutznick*), which provided for quotas to be used for minority-owned firms that competed for government contracts.[8]

In recent years the issue of affirmative action was again situated in the university setting, this time at the University of Michigan involving a point system that gave greater weight to students of color over whites, although the whites may have scored higher on standardized tests. The Court, in a close 5-4 decision in 2003 (*Gratz v. Bollinger*), struck down the point system as another example of unconstitutional quotas, but at the same time upheld a University of Michigan Law School admission policy that used race as one factor in its admission process. In both cases the justices did hold firm to the view that the university had a legitimate right to try and create a diverse student body, but in the case of undergraduate admissions the Court felt that the point system placed a higher weight on race, which violated the equal protection clause of the Fourteenth Amendment. The University of Michigan ruling at the undergraduate level has forced many institutions of higher learning to abandon quota-like procedures and rely more on close examination of students' academic record, letters of recommendation and extra-curricular activities.[9]

In some states such as California, affirmative action has been completely removed as official state policy. Ward Connerly, a black businessman and one of the regents of the University of California system, worked for years to remove affirmative-action procedures from the admission process. Connerly became concerned with existing affirmative-action policies when he met white and Asian students who had been denied entry to the university system, although they scored high on tests and had high academic credentials. After years of intense battles among the regents and various pro–affirmative-action groups in the state, Connerly was successful in removing affirmative-action guidelines from university policy. Furthermore, Connerly was the driving force behind Proposition 209, which in 1996 banned the use of affirmative action statewide.[10]

African-American and liberal critics of Connerly and his campaign to end affirmative action in California complain that the number of minority applications and admissions in the California system has declined in recent years (though not at all campuses in the system), creating a new era of limiting access for minorities to higher education. As for Connerly and his supporters, they are convinced that admission to higher education should not be the result of preferential treatment, but rather be the result of competition and personal responsibility. For now, with the University of Michigan decision and the actions taken in California, affirmative action has moved to the background, but the issues of discrimination and access to higher education and employment opportunities remain simmering below the surface of race relations in the United States. For example, in 2008, five states–Arizona, Colorado, Missouri, Nebraska and Oklahoma–sought to end affirmative action by using ballot initiatives to stop the use of state tax revenue for programs that offer race-based preferential treatment.[11]

Contemporary race relations in the United States have been linked not only to Supreme Court cases and state action but also to the Congress, which in 2006 was embroiled in a debate over the reauthorization of the Voting Rights Act. The Voting Rights Act, which was originally made law in 1965, had expired and was up for renewal. If passed, the law would be extended for another twenty-five years. However, after initial bipartisan support for the law, southern Republican legislators balked at approving the bill, stating that it singled out their region as the center of voting discrimination and irregularities and that the legislation would open the way toward federal ballots being printed in languages other than English. Some Republican legislators from Georgia and Texas were upset that the voting irregularities in Florida during the 2000 presidential election were being linked unfairly to their states because the reauthorization allowed the Justice Department to review any changes to voting procedures in nine southern states that had a history of voting discrimination.[12] However, despite the rebellion among southern Republicans, the Republican leadership and President Bush pushed vigorously to end the standoff and in a Rose Garden ceremony President Bush signed into law the Fannie Lou Hamer, Rosa Parks and Coretta Scott King Voting Rights Act Reauthorization and Amendments Act of 2006.[13]

Data Bank

The gap between African-Americans and the rest of the American population has historically been significant. Some examples of the differences are given here:

	Year	Blacks (in %)	Total population
Home ownership	2003	41.8	68.3
College graduates	2003	17.3	27.2
Poverty	2003	24	14
Percapita personal income	2006	$16,035	36,629

Source: U.S. Census Data

Although much of the struggle for equal treatment and equal opportunity has fostered intense debate and partisan wrangling in the institutions of government, some of the most heated debates occur in the everyday lives of African-American citizens, revealing the continuing differences and divisions between black America and white America. One of the most serious examples of the deep divide between the races in recent years has been over racial profiling by local and state police departments. The term *racial profiling* refers to the use of certain race-based characteristics by law enforcement authorities in determining whether a person of color is likely to commit a crime. Police have justified the use of racial profiling as a means of preventing crimes or pursuing criminals who have allegedly committed a crime. Civil rights advocates such as the American Civil Liberties Union (ACLU) and representatives of the African-American community such as the NAACP have criticized the practice as racist and in direct violation of the Fourth Amendment guarantee against illegal search and seizure.[14]

Both organizations cite numerous examples of police over-reaction and brutality when racial profiling has been used. The lethal shooting of African immigrant Amadou Diallo by New York City police officers, who wrongly suspected that he was a rapist, was viewed by many in the African-American community as an example of racial profiling. Diallo, although unarmed, was killed in the doorway to his home while coming back from work. In New Jersey, State Police were engulfed in a controversy over racial profiling as numerous black motorists accused the police of harassment during unnecessary vehicle inspections along the New Jersey Turnpike. An investigation found that many state troopers were ordered to pull over black motorists. Eventually the controversy led to the appointment of a federal monitor and an agreement by the State Police to put into place new rules about detaining drivers based on race, unless those individuals fit a specific description of a wanted criminal. Although New Jersey became the target of the racial profiling debate, many blacks throughout the country complained about their vulnerability when Driving While Black (DWB). Despite the heightened concern over racial profiling abuses and some reforms, an ongoing debate continues over such practices, but now the accent has shifted to Middle Eastern and Hispanic men. Law enforcement authorities justify the practice as essential to the anti-terrorist security and immigration efforts, but Muslim and Hispanic leaders like African-Americans, view the practice as a violation of personal liberties and rights granted under the Constitution.[15]

Even more disturbing for the African-American community is the rise in hate crimes and racial threats. In recent years there has been a marked increase in cross burnings and spray paintings of racial epithets on African-American homes and properties. There has been a rise in the placement of rope nooses at the homes of blacks or in schools with black students. The nooses are grim reminders of the lynchings that occurred in the South of blacks who dared to challenge the system of segregation. In response to such actions, states have passed hate-speech laws based on their interpretation of the Supreme Court's doctrine of "fighting words." Under this doctrine the government can prohibit and eventually prosecute those individuals who engage in activities that foment fights or affect the public peace. As a result of this interpretation, a number of states have passed hate-crime laws, in large part to address racist activity or speech.[16]

On the economic front there has also been some progress. Despite the considerable gap in income and other key indicators of wealth, in the last twenty years an African-American professional and middle class has emerged, that holds out hope for other African-Americans about the prospects of making it in the American economic and social sphere. There are now black CEOs of major U.S. companies, black multi-millionaires and many stories of rags-to-riches blacks who have used their entrepreneurial skills and hard work to become financial successes. Although far too many blacks remain stuck in poverty and evidence of the gap between the rich and the poor continues to grow in the United States, the success of some blacks holds out hope that moving up the economic ladder in the American system is not beyond the realm of possibility. Unfortunately, there continue to be signs that blacks face discrimination in housing, credit and mortgages. Housing in particular has become troublesome as blacks remain the most residentially segregated group in the United States. Although some of this separation is the result of blacks feeling more comfortable living in communities with higher concentrations of blacks, there is also the reality of blacks facing subtle discrimination as they seek homes, bank loans and mortgages in communities where whites dominate.[17]

Challenges to existing affirmative-action policies also continue, such as school assignment formulas designed to create a diverse and more equal racial balance in public schools. In 2007 the Supreme Court in a 5-4 decision struck down such assignments in cases from Seattle and Louisville. The majority of the Court said that such desegregation plans discriminated against white students and denied them the ability to choose the schools they wished to attend. Justice Roberts, writing for the majority, said that students should not be told "where they could and could not go to school based on the color of their skin." Writing for the minority, Justice Stevens said that the majority side was trying "to rewrite history" and deny the fundamental principles in the historic *Brown* decision of 1954.[18]

On the political front, from voting rights to the institutionalization of a wide range of civil rights, there has been considerable progress. African-Americans are now at the highest levels of government as evidenced by Supreme Court Justice Clarence Thomas and Secretaries of State Colin Powell and Condoleezza Rice. African-Americans are also well presented at the state and local levels, including big-city mayors, county commissioners, education leaders and high-level law enforcement officials. Blacks still remain under-represented in government (especially as governors; Deval Patrick of Massachusetts is only the second African-American to head a state government).

Of course the election of Barack Obama as the forty-fourth president in many respects "changed everything" in race relations in the United States. The election of Barack Obama is now viewed as a watershed event in the United States as it proved to many in the country that race is not a barrier to achieving the highest elected office in the land. Obama's victory energized the African-American community and filled many with new hope that an era of real racial harmony had arrived. But despite the Obama Presidency there are still perceived barriers to full equality in the African-American community and disappointment among some black leaders at the President's civil rights agenda. A Gallup poll in 2007 showed that whereas 75% of white Americans polled said that race relations were good, only 55% of blacks agreed. The percentage of blacks agreeing to the question about the condition of race relations was the lowest response since 2001, when 70% of blacks said relations with whites were good.[19] Apparently, white America thinks that race relations are moving along quite well, whereas blacks see the problems and experience subtle discrimination on a daily basis. Also, polling data in the early days of the Obama presidency showed that many white Americans "felt differently" about race relations and that Obama's election was responsible for "speeding change." Barack Obama said it best about the current state and future of race relations in the United States. In a memorable speech in Philadelphia during the campaign, Obama said the following:

I have never been so naïve as to believe that we can get beyond our racial divisions in a single election cycle, or with a single candidacy–particularly a candidacy as imperfect as my own. . . . I have brothers, sisters, nieces, nephews, uncles, cousins, of every race and hue, scattered across three continents, and for as long as I live, I will never forget that in no other country on earth is my story even possible.[20]

The report card of race relations in the United States is thus filled with incompletes as progress in creating a truly equal America is far too slow and filled with unmet goals. Taken over time, particularly since the *Brown v. Board of Education* case and the civil rights victories of the 1960s, it is possible to state that considerable progress has been made in improving race relations in the United States. Blacks and whites generally get along (although often from a distance) and the days of race riots appear to be a bad memory. Yet so much needs to be done to erase the economic gap, the subtle discrimination and the occasional outbursts of blatant racism.

Despite Barack Obama's stunning election victory and the hope that it brought to race relations in the United States, it appears safe to state that America will continue to have a race problem and will have to face the fact that much more needs to be done to bring black and white together.

The Great Debate

Many Americans are cautiously optimistic that the election of Barack Obama signals that the United States has turned the corner on race relations and that a new era of cooperative race relations has begun.

Debate Topic

Does the presidency of Barack Obama signal an end to racial tensions and racial discrimination in the United States?

Critical Thinking Questions

1. Recent polling data suggest that younger Americans are color blind. Do you agree?
2. Why do think that the largest percentage of poor people in the United States is African-American?
3. Is it fair to use affirmative-action policies to give preference to minorities in hiring and admissions to colleges and professional schools?
4. Where do you stand on racial profiling of African-American men by police and the contention by blacks that DWB remains a racial problem in the United States?
5. Census data show that by 2040 whites will be a minority in the United States. Do you foresee any problems with race relations associated with this shift in the racial composition of the country?

Connections

The premier advocate for African-Americans is the NAACP. Visit its site at http://www.naacp.org

A website that examines a range of issues and concerns of African-Americans is at http://www.africanamericans.com

The American Civil Liberties Union has a comprehensive website devoted to racial justice. See http://www.aclu.org/racial-justice

The National Urban League has been in the forefront of African-American community issues and is also a leading advocate for blacks. See http://www.nul.org

Government policy related to race relations and racial justice is centered at the U.S. Commission on Civil Rights. Visit their site at http://www.usccr.gov

Some Books to Read

Myers, Samuel, *Civil Rights and Race Relations in the Post-Reagan-Bush Era* (Westport, CT: Praeger, 2007).

National Urban League, *The State of Black America 2007: Portrait of the Black Male* (Silver Spring, MD: Beckham Publications Group, 2007).

National Urgan League, *The State of Black America in 2008: The Black Women's Voice* (New York: National Urban League, 2008).

Messer-Kruse, Timothy, *Race Relations in the US: 1980–2000* (Westport, CT: Greenwood Press, 2008).

Ogeltree, Charles J. Jr., *All Deliberate Speed: Reflections on the First Half Century of Brown v. Board of Education* (New York: Norton, 2004).

Notes

1. See a compendium of King's speeches in Clayborne Carson and Kris Shepard, ed., *A Call to Conscience: The Landmark Speeches of Dr. Martin Luther King, Jr.* (New York: Time Warner, 2001).
2. A highly critical study of the black experience in the period of the civil rights movement is found in Andrew Hacker, *Two Nations: Black and White, Separate, Hostile, Unequal* (New York: Scribners, 1992).
3. See Taylor Branch, *At Caanan's Edge: America in the King Years, 1965–1968* (New York: Simon and Schuster, 2000).
4. U.S. Census Bureau, Historical Poverty Tables, Table 24, and U.S. Census Bureau Statistical Abstract of the United States, 2005, Table 671.
5. For a criticism of affirmative action and other government policies related to race relations, see Stephen Thernstrom and Abigail Thernstrom, *America in Black and White: One Nation, Indivisible: Race Relations in America* (New York: Simon and Schuster, 1997).
6. For a comprehensive discussion supporting affirmative action see "In Defense of Affirmative Action," *In Motion Magazine*, http://www.inmotionmagazine.com/pr.html. See also Harry Holzer and David Newmark, "Assessing Affirmative Action," *Journal of Economic Liberalism* 38, 2000, pp. 245–269. Also Juan Williams, "The Affirmative Action Debate," *Washington Post National Weekly Edition*, August 3–9, 2009, p. 26.
7. *Regents of the University of California v. Bakke* 438 U.S. 265 (1978).
8. *Fullilove v. Klutznick* 488 U.S. 488 (1980).
9. *Gratz v. Bollinger* 539 U.S. 306 (2003).
10. Connerly's position on affirmative action in California are outlined in "Racial Preferences Are Dead," *Reason Online*, http://www.reason.com/news/show/30527.html
11. Stephanie Simon, "Five State Bid to Ban Affirmative Action," *Boston Globe*, January 20, 2008, A1.

12. Carl Hulse, "Rebellion Stalls Extension of Voting Rights Act," *New York Times*, June 26, 2006, http://nytimes.com/2006/06/22/washington/22vote.html

13. See Lynn Sweeton, "Bush: Signs Voting Rights Act Reauthorization. Pelosi, Reid Call for Justice Department to Enforce Provisions,"*Chicago Sun Times*, June 27, 2006, http://blogs.suntimes.com/sweet/2006/07/bush_signs_voting_rights_act_r.html

14. See Ronald Weltzer and Steven Tuck, *Race and Policing in America Conflict and Reform* (New York: Cambridge University Press, 2006).

15. See the discussion of racial profiling in American history and also in the current 9/11 atmosphere related to Muslim-Americans in "What's at Stake" in Christine Barbour, et al. *Keeping the Republic* (Washington, D.C.: Congressional Quarterly Press, 2006), pp. 207–208, 261–262.

16. The landmark decision related to hate crimes was out of Minnesota. See *R.A.V. v. City of St. Paul* 60 LW 4667 (1994).

17. As reported in the *Boston Globe*, June 29, 2007, p. A1.

18. As reported in http://pollingreport.com/race.htm. See also the debate contained in the briefs filed before the U.S. Supreme Court concerning the Seattle race-based school issue–National Education Association, et al. Amicus curiae brief to the U.S. Supreme Court in *Parents Involved in Community Schools v. Seattle School District No. 1* (2007) and Asian American Legal Foundation, Amicus Curiae brief to the U.S. Supreme Court in *Parents Involved in Community Schools v. Seattle School District No. 1* (2007).

19. "Obama Presidency Nudging Views on Race, Poll Finds," *New York Times*, April 28, 2009, A1.

20. See Gary Wills, "Two Speeches on Race," *New York Review of Books*, May 1, 2008, pp. 4–6.

9 REFORMING **EDUCATION**

Issue Focus

The link between education and national development is clearly established in the United States. An educated workforce provides the foundation upon which the country can compete effectively in the new global economy and expand the level of prosperity to a growing number of Americans. However, because of the heightened importance of education in American life, public schools are facing intense scrutiny as critics point to a range of deficiencies from low test scores to increased dropout rates. As a result, new options for educating America's youth have come to the fore. What was once general agreement on the positive contributions of public education are today undergoing challenge and change.

Chapter Objectives
This issue chapter will seek to:
1. Describe the problems associated with public education in contemporary America, especially since the Nation at Risk study was published in the 1980s.
2. Present the numerous federal, state and local initiatives that have been developed to reform public education.
3. Discuss obstacles to reform that remain as the United States seeks to develop an educational system that will keep the challenges of the 21st century.

SOME BACKGROUND

In 1983 Ronald Reagan appointed a commission to examine the state of education in the United States. The commission came back with a scathing critique entitled "A Nation at Risk." The report stated in part, "Our Nation is at risk. The educational foundations of our society are presently being eroded by a rising tide of mediocrity that threatens our very future as a Nation and a people." The critique of education in America, showed that test scores were dropping significantly and that many other countries, some far below the United States in national income, were making remarkable progress in preparing their students for the demands of an ever-increasing global economy. The report was designed to shock the country into taking bold steps to improve education and address what many policy analysts felt was the most important public issue facing the country.[1]

"A Nation at Risk" stimulated a national conversation about what needed to be done to get the country's educational system back on track. Liberals talked about pumping billions of dollars into improving school buildings, hiring more teachers and updating equipment and technology. Conservatives stressed that the public education system had to be completely changed, and they pushed for charter schools that were outside the domain of union influence, vouchers that allowed parents the financial flexibility to remove their children from a local school to go to another school and most important, high-stakes testing that accented the importance of teacher and administrative accountability to reach certain benchmarks of academic success. Although there was no shortage of solutions to the education problem facing the United States, "A Nation at Risk" placed what happens in our schools and with our students at the forefront of a national policy debate.

In 2002 Senator Edward Kennedy of Massachusetts and Representative George Miller of California, both Democrats, worked cooperatively with the Bush administration to push through the landmark education bill No Child Left Behind. The law was not only an example of bipartisanship in a policy area where there was general agreement that major reform was essential, but it also established teacher and school accountability through testing as the foundation of assessing educational progress. Those schools that did not show "adequate yearly progress" were deemed failing and would face both the stigma of poor-quality education and a cut in federal funding. The No Child Left Behind law was a major shift in the role of the federal government in education as it became much more involved in what had often been viewed as a state and local responsibility.

In 2008 Kennedy and Miller were in the forefront of a legislative movement to overhaul No Child Left Behind as they and other Democrats targeted the Bush administration and the Department of Education for failing to provide adequate budgetary resources for the law and for not understanding the special challenges faced by urban schools and the unique circumstances of low-income immigrant and special needs students. As Senator Kennedy said in his support for a reform of No Child Left Behind, "We still have the concept of accountability, but what we need to do is get away from labeling, get away from the punitive aspects and give help and assistance to the neediest schools. We're now on a pathway to make some sense on this." Legislators such as Kennedy were responding to a groundswell of opposition to No Child Left Behind as teachers, administrators and parents complained about the law's emphasis on rigid adherence to testing standards, whereas state and local authorities criticized the government for creating unfunded mandates as the Bush administration promised money to assist in implementing the standards and then held back on the appropriations.[2]

Public education in the United States has a proud heritage that dates back to Horace Mann in the 1830s and has remained since that time the dominant channel for providing young people with the skills they need to enter the world of work. Moreover, public education has often been viewed as the "great equalizer" as it has offered Americans of any race, color, creed or religious affiliation the opportunity to expand their personal horizons and achieve their dreams. Today, however, public education is not only under attack for failing in its mission of preparing young people with the necessary skills to succeed in a highly competitive world, but it is also challenged by numerous alternatives from the private sector, the religious community and even homeschooling. Americans remain committed to public education and often place it high on their list of policy priorities, but public education has become an issue where there is an endless supply of new reforms and options, and there is no shortage of contrarian views on how to fix an education system that many see as in desperate need of repair.

On the Record

As the first commissioner of education in Massachusetts, Horace Mann is often considered the father of public education in the United States. Mann was a tireless advocate for education and its ability to improve the lives of the citizens of Massachusetts. One of his most famous quotes about the value of education is cited here:

> Education then, beyond all other devices of human origin, is the great equalizer of the conditions of men, the balance-wheel of the social machinery.

DEBATES, DIFFERENCES AND DIVISIONS

Among all the proposals for education reform in the United States, it is safe to say that the driving force behind reform is standardized testing. One of the outgrowths of the "A Nation at Risk" report was the move by states to require students to take regular testing mechanisms to gauge their proficiency in key subject areas such as English, mathematics and science. Many states have also made passing tests a requirement for graduation, thus introducing the term *high-stakes testing*. The testing movement was based on the view among many legislators at state and local levels that school systems had to be held accountable for certain established benchmarks of educational progress; in their view, the normal report card and parental visit was not sufficient. As a result, throughout the country a new educational industry was formed; state boards of education developed standardized tests and began administering them to the students. Along with the tests, state education policy makers created set curricula in the major content areas to ensure that teachers were teaching and students were learning the same material.[3]

Standardized testing quickly became the target of criticism from teacher unions, minority leaders and opponents of a one-size-fits-all testing procedure. The position of the critics was that testing was not only unfair to minorities, those with special disabilities and students with test-taking phobias, but also that the emphasis on creating standardized curricula forced teachers to "teach to the test," leaving little room for teaching ancillary material related to the curricula, extended discussion or analysis of a topic or the introduction of subject matter that was outside the established framework. Moreover, critics pointed to the fact that test scores were increasingly being used as the basis for determining merit pay for teachers and as a result fostered heightened competition among school districts to achieve high scores–two objectives that teacher unions roundly opposed because in their view the education would be driven by a learning environment that was more about scores than mastering a body of knowledge. The National Education Association (NEA) has become the primary voice of opposition against standardized testing, emphasizing that reliance on test scores as the focus of education reform ignores other proven strategies such as smaller class sizes, more services for at-risk students, increased teacher professional development and more reliance on a range of assessments.[4]

However, despite the criticism, advocates of standardized testing pressed forward and continued to receive support from state legislatures and the federal government. Many states in fact expanded their testing programs and required higher scores for a student to be defined as proficient. Results from similar tests in other countries that compete with the United States often drive the push for tougher standardized test scores. The standardized test scores from other countries in mathematics and science are used to show that the United States has to pick up ground and maintain its focus on accountability in order not to fall further behind many of the major industrial countries in the world. More importantly, support for standardized testing has been associated with a business approach that is based on measurable progress much like a profit-and-loss report or a quarterly dividend assessment. Learning must be data driven, so the argument goes, and reliance on subjective, teacher-controlled evaluations is not considered an acceptable method of determining proficiency in a subject area or the extent to which remedial action needs to be taken to improve proficiency in the subject area.[5]

FYI

An organization called the Program for International Student Assessment tests fifteen-year olds from thirty major industrialized countries that are members of the Organization of Economic Cooperation and Development (OECD). The tests are in mathematics and science. In the tests given in 2007, U.S. students achieved an average score that was lower than that of sixteen other OECD countries, and in mathematics the American students achieved a score that was lower than that of twenty-three other countries. The leader in science was Finland, followed by Hong Kong and Canada. The leader in mathematics was also Finland, followed by Taiwan, South Korea and Hong Kong.

Source: OECD

Following further along the business model that has influenced the debate on educational reform is the introduction of school choice. In large part because of the dissatisfaction with the public school system, especially in the inner cities of the United States, there has been a movement supported by parents groups, the business community and conservative educational reformers to create the opportunity to move from a public school to a private or parochial school. To support this move, the federal court system has validated some aspects of financing private or parochial schools through public tax dollars. In a series of cases in the 1980s and 1990s the Supreme Court held that a parental tax deduction for education purposes was constitutional, even though the overwhelming majority of the deductions claimed by the parents were for expenses related to their children attending nonpublic schools. In the 1990s the Court also ruled in favor of a state providing a sign language teacher, even if that teacher worked in a parochial school. And in perhaps the most important decision, in 1993, in *Agostini v. Felton* the Supreme Court ruled that the state of New York could provide remedial education instructors in parochial schools and allow those teachers to teach on school property.[6]

The key to the process of moving out of a school district to what are perceived to be better schools is a voucher to cover the tuition at the private or parochial school. The voucher system, besides introducing choice to parents, removes the financial equivalent of what the public school receives to educate the student who is leaving the system and shifts it to a private or parochial school. In the end the voucher system not only empowers the parents but also provides a transfer of money from public education to private or parochial education.[7] At present there has been only limited implementation of a school voucher system. In the 1990s only two states, Wisconsin and Ohio, started voucher programs, and in both states the issue headed to the state courts for a challenge led by teacher unions and groups that were concerned that the doctrine of separation of church and state was being violated by using public monies to support religious schools.

The key decision regarding school choice and vouchers came in 2002 when the U.S. Supreme Court in *Zelman v. Simmons-Harris* voted 5-4 that the Cleveland voucher system was constitutional.[8] The argument made by the majority of the justices was that the primary purpose of parents' decision to educate their children was a secular one and the choice of a private or parochial school did not violate the principle of separation of church and state. However, despite the Court decision, school choice and vouchers have not spread across the country. In 2006 the Florida Supreme Court struck down the Opportunity Scholarship Program that provided for vouchers. The court held that the voucher system violated the state constitution and upheld the principle of state money being used only for public schools. There have also been some recent defeats of school vouchers at the ballot box. In 2000, California voters, by a vote of 70% to 29%, rejected an expansive voucher program that would allow the transfer of public money to a private or parochial school without regulations regarding the accreditation or need. And finally, in 2007 the voters in Utah rejected an annual $3,000 tuition subsidy. The Utah vote was considered important because of the conservative nature of the state and the heavy influence of the Mormon religion in the political arena.[9]

However the struggle to move vouchers into the front ranks of the school choice movement has taken a new tack. In New Jersey in 2007 parents in twenty-five underperforming public school districts filed suit in court, rather than use a statewide referendum as in Utah. The suit argued that because the public schools were denying students their constitutionally mandated right to a quality education, the court in New Jersey should refund the tax money the parents paid to the local communities so that the parents could use that money to pay for tuition at a private or parochial school. Those who follow the voucher issue say that the suit in New Jersey has a real possibility of gaining the support of the court since it has intervened in other school financing cases, especially one in which it required the state to spend more money on poor school districts to even out the spending with more affluent districts. Public support for vouchers in New Jersey is still below 50%, but advocates are hoping that an activist court in that state will give a boost to the school choice movement.[10]

Despite the setbacks and uncertainty associated with state-funded voucher programs, an expansion of school choice initiatives has been supported by individual donors or private foundations. Most of these school choice programs are directed at inner-city schoolchildren where opposition to public schools is greatest and where private and parochial schools have sought to carve out an educational niche designed to offer alternatives to parents. Also, private individuals and foundations have begun to establish separate schools in the inner city and provide students with tuition assistance or full scholarships. Besides Cleveland and Milwaukee, which has the highest number of privately funded choice schools, private groups and foundations have established choice schools in Dallas, Buffalo, Oakland, New York and even in smaller cities such as Midland, Texas. In most of these cities there has been proven success with these privately funded urban schools as inner-city youths have in many cases excelled in the classroom and have gone on after graduation to attend two-year or four-year colleges.

Data Bank

In 2006 the national average cost per pupil for elementary and secondary education in the United States was $9,963. The highest cost per pupil was in Vermont, which spent $15,139. The lowest cost per pupil was in Utah at $5,964. The costs per pupil for Vermont and Utah were adjusted to reflect regional cost differences.

Source: U.S. Department of Education

In the wake of the difficulties faced by supporters of vouchers, support-ers of school choice have pushed successfully to develop publicly authorized charter schools. Charter schools are non-religious public schools that offer par-ents and students choice, but are structured in ways that separate them from traditional public schools. Charter schools have fewer regulations, more flexi-ble union contracts and stress instructional innovation and parental involve-ment. The designation of a charter school means that a state or local school board grants a charter for a set period of time (usually three to five years), and within that period the school must show that it has met the mission goals that have been set in its application for the charter. The underlying relationship that drives the charter school movement is that in return for more autonomy to experiment, there is an expectation of accountability and improved education.

The charter school movement started in the 1980s when Philadelphia des-ignated a number of its underperforming schools as schools within schools, termed *charter schools*, and fostered a climate of innovation and autonomy. Later, in Minnesota, charter schools were established based on the concepts of oppor-tunity, choice and responsibility. In 1991 Minnesota passed the first charter school law. By 1995 nineteen states signed laws establishing charter schools and implemented a process for schools to obtain a charter based on specific mission statements and mission objectives. Today 1 million students are enrolled in more than 3,500 charter schools in 40 states plus the District of Columbia and Puerto Rico. The charter school movement has also been supported at the fed-eral level. President Clinton in his State of the Union address in 1997 called for the creation of 3,000 charter schools. President George W. Bush continued his support for the charter school movement with his 2002 proposal for $100 mil-lion for what he called the Credit Enhancement for Charter Schools Facilities Program. And President Barack Obama, despite strong pressure from teacher unions, has signaled his support for charter schools and for their expansion. He has initiated a highly competitive funding program called Race to the Top, which awards states grants based in part on their support for charter schools and other innovative teaching strategies.[11] Since 1994 the U.S. Department of Education has provided federal support of $6 million in assistance to states and communities to advance the charter school movement.[12]

It is fair to state that the charter school option is catching on across the United States. Because many charter schools are small in size and often accent a particular mission such as international studies, music and the arts and envi-ronmental change, they are attractive to both students and parents who want to mix new assessment techniques and more innovation with specialized edu-cational experiences. Even some teacher unions are proposing charter school options within existing public school systems that allow teachers the ability to experiment with new teaching styles and instructional methods. However, reluctance on the part of many teacher unions and their supporters in state leg-islatures to fully embrace the charter school movement continues, and as a result, efforts have been made to limit the number of charters made available to prospective groups anxious to start a new school. However, the fact that many of these newly established schools have registered clear, positive results has made them a popular alternative to the public school system, while weakening the argument for a voucher-based system of educational reform.

Although vouchers and charter schools have garnered the bulk of the attention in the school choice movement, it is also necessary to comment on a third alternative to the traditional public school: homeschooling. As the name implies, homeschooling is providing a child an education within the home setting, usually by a parent. Parents must receive permission from the local school district or state authority to conduct a homeschool program with their child or children, which includes an examination of the curriculum that will be followed, the books used and the testing that will be employed to determine progress. However, despite these administrative hurdles, homeschooling has become increasingly popular with parents who are concerned with the problems associated with public education, the safety environment in the schools and in many cases the lack of religious training or values training in the traditional public schools.

The homeschooling movement began as a result of the work of education critics John Holt and Raymond and Dorothy Moore. Holt and the Moores wrote controversial books on how children learn and the limitations of the traditional public education system. Both argued that formal schooling was harmful to the development of the child and that the nurturing attachments developed between parent and child, especially at the elementary level, were far more beneficial than those within the public school classroom. As a result of the work of Holt and the Moores and their aggressive promotion of their views, a new movement based on homeschooling and direct parental involvement in the education of children took hold. Moreover, as the evangelical religions gained increasing prominence in the United States, there was a significant exodus from the public schools, which were viewed as harmful to the moral and ethical development of children.[13]

Homeschooling has seen remarkable advancement as an educational alternative. U.S. Department of Education data show that from 1999 to 2003 the number of homeschooled students increased from 850,000 to 1.1 million, and the National Home Education Research Institute, the educational think tank advancing homeschooling, stated in a report in 2006 that an estimated 2.4 million children in the United States were educated at home. As advocates of homeschooling state, there are clear advantages to one-on-one tutoring in the home environment, the accent on student-paced learning and the benefits of using on a regular basis the vast resources often available in the community such as museums, science centers, college resources and other institutions where field trips can be arranged.

Homeschooling definitely has its critics, especially from public school educators who question the academic quality of parental teachers, the lack of socialization and the concern over excessive emphasis placed on religious instruction at the expense of mainstream subject matter.[14] However the National Home Education Research Institute contends that homeschooled children do well on standardized tests and have little difficulty entering college and succeeding in the college environment. The apparent success of the homeschool movement has begun to influence public opinion. A Gallup poll in 2001 showed that since 1981, when the movement was first getting off the ground, opposition to homeschooling has dropped from 73% to 54%.[15] Homeschooling remains the school choice option with the least support among Americans with school age children, but support continues to move upward and its success rate in terms of providing solid education results can no longer be ignored.

Amidst all the school choice options and the controversy and disagreement that has accompanied them, the key to education reform in the United States remains in the public schools. Many states have made K-12 education a high priority and have directed increased funding to school systems. However, issue disputes continue to be centered on fairness in terms of disparities in funding among rich and poor districts, the frequent roller coaster effect of budgets with good years and bad years of legislative and community support and the ongoing debate over teacher competency, certification and merit. However within this atmosphere of fairness, funding and the workplace conditions of teachers, there are numerous examples throughout the country of real reform and effective change that brings hope to those committed to improving and revitalizing the public school system in the United States.

Both Washington, D.C., with its youthful and no-nonsense Chancellor Michelle Rhee and New York City with its hard-driving Chancellor Joel Klein are often cited as examples of the future of education reform in the United Staes.[16] Because New York City has one of the largest public school populations in the nation, the changes occurring there may likely become a model for the rest of the country. Mayor Michael Bloomberg announced in 2007 that he intended to make all the public schools in the city charter schools. The current number of charter schools is sixty, but the students in those schools have shown a remarkable level of academic improvement as autonomy and greater accountability have turned a number of schools around, especially in poor neighborhoods such as the Bedford-Stuyvesant district in the Bronx. In 2002 less than 40% of students in grades 3 through 8 were reading and performing math problems at their grade level, but five years later the percentage had increased to 65% in math and 50% in reading. Moreover, graduation rates are the highest they have been in more than twenty years, and the entire New York school system is now outperforming other major urban school systems in the state such as Syracuse, Buffalo and Rochester.[17]

The school reform effort began when Bloomberg got effective control of the New York school system and quickly moved the headquarters from Brooklyn to a building next to city hall. Next, he set up a report-card system to evaluate public schools and gave out grades to each school that reflect their academic performance and the input of students, parents and teachers. Those schools that get a high grade receive an increase in their yearly budget, principals get a bonus and teachers receive merit pay. Those schools that get a bad grade for two consecutive years face significant change; the principal may be fired and the new principal will be required to submit a remedial school improvement plan. If the trend of the school continues downward after two more years, the school will be closed. So the accountability initiative is not punitive, Bloomberg secured private funds to develop a leadership academy to train current and future principals and assist them in moving their schools forward under the new accountability program.[18]

Besides centralizing control of the school system in city hall and implementing a tough accountability program, Mayor Bloomberg also brought the private sector into the reform movement. Bill Gates of Microsoft, Eli Broad, a billionaire from Los Angeles with ties to New York (who established a $500,000 college scholarship fund), and numerous wealthy hedge fund leaders contributed millions of dollars to support experimental programs in the charter schools. With sufficient private funds, implementors of many of the key changes did not have to rely on public money, which thereby limited contentious partisan debate. The combination of mayoral control, local autonomy, accountability and private financial support has proved to be, at least in the short run, an effective road map for educational success, especially in a diverse, urban setting where there are numerous pockets of poverty and violence. New York City will likely be closely watched in the coming years to see whether this model can be sustained and whether continued academic progress is made by the students in that city.[19]

Each of the issues we have dealt with so far is complex and fosters serious divisions in American politics and society. Education improvement and education reform, however, is so different and divisive because it is recognized as the key investment of the United States in its future. A wide spectrum of leaders from government to business to law enforcement to social workers realize that making education work and producing educated graduates is a critical ingredient for our national success in an ever-competitive world. Because of the importance of education, multiple alternatives for change and reforms are being presented on the local, state and national stages. The American public recognizes that getting education right means that the nation will continue to remain vital, prosperous and strong.

Public education has without a doubt been struggling for the last thirty years. The country where public education got its start and developed a model for the rest of the world has failed too many of its young people. In 2008 it was reported that a majority of Americans felt that the public schools were doing only a "fair to poor job." Much of the concern by the poll respondents was in the area of weak mathematics proficiency and too much time being relegated to remedial courses.[20] The poll revealed that from the perspective of the American people there is plenty of blame to go around as the reasons why public education has disappointed so many of its citizens. However it is important to emphasize that despite these negative perceptions of American schools, there continue to be hopeful signs of improvement in the schools and classrooms of the United States; in particular, standardized test scores have been slowly moving upward, with some states experiencing significant advances.[21] There is also promising evidence, as shown by standardized testing, that some individual states such as Massachusetts are surpassing many of the countries that traditionally have bested the United States.

As for the Obama administration, there is reason to hope that the reform effort will continue unabated. Secretary of Education Arne Duncan, the former head of the Chicago public schools, has pledged to push forward with charter schools, merit pay for teachers and limiting the gap between rich and poor schools. Obama and Duncan have also proposed major changes in the No Child Left Behind law, particularly in the area of how schools are judged as a result of assessment tests. They have proposed that the 2014 deadline for bringing every American child up to an agreed-on standard of universal proficiency in a series of key subjects should be eliminated and replaced with a national standard of "college and career ready."[22] Governors have also extended considerable support for the Obama administration's proposal to establish national academic standards for key disciplines such as English, mathematics and science so that assessment testing could be conducted based on a set body of knowledge that all students in the country should be responsible for learning. Obama has made education reform one of his top priorities and given Secretary Duncan wide latitude in bringing change to U.S. public schools. Obama has also targeted major injections of stimulus money toward education and increased the Department of Education funding substantially. Both Obama and Duncan owe their success to solid education, although largely in private schools, and as a result have pledged to drive education forward, no matter what obstacles may lay ahead from teacher unions or dwindling national, state and local resources.[23]

There may be debates and differences and divisions over how to improve U.S. schools, but there is no shortage of desire and energy to make the public education system work. Although the No Child Left Behind Act is currently the target of criticism and redesign, the title of this landmark legislation is appropriate. The country, its governmental leaders at all levels and a wide range of community leaders agree that the United States cannot leave any child behind; it must do its utmost to ensure that every American has a quality education as a stepping-stone to the opportunities Americans as a nation promise to all citizens.

The Great Debate

The No Child Left Behind Act places primary emphasis on accountability through standardized testing. Yet many critics of testing say that it is deeply flawed in terms of test preparation time, teaching to the test, high-stakes testing linked to graduation and erratic funding to assist students who have difficulty passing the test.

Debate Topic

Should standardized testing remain as the foundation for assessing the academic progress of students in the United States?

Critical Thinking Questions

1. What factors do you see as responsible for the low ranking of the United States on international education assessment scores?
2. Is the answer to better education in the United States more public money or more competition from charter schools and vouchers?
3. Do you agree with the assessment in recent polls that show that a majority of Americans feel public schools are doing a "fair to poor job"?
4. Do you believe that teacher unions, which are often opposed to charter schools, vouchers and standardized testing, are the main roadblock to education reform?
5. What recommendations would you make to fix American public schools?

Connections

The U.S. Department of Education is a valuable source for policy discussions on public education. See http://www.ed.gov

The NEA is the leading advocate for public education in the United States. Their website can be reached at http://www.nea.org

The case for vouchers is made by the organization Rethinking Schools Online. See http://www.rethinkingschools.org

The primary organization advocating for charter schools is Charter Voice. The website can be reached at http://www.chartervoice.org

The Center for Education Reform is an invaluable site for presenting the latest issues in educational policy. The website is at www.edreform.com

Some Books to Read

Mitchell, Bruce, *Unequal Opportunity: A Crisis in America's Schools* (Westport, CT: Bergin & Garvey, 2002).

Jeffrey R. Henig, *Rethinking School Choice* (Princeton, NJ: Princeton University Press, 1995).

A Nation at Risk: The Imperative for Education Reform (U.S. Government Printing, 1983).

Ravitch, Diane, *The Death and Life of the Great American School System* (New York: Basic Books, 2010).

Gordon, David, *A Nation Reformed: American Education 20 Years after a Nation at Risk* (Boston: Harvard Educational Publishing Group, 2003).

Notes

1. *A Nation at Risk: The Imperative for Educational Reform* (U.S. Government Printing, 1983).
2. "No Child Left Behind Authors Work on a Revision," *Boston Globe*, July 16, 2007, p. A1.

3. Aaron Bernstein, "Lou Gerstner's Classroom Quest," *Business Week*, April 7, 2005, http://www.businessweek.com/bwdaily/dnflash/apr2005/nf2005047_7811_db016.htm

4. The National Education Association's position on testing can be found in a position paper entitled "NEA Position on 'Highly Qualified Effective Teacher' Mandate," A Response to the No Child Left Behind Commission, http://www.nea.org/home/18018.htm

5. See Ludger Woessman, "Why Students in Some Countries Do Better: International Evidence on the Importance of Education Policy," *Education Matters*, Summer, 2001, Vol. 1, # 2.

6. *Agostini v. Felton* 521 U.S. 203 (1997).

7. "What about Tax Funded Vouchers, Tax Credits and Charter Schools," Alliance for the Separation of Schools and State, http://www.honestedu.org/misc/vouchers.php

8. *Zelman v. Simmons-Harris*, 536 U.S.639 (2002).

9. "Pro-Choice," *Economist*, June 9, 2007, p. 38.

10. Ibid.

11. Michael Shea and Nick Anderson, "President Obama Discusses New 'Race to the Top' Program", Washington Post, July 23, 2009, http://www.washingtonpost.com/wp-dyn/content/2009/07/23/2009072302938.html

12. The history of the charter school movement can be seen at http://www.uscharterschools.org/pub/uscs_docs/o/index.htm

13. See a discussion of the National Home Education Research Institute and an evaluation of the data provided by the Institute in a report from the Cato Institute, http://cato.org/pubs/pas/pa-294.html

14. See Rob Reich, "The Civic Perils of Homeschooling," *Journal of Educational Leadership*, Vol. 59, Issue 7, p. 56.

15. The success of homeschooling is examined by the educational journal *Ed Week*. See http://www.edweek.org/rc/issues/home-schooling/

16. For a look at the controversial chancellor of Washington's public schools, see the *Time Magazine* cover story on Michelle Rhee, November 26, 2008.

17. "Six Books a Week," *The Economist*, May 10, 2008, p. 40.

18. A discussion of New York City teacher unions is presented at "Learning Their Lessons," *The Economist*, July 19, 2008, p. 43.

19. "Red Ties and Boys Pride," *Economist*, May 10, 2008, p. 40.

20. As reported in the *Boston Globe*, June 28, 2008, p. A16.

21. Marjorie Coeyman, "Twenty Years after 'A Nation at Risk,'" http://www.csmonitor.com/2003/0422/p13s02-lepr.htm

22. Gail Russell Chaddock, "Obama's No Child Left Behind Revise: A Little More Flexibility," Christian Science Monitor, March 15, 2010, HYPERLINK "http://www.csmonitor.com/usa/Politics/2010/0315/Obama's-No-Child-Left-Behind-revise-a-little-more-flexibility" http://www.csmonitor.com/usa/Politics/2010/0315/Obama's-No-Child-Left-Behind-revise-a-little-more-flexibility

23. For a critical evaluation of Arne Duncan and his vision for education reform in the United States, see "The Golden Boy and the Blob," *Economist*, May 9, 2009, p. 36.

10 ABORTION RIGHTS

Issue Focus

The issue of a woman's right to control her own reproductive decisions versus the rights of an unborn fetus has divided Americans for almost forty years. This clash of viewpoints has been at the center of the national political debate since the landmark Supreme Court decision *Roe v. Wade*. There is little middle ground between the right of a woman to choose to abort a fetus and the right to protect life in the womb. Advocates on both sides of the debate have made this issue a litmus test of whether a state official, a member of Congress, a Supreme Court nominee or a presidential candidate should be supported by the right-to-choose or right-to-life movement. This battle continues with little sign of letting up.

Chapter Objectives
This issue chapter will seek to:
1. Examine the long struggle between right-to-life and pro-choice groups over abortion rights in the United States.
2. Discuss the political and legal positions policy makers and jurists take concerning abortion rights.
3. Explore some of the new areas of controversy over abortion rights and the responsibilities of medical professionals regarding abortion counseling.

SOME BACKGROUND

In 1973 the Supreme Court outlawed most of the existing state abortion laws in its famous *Roe v. Wade* decision. In a 7-2 ruling regarding Texas law, the Court restricted state legislative interference in a woman's right to an abortion in the first three months of pregnancy, but did allow states to restrict second- and third-trimester abortions under certain circumstances. Almost immediately the number of abortions performed in the United States increased dramatically. In 1981, 29.3 abortions were performed per 1,000 births. In 1990 1.6 million abortions were performed, the highest number in one year. In recent years, however, the number of abortions has declined somewhat. In 2007 the Centers for Disease Control and Prevention reported that the number of reported abortions was 1.2 million, the lowest number since 1976. Despite the decline, the number of abortions performed since 1973 is approximately 50 million.[1]

With the *Roe v. Wade* decision and the steady increase in legal abortions, the abortion rights debate in the United States began in earnest as state legislatures, the Congress and the courts took steps that defined more precisely a woman's right to abort her pregnancy. This intense passion over abortion rights continues today as pro-choice and right-to-life groups mount national campaigns to either protect a woman's right to choose or strip women of that right. Despite the ruling in the *Roe* case and subsequent legislative and court action, the abortion rights debate has not been removed from political agendas; it may move back and forth from a high priority to a lesser status in political circles, but it remains an issue that political parties, candidates for public office and government officials cannot ignore.

A woman's right to an abortion has always been controversial in the United States. Dating back to the 1820s there were state laws controlling abortion rights and setting time limits on when abortions could be performed. By the early 1900s, however, most states had outlawed abortions, and there was general agreement that abortion was an unsafe medical procedure that put women at risk. Even leading feminists at the time such as Susan B. Anthony and Elizabeth Cady Stanton were opposed to abortion as they turned their attention to other causes of equality such as gaining suffrage and breaking down other social and economic barriers to full equality. However, as the United States moved into the 1960s and the so-called sexual revolution began to take hold with its emphasis on personal freedom, more and more pressure was placed on public officials at the state level to expand abortion rights and allow women to control reproduction. By 1965, however, all states had passed restrictive laws banning abortion.[2]

With states refusing to make abortions available to women, it was up to the Supreme Court to take on this volatile issue. However, although the Court established a key legal precedent with its decision in the *Roe* case, it also created a firestorm of controversy as the nation debated not just the elements of the law, but the morality of allowing women to control the reproductive process in the early stages of pregnancy. The decision unleashed a torrent of opposition from religious groups (particularly the Catholic Church), which saw in the Supreme Court decision a rejection of life and a refusal to recognize the rights of the unborn fetus. Interest groups such as the National Abortion Rights Action League (NARAL) and National Right to Life Committee quickly began forming on either side of the debate. Kate Michelman of NARAL attributed the intensity of the debate to conservatives who were "driven by those who have never accepted reproductive rights as essential individual rights, and have seen the benefit of abortion as an organizing tool for a much larger social vision–a vision that rolls back civil rights gains, women's rights, rights of the disabled and environmental protections." Gary Bauer of the conservative American Values group placed the abortion battle squarely in the political arena when he stated, "the right to life is the most fundamental, natural human right upon which all other rights are based."[3]

The scope of the social and political divisions over abortion rights became so wide that yearly rallies and demonstrations were held each

January to mark the anniversary of the *Roe v. Wade* decision. In this contentious environment there were unfortunately numerous instances of confrontation and conflict as pro-life groups such as Operation Rescue staged sit-ins and other intimidating measures at abortion clinics to stop women from entering buildings to have abortions. There were also periods of violence as Planned Parenthood clinics were bombed in North Carolina and clinic workers were killed at the Planned Parenthood facility in Boston. In many states, legislatures had to enact laws creating safe zones that separated pro-life protesters from women seeking to enter abortion clinics. Although pro-life advocates challenged these safe zones as violations of free speech, courts upheld them as necessary to protect the safety of women who were exercising their new-found right to an abortion.

The right to an abortion granted through *Roe v. Wade* quickly entered the political arena. In the years immediately after the *Roe* ruling, candidates running for office or long-term incumbents often defined their campaigns around the abortion issue and were victorious or defeated based on their position on choice versus life. The pressure from right-to-life proponents eventually influenced Congress to take action. Under the leadership of Representative Henry Hyde of Illinois, Congress passed legislation banning the use of public funds for abortions and removed insurance coverage for federal employees to obtain an abortion. Many states followed suit and removed public funding for abortions, thus limiting the availability of abortions for many American women.

Since *Roe v. Wade*, the Supreme Court has addressed a number of issues related to abortion and made some clarifying and limiting decisions. In the 1980s state legislatures enacted laws to make it difficult to obtain an abortion by requiring that abortions be conducted in hospitals rather than clinics and that a 24-hour waiting period be observed in hopes that women would change their minds about aborting their fetus after receiving information on fetal development from the hospital. In 1992 in *Planned Parenthood v. Casey*, the most important decision regarding abortion rights since *Roe v. Wade*, the Court approved many of these restrictive regulations and also trimmed back the trimester formula that was the core of the abortion rights decision in *Roe v. Wade*.[4] However, the Court validated the fundamental right for a woman to have an abortion as consistent with the concepts of liberty and the right to privacy as suggested in the due process clause of the Fourteenth Amendment.

The change in *Roe v. Wade* was brought on by the viability issue as advanced medical technology made it possible to keep a fetus viable five to six weeks earlier than the first trimester, or twenty-eight weeks. As a result, the Court ruled that the 1973 formula was obsolete and therefore should not remain as the basis for supporting abortions. But the Court clearly emphasized that it was not overturning the right of women to seek abortions in the United States. As the judges stated in their majority opinion, "If the right to privacy means anything, it is the right of the individual, married or single, to be free from unwarranted governmental intrusion into matters so fundamentally affecting a person as the decision whether to bear or beget a child."[5]

With abortion rights secure (at least for a time) with the Casey decision, attention turned to the Congress where conservatives worked to achieve a ban on partial birth abortions. Partial birth abortions, which in the medical community are called intact dilation and extraction, are rare procedures usually performed to protect the life of the mother, in which the fetus is taken out of the womb and a saline solution is injected into the skull to end life. During the Clinton administration bills banning partial birth abortion were vetoed as the president maintained his support for a woman's right to choose. But with the arrival of George W. Bush in the White House, the legislative dynamics changed. In 2003 a partial birth abortion ban bill was passed by Congress and signed by the president. The bill was initially blocked by a federal judge and the case went to the Supreme Court. In 2007 in a key decision (*Gonzales v. Carhart*) the Supreme Court by a 5-4 margin upheld the Partial Birth Abortion Ban Act, and the majority stated that the ban did not interfere with the precedents set with the *Roe* and *Casey* decisions. Opponents of the ban saw this victory in the Supreme Court as a signal that abortion rights were under threat and that it was only a matter of time before a case dealing with a woman's right to an abortion would make its way to the court and face a new level of scrutiny.[6]

Actions on abortion rights were also taken at the state level as states such as South Dakota and Nebraska passed strict anti-abortion legislation that permitted no abortions and penalized doctors who performed the procedures and women who sought abortions. In South Dakota in 2006 Governor Mike Rounds signed a law supported by anti-abortion advocates that would have made performing an abortion a felony. The law also allowed little leeway as it banned abortions even if the life of the mother was in danger. The law divided the state and initiated an intense referendum campaign to determine the will of the people of South Dakota. The referendum was eventually rejected by the voters, but was seen nationally as representative of individual states seeking to end abortion rights without waiting for the federal courts to act.[7]

On the Record

Justice Harry Blackmun wrote the majority opinion in the *Roe v. Wade* case. His opening remarks regarding the task before him and the Court are given here:

> We forthwith acknowledge our awareness of the sensitive and emotional nature of the abortion controversy, of the vigorous opposing views, even among physicians, and of the deep and seemingly absolute convictions that the subject inspires. One's philosophy, one's experiences, one's exposure to the raw edges of human existence,

(continued)

On the Record   (continued)

one's religious training, one's attitude toward life and family and their values, and the moral standards one establishes and seeks to observe, are all likely to influence and to color one's thinking and conclusions about abortion. . . . Our task, of course, is to resolve the issue by constitutional measurement, free of emotion and of predilection.

DEBATES, DIFFERENCES AND DIVISIONS

The abortion debate, as presented by Justice Blackmun in the earlier quote, has many sides–ethical, medical, philosophical, religious and personal. But as an issue that was addressed on numerous occasions by the Supreme Court and has become a lightning rod of partisan discord in the Congress and among the presidential candidates, there are some critical elements to the abortion debate that are centered in the Constitution and the interpretation of the Constitution by the justices at all federal court levels. Central to the disagreement over abortion rights is the privacy issue. It must be emphasized that nowhere in the Constitution is the term *privacy* used and no amendment to the Constitution provides a specific right to privacy. But in *Roe v. Wade* and decisions leading up to that historic decision, justices on the Supreme Court found the right to privacy to be inherent in the Constitution and based its decision to support abortion rights in part on this newly found right to privacy.

The right to privacy and its connection to abortion rights is founded on the 1965 *Griswold v. Connecticut* decision. The Supreme Court overthrew a Connecticut law that banned the use of contraceptives, saying that it violated the privacy rights of individuals, in this case married couples seeking to purchase contraceptives. Writing for the majority Justice William O. Douglas found that the right to privacy was created from the language and intent in the First, Third, Fourth, Fifth and Ninth Amendments. Douglas, some say using tortured language and questionable interpretation of the Constitution, stated that there existed "penumbras, formed by emanations from those guarantees that help give them life and substance." In other words, the language contained in those five amendments signal that the Constitution does provide for the right to privacy. In particular, Justice Douglas used the Ninth Amendment to support his case when he quoted its language, which declares that "the enumeration in the Constitution of certain rights, shall not be construed to deny or disparage others retained by the people."[8]

Justice Douglas's defense of the right to privacy carried over seven years later in the *Roe v. Wade* case when Justice Blackmun, in defending his position overturning the Texas law that limited a woman's right to make reproductive choices, said the following:

The Court has recognized that a right of personal privacy, or a guarantee of certain areas or zones of privacy does exist under the Constitution . . . whether it be founded in the Fourteenth

Amendment's concept of personal liberty and restrictions on state action . . . or as the District Court determined, in the Ninth Amendment's reservation of rights to the people, is broad enough to encompass a woman's decision whether or not to terminate her pregnancy.[9]

The abortion rights decision in *Roe v. Wade* not only created an intense controversy over the Court's protection of a woman's right to choose but also led to a serious debate among constitutional scholars, especially those with conservative credentials, about whether a right to privacy exists in the Constitution. Justices and constitutional scholars who were often termed *strict constructionists* or supporters of the *original intent of the founding fathers* stated that if the right to privacy is not mentioned in the Constitution, then the right does not exist, therefore nullifying the founding principle on which *Roe v. Wade* was adjudicated. As the terms suggest, strict constructionists and supporters of original intent believe that the Constitution must be viewed literally and that the original intent of the Constitution can be determined only by the words used by those who wrote the document and its amendments.

One of the primary advocates of the strict construction and original intent perspectives on the right to privacy is former federal judge Robert Bork, who was unsuccessful in gaining Senate approval to the Supreme Court when Ronald Reagan nominated him in 1987. Bork was rejected in large part because liberal Democrats on the Senate Judiciary Committee were able to convince a majority of the Senate that Bork's views were out of step with a "living constitution" that expands rights and applies constitutional principles to modern-day conditions and circumstances. Bork was unyielding in his rejection of the privacy rights that bolstered the *Roe v. Wade* decision and stressed that justices on the high court must be guided by the Constitution as written, not as they would like it to be written or as they choose to interpret its language. Today, Bork remains an unabashed proponent of strict constructionism and original intent and continues his criticism of the *Roe v. Wade* decision as deeply flawed in terms of its support for privacy rights and from that abortion rights.[10]

Because the Supreme Court has been at the core of the abortion rights debate in the United States, appointments to the highest court have become politicized as both Democrats and Republicans seek to influence the appointment process and ensure that justices are either pro-choice or pro-life. The failure of Robert Bork to win approval by the Senate was just the beginning of long struggle over whether a shift in the balance of the Supreme Court to a pro-life majority would end abortion rights and overturn the precedent-setting *Roe v. Wade* decision. The partisan debate over abortion rights and judicial appointments came to a head during the hearings to approve or reject President George W. Bush's nomination of Samuel Alito to the high court. Alito was the replacement for Justice Sandra Day O'Connor, who in the past had supported abortion rights and joined the majority in the *Casey* decision. Liberal Democrats on the Senate Judiciary Committee viewed Alito as a quiet supporter of the pro-life position and sought to ascertain through tough questioning whether he would overturn *Roe v. Wade*. Alito maintained his openness to both sides of the issue but would not make a public commitment on how he might vote on a case associated with abortion rights. Critics of Alito among pro-choice advocates, however, pointed to positions that Alito had taken as a federal judge in abortion-related cases that signaled his opposition to the judicial philosophy used in *Roe v. Wade*. This concern was born out in 2007 when Alito joined the majority, including Chief Justice John Roberts, also a Bush appointee, in upholding the Partial Birth Abortion Ban Law.[11]

The political and legal struggle to set the proper balance between the rights of the mother and the rights of the fetus has also been part of the debate over abortion rights. Pro-choice advocates state that the right of the mother, who is a fully formed human, must be considered more important than the right of the fetus, who they view as a "potential human." Denying a woman the right to an abortion, according to the pro-choice argument, would treat pregnant women as if they were less than a person and elevate a fetus to the same status as the mother. Pro-life advocates, however, see the fetus as protected under the Constitution because there is human life in the mother's womb, and as time goes on that fetus takes on many of the physical characteristics of a human. The fact that the fetus has not left the womb does not, in the view of the pro-life position, negate its inalienable right to life, and because of medical and scientific breakthroughs that impact viability, the call for fetal rights becomes more pronounced.

Data Bank

From the start, abortion policy has been the subject of regular assessments of American public opinion as each side in the debate used polling data to support their position in the courts and in national and state legislatures. Three recent polling studies using different questions to determine the position of the American people toward abortion are given here.

In a 2006 Gallup poll a representative sampling of Americans was asked whether they thought abortions should be "legal under any circumstance," "legal under certain circumstances" or "always illegal." The results were as follows:

Legal under any circumstance–24%
Legal under certain circumstances–55%
Always illegal–20%

In 2007 a CBS News poll asked Americans "their personal feelings about abortion."
The results were as follows:

31%–abortion should be permitted in all cases.

16%–abortion should be permitted but subject to greater restrictions than at present.

30%–abortion should be permitted only in cases such as rape, incest, or to save the woman's life.

12%–abortion should be permitted only to save the woman's life.

5%–abortion should never be permitted.

In a 2009 Gallup Poll:

51% of the respondents stated that they were pro-life.

42% of the respondents stated that they were pro-choice.

This polling data was the first turnaround for the Gallup poll in the views expressed by Americans toward the abortion issue, as now a majority of Americans describe themselves as pro-life.

Source: Boston Globe, May 16, 2009, A8

Although much of the controversy surrounding abortion and abortion rights has been out in the political arena and before the federal courts, there is a racial and economic element to the debate that cannot be ignored and is at the core of the pro-choice position. Many of the women who seek abortions are young minorities. Data from 2000 to 2001 show that the rate of abortion was 49 per 1,000 for blacks and 33 per 1,000 for Hispanics. Among white women the rate of abortion was 13 per 1,000. Many of the black and Hispanic women reported that their desire to have an abortion was related to the fact that they could not afford a baby or that the father had left the scene and they were unable to provide financially for the care of the child. Pro-choice advocates use these data to support their view that abortion rights are absolutely essential to provide poor black and Hispanic women with the option of terminating their pregnancy and not bringing a life into the world that would immediately be at an economic and social disadvantage. Although pro-life supporters do not deny these data on race and economic status, they stress the importance of taking the baby to full term and then placing the child up for adoption.[12]

What complicates the racial and economic factors in the abortion rights debate is that as a result of federal and state laws that deny funding of abortions, many poor women do not have access to safe abortions should they want to terminate their pregnancy. Currently, only seventeen states offer coverage for poor women to have abortions, with California, Illinois and New York being the largest states with health care provisions that provide financial assistance for abortions. In general, white women have higher incomes or a network of support that would allow them to pay for an abortion. Pro-choice supporters thus see the inequity in the current availability of abortion coverage as women of color are forced to travel long distances to states that have such benefits or carry an unwanted pregnancy to full term. Again, the pro-life position does not address the racial and economic disparity issue, but stresses the importance of fetal rights and the necessity of not terminating a pregnancy.[13]

FYI

The two major political parties have taken very different positions on abortion rights in their party platforms, revealing the vast differences that exist in political and governmental circles over this controversial issue.

The position of the Democratic Party as presented in their 2008 party platform is as follows:

> Because we believe in the privacy and equality of women, we stand proudly for a women's right to choose, consistent with *Roe v. Wade*, and regardless of her ability to pay. We stand firmly against Republican efforts to undermine that right. At the same time, we strongly support family planning and adoption incentives. Abortion should be safe, legal and rare.

The position of the Republican Party as presented in their 2008 party platform is as follows:

> We must keep our pledge to the first guarantee of the Declaration of Independence; that is why we say the unborn child has a fundamental, individual right to life which cannot be infringed. We support a human life amendment to the constitution and we endorse legislation to make it clear that the 14th Amendment's protections apply to unborn children.

Currently, the abortion debate in the United States is in a "wait-and-see" mode as the addition of Chief Justice John Roberts and Justice Samuel Alito to the Supreme Court have encouraged the pro-life movement that there will soon be an overturn of *Roe v. Wade*. However, although the Court appears to have shifted to the right and may be more amenable to reviewing and perhaps voiding *Roe v. Wade*, this is not a certainty. Although Justice O'Connor has left the Court and taken her pro-choice position with her, there is still a substantial divide in the Court with Justice Anthony Kennedy, a Catholic, holding the key swing vote. Sometime in the future there is likely to be a case that will test *Roe v. Wade*. And President Obama's appointments to the current Supreme Court, Sonia Sotomayor and Elena Kagan, are viewed by many experts as staunch supporters of choice and therefore will likely maintain the tenuous majority in favor of a woman's right to an abortion.

In a related abortion controversy President Obama signaled early in his presidency that he was going to eliminate the "conscience clause" from federal regulations. On the last day of his presidency George W. Bush signed an executive order protecting health care workers who object to abortion and other birth control practices on religious or personal conscience grounds. The decision by Bush invalidated fifty-four laws in thirty-seven states that provide for access to contraceptives and gave health care workers the right to refuse their medical services as a matter of conscience. The wording of the Bush regulation stated that abortion is properly defined as "any of the various procedures–including the prescription, dispensing and administration of any drug or the performance of any procedure or any other action–that results in the termination of life of a human being in utero between conception and natural birth, whether before or after implantation."[14]

Obama's intention to reverse the conscience clause was supported by most of the major medical professional organizations such as the American Medical Association. These groups stated that doctors, nurses and other medical professionals have an obligation to provide information that gives patients the full range of options available to them regarding contraception and pregnancy. But some doctors groups that are linked to religious organizations and the Catholic Church criticized Obama for limiting what they viewed as the constitutional rights of free speech and freedom of religion. These groups suggested that doing away with the conscience clause would be akin to moving toward a totalitarian state.

Abortion rights also entered into the health care reform debate as pro-life Democrats joined conservative Republicans to demand that the bill would not allow government-subsidized insurance that would pay for abortions. In last-minute discussions with Democrats, President Obama pledged that he would sign an executive order banning any federal support for abortion, a move that help swing pro-life members of the House of Representatives to vote for the bill.[15]

Much speculation has been observed in recent years about what the abortion issue would look like should *Roe v. Wade* be overturned. Most observers of this issue believe that a decision voiding *Roe v. Wade* would allow the states to make their own laws regarding abortion rights. Those states that now restrict abortions either through funding mechanisms or by not encouraging doctors or health professionals from starting clinics that perform abortions would certainly move quickly to build on an anti–*Roe v. Wade* decision coming from the Supreme Court. But those states that currently provide access and funding, especially large, liberal-leaning states such as California, New York and Illinois would likely not choose to strip a woman of her reproductive rights. According to a 2004 Center for Reproductive Rights study entitled "What If Roe Fell? The State by State Consequences," abortion rights appear secure in twenty states but in the other thirty states, "women are at risk of losing their right to choose an abortion after a reversal of *Roe*."[16]

The result of an overturn of *Roe v. Wade* would thus likely be a compartmentalization of abortion rights in the United Staes, with many southern, midwestern and mountain states forbidding abortions and other states on both coasts maintaining the right example, in 2010 the Governor of Nebraska signed legislation that would bar abortions at or after twenty weeks and require women seeking an abortion to be screened for mental health and other issues before having an abortion. This bill is certain to be challenged in the federal courts.[17] Interestingly, what started in 1972 as a state issue that was overturned by a federal court, may, if *Roe* is ever overturned, return the country to a time when states set abortion policy, with the only difference being that there would likely not be a universal ban, as outposts of abortion rights would remain.[18] The fate of *Roe v. Wade* is unknown, but it is certain that the decision has divided America and will continue to divide America no matter what happens in the future.[19]

The Great Debate

The struggle over abortion in the United States is rooted in the issue of rights–the women's right to reproductive freedom or the fetus's right to life.

Debate Topic

In the battle over rights, does a women's right to choose to have an abortion supersede that of the fetus in the womb to live?

Critical Thinking Questions

1. Does human life begin at conception?
2. If the U.S. Constitution does not mention privacy rights, do Americans have them?
3. Are you in favor of overturning *Roe v. Wade*? What would be the consequences of such a reversal?
4. Should medical professionals have the right to refuse to participate in hospital programs that violate their conscience regarding abortion and contraception?
5. Is the argument that abortion rights should be retained as a means of providing poor women with opportunities to terminate their pregnancy and avoid the economic challenges that come with having a baby a valid one?

Connections

One of the primary advocates for women's rights, and in particular a woman's right to choose, is the National Organization of Women, which can be accessed at http://www.now.org

NARAL is the primary pro-choice organization in the United States. Its site is http://www.naral.org

The Pro-Life Action League is the primary pro-life organization in the United States. Its site is http://prolifeaction.org

The Guttmacher Institute researches state policies toward abortion and conducts other valuable research on the abortion issue. Visit its site at http://www.guttmacher.org

Operation Rescue is the most controversial of the anti-abortion groups because of its militant opposition to abortion. See its site at http://www.operationrescue.org

Some Books to Read

McBride, Dorothy, *Abortion in the United States: A Reference Handbook* (Santa Barbara, CA: ABC-CLIO, 2007).

Hendershott, Ann, *The Politics of Abortion* (New York: Encounter Books, 2006).

Rose, Melody, *Safe, Legal and Unavailable? Abortion Politics in the United States* (Washington, D.C.: Congressional Quarterly Press, 2006).

Solinger, Rickie, *Beggars and Choosers: How the Politics of Choice Shapes Adoption, Abortion and Welfare in the United States* (New York: Hill & Wang, 2002).

Burns, Gene, *The Moral Veto: Framing Contraception, Abortion and Cultural Pluralism in the United States* (New York: Cambridge University Press, 2005).

Notes

1. Rob Stein, "Number of Abortions Lowest in Decades," *Boston Globe*, January 17, 2008, A2.
2. For background see David Garrou, *Liberty and Sexuality: The Right to Privacy and the Making of Roe v. Wade* (New York: MacMillan, 1994).
3. See Carolyne Zinko, "The Ideological Rumble: The Abortion Issue," http://articles.sfgate.com/2006-01-08/news/17275463_1_abortion-rights-case-abortion-wars-alito-nomination. See also Alesha E. Doan, *Opposition and Intimidation: The Abortion Wars and Strategies of Political Harassment* (Ann Arbor, MI: University of Michigan Press, 2007).
4. *Planned Parenthood v. Casey* 505 U.S. 883 (1992).
5. Ibid.
6. *Gonzales v. Carhart* 530 U.S.914 (2000).
7. Evelyn Nieves, "South Dakota Abortion Bill Takes Aim at Roe," *Washington Post*, February 23, 2006, A01.
8. See a background discussion of the right of privacy at "Exploring Constitutional Conflicts," http://www.law.umkc.edu/faculty/projects/ftrials/conlaw/rightofprivacy.html
9. *Roe v. Wade* 410 U.S. 113 (1973).
10. Linda Greenhouse, "Why Bork Is Still a Verb in Politics, Ten Years Later," *New York Times*, October 5, 1997. Also see a video presentation of the Bork controversy entitled "The Honorable Court," Greater Washington Educational Telecommunications Association, 1988, Program # 1.
11. Jason Deparle and David Kirkpatrick, "In Battle to Pick Next Justice, Right Says," New York Times, June 27, 2005, A01. For background see Charles S. Franklin and Liane Kosaki, "The Republican Schoolmaster: The Supreme Court,

Public Opinion and Abortion," *American Political Science Review* 83 (1989), 751–772.

12. See data and analysis on race and abortion at http://www.abortionfacts.com/statistics/race.asp

13. Heather D. Boonstra, "The Heart of the Matter: Public Funding of Abortion for Poor Women in the U.S.," *Guttmacher Policy Review*, Winter, 2007, Vol. 10, #1.

14. Rob Stein, "New Front in the Abortion War," *Washington Post National Weekly Edition*, August 4–10, 2008, p. 35.

15. David Kirkpatrick, "Health Care Overhaul Revives Abortion Debate," *New York Times*, November 24, 2009, A1.

16. See the discussion on the possible fall of *Roe v. Wade* in *USA Today*, July 7, 2005, http://www.usatoday.com/news/opinion/editorials/2005-07-26-forum-roe-x.htm

17. See Cynthia Gorney, *Article of Faith: A Frontline History of the Abortion Wars* (New York: Simon & Schuster, 2000).

18. See Nate Jenkins," Nebraska Governor Signs Landmark Abortion Measure" Boston Globe, April 14, 2010 A2.

19. There are some signs that the anti-abortion forces may be changing tactics from working toward a ban to strategies that reduce the number of abortions. See Jacqueline Salmon, "A Truce in the Abortion Wars," *Washington Post National Weekly Edition*, November 24–30, 2008, p. 17.

11 GUN RIGHTS

Issue Focus

It is safe to say that America is a country of guns and gun owners. Millions of Americans proudly profess their right to bear arms. But the passionate belief in gun ownership has a huge downside. The United States has developed a reputation around the world as a violent country where liberal gun ownership laws create the opportunity for criminals and ordinary citizens to use handguns and even assault rifles to engage in illegal activities or settle a personal score. Despite thousands of gun-related deaths each year, Congress has been unable and unwilling to put in place tough measures that would restrict gun purchases or requirements that potential gun owners would be forced to follow. The issue of gun ownership has now shifted to the federal courts, where the justices are defining the meaning and the scope of the Second Amendment regarding the right to bear arms.

Chapter Objectives
This issue chapter will seek to:
1. Document the longstanding dispute over the meaning of the Second Amendment right to bear arms.
2. Update the controversy involving gun rights by examining the dispute between the National Rifle Association, the powerful pro-gun lobby, and groups, such as the Coalition to Stop Gun Violence, that are opposed to expanded rights of gun ownership.
3. Discuss the latest issues involving gun rights, particularly in light of a key Supreme Court decision that for the first time addressed the issue of what the Second Amendment means.

SOME BACKGROUND

One of the exasperating characteristics of the Bill of Rights is that it is often difficult to determine what the Founding Fathers were thinking when they wrote the basic elements of Americans' personal freedoms. This is certainly the case with the wording of the Second Amendment and its definition of gun rights. The Second Amendment states: "A well regulated Militia, being necessary to the security of a free State, the right of the people to keep and bear arms, shall not be infringed."

A reader and interpreter of the Second Amendment is likely drawn to the opening phrase about a "well regulated Militia" and the closing phrase that establishes "the right of the people to keep and bear arms." The question that has befuddled constitutional scholars and fostered a vigorous if not contentious debate over gun rights in the United States is whether the authors of the Bill of Rights were granting the right to bear arms only to a well-regulated Militia or were extending that right to all citizens of the United States.[1]

Supporters of gun rights in organizations such as the National Rifle Association (NRA) see the Second Amendment as granting citizens the right to "keep and bear arms" and that the right "shall not be infringed," meaning that gun ownership should be unrestricted. Opponents of gun rights such as the Coalition to Stop Gun Violence concentrate their position on the opening phrase of "a well regulated Militia" and state that the Founding Fathers never intended gun rights to be universal in the United States, but to be only within the confines of the state militias, the forerunners of what is now the U.S. National Guard.

This critical interpretive divide over what the Second Amendment means has created one of many issue battlegrounds in the United States. Both sides in this debate about gun ownership differ not only on the issue of what the Founding Fathers meant in the Second Amendment, but they also are at odds over a range of subsidiary concerns such as whether guns are the causal factor in the high rate of violent crime in the United States, whether a citizen's best defense against a criminal act is the possession of a handgun, whether various forms of automatic weapons should be viewed as protected under the Second Amendment and whether the government has the power to require certain safety features on guns and background checks for potential gun owners. Although all these issues flow from the central question of the right to bear arms under the Constitution, the debate over guns has become multi-faceted and highly divisive.

While the courts have seen fit to become involved in defining the character and limits of certain rights such as in the case of abortion, the judicial interpretation of the Second Amendment has been rather sparse as justices at both the state and federal level have sought to stay out of the minefield of gun rights. To fill the legal gap, public policies regarding gun rights have been developed in Congress, thereby creating a political rather than a constitutional resolution of how to properly apply the Second Amendment in the United States. In three cases from the 19th century the Supreme Court ruled narrowly that the Second Amendment restricts only the federal government, not the states, in matters related to gun rights. Those decisions came during what was termed the pre-incorporation period, when the Court chose not to expand the Bill of Rights to include state action. As a result of these decisions, the Supreme Court chose not to address the key issue of what the Second Amendment means nationally and how the wording should be applied to all Americans. Only in 1939 did the Supreme Court take on the first case in which the Second Amendment was addressed specifically, and the Court sought to bring some definitional precision to the language. In *United States v. Miller* the Court examined whether a sawed-off shotgun owner (Miller) could be indicted under the National Firearms Act of 1934.

Unfortunately, the resolution of the constitutional issue was murky because Miller died, and the Supreme Court upheld the federal law without a definitive resolution of the key issue of what the Second Amendment means and how it should be applied.[2]

In the contemporary period the issue of gun rights rose to national prominence with the assassination of President John F. Kennedy as his alleged killer, Lee Harvey Oswald, purchased the rifle that was used to murder the president from a mail-order catalog. Later in 1968 when both Dr. Martin Luther King Jr. and President Kennedy's brother Robert Kennedy were assassinated, Congress passed the Gun Control Act, which banned the interstate sale of firearms, the importation of military surplus weapons and gun ownership by minors and felons. Then again in 1981, when President Reagan was wounded and his press secretary Jim Brady was permanently disabled, there was a call for further gun restrictions, but it was not until the Clinton administration came to power that the Brady Act was passed, which required a five-day waiting period to purchase handguns and that local law enforcement agents conduct background checks of gun purchasers. Clinton was also successful one year later in passing a crime control bill that prohibited the importation of semi-automatic assault weapons.[3]

These legislative victories for the opponents of gun rights, however, were often matched by laws in states that defended gun ownership and expanded gun rights. In 1986 Congress passed the Gun Owners Protection Act, which in effect overturned the Gun Control Act of 1968 and permitted the interstate sale of rifles and shotguns. Also in the 1980s and 1990s over two-thirds of the states passed laws allowing citizens the right to carry concealed weapons without proof that there was a special need for such a privilege.[4] And in 1997 the Supreme Court in *Printz v. United States* struck down the key element of the Brady Act when it found that the requirement that local police officials conduct background checks was a violation of state's rights. In each of these shifts in policy the NRA showed its immense lobbying power and legal clout as it fought successfully to turn the tide against gun control legislation.[5]

The battle between gun owners and gun control advocates is relentless as each side marshals data on crime and violence, presents examples from American everyday life that supports their position and targets members of Congress with threats of electoral retribution if they do not support gun rights or gun control. Perhaps no issue on the American scene carries with it such dire predictions if laws are passed either restricting gun ownership or expanding the right. However, with the FBI estimating that more than 200 million guns are owned by Americans and approximately 93 million people in the country live in households where a gun is present, it is safe to say that we are a nation of gunowners. The issue thus becomes whether we regulate gun ownership and, if we do regulate, how will we regulate. Both of these questions are at the core of the issue of the right to bear arms.

On the Record

There is no scarcity of opinion on the issue of what the Second Amendment means and how it should be applied in American society. Here are two opinions from the opposing groups associated with the gun rights controversy:

"The Second Amendment preserves the greatest human right–the right to defend one's own life."–Tanya Metaksa, lobbyist for the National Rifle Association.

"Gun violence is not a constitutional issue; it is a public health and safety issue. . . . The 35,000 Americans fatally shot every year are real."–Dennis Henigan, Brady Center to Prevent Gun Violence.

DEBATES, DIFFERENCES AND DIVISIONS

The two quotes from both sides of the gun rights argument capture the essence of the differences and divisions that mark this controversial issue. Supporters of gun ownership possess an unwavering belief that Americans have the right to defend themselves and that the Constitution provides them with that right. Like Tanya Metaksa, gun owners believe that possessing a firearm provides personal security; taking away or compromising that right would thus place individuals in danger from the criminal element. But for Dennis Henigan, gun ownership is fraught with danger as easy access to firearms fosters their use in the home, the workplace and social settings. Gun violence has reached epidemic proportions, and thus strict controls are essential if Americans are to be truly safe.

Around these two arguments both sides in the gun debate present mountains of evidence and personal accounts that support their case. The NRA has reams of testimony from supporters of gun ownership who testify that their possession of a firearm foiled a robbery or saved their life from an attacker. In its newsletter and other mailings, the NRA regularly runs stories of how gun ownership was responsible for saving a life or warding off a criminal attack. Opponents of gun rights will counter this issue with an equal number of examples of random violence associated with easy access to guns as deranged individuals kill fellow workers over an employment issue or students seek revenge by killing classmates who bullied them in school. The Columbine High School shootings in 1999 and the tragic massacre at Virginia Tech University in 2008 are often used by opponents of gun control as examples of the need to control weapons. Both sides are capable of making a credible case that possessing a gun either provided personal security from a criminal attack or led to a horrific rampage.

As it may be obvious by now, the gun rights debate is driven by the constant clash between the two primary interest group organizations, the NRA and the Brady Campaign to Prevent Gun Violence. The aforementioned Coalition to

Stop Gun Violence is also a key opponent. There is little question among experts who study interest group politics in the United States that the NRA is one of the most powerful and effective advocates for its position of broad gun rights. With a national membership of over 4 million gun owners and supporters of gun ownership and a staff of 300 lobbyists, researchers and public relations experts, the NRA has proven its ability to pressure Congress and state legislatures to reject measures that would limit gun ownership. On many occasions the NRA has mounted effective get-out-the-vote campaigns at the grassroots level, relying on its supporters to send postcards, letters and emails to incumbents and candidates, threatening them with electoral retribution should they vote against gun owners' interests. Members of Congress and state legislatures openly admit that the get-out-the-vote efforts of the NRA have had a significant impact on getting pro-gun right officials into political office.[6]

The anti-gun groups such as the Brady Campaign to Prevent Gun and the Coalition to Stop Gun Violence are akin to the biblical Daniel facing Goliath. Like the NRA, the Brady Campaign puts out a stream of information on its interpretation of the Second Amendment; the linkages between crime, violence and guns and the intransigence of the NRA to even consider moderate regulatory provisions such as background checks, bans on automatic weapons and the end of trade-show gun purchases, which are often the source of easily purchased weapons. Although James Brady and his wife Sarah have been tireless advocates for gun control and have developed a capable interest group organization, the Brady Campaign to Prevent Gun Violence, with substantial funds and staff to mount an effective counterforce to the NRA, the organization is outspent by the NRA and other pro-gun rights groups. A 2006 study by the non-partisan Center for Responsive Politics, which monitors lobbying and spending for lobbying, found that the pro-gun lobby led by the NRA outspent the anti-gun lobby led by the Brady Center by a ratio of 3 to 1.[7]

Alongside the supporting testimonials and everyday examples used by the advocates of gun rights and gun control is a large body of scholarly studies that have also become part of the national debate over the Second Amendment. Two major areas of research and research debate surrounding gun ownership are the relationship between crime and gun ownership and the connection between violence and gun ownership. Dr. Gary Kleck, a noted criminologist from Florida State University, has studied the issue of whether guns have enhanced personal security. Kleck estimated in his study that as many as 2.5 million Americans used a gun in self-defense or to ward off a criminal. He also found that the mere showing of a gun helped the owner to enhance personal security as potential criminals were scared off.[8] Kleck's research, however, has been challenged by other scholars such as David Hemenway who questioned Kleck's data because Kleck's connection between gun use and self-defense resulted from the testimony of gun owners, not from police investigation or other independent analysis. Hemenway does admit that some valid association exists between gun ownership and self-protection. However, in his book *Private Guns, Public Health*, Henenway concludes that the more guns available, the greater the chance for a range of violent actions.[9]

The issue of keeping guns in the home and the incidence of violence is also creating scholarly division in the gun control debate. Writing in the *New England Journal of Medicine,* Arthur Kellerman, an emergency room doctor, asserted that people who keep a firearm at home significantly increase the chances of a homicide. Kellerman's findings were challenged by a range of critics who stated that the doctor failed to recognize the deterrent effect of keeping guns in homes as residents used firearms to protect property and save the lives of their loved ones. Kellerman, however, refused to budge on his position that guns in the home can be directly linked to incidents of firearms accidents, spousal killings and suicide. Suicide in particular has been seen as directly related to gun availability. Data from 2003 show that nearly 54% of the suicides in the United States are committed with guns.[10]

Data Bank

In recent years opponents of gun rights have accented the impact of firearms violence on children and have compared them with other nations that have tougher gun laws. Some data points on gun violence and the safety of children in the United States and elsewhere in the world follow.

According to data provided by the Children's Defense Fund and the National Center for Health Statistics, the number of children and teens killed by gunfire in 2002 in the United States is 3,012, whereas between 1979 and 2001 the number is 90,000.

Data from the Centers for Disease Control and Prevention show that the rate of death due to firearms among children under the age of fifteen is nearly twelve times higher in the United States than that in twenty-five other industrialized countries.

The American Medical Association reported that between 36% and 50% of male eleventh graders in the Unites States stated that they could get a gun with ease if they wanted one or needed one.

The U.S. Department of Education in 2000 issued a report that stated that in 1998–1999, 3,523 students were expelled for bringing a firearm to school; this was a decrease from the previous year when 5,724 students were expelled for bringing a firearm to school.

Although the scholarly and medical debates continue and are used by both sides in the gun rights debate, other concerns regarding gun availability have been raised in recent years. Two issues in particular have become major points of contention between the pro- and anti-gun groups–gun-show purchases and background checks of individuals with a history of mental illness. For a number of years gun control advocates have been pushing state authorities to close the loophole that allows anyone, including those individuals who have been denied a gun license by an authorized gun dealer, to attend a private gun show and purchase a weapon from the trunk of a dealer's car without any background check. Police chiefs and the federal government's Bureau of Alcohol, Tobacco, Firearms and Explosives have for years sought to bring stronger controls to the gun-show trade, but without success. Currently, only fifteen states require background checks of gun purchasers at gun shows.

In 2008 the governor of Virginia, Timothy Kaine, introduced legislation to the state's General Assembly to close the loophole and require background checks of individuals purchasing weapons at gun shows. Not surprisingly, advocates of gun ownership opposed the governor's proposal. Philip Van Cleave of the Virginia Citizens Defense League took a position that has become familiar in the gun debate when he stated, "Criminals don't get guns at gun shows. . . . It's [the proposed legislation] not going to do anything about crime." The legislation to close the loophole on gun shows was also in response to the Virginia Tech shootings and the lax state laws regarding background checks of the mental history of individuals purchasing firearms. The killer Seung Hui Cho, a Virginia Tech student, had a history of mental illness, and even though he purchased the automatic weapons used in the massacre at an authorized gun shop, his past history of mental illness was never brought to light during the background checks. The issue of adding the mental health history to the background check of potential gun purchasers was criticized by gun ownership advocates who stated that the answer to avoiding future massacres by mentally deficient individuals is better mental health counseling, not expanding the background-check process.[11]

The vast difference between state laws and the impact that those laws have on gun availability is also at issue in the gun rights versus gun control debate. According to the NRA, over 20,000 gun laws are on the books in the United States, which from its perspective proves that gun control does exist. However the issue is not so much the number of laws, but the state-to-state differences in the laws and the restrictions that follow from those laws. Law enforcement officials consider the intra-state movement of guns as one of the most serious challenges faced by communities seeking to limit access of guns to criminals. Massachusetts, for example, has one of the toughest gun control laws in the United States and has passed landmark legislation requiring handgun safety features on all guns purchased in the state. However, in recent years the city of Boston has been hit with a wave of gang-related shootings in which the guns in question were likely purchased out of state and brought into the city. Public officials in Boston decried the easy access that gang members had to guns in neighboring states, but they could do little to counteract laws in neighboring states that were not as restrictive as those in Massachusetts.[12]

Besides having vastly different gun laws among states that cause problems for law enforcement officials, the United States has also been heavily criticized in the international court of public opinion because of its inability and unwillingness to pass strong gun control legislation. Many nations in the industrialized world have strong gun control laws that make it difficult, if not impossible, for their citizens to legally purchase a firearm. Opponents of gun rights often point to England, Japan and Germany as examples of countries that have strong gun control laws and also little violent crime. Americans are often portrayed outside the country as living in a gun culture. Today Europeans in particular view Americans as obsessed with guns and unconcerned about how the gun culture has become a permanent part of American life in movies, television, video games and music. With each example of a random killing or a massacre of tragic proportions, the world wonders why the United States does not implement more restrictive gun laws. But when guns are part of a national heritage and are viewed as an accepted means of self-defense, negative international opinion does not sway national or state legislators to follow the example of other nations and implement stricter gun laws. It is important to stress, however, that the United States does not lead the world in homicides. According to U.N. data, in 2000 Russia had 20.15 homicides per 1,000 deaths, Venezuela had 31.61 and Jamaica 32.4; whereas the United States, using 2004 data, had 5.5 homicides per 1,000 deaths.[13]

FYI

In response to gun deaths and general criminal behavior in which firearms are used, many communities across the country have implemented programs that teach gun safety, seek to limit the availability of guns or engage in proactive work with at-risk youths who have the greatest potential to purchase and use guns.

The Brady Center to Prevent Gun Violence (a think tank associated with the Brady Campaign) has developed a program called Steps to Prevent Firearms Injury (STOP) that works with parents to provide counseling on how to work with their children to avoid firearms injuries.

The city of Boston in the 1990s instituted Operation Ceasefire that targeted areas in the inner city with increased police presence and gang-mentoring programs designed to limit access to guns and educate youths to the dangers of gang or gun violence. Boston continues to use this approach under different names and different programs but with only limited success.

Mayors Against Illegal Guns Coalition was formed in 2006 by 210 mayors from 40 different states with the expressed goal of "making the public safe by getting illegal guns off the streets."

Project Safe Neighborhoods is a federal program that was instituted in 2001 and supported by the Bush administration to use the resources of the government, particularly the Department of Justice, to hire prosecutors and provide assistance to state and local authorities especially in the area of community outreach. Since its inception the federal government has allocated over $1.5 billion in assistance.

Source: Boston Police Department

Like most of the issues that are part of the American political process, the debate over gun rights and gun control is complex, and as a result a broad policy consensus is difficult to achieve. However, despite the differences and divisions, the Second Amendment, its meaning and application in American society, is at the heart of the gun debate. Observers of the gun debate often point to the reluctance of the Supreme Court to take the matter head on and define more precisely its interpretation of the founders' meaning of "a well regulated Militia, the right of the people to bear arms." Proponents of gun control have accused the NRA of being opposed to a Court examination of the Second Amendment, sensing that the justices would agree with them that the founders meant only that a militia had the right to bear arms. The NRA, however, responds with extensive historical evidence that shows gun owners are on solid constitutional ground and that a Supreme Court review of the Second Amendment would favor their position.[14]

The NRA got its chance in 2007. In a case from Washington, D.C., the U.S. Appeals Court ruled in *Parker v. District of Columbia* that laws in Washington, D.C., that prohibit personal gun ownership were unconstitutional. The D.C. law limited gun ownership only to retired police officers; prohibited the carrying of a firearm, even in one's home; and required that a gun be kept unloaded and disassembled unless used for what was termed by the court as "lawful recreational purposes." The court stated in its ruling that the first phrase in the Second Amendment referring to the Militia was not, in its view, a limiting factor in personal gun ownership for self-protection and that the recognition of the Militia and gun ownership should not be the sole basis for determining the right of the people to bear arms.[15] The Parker decision had limited application to the District of Columbia and was appealed to the Supreme Court. In 2008, however, the Supreme Court ruled in a 5-4 decision (*District of Columbia v. Heller*) to strike down the Washington, D.C., gun ban and upheld the right of citizens to purchase and keep a gun to protect themselves and their property. Speaking for the majority, Justice Scalia stated that the Second Amendment protects an individual's right to possess and use firearms for lawful reasons "unconnected with service in the militia." The decision was hailed by gun owners as the first firm definition of the Second Amendment and a validation of gun rights. Opponents of the ruling were dismayed with the Court's narrow decision and felt that it would only increase gun violence in America.[16]

Although gun rights advocates consider the *Heller* case as a landmark decision that will change the shape of gun rights in the United States, its application to gun ownership has yet to have a significant impact on other court decisions. In more than eighty cases since the *Heller* decision, federal courts have, according to law professor Adam Winkler, upheld federal laws banning gun ownership by people convicted of felonies and misdemeanors, by illegal immigrants and by drug addicts. Courts have also supported laws that banned machine guns and sawed-off shotguns, restrictions on carrying guns near schools and post offices and regulations that seek to control concealed and unregistered weapons. As Winkler states, "the Heller case is a landmark decision that has not changed very much at all."[17]

The real test for Second Amendment rights will happen when the Supreme Court makes a decision on a case in Chicago (*McDonald v. Chicago*) that will determine whether the right to bear arms extends to state and local laws. In preliminary arguments in March 2010 a majority of justices questioning attorneys on both sides of the case appeared to take the position that the gun laws that permitted the ownership of a weapon as a means of personal protection were indeed supported by the Second Amendment. Although liberal justices such as Stephen Breyer continued to question whether the second amendment applied only to a "well regulated militia," Justice Antonin Scalia and others on the Court stressed the right of individuals to protect themselves in their homes.[18]

Although gun opponents could in future years be dealt a serious blow to their efforts to control the sale and ownership of guns in the United States, public opinion polls consistently show that approximately two-thirds of Americans believe that they possess the right to bear arms and that any decision that would seriously compromise that right would be challenged and lead to an intense political division in the country.[19] Like the pro-life advocates, the proponents of broad gun rights are passionate about the rights that they believe are granted in the Second Amendment and would never allow government to engage in any policy that took away that right. Numerous bumper stickers on the road today champion gun rights and the ferocity with which some gun owners would fight any attempt to limit their gun ownership ("Fight Crime–Shoot Back," "I Love My Country, But I Fear My Government" and "Stop Gun Control Because Freedom Is a Terrible Thing to Waste"). Moreover, the election of Barack Obama spurred a run on gun purchases by Americans who believe that he will take steps to further restrict gun ownership. Obama, however, signed into law the right of gun owners to carry weapons in national parks, although he may have been forced to sign the legislation, because it was attached to a credit card reform bill that he had pledged to support.[20]

However, although the high level of passion concerning gun rights continues, gun control advocates are quick to remind gun owners that their aim is not confiscation and the creation of an all-powerful government that would serve as a kind of Big Brother of gun restrictions. Rather, those from groups emphasize stricter controls on gun ownership similar to those that are associated with getting a driver's license. They also seek a ban on automatic weapons and other quick-firing weapons whose only purpose is to kill people more efficiently, along with an end to the gun-show trade that creates a huge underground market for illegally obtained firearms. The fundamental premise of the gun control advocates is that groups such as the NRA have drawn a broad line in the sand and have refused to accept even modest restrictions that are designed to ensure that guns are only in the hands of individuals who would not use them to commit crimes and violent acts.[21]

This line-in-the-sand strategy of the NRA has had remarkable success and any change in that strategy to achieve some sort of middle-road compromise on gun control is highly unlikely. The NRA knows that its ability to mobilize grassroots supporters has worked effectively to remind legislators that a gun control position would be political suicide. As for the gun control advocates, they have yet been able to match the clout of the NRA. Public opinion polls do show that Americans are in favor of reasonable restrictions on gun use and abhor the mass killings that have occurred because of America's lax gun laws. But this viewpoint has not translated into new gun control legislation, meaning that the gun rights versus gun control battle will continue unabated for years to come, with each side pressuring national and state legislatures to hold the line or implement new restrictions. Not only will the debate and divide between gun rights and gun control be around for a long time, but it is safe to state that a resolution that is acceptable to both sides in the debate will remain elusive.

The Great Debate

Although the Supreme Court has made an expansive interpretation of the right to bear arms, ongoing debates remain about the proper application of the Second Amendment and the kind of restrictions that should be enforced.

Debate Topic
Should Americans have unlimited gun ownership rights, and if limitations on gun ownership are appropriate, what should those limitations be?

Critical Thinking Questions

1. How do you interpret the language of the Second Amendment regarding the right to bear arms?
2. Should gun ownership be controlled in a manner similar to getting a driver's license?
3. Do you believe that violent crime would decrease if there were a ban on guns, or would innocent people be the target of criminals who have obtained guns illegally?
4. What is your view of the Washington, D.C., gun case decision? Did the majority of the court get it right about the Second Amendment and the right of homeowners to protect themselves and their property?
5. Why does the United States not follow other industrialized countries and ban the purchase and ownership of guns?

Connections

The NRA is viewed by many as the most effective gun rights lobbying organization in the United States. Its site is at http://www.nra.org

The NRA is opposed in the gun debate by the Coalition to Stop Gun Violence. Its site is at http://www.csgv.org

The government agency charged with gun policy on the national level is the Bureau of Alcohol, Tobacco, Firearms and Explosives (ATF). Its site is at http://www.atf.gov

An organization that monitors gun laws and gun initiatives at the state and national levels is gunpolicy.org. Its site is http://www.gunpolicy.org

The Center for Gun Policy and Research is an independent think tank at Johns Hopkins University that concentrates on gun violence. Visit its site at http://www.jhsph .edu/gunpolicy

Some Books to Read

Feldman, Richard, *Ricochet: Confessions of a Gun Lobbyist* (New York: Wiley, 2007).

McClung, Andrew, Kopel, David and Denning, Brannon, *Gun Control and Gun Rights: A Reader and Guide* (New York: NYU Press, 2002).

Young, David, *The Founders' View on the Right to Bear Arms: A Definitive History of the Second Amendment* (Ontonagon, MI: Golden Oak Books, 2007).

LaPierre, Wayne, *Shooting Straight: Telling the Truth about Guns in America* (Washington, D.C.: Regnery Publishing, 2007).

Tushnet, Mark V., *Out of Range: Why the Constitution Can't End the Battle over Guns* (New York: Oxford University Press, 2007).

Notes

1. For background see the discussion of the Second Amendment at the website Findlaw, http://caselaw.lpfindlaw.com/data/constitution/amendment02
2. A historical guide to the early decisions related to the Second Amendment can be found at http://www.usconstitution.net/consttop_2nd.html. Also see federal court cases regarding the Second Amendment at the Second Amendment Foundation site http://www.saf.org/2ndAmendSupremeCourtTable.html
3. See the Brady Handgun Control Act 103–159, House of Representatives 1025, 103 Congress.
4. See Gun Law News for a discussion of the Firearm Owners Protection Act of 1986, http://www.guncite.com/journals/hard/fopa.html
5. *Printz v. United States* 117 S.CT. 2365 (1997).
6. See the NRA website, http://www.nra.org
7. See the Center for the Prevention of Gun Violence, http://www.bradycenter.org. On the issue of spending between the NRA and the Center for the Prevention of Gun Violence see the Center for Responsive Politics, http://www.opensecrets .org/news/issues/guns/lobbying.php

8. Gary Kleck, "What Are the Risks and the Benefits of Keeping Guns at Home," http://www.guncite.com/kleckjama01.html

9. Gary Hemenway, *Private Guns, Public Health* (Ann Arbor, MI: University of Michigan Press, 2006).

10. Arthur Kellerman, "Gun Ownership and the Risk Factors for Homicides at Home," *New England Journal of Medicine*, October 7, 1993.

11. Anita Kumar "Kaine to Push Background Checks at Gun Shows," *Washington Post*, January 9, 2008, B05.

12. For a discussion of the Massachusetts gun laws see http://www.bradycampaign .org/legislation/state/viewstate/php?st=ma

13. See http://guncite.com/gun_control_gcgvinco.html

14. See "Federal Court Cases Regarding the Second Amendment," National Rifle Association Institute for Legislative Action, http://www.nraila.org/Issues/ FactSheets/Read.aspx?ID=52

15. *Parker v. District of Columbia* 478D.3d 370 (D.C. CIR.2007).

16. Robert Barnes, "Justices Reject D.C. Ban on Handgun Ownership," *Washington Post*, June 27, 2008. The ruling can be found in *District of Columbia v. Heller* 07-290.

17. "Gun Ruling was Called a Landmark, But That Remains to be Seen," *New York Times*, March 17, 2009, A14.

18. See http://www.CNN.com/2007/US/12/16/guns.poll/index.html

19. Adam Liptak, "Justices Lean Toward Extending Gun Rights," *New York Times*, March 3, 2010, A1.

20. Ian Urbina, "Fearing Obama Agenda, States Push to Loosen Gun Laws," *New York Times*, February 10, 2010, A1.

21. "Exploding the NRA's Constitutional Myth," Brady Center to Prevent Gun Violence Legal Action Project, http://www.gunlawsuits.org/defend/second/ articles/exploding/php

12 GAY **RIGHTS**

Issue Focus

First there was the civil rights movement, then the women's movement and now in the 21st century, the gay rights movement. The gay and lesbian population has become one of the most visible groups seeking to advance their agenda in the American political arena. The key component of this agenda is recognition of gay marriage. Although a few states have recognized the legality of gay marriage, there is widespread opposition to allowing gay couples to obtain marriage licenses. Opposition to gay marriage is based on the view that such state-sanctioned unions are contrary to the western tradition of male-female marriage. However, just like civil rights and women's rights, gay rights is currently a battleground of opposing views on how far government should extend personal rights and legal guarantees.

Chapter Objectives
This issue chapter will seek to:
1. Describe the struggles of the gay and lesbian community to achieve equal rights in the United States.
2. Discuss the contentious issue of gay marriage, which is at the heart of the struggle for gay rights.
3. Examine the current political and legal status of gay rights and gay marriage in the United States.

SOME BACKGROUND

The push for gay rights and the subsequent battles over public policies that establish or extend gay rights is a relatively new issue area in American politics. Although the gay community has long been an active participant in the public arena seeking to break down the barriers of discrimination, only in the last forty years have individual leaders and organized groups pressured government at all levels to place their issues on the front burner of national priorities. Although only about 5% of Americans self-identify themselves as being gay, lesbian or bisexual, they have become a force in American politics. Gays have given generously to political campaigns, primarily on the Democratic side, and they have been determined in their activism to advocate for issues that they believe are essential to breaking down barriers of discrimination and hate.

However like most minorities in the United States who seek recognition and power and work to change the rules of society and politics, gays have encountered obstacles and stiff opposition. From religious groups to conservative organizations, the political agenda of the gay community has been challenged in large part over lifestyle issues and the push for equal marriage rights, which is seen as a threat to the traditional family and heterosexual relationships. Although the push and pull of gay rights in the United States is still in its formative stages, both sides in this struggle are seeking to define the moral and legal parameters of the debate, pointing out key policy differences and assessing the political impact of a divisive national issue.[1]

The issue of gay rights first entered the political arena not as a specific policy debate but as a result of the onset of HIV/AIDS in the United States. In the early 1980s, when the first signs of the disease were spotted, HIV/AIDS hit hard in the gay community as thousands of men died from this virus, which can break down the body's immune system and lead to a long, horrible illness that likely ends in death. From 1981 to 2005 over 1.5 million cases of HIV infection were reported in the United States and over 500,000 deaths occurred when the HIV virus led to the onset of AIDS. The AIDS epidemic politicized the gay community as the Reagan administration seemed unconcerned about the spread of the disease and its impact on homosexuals. Numerous protests were held in major cities and in Washington to press the Reagan administration to take action against the spread of AIDS. Furthermore, leaders of the gay community criticized the Food and Drug Administration (FDA) for not moving quickly enough to approve new drugs that in preliminary tests showed promise in arresting the advance of the AIDS virus in those who contracted the disease. Eventually, promising "cocktails" containing a range of pills that attacked the virus, entered the market and slowed the death rate from AIDS. However, for members of the gay community, the battle over HIV/AIDS drugs convinced them that they needed to be much more vocal and better organized to get the attention of government to fight what they viewed as discrimination against their sexual orientation.[2]

The Clinton administration thrust the gay issue into the forefront of the American issue arena, as one of the first acts of the new president was to issue a "Don't Ask, Don't Tell" policy regarding gays in the U.S. military. (Clinton was fulfilling a campaign pledge made to gays, who in return gave him overwhelming electoral support in the 1992 election.) In effect the presidential order required the military to not seek out or require public admission of the sexual preference of its soldiers, but rather to leave the matter private. The Clinton initiative on gays replaced the longstanding position of the military contained in military policy handbooks, which prohibits anyone who, "demonstrates a propensity or intent to engage in homosexual acts" from serving in the armed forces of the United States, because such behavior would "create an unacceptable risk to the high standards of morale, good order and discipline, and unit cohesion that are the essence of military capability." Despite opposition through the ranks of the military, the "Don't Ask, Don't Tell" policy of the Clinton administration did show that the new president was sympathetic to the concerns of the homosexual community and that sexual orientation should be considered a private matter and not be used as a guidepost for military enlistment or military evaluation purposes.[3]

Gays also gained a key victory in 1996 when the Supreme Court struck down an amendment to the Colorado state constitution that would have prevented gays from bringing civil suits charging discrimination in employment and housing. Conservative groups opposed to gay rights had pushed for the amendment and were successful in a state referendum that changed the state constitution. The Supreme Court, however, viewed the amendment as denying a class of people their rights as citizens to be treated equally and protected by the laws in a manner similar to other identifiable groups. The Colorado victory for gay rights was further enhanced in 2003 when the Court in a landmark case, *Lawrence v. Texas*, overturned a previous decision (*Bowers v. Hardwick*) that upheld Georgia statutes supporting sodomy laws that were clearly intended to punish gays who engaged in sexual activity, even in the privacy of their homes. In the *Lawrence* decision the Court stated that the Georgia law violated the fundamental right to privacy and set the stage for many states either ignoring sodomy laws or removing them from the statute books. The decision by the Court was a signal to states that sexual orientation should not be the subject of state regulation.[4]

The push for gay rights was not without its roadblocks or disappointments. In 1996 the Republican-dominated Congress passed the Defense of Marriage Act (DOMA), which defined marriage at the federal level as a union between a man and a woman and advised states to ignore or not recognize gay marriages performed in other states, even though at that time no states allowed gay marriages. Although many opponents of gay marriage saw DOMA as a powerful statement designed to weaken the position of gays, the legislation has often been overshadowed by state laws. Also, legal scholars have analyzed DOMA as requiring Supreme Court review to determine its constitutionality because it sought to deny the opportunity of gay married couples to invoke the Constitution's "full faith and credit clause" and insist on having their marriages valid in all fifty states.

Although gays did attain some key victories through the courts and in the Clinton administration, the gay rights movement suffered a setback in 2000 when the Supreme Court supported the policy of the Boy Scouts of America that prohibited gay men from becoming Boy Scout leaders. The Court sided with the Boy Scouts and stated that the tenets and philosophy of the group, which accented traditional sexual orientation, allowed them under First Amendment grants of free speech to foster a policy of exclusion of gays from leadership positions. The Boy Scout decision was vilified in the gay community as perpetuating the myth that gays would use their positions as group leaders to engage in homosexual acts and attempt to socialize young boys into the gay lifestyle.[5]

However, despite some setbacks in Congress and the courts, the gay rights movement gained an unprecedented court victory in 2003 when the Massachusetts Supreme Judicial Court narrowly voted to support gay marriage as a civil right based on its view that denying gays the right to marry was a violation of the equal protection and due process clauses in the Massachusetts constitution. Although the decision was hailed by the gay community and almost immediately led to hundreds of state-validated marriages, it was strenuously opposed throughout the United States by those who saw the decision as destroying the western tradition of male-female marriage and a further example of unwarranted judicial activism.[6] The Massachusetts decision quickly set into motion a wave of anti-gay-marriage groups and initiatives at state and federal levels designed to ensure that such decisions or legislative acts would not spread further. President George W. Bush, for example, initially pushed for an amendment to the Constitution barring gay marriage and defending traditional marriage; numerous states quickly passed laws banning gay marriage.[7]

Because of the Massachusetts Supreme Judicial Court decision validating gay marriage, the issue of gay rights in the United States has moved to the next level of intensity. For example, the California Supreme Court in 2008, in a narrow decision, supported the "right of gays to marry," once again setting off a political debate as opponents of same-sex marriage sought to influence a statewide referendum that would overturn the court's position.[8] In a highly contentious referendum process, California voters opposed to gay marriage defeated the proponents of the supreme court decision. In May 2009 the California Supreme Court upheld the referendum. Although both sides in the California gay marriage debate remain locked into their positions and are continuing the debate in the courts and in another likely referendum, other states such as Connecticut, Vermont, Iowa, Maine and New Hampshire have joined Massachusetts in approving gay marriage as a civil right. Advocates of gay marriage, however, faced new setbacks in New York and New Jersey, where the legislatures refused to advance bills that would sanction the right of gays to marry.[9]

Because the issue of gay rights encompasses the sexual orientation and relationships of a minority in a country where the vast majority of citizens are heterosexual and where the tradition of male-female marriage is considered the bedrock of western civilization, the attempt to eliminate discrimination, extend equality and revise traditions has created a passionate national debate and divided the country over fundamental differences. As additional states address the issue of gay marriage, battle lines will be drawn and intense debates are certain to push this contentious issue to the forefront of national politics.

On the Record

Chief Justice Margaret Marshall wrote the majority decision in the Massachusetts Supreme Judicial Court ruling (*Goodridge v. Department of Public Health*) that supported same-sex marriage. The core of her argument in defense of gay marriage is given here:

Marriage is a vital institution, the exclusive commitment of two individuals to each other, it nurtures love and mutual support, it brings stability to our society. For those who choose to marry and for their children, marriage provides an abundance of legal, financial and social benefits. In return it imposes weighty legal, financial and social obligations. The questions before us is whether, consistent with the Massachusetts constitution, the Commonwealth may deny the protections, benefits and obligations conferred by civil marriage to two individuals of the same sex who wish to marry. We conclude that it may not. The Massachusetts Constitution affirms the dignity and equality of all individuals. It forbids the creation of second class citizens. In reaching our conclusion we have given full deference to the argument made by the Commonwealth. But it has failed to identify any constitutionally adequate reason for denying civil marriage to same sex couples.

DEBATES, DIFFERENCES AND DIVISIONS

Although the gay rights movement is wide-ranging in scope and designed to eliminate all forms of discrimination against homosexuals, the gay marriage component of this movement has galvanized public opinion, fostered the formation of numerous interest groups representing the two sides in the debate and developed moral, social and religious arguments on both sides of the issue. There is no doubt that among the American public, opposition to same-sex marriage is substantial, but trending downward. A Pew Research Center poll in 2004 found that 63% of Americans were opposed to same-sex marriage; in 2006 the level of opposition declined to 51%, with nearly 40% supporting gay marriage. If the issue is viewed from a generational perspective, older Americans are clearly uneasy with gay marriage and form the largest bloc of the opponents, but younger Americans, those from the so-called millennial generation (people born between 1980 and 2000), have little concerns about gay marriage and provide the bulk of support.[10]

Although there may be signs of some softening of opposition to gay marriage, there is also growing support across the spectrum of age groups in the United States for civil unions as an alternative to marriage. A civil union is a legal arrangement that falls short of traditional marriage in which the relationship between two gay individuals is recognized by the state and provides a range of legal, financial and insurance protections for the couple. Many legal and gay rights experts believe that civil unions rather than gay marriage may be the short-term solution in the fight for homosexual rights in the area of sanctioning personal relationships, because civil unions are more palatable to a skeptical public. Many public officials have also climbed aboard the civil union bandwagon, knowing that the majority of their constituents are opposed to gay marriage. Civil unions, quite simply, are a safe compromise.

In the area of interest group activity related to same-sex marriage, both sides have highly aggressive organizations to lobby national and state legislatures and mobilize grassroots supporters. Human Rights Campaign is one of the most prominent gay rights groups involved in political activity. This group and its president Joe Solmonese have been especially active in fighting against the various ballot issues introduced in the states to ban same-sex marriage, and also President Bush's short-lived attempt to introduce a constitutional amendment, The Marriage Protection Amendment, that would have created a national ban on same-sex marriages. Although Solmonese was successful in quashing the constitutional amendment initiative, as it fell far short of the two-thirds support in both houses of Congress, he and his group were less successful in stopping state legislatures around the country from passing laws banning same-sex marriage.[11] Currently twenty-six states have constitutional amendments that bar the recognition of same-sex marriages and mandate that marriage is valid only when it is between a man and a woman.

The National Gay and Lesbian Task Force is also prominent in advancing gay rights. Founded in 1973, the Task Force is committed to enhancing "the grassroots power of the lesbian, gay, bisexual and transgender community." The Task Force trains its members to provide information and talking points to state and federal officials regarding legislation to protect and expand gay rights. The Task Force and its director Rea Carey have developed an aggressive lobbying effort at all levels of government, and its policy institute has been recognized as one of the few think tanks that is dedicated to providing accurate data and analysis regarding the gay community, including such issues as hate crimes, HIV/AIDS and discriminatory practices. The Task Force has championed the cause of gay marriage throughout the United States and worked on some of the more narrow issues related to gay marriage such as inheritance, health insurance and community property.[12]

Both the Human Rights Campaign and the National Gay and Lesbian Task Force have been active in pressing Congress to pass legislation that prohibits discrimination in the workplace and hate crime bills[13] that protect gays and other minorities from violent attacks. The Employment Non-Discrimination Act (ENDA) has been in the legislative pipeline since the late 1990s and targets discrimination based on sexual orientation. There has been insufficient support for the legislation, and as a result the bill has languished in committee. In the area of anti-hate legislation, the two groups have sought support for the Local Law Enforcement Hate Crimes Prevention Act. The legislation extends the definition of federal hate crimes in federal statues to include sexual orientation, gender identity and disability. The bill did receive a positive vote in the House of Representatives in 2005, but died in the Senate. In 2009 with the Obama administration lending support, the bill was reintroduced and renamed after Matthew Shepard, a young man in Wyoming who was beaten to death because of his sexual orientation. The bill passed with strong congressional support and was signed by President Obama in October 2009.[14] The slow movement and limited success of including gender orientation along with anti-discrimination and hate crimes in legislation shows the difficulty of advancing the political agenda of homosexuals within the American governing system.[15]

A number of activist groups oppose same-sex marriage, and many of them are linked to the evangelical movement with its accent on family values and marriage between a man and a woman. The most prominent of these groups are the Alliance for Marriage, American Values, the Family Research Council and Focus on the Family. The official position of the Alliance for Marriage is that "the benefits of marriage for husbands, wives and children derive from the fact that marriage unites the two haves of the human race to share in raising children." The president of Alliance for Marriage, Matt Daniel, worked closely with the Bush White House on the Marriage Protection Amendment and has been an outspoken critic of gay marriage, citing its negative impact on the traditional family and social stability.[16] American Values, headed by Gary Bauer, a long-time conservative leader, is an organization that advocates not just for marriage between a man and a woman but also opposes abortion, stem cell research and euthanasia.[17] The Family Research Council, led by Tony Perkins, a frequent advisor to President Bush on matters of faith and family, has strong ties to the evangelical movement. It states that it "champions marriage and family as foundations of civilization, the seedbed of virtue and the wellspring of society" and believes that "Government has the duty to promote and protect marriage and family in law and public policy."[18] Finally, James Dobson's Focus on the Family is perhaps the most visible and well-known group opposed to same-sex marriage. Dobson has a frequent media presence, and many conservatives and evangelicals believe he has taken over as the voice of Christian right after the death of Reverend Jerry Falwell.[19]

Organized religion also plays a role in the mix of groups that are on either side of the debate regarding same-sex marriage. The Catholic

Data Bank

At present five nations provide full legal recognition for same-sex marriages–Belgium, Canada, Netherlands, South Africa and Spain– whereas sixteen other countries, primarily in Europe, have followed the path of civil unions and what has come to be called registered partnerships.

Church, in particular, has taken a very strong position against gay marriage, and in many dioceses across the country, bishops and other church leaders have sought to use the pulpit to encourage their faithful to write state and federal officials in hopes of heading off any future legislation that would endorse or permit same-sex marriage. In Massachusetts, after the court decision permitting same-sex marriage, the Catholic Church was very aggressive in pushing for a constitutional amendment that would limit marriage to a union between a man and a woman. In one of the most contentious debates in Massachusetts legislative history, the opponents of same-sex marriage, with considerable support from the Catholic Church (church property was used to gather signatures for the initiative petition and to hold organization meetings), were nearly successful in getting a referendum question on the ballot that would have ended same-sex marriage. After two attempts, the opponents of same-sex marriage failed to get the initiative petition on the ballot.[20]

The evangelical churches, primarily in the South, Midwest and West, were equally active in the same-sex marriage debate. The Southern Baptist Convention, the largest organized evangelical church, along with many of the pastors of mega-churches run by well-known television preachers such as Pat Robertson and Franklin Graham, took firm stances against gay marriage and used their extensive media, Internet and fund-raising entities to drum up support for legislation that would ban any form of same-sex marriage in various states. The considerable influence of the evangelical ministers was further enhanced when many African-American religious leaders also came forward in opposition to gay marriage, despite the pleadings of gay rights leaders that their fight was no different than that of blacks during the civil rights era. African-American ministers rejected this idea and held firm to their biblical beliefs that gay relations and gay marriage violated the words and the intent of the Bible.[21] The Protestant ministries that supported gay marriage such as the Anglican Church experienced deep fissures in their religious communities. The appointment of a gay minister as bishop of the Anglican Church in the United States caused a major rift and forced some members of the church to break away and seek to form a new more conservative Anglican Church with ties to Africa and African bishops.

FYI

Many within the gay community state that their politicization began in 1969 in New York City when a riot broke out at a bar frequented by homosexual men who were reacting to constant harassment from police officers. Today the FBI regularly collects data and monitors hate crimes against minorities, including gays, on a yearly basis. The 2006 figures for hate crimes against members of the gay community are given here:

Incidents, Offenses, Victims and Known Offenses (by bias motivation, 2006)

	Incidents	Offenses	Victims	Known Offenses
Anti-male homosexual	747	881	913	914
Anti-female homosexual	163	192	202	154
Anti-homosexual	238	293	307	268
Anti-bisexual	21	21	21	18

Note: – Many in the gay community challenge the FBI hate crimes data, stating that in their view a large number of hate crimes against gays go unreported or underreported. Many gays feel that if they did report the crimes, police would not act on the accusations.

Every issue in American politics is accompanied by passion, intensity and activism. The movement for gay rights, and in particular same-sex marriage, however, has generated more passion, intensity and activism than many of the other issues in the political arena. Because gays are a small minority of the population and live a lifestyle that is not part of the mainstream, they face not just the expected obstacles that all minorities have encountered in the Unites States in their struggle for rights and acceptance, but also enormous legal roadblocks and deep-seated public antagonism that makes their struggle of Herculean proportions. It is thus not an exaggeration to state that the gay rights movement in the United States will have to endure many more years of struggle and disappointment before it reaches its goals.[22]

As evidence of the difficulty gays faced in gaining what they consider their complete equality, the Obama administration was roundly criticized by the leaders in the movement who were disappointed at the slow pace of change under a president that they considered to be a staunch advocate. Although Obama did sign a memorandum in June 2009 that extended benefits related to visitation and dependent care rights to all federal employees who are gay, he refused to move forward with ending the "Don't Ask, Don't Tell" policy in the military and was slow to move forward with lobbying efforts to repeal the DOMA. John Aravolis, a Washington-based lobbyist for gay rights, summed up the frustration of gays about the Obama administration's efforts to advance their cause when he stated, "When a president tells you he's going to be different, you believe him. It's not that he didn't follow through on his promises, he stabbed us in the back."[23]

As a result of pressure from the gay community and also changes in public perceptions of gays in the military, the Obama administration lobbied the Pentagon to review its policy of "Don't Ask, Don't Tell." In February 2010, speaking before a congressional committee, Secretary of Defense Robert Gates and Joint Chiefs of Staff Admiral Mike Mullen pledged to end the sixteen-year policy of "Don't Ask, Don't Tell." At the hearing Admiral Mullen stated, "No matter how I look at the issue, I cannot escape being troubled by the fact that we have in place a policy that forces young men and women to lie about who they are in order to defend their fellow citizens."[24]

The movement for gay rights and specifically same-sex marriage runs up against some of the most basic bedrocks of our society and indeed western civilization. Although there is no doubt that homosexuality has always been part of our society and is not a behavioral abnormality (as some claim) that can be cured, the fact that gays are seeking societal acceptance and demanding equal rights challenges the views of many Americans who either do not understand homosexuality or are comfortable with their prejudices against homosexuals. The sight of gays showing public affection or seeking to make a longstanding relationship legal is difficult for many Americans to accept, especially when they have been acculturated in a lifestyle and marriage compact that has always been based on one man and one woman.

However, as advocates of gay rights and same-sex marriage often emphasize, the movement to expand and guarantee homosexual rights in the United States is no different than the civil rights movement. Southerners had been acculturated in a social environment that viewed African-Americans as holding a lesser station in life and thus could be treated differently. Many in the South certainly showed overt prejudice and an unwillingness to embrace a new way of thinking about African-Americans and a new way of integrating them fully into society. But a combination of time, generational change, activist pressure, the intervention by the federal government, the leadership of many enlightened Southerners and the eventual recognition of most in the South that they had treated African-Americans unjustly brought numerous advances in civil rights and a string of laws that tore down the walls of segregation and discrimination.

The advocates of gay rights are hoping that the combination that brought change to the South will turn the tide in favor of accepting homosexuals fully into American society and providing them with the equal rights they have been denied. However, just like the civil rights movement, change will not come quickly or without setbacks or conflict. Those in the minority in the United States have always had to struggle to make the political system recognize their needs and rights. Gays in the United States are fully cognizant of the civil rights model with all its challenges and eventual successes. However, gays also realize that their movement is relatively new and is facing stiff opposition. The question thus becomes, how long will gays be willing to wait to achieve what they feel are their rights and will those who oppose gay rights be willing to change their positions and accept homosexuals fully into American society?

The Great Debate

The gay marriage debate is often framed around the issue of state courts ignoring the wishes of the people in referendums or public opinion polls, while supporting the right of gays to marry.

Debate Topic

Is gay marriage a right that should be sanctioned by the state even though a majority of citizens are opposed?

Critical Thinking Questions

1. Does a state-sanctioned gay marriage weaken the western tradition of man-woman marriage?
2. Is a civil union rather than marriage an acceptable compromise to ensure gay couples their economic and social rights?

3. Should states that have passed anti-gay marriage laws recognize the marriages of gay couples in states that permit gay marriage?
4. How do you account for the generation gap in support of gay marriage, with older Americans having larger percentages of opposition compared to younger Americans?
5. Do you believe gay marriage will be permitted in the future throughout the United States?

Connections

One of the more prominent advocates for gay rights is the Gay & Lesbian Alliance Against Discrimination. Visit its site at http://www.glaad.org

The most visible gay rights organization is the National Gay and Lesbian Task Force. See its site at http://www.thetaskforce.org

The status of gay marriage laws can be accessed at http://www.stateline.org

A useful site to examine recent developments on the gay rights issue is http://gayrights.org

The most visible anti-gay marriage organization is the National Organization for Marriage. Their website is at www.nationformarriage.org

Some Books to Read

Rimmerman, Craig, *The Lesbian and Gay Movements: Assimilation or Liberation* (Boulder, CO: Westview Press, 2007).

Richards, Lawrence, *The Case for Gay Rights: From Bowers to Lawrence and Beyond* (Lawrence, KA: University of Kansas Press, 2005).

Wolfson, Evan, *Why Marriage Matters: America, Equality and Gay People's Right to Marry* (New York: Simon & Schuster, 2005).

Smith, Miriam, *Political Institutions and Lesbian and Gay Rights in the United States and Canada* (New York: Routledge, 2008).

Gerstmann, Evan, *Same-Sex Marriage and the Constitution* (New York: Cambridge University Press, 2009).

Notes

1. For the history of the gay rights movement see Vern Bullough, ed. *Before Stonewall: Activists for Gay and Lesbian Rights in Historical Context* (New York: Harrington Press, 2002). See also Diane Helene Miller, *Freedom to Differ: The Shaping of the Gay and Lesbian Struggle for Civil Rights* (New York: NYU Press, 1998).
2. See Robin Toner and Robert Pear, "A Reagan Legacy Tainted by AIDS, Civil Rights and Union Policies," *New York Times*, June 9, 2004.

3. For a comprehensive discussion of the Don't Ask, Don't Tell policy see the database project from Stanford Law School, http://www.dont.stanford.edu

4. *Lawrence v. Texas*, 539 U.S. 588 (2003). The DOMA legislation is monitored and analyzed at http://www.domawatch.org/index.php

5. *Boy Scouts of America, et al. v. Dale* 530 U.S. 640 (2000).

6. *Goodridge v. Department of Health* 798 N.E. 2nd 941 (MASS 2003).

7. Laura Dolan, "California Overturns Gay Marriage Law," *Los Angeles Times*, May 16, 2008, http://www.latimes.com/news/local/la-me-gaymarriage16,0,6182317.story

8. Jesse McKinley, "Marriage Ban Inspires New Wave of Gay Rights Activists," *New York Times*, December 10, 2008, A22.

9. See for example, Jeremy Peters, "New York Senate Turns Back Bill on Gay Marriage," *New York Times*, December 3, 2009, A1.

10. Cited in a Pew public opinion poll. See "Less Opposition to Gay Marriage, Adoption and Military Service," http://people-press.org/report/273/less-opposition-to-gay-marriage-adoption-and-militaryservice

11. See the Human Rights Campaign website, http://www.hrc.org

12. See the National Gay and Lesbian Task Force website, http://www.taskforce.org

13. The American Civil Liberties Union monitors the ENDA. See http://www.aclu.org/lgbt/discrim/29544res20070424.html

14. Matthew Shepard and James Byrd Jr. Hate Crimes Prevention Act" at the Human Rights Campaign website. http://www.hrc.org/issues/5660.htm

15. See the Civil Rights Coalition for the 21st Century at http://www.civilrights.org/issues/hate

16. See the Alliance for Marriage website at http://www.allianceformarriage.org

17. See the American Values website at http://www.americanvalues.org

18. See the Family Research Council website at http://www.frc.org

19. See the Focus on the Family website at http://www.focusonthefamily.com

20. See Kristen Lombardi, "The Catholic War Against Gay Marriage," *The Boston Phoenix*, March 26-April 1, 2004, http://www.thebostonphoenix.com/boston/news_features/top/features/documents/03702314.asp

21. See Michael Paulson, "Black Clergy Rejection Stirs Gay Marriage Backers," *Boston Globe*, February 10, 2004, http://www.boston.com/news/local/articles/2004/02/10/black_clergy_rejection_stirs_gay_marriage_backers/

22. For the most recent update on the same-sex marriage in the United States, see David Cole, "The Same-Sex Future," *New York Review of Books*, July 2, 2009, pp. 12–16.

23. Philip Elliott, "Same-sex Activists Angry at Obama," *Boston Globe*, June 18, 2009, A6.

24. See Elizabeth Bumiller, "Top Defense Officials Seek to End 'Don't Ask, Don't Tell,' " *New York Times*, February 2, 2010, A1.

13 CAPITAL **PUNISHMENT**

Issue Focus

The issue of capital punishment in the United States is undergoing a thorough review. After over thirty-five years of state-sanctioned executions, a number of states have declared moratoriums on the use of capital punishment or have been content to let court proceedings drag on, thus delaying the imposition of the death penalty. The decline in capital punishment is the result of new DNA testing that has proven some on death row as innocent, questions regarding racial discrimination and misidentification, and lax legal representation of accused criminals. Together these concerns have raised the question as to whether innocent individuals may have been put to death. Americans, however, continue to support capital punishment as the ultimate verdict for those who have committed heinous crimes.

Chapter Objectives
This chapter will seek to:
1. Chronicle the recent history of capital punishment in the United States and the extent of the use of the death penalty by the states.
2. Present the points of contention between the proponents and opponents of capital punishment, particularly associated with moral, deterrence and racial issues.
3. Describe the current status of capital punishment in light of new scientific advances in DNA detection and legal challenges based on questions of due process of the law.

SOME BACKGROUND

Just as the Second Amendment has posed a challenge for interpretation and application, so too has the Eighth Amendment, which prohibits "cruel and unusual punishment." The interpretation of exactly what is meant by "cruel and unusual punishment" has served as the basis for the ongoing debate over the issue of capital punishment. At issue with capital punishment is the question of whether the state has the constitutional right (and also the moral right) to take the life of an individual who has been convicted in a court of law of a capital crime (such as various categories or legally defined degrees of murder). Because the writers of the Bill of Rights did not specify what types of punishments were appropriate in capital cases, or for that manner in any criminal case, it is the responsibility of the courts to infer meaning to the words cruel and unusual punishment.

The Eighth Amendment, which also bans excessive bail for prisoners, was included in the Bill of Rights as a response to the harsh treatment of prisoners under British rule both in the colonies and England. But once the British were defeated and the Bill of Rights was enacted, states did not shy away from using a wide array of punishments for capital crimes, including hanging and execution by firing squad. The use of capital punishment was widespread in the United States well into the 20th century. Between 1930 and 1968, 3,859 people were executed in the country. But after World War II, the number of executions decreased markedly. By the 1960s there was a significant decline in executions as state legislatures banned various procedures, governors commuted death sentences to life in prison without parole or courts intervened to stay executions.[1]

In 1967 Luis Monge was the last individual to die (in the gas chamber) in Colorado before the issue of capital punishment entered the federal court system and a series of test cases were brought challenging capital punishment as violating the Eighth Amendment ban on cruel and unusual punishment. Opponents to capital punishment, such as the Legal Defense Fund, the National Association of Colored People (NAACP) and the American Civil Liberties Union (ACLU), argued that state laws were not only a violation of the Eighth Amendment but were biased against African-Americans in violation of the Fourteenth Amendment guarantee of "equal protection of the laws." State governments, especially from southern and western states, responded that they had the right to impose capital punishment and were responding to overwhelming support from voters in referenda.

The Supreme Court took both of these positions into consideration in 1972 in *Furman v. Georgia*, as it examined whether Georgia's capital punishment law was in violation of the Eighth Amendment. The case involved the use in Georgia of a "unitary trial" in which the jurors not only found the individual charged with a capital crime guilty or innocent, but also decided on the form of punishment, if that individual was found guilty. In a 5-4 decision the justices revealed that they could not arrive at a consensus on capital punishment, although they did agree that the Georgia law was vague in defining what crimes were deserving of capital punishment and that the unitary trial procedure leading to a decision on the death penalty was "arbitrary and capricious."[2]

Although the *Furman* decision led to four years (1972–1976) when no individual was executed, thirty-eight states went back to the legislative drawing board and produced new laws that they felt would be approved in future test cases by the Supreme Court. These laws included more specific language on the crimes worthy of capital punishment, and created a bifurcated sentencing system in which jurors were asked to decide on guilt and innocence in one trial and then at a second trial determine whether execution was indeed appropriate. In 1976 in *Gregg v. Georgia* the Supreme Court upheld the new Georgia law and those that followed similar procedures, thereby opening up the floodgates of executions in the United States. From 1976 to 2007 there were 1,099 executions in the United States, with the state of Texas leading the way with 405 executions through 2007.[3]

Although a significant majority of Americans support capital punishment—a 2005 Gallup poll found that 74% of the respondents supported the death penalty for murder—at present state lawmakers are reevaluating their laws and execution practices. A number of states have moratoriums on executions, and some states, such as Illinois, have commuted death sentences to life in prison without parole. Also in 2007, the New Jersey state legislature banned outright the use of capital punishment. A combination of factors has generated this review of capital punishment, including the more prominent use of DNA analysis, which has proven that some convicted criminals (including some on death row) were unjustly imprisoned, the increasing scrutiny of the manner in which defense lawyers have represented individuals charged with capital crimes, especially poor blacks and Hispanics, and the effectiveness of lethal injection as a painless form of execution. State officials are now more cautious about executing individuals as capital punishment groups have called attention to the problems associated with the death penalty and the real possibility that innocent individuals either have been executed or are awaiting execution.[4] In 2008 the number of executions in the United States dropped to 37, the lowest number since 1994, and a total of 111 death sentences were handed down, the lowest since 1976.[5]

Just as the issue of capital punishment is under review, so too are the arguments that have been used to either support the death penalty or work for its end. In many respects the issue of capital punishment is at a crossroads, in much the same way it was during the time after the *Furman* case and before the *Gregg* decision. Government officials at all levels are taking a hard look at capital punishment to determine whether this ultimate sanction against a criminal convicted of a capital offense is not only unconstitutional but also seriously flawed. Because public opinion remains supportive of capital punishment and many Americans do not see the death penalty as cruel and unusual punishment, this issue will remain hotly contested in the coming years even though doubts about the accuracy and fairness of its application are mounting.

On the Record

Former Governor of Illinois George Ryan, in one of his last acts as governor, commuted the sentences of death-row prisoners to life in prison without parole. Ryan's change of position on the death penalty was heavily influenced by the fact that between 1997 and 2000 thirteen death-row inmates were found innocent of the charges against them. Upon making the decision to commute the sentences, Governor Ryan said the following:

> I cannot support a system, which in its administration, has proven so fraught with error and has come so close to the ultimate nightmare, the state's taking of an innocent life.

Source: "The Moratorium Gambit," *New York Times Magazine*, December 9, 2001, 82

DEBATES, DIFFERENCES AND DIVISIONS

The arguments that have been made for and against capital punishment reveal the complexity of the issue and also the intense emotions that are associated with the state sanctioning the execution of a convicted murderer. The debates that have formed around the issue of capital punishment in large part involve moral concerns, the deterrent effect, racial and class bias, comparison with other nations and cost efficiency. Within each of these issues, there are vast differences of opinion, as proponents of capital punishment, especially the family members of a murder victim, approach the execution of the convicted criminal as bringing closure to a traumatic event, whereas opponents see capital punishment as simply revenge akin to the biblical eye-for-an-eye viewpoint that lessens the value of life and in the end allows for no chance of rehabilitation or redemption.

The moral debate surrounding the death penalty is often framed as an issue of whether the state should have the right to take a life and whether that act is indeed cruel and unusual punishment. The questions raised when a murder is committed and the murderer is convicted are what is the proper punishment and does the punishment fit the crime. Proponents see capital punishment as removing a violent killer from society's midst and achieving a form of justice that indeed is moral and proper in a civilized culture. They believe that society must retaliate with the highest form of sanction to show the gravity of the crime and the revulsion that law-abiding citizens have for such heinous acts. On the other side of the argument is the view that capital punishment brings society down to the level of the killer and cheapens life by engaging in an execution that is in itself murder and makes the state an enabler of death. Both moral arguments have merit as one talks about the importance of justice and society registering its abhorrence for murder, whereas the other places emphasis on the inalienable right to life and the importance of society not being a party to murder.[6]

The concern over wrongful death is also associated with other cogent arguments. Opponents of the death penalty point to data that show from 1973 to 2005, 123 convicted murderers in 25 states were released from death row as a result of new evidence that proved their innocence. Furthermore, a study done in 2000 found that in more than two-thirds of 4,500 capital cases, the sentences were overturned.[7] In some of these cases the new evidence is DNA related; this use of new scientific procedures has proven with certainty that the blood or other bodily fluids from the convicted individual did not match evidence brought into testimony during the trial. There is also evidence of individuals being freed from death row as new witnesses come forward or others recant their testimony. Finally, there have been numerous cases of mistaken identity, especially in cases involving African-Americans, in which witnesses, who were often white, have failed to recognize differences in appearances of black men and have given testimony that years later was proven incorrect. All these examples bring doubt into the matter of whether even one instance of wrongful death is enough of an argument to stop the death penalty.

There is also evidence that the American people are beginning to recognize that innocent individuals have been executed. A Gallup poll taken in 2000 showed that the number of Americans who believe that innocent people have been executed was 91%, an increase from 82% in 1995. Opponents of the death penalty are hoping that the combination of DNA-related cases in which individuals have been released from death row and the increasing level of doubt among Americans about wrongful death may be the moral spur to end capital punishment in the United States.[8]

Although the moral, scientific and procedural arguments often drive the capital punishment debate and galvanize emotions on both sides, the issue of whether the death penalty serves as a deterrent to capital crimes has received the most attention from experts. The deterrence argument is based on the premise that the threat of execution will serve as the most effective means of stopping capital crimes. However, although there is a commonsense component to this premise, criminologists and other social science researchers have been unable to agree whether state-sanctioned executions impact the incidence of capital crimes. Studies have failed to show that states with capital punishment laws have a lower rate of homicide than those without such laws. Some studies do show a slight reduction, but no research has been able to prove a direct link between capital punishment and a consistent and comprehensive decline in the homicide rate. Recently, however, a number of new studies have been performed by various groups of economists on the deterrent effect of capital punishment with findings that support the connection between the death penalty and a reduction in homicides. The studies showed that in Texas, for example, where the rate of punishment for capital crimes is high, independent researchers found that the use of the death penalty may have prevented from three to eighteen murders per year.[9]

Opponents of linking capital punishment to deterrence cite the fact that most homicides occur as crimes of passion and are not pre-meditated acts. Therefore murderers do not consider, nor are they influenced by the death penalty as they kill in a jealous rage or act out some deep-seated hatred. Also opponents of the death penalty rely on those scholars who question the research linking deterrence and a drop in the capital crime rate. Despite the new findings, mentioned earlier, supporting the position that capital punishment may indeed deter homicides, critics such as John Donohue III, a law professor at Yale University, question these findings, stating because the death penalty, "is applied so rarely that the number of homicides it can plausibly have caused or deterred cannot reliably be disentangled from the large year to year changes in the homicide rate caused by other factors."[10]

A further issue associated with capital punishment is that fact that convicted criminals who are on death row work the judicial system to delay their executions, thus counteracting the deterrent effect of swift punishment. Proponents of the death penalty state that the regular stays of execution and delays while the courts examine new evidence or challenges to the original conviction only weaken the deterrent impact of capital punishment. Those in favor of capital punishment believe that the deterrent effect would be much more visible if the process of implementing the death sentence moved quickly after the conviction and those on death row were permitted only one challenge to the decision of the courts. At present, most death sentence cases take at minimum about ten years before the execution of the convicted criminal is carried out, meaning that the number of criminals awaiting execution continues to expand. A study by the Urban Institute found that in Maryland, implementing the death penalty after years of judicial challenges cost the state $186 million from 1878 to 1999, an average of $3 million per case. Other states such as Colorado and Kansas, which are debating ending capital punishment, anticipate considerable savings from the almost endless judicial challenges and delays and recommend shifting the money related to death penalty enforcement to other forms of crime prevention.[11]

In 2007 the average wait on death row was 17.2 years; thirty people were awaiting execution for over twenty-five years. As a result of this backlog of cases, a federal appeals judge in California sparked controversy when he called for more resources to hire defense lawyers to deal with the death penalty cases speed up the appeal process to ensure that execution orders were carried out with greater speed. In California and other states that have capital punishment laws, governmental leaders who are opposed to the death penalty have fostered a system that makes the likelihood of executions slim as court delays are tolerated and funding to hire personnel to break the logjam of cases is never approved.

TABLE 13.1   State-by-State Status of Capital Punishment

States where the death sentence has been carried out between 1976 and 2007

Alabama	Illinois	Nebraska	South Carolina
Arizona	Indiana	Nevada	Tennessee
Arkansas	Kentucky	North Carolina	Texas
California	Louisiana	Ohio	Utah
Colorado	Montana	Oklahoma	Virginia
Georgia	Mississippi	Oregon	Washington
Florida	Missouri	Pennsylvania	Wyoming
Idaho			

States where there is a death sentence but no executions have occurred between 1976 and 2007

Connecticut	Kansas	New Mexico	North Dakota
Delaware	New Hampshire	New York	South Dakota

States where the death penalty is now illegal

Alaska	Massachusetts	Minnesota	Vermont
Hawaii	Maine	New Jersey	West Virginia
Iowa	Michigan	Rhode Island	Wisconsin

The most highly charged aspect of the capital punishment debate involves the fact that a large percentage of those on death row or already executed are African-American males. The most recent data on the racial makeup of those on death row or already executed show that African-American males made up 42% of death-row inmates and 34% of those executed since 1976. Other studies have shown that although race may be a factor, socio-economic class must also be considered as the poor, whether white or black, do not have the financial resources to hire the best lawyers and thus must rely on public defenders. Critics of the capital punishment laws in the various states point to evidence that public defense lawyers have shown a consistent failure to adequately represent their indigent clients. Without proper investigative resources and with huge case-load demands, many public defenders do not have the capability to mount the kind of defense a wealthier, usually white, defendant can present.[12]

The ACLU, which often represents individuals facing the death penalty, has for years pointed to the connection between faulty defense representation and the prospect of the accused facing capital punishment. As the ACLU states in its position paper on capital punishment, "the quality of legal representation (in the USA) is a better predictor of whether or not someone will be sentenced to death than the facts of the crime." Although the ACLU was referring to the problems of defense representation for all those convicted of a capital offense, it has been especially concerned about the fate of African-Americans who often rely on public defenders.[13] In 1987 the Supreme Court took up the case of *McCleskey v. Kemp* in which the issue of race and the death penalty was presented. Opponents of the death penalty showed that blacks received the death penalty more than whites, but in a 5-4 decision Court was not convinced that racial bias was a factor in applying the death penalty to capital cases.[14]

Data Bank

According to Amnesty International, a human rights organization that monitors capital punishment laws as part of its mission to end what it considers official abuses of basic human rights, seventy-seven countries impose the death penalty for capital crimes, and those countries are mostly in the Middle East, Africa and Asia. The United States and Japan are the only industrialized countries that retain capital punishment, although Japan's use of the death penalty is markedly less than that of the United States. In the last thirty years, over 118 countries have abolished capital punishment. The most recent countries to do away with capital punishment are the Philippines in 2006, Armenia in 2003 and Cyrus in 2002. Of the seventy-seven countries that retain the death penalty, twenty-three have not carried out executions in over ten years; these countries include the Russian Federation, Sri Lanka and Tunisia.

The most recent aspect of the capital punishment debate is associated with the constitutionality of lethal injection. Since 1978 each of the states that permit capital punishment has employed lethal injection as a means of execution. The so-called three-drug cocktail used by prison officials to carry out the death penalty order, however, came under intense scrutiny in 2007 as there was evidence that the procedure is not a painless way to end the life of a convicted murderer but rather it masks the pain the individual experiences before death. As death penalty consultant Lisa McCalmont of the University of California at Berkeley Law School stated, condemned inmates are, "alive all the way through the process, feeling pain until the bitter end." Prison officials around the country disputed the allegations that lethal injections caused pain before death sets in and charged that challenging the procedure as a violation of the Eighth Amendment prohibition against cruel and unusual punishment was just the latest attempt to end capital punishment in the United States.[15]

Despite the position of officials in the states that the use lethal injection is humane and does not violate the principles of the Eighth Amendment, the Supreme Court entered the controversy by stopping execution by lethal injection of convicted killers in Kentucky, Nevada and Virginia. Other states on their own stopped executions using lethal injection until the Supreme Court issued a decision on the constitutionality of lethal injection in a case in Kentucky (*Baze v. Rees*). This temporary moratorium on lethal injections was viewed by opponents of capital punishment as a breakthrough in ending the practice, but state officials and proponents of capital punishment saw this delay only as a temporary setback. In April 2008 the Supreme Court in a 7-2 decision upheld the three-drug protocol used in lethal injection.[16]

FYI

When an inmate is lethally injected, he or she is strapped to a gurney and given a three-step chemical cocktail. First, sodium thiopental, a barbiturate, is administered, which makes the inmate unconscious. Then pancuronium bromide is injected, which stops breathing and causes paralysis. Lastly, potassium chloride is added, which induces cardiac arrest and death. The injection of pancuronium bromide has caused the issue as opponents of the death penalty state that in a number of executions the drug masks pain the inmate endures. As an alternative to the current cocktail, prison officials are considering using barbiturates to depress the nervous system, followed by certain inhalant anesthetics to terminate breathing and create cardiac arrest. Prison officials think that taking the pancuronium bromide out of the cocktail will do away with the pain that may occur during the execution process.

Despite the Supreme Court's support for lethal injection, the issue of capital punishment continues to have opponents and supporters. New Jersey banned capital punishment completely and replaced it with life in prison without parole. With the new law, New Jersey became the first state in forty years to reject capital punishment. Governor Jon Corzine, in signing the law stated, "this is a day of progress for us and for the millions of people across our nation and around the globe who reject the death penalty as a moral or practical response to the grievous, even heinous, crime of murder." New Jersey's decision took eight individuals off death row and commuted their sentences. However, the decision was not without outcries from the families of murder victims. Marilyn Flax, whose husband was murdered in 1989 by death row inmate John Martini, stated, "I will never forget how I've been abused by a state and a governor that was supposed to protect the innocent and enforce the laws." Also Richard Kanka, whose daughter Megan was raped and murdered and was the driving force behind Megan's Law that requires law enforcement agencies to notify the public about the presence of convicted sex offenders in local communities, said that Corzine's signing of the law was "Just another slap in the face to the victims."[17]

There is no doubt that the debate over capital punishment is beginning to be muddled again as it was during the 1970s as the courts re-examine lethal injection, states such as New Jersey ban the death penalty and polls start to show some signs of questioning whether innocent individuals have been executed. However, it is important to point out that the number of Americans who remain supportive of capital punishment continues to be in the 70% range. Some hold to the eye-for-an-eye biblical position wherein capital punishment is seen as a matter of simple justice, others are convinced that the death penalty is a deterrent to future crimes whereas still others, especially the families of victims, see executions as a form of closure. As with the support for gun rights, many Americans continue to believe that capital punishment is what the founding fathers intended and that it is a policy that should not be tinkered with, much less abandoned.

Because capital punishment laws are centered in the states and changes in the laws will come from state action, the decision of the Supreme Court on lethal injection or any other future challenge to the death penalty will likely spur states to make adjustments to their procedures or legal processes that lead to an execution. However, although capital punishment laws and policies are being re-examined, convicted murderers on death row will seek to use the legal system to delay their executions and state officials and the supportive courts will seek to speed up the time between conviction and execution. As these maneuvers continue, the proponents and opponents of capital punishment will push forward with their lobbying efforts and court challenges, all in an effort to define more precisely what cruel and unusual punishment means and how it should be applied in 21st century America.[18]

The Great Debate

Supporters of capital punishment often point to the killing of children by sex offenders, the murder of police officers, heinous executions and serial killings as examples in which capital punishment should be permitted.

Debate Topic

Under what circumstances, if any, should capital punishment be permitted by the states?

Critical Thinking Questions

1. Is the death penalty inherently immoral?
2. Is lethal injection a more humane form of capital punishment?
3. Should the punishment for a capital crime be life in prison without parole rather than some form of life-ending punishment?
4. Substantial data show that African-Americans are not properly defended in murder trials and thus are more likely to be found guilty of a capital crime. Is this a key argument against capital punishment?
5. Do you believe that capital punishment will eventually be stopped by most states?

Connections

For accurate and timely data on capital punishment see the U.S. Department of Justice— Bureau of Justice Statistics at http://www.ojp.usdoj.gov/bjs/cp.htm

The leading organization supporting the death penalty is Pro-Death Penalty; its website is at http://www.prodeathpenalty.com/

The foremost critic of capital punishment is the ACLU. Its position on capital punishment can be seen at http://www.aclu.org/capital/general/35665res20080530.html

An outspoken critic of capital punishment is Human Rights Watch. See its position at http://www.hrw.org/campaigns/deathpenalty

For the most accurate account of individual deaths through capital punishment in the United States see the site of the Death Penalty Information Center, http://www.deathpenaltyinfo.org/article.pjp?did=1666

Some Books to Read

Villa, Bryan, *Capital Punishment in the United States: A Documentary History* (Westport, CT: Greenwood Press, 1997).

Palmer, Louis J. Jr. *Encyclopedia of Capital Punishment in the United States* (Jefferson, NC: McFarland & Company, 2001).

Harrison, Maureen and Steve Gilbert, eds. *Death Penalty Decisions of the Supreme Court* (New York: Excellent Books, 2003).

Sarat, Austin, *When the State Kills: Capital Punishment and the American Condition* (Princeton, NJ: Princeton University Press, 2002).

Prejean, Helen, *Dead Man Walking, an Eyewitness Account of the Death Penalty in the United States* (New York: Vintage, 1994).

Notes

1. For background and historical data see the Death Penalty Information Center, http://www.deathpenaltyinfo.org/article.php?did=1666.
2. *Furman v. Georgia* 408 U.S. 238 (1972).
3. Death Penalty Information Center, op.cit.
4. See Frank R. Baumgartner, Suzanna L. DeBoef and Amber E. Boydstun, *The Decline of the Death Penalty and the Discovery of Innocence* (New York: Cambridge University Press, 2008).
5. Carol Williams, "Capital Punishment Continues Decline in the U.S.," *Boston Globe*, January 2, 2009, A2.
6. Still considered the seminal book on the morality of capital punishment, see Walter Berns, *For Capital Punishment: Crime and Morality of the Death Penalty* (New York: Basic Books, 1979).
7. See Amnesty International's study on innocence and capital punishment, http://www.amnesty.org/library/Index/engAMR.510691998(Nov1998). Also see Harry Weinstein, "Death Penalty Overturned in Most Cases," *Los Angeles Times*, June 20, 2000, A1. For background see James S. Leibman, "A Broken System: Error Rates in Capital Cases 1973–1995," http://www.thejusticeproject.org
8. See Barry Scheck, Peter Neufeld and Jim Dwyer, *Actual Innocence: Five Days to Execution and Other Dispatches from the Wrongly Convicted* (New York: Doubleday, 2000).
9. See Adam Liptak, "Studies Spark New Execution Debate," *Boston Globe*, November 18, 2007, A21.
10. Studies Spark New Execution Debate, op. cit.
11. "Saving Lives and Money," *The Economist*, March 14, 2009, p. 32.
12. The NAACP has taken an active role in criticizing the fact that large numbers of African-Americans are on death row. See "NAACP Remains Steadfast in Ending the Death Penalty and Fighting Injustice in America's Justice System," http://www.naacp.org/news/press/2007-06-28/index.htm
13. See the ACLU Capital Punishment Project at http://www.aclu.org/capital/index.html
14. *McCleskey v. Kemp* 481 U.S. 279 (1987).
15. Darryl Fears, "The Lethal Injection Debate Intensifies," *Washington Post National Weekly Edition*, October 22–28, 2007, p. 35.
16. See a discussion of the Supreme Court's lethal injection decision at http://commonlaw.findlaw.com/2008/04/supreme-court-u.html
17. Tom Hester, "New Jersey Become First State in 42 Years to Ban Death Penalty," http://seattletimes.nwsource.com/html/nationworld/2004078298_webdeathpenalty17.html See also the debate in Texas over capital punishment.

James C. McKinley Jr., "Controversy Builds in Texas Over Execution,"*New York Times*, October 20, 2009, A14.

18. See the debate between Stephen B. Bright, Director of the Southern Center for Human Rights, and John McAdams, Professor of Political Science, Marquette University, during congressional hearings on "An Examination of the Death Penalty in the United States" before the U.S. Senate, Committee on the Judiciary, Subcommittee on the Constitution, February 1, 2006.

14 MONEY **AND** POLITICS

Issue Focus

Running a democracy is not supposed to be a matter of dollars and cents, but indeed American democracy has become a costly venture. Billions and billions of dollars are spent every election period to pay for the campaigns of those running for office, whether at the local, state or national level. Injecting money into the democratic process has led to numerous problems, from corruption of public officials to influence peddling by lobbyists seeking to sway the votes of politicians. The influence of money in American politics has become so problematic that questions are often raised about who really matters in the United States—the American people or those who use money to advance their special interests.

Chapter Objectives
This issue chapter will seek to:

1. Explain the impact of campaign contributions and fund-raising to the character of contemporary American politics.

2. Describe the attempts to define and control the limits of campaign fund-raising and spending in American politics.

3. Discuss the issues of public financing of campaigns and other reforms suggested as remedies to the abuses associated with money and politics.

SOME BACKGROUND

As the old saying goes, money is the mother's milk of politics. Although a bit graphic, money can indeed be linked to that which nourishes and sustains politics and politicians. Without huge infusions of money, American election campaigns would not be able to support an army of organizational workers, numerous specialized consultants, constant polling, endless media advertising, coast-to-coast travel and all those necessary miscellaneous costs from funny hats and t-shirts to envelopes and stamps. In the 2000 election for the presidency the bill for capturing the White House was, according to Federal Election Commission data, approximately $450 million; in 2004 the amount increased to $650 million and the 2008 bill surpassed the $2 billion mark. These figures do not include races for the House of Representatives and the Senate or the money spent by ancillary organizations that seek to assist the candidate of either party by running their own advertising campaigns. In 2004 and 2006 the cost of all Congressional races reached $4 billion, with the average cost of winning a House seat over $1 million and a Senate seat around $8 million. Remember that members of the House and Senate receive an annual base salary that increased to $174,000 in 2009. By any measure this is a great deal of money to spend to win a job that pays a substantial, but not exorbitant salary.[1]

The connection between money and American politics has a long history going back to the days of Andrew Jackson and his "spoils system," in which potential office seekers paid a handsome amount to get a government job. In the more modern era, campaign contributions to candidates for pubic office were largely unregulated, leading to stories of bags full of money being given to them and a variety of expensive perks (vacations, gifts, homes) being offered to politicians with the clear understanding that something was expected in return. The triggering event for financing reform came after the Watergate scandal when an organization associated with Nixon re-election campaign of 1972 (Committee to Re-Elect the President–CREEP) was found to have engaged in illegal activities. In the wake of the Watergate and CREEP scandals, Congress passed the Federal Election Campaign Act of 1972, which required disclosure of all contributions over $100 to federal candidates and allowed citizens to check off a $1 deduction that would be used to finance presidential elections. A companion Federal Election Campaign Act (FECA) in 1974 established the Federal Elections Commission, provided for public financing of presidential elections and set specific limits on campaign contributions to federal candidates.[2]

However, with each step forward for campaign finance reform there was often a step backward as either court decisions or loopholes in the existing laws allowed money to remain a critical ingredient in the electoral process. In 1976 in a landmark decision on campaign finance (*Buckley v. Valeo*), the Supreme Court struck down the section of the 1972 Federal Election Campaign Law that sought to place a limit on the personal contributions that individuals running for office could spend on their campaigns. The Court also struck down sections of the 1972 law that set limits on overall spending and on contributions by private groups. In the decision the Court invoked the First Amendment, stating, "The candidate, no less than any other person, has a First Amendment right to engage in the discussion of public issues and vigorously and tirelessly to advocate his own election." The use of the First Amendment free speech argument as the constitutional foundation for campaign contributions served as the basis for Congress refusing to engage in a sweeping financing reform or moving to comprehensive public financing of elections. As a result of the Supreme Court decision, spending one's own money or permitting individuals, corporations or other entities to write campaign checks was seen as part of the constitutional protection of free speech–another form of political expression.[3]

Although the *Buckley* decision weakened the 1972 law considerably, it did place some limits on individual contributions, especially from major donors. However, loopholes in the law were quickly found that allowed money to be given directly to political parties, rather than to candidates. The parties then transferred the bulk of the money, which was intended for party building, directly to the candidates. This "soft money" transfer from parties to candidates became the avenue for huge contributions from wealthy donors, corporations and unions, and continued the process of unrelenting spending on federal campaigns. The use of soft money became so important to fund-raising for political parties and the candidates that the reform effort again gathered steam as "good government" watchdog groups became convinced that money had corrupted the political system and made incumbents and candidates for office beholden to donors–individual, corporate or interest group.[4]

In 2002 Republican Senator John McCain of Arizona and Democrat Russ Feingold of Wisconsin pushed campaign reform legislation through Congress. As a result the Bipartisan Campaign Reform Act (BCRA) was enacted, which ended the practice of providing political parties with soft money. However, as a compromise measure, the legislation also raised the individual contribution limit to $2,300 (to candidates in the primaries and the general elections) and allowed contributions to national and state political parties. In total under the BCRA, an individual could contribute up to $108,200 in one biennial period. Not surprisingly, the BCRA faced new constitutional questions and schemes to find ways to get money into the hands of candidates.[5]

The latest end run around campaign finance reform is the 527 Organization. Named after Section 527 of the IRS Code, groups that form under this tax section cannot be formally aligned with a political party or a candidate, but they can advocate for a particular cause and in the process the candidates who are supportive of the cause. The 527 Organizations provide the financial resources to mobilize voters through direct mail, television advertising and other media outlets. As a result of the IRS Code, 527 Organizations are not limited in the amount of money they can spend on advocacy campaigns and they have been very successful in getting their messages out along with those messages of candidates supportive of their causes. The most notable of the 527 Organizations was the Swift Boat Veterans who in the 2004 presidential campaign cast doubt on the veracity of John Kerry's war record and the medals he received for bravery. Most observers of the campaign believed that the Swift Boat television ads painted Kerry in a bad light and contributed in part to his electoral loss.[6]

The history of campaign finance and campaign finance reform is thus one of fits and starts, progress and failure; but there is one constant–a search for new loopholes and new opportunities to skirt the law and raise money for candidates. The result of all the efforts to reform and evade the way the United States finances federal elections has led to numerous incidents of political corruption and an occasional wave of political scandals. But more importantly, the relentless pursuit of ways to continue funneling huge amounts of money into the political process has led to a weakening of public confidence in the electoral and legislative systems. The United States has thus become a nation where money talks in politics, and efforts to control money have been difficult, if not impossible.

On the Record

John Stewart of the popular Comedy Central program *The Daily Show* and author of the humorous *America (The Book) A Citizen's Guide to Democracy Inaction* had this take on the venerable fund-raising institution, the political fund-raiser:

> Political fundraisers take many forms, but the most common is the dinner. Supporters gather in a crowded auditorium or banquet hall to eat chicken. If they're lucky, the candidate will breeze in at the end to spend five minutes pumping hands and slapping backs before jetting off to another fund-raising dinner. This experience costs $2000.

DEBATES, DIFFERENCES AND DIVISIONS

When Americans give money to candidates for office, either individually or through a corporation, union or trade association, they are not doing so for altruistic or high-minded purposes. The name of the political game in Washington is access, and with that access to government officials, the hope of influencing public policy. Nothing is innately wrong or illegal about giving contributions to candidates for political office. The First Amendment to the Constitution encourages petitioning government, which in this case does not mean signing a long letter, rather it means a check. The problem with campaign contributions is that most Americans do not have the resources to give money to candidates for public office, and even if they do, it is usually a modest amount. The result is that most Americans do not enjoy the access to government officials and the prospect of influencing public policy because they cannot match the contributions of the major economic players in the Washington political process.

As evidence of this political inequity, the Center for Responsive Politics published a list of the top campaign contributors from 1989 to January 2008. The list, compiled by the Federal Election Commission, is a who's who of the major interest groups that have wide access to members of Congress and certainly have the opportunity to make their case on specific public policy issues and in the process perhaps sway votes in favor of their organization and its membership.

American Federation of State, County and Municipal Employees	$39,152,384
AT&T	$38,749,107
National Association of Realtors	$31,749,107
American Association for Justice	$28,290,139
Goldman Sachs	$27,365,532
National Education Association	$27,335,762
International Brotherhood of Electrical Workers	$27,272,206
Laborers' Union	$26,186,839
Service Employees International Union	$25,392,043
Carpenters & Joiners Union	$25,384,232

Source: Center for Responsive Politics, http://www.opensecrets.org/orgs/index.asp

Another way to look at campaign contributors is to examine individual donors. Again the Center for Responsive Politics, using Federal Election Commission data, published a list of those individual donors who gave $50,000 to federal candidates and parties during one or more election cycles. The workplaces of these individual donors that appear multiple times on the list are the following:

Microsoft

Time Warner

Archer Daniels Midland

Metropolitan Life

Philip Morris

Citigroup

Morgan Stanley

Bristol-Myers Squibb

Enron

Credit Suisse Group

Vivendi

American Financial Group

Walt Disney Co.

Eli Lilly and Co.

MBNA Corp.

This list of corporate donors is a cross section of computer, finance, pharmaceuticals and media companies who view the contributions as assisting their corporations on a range of legislative, regulatory and public relations issues. All of these companies want something from government and see campaign contributions as a smart business practice. The only problem with these lists is that they are made up of powerful businesses, unions, trade associations and top-level managers at Fortune 500 corporations. The difficult democratic question can thus be asked: if average Americans cannot play the political campaign contribution game, how can their interests be protected and how do they gain access to government policy makers? The answer to this question is that most Americans cannot play the money/access/influence game that drives Washington policy making and that the national interest is often pushed aside in favor of special interests.

Data Bank

A public opinion poll conducted by Rasmussen Reports in 2006 found that only 27% of those Americans surveyed believe that the elected officials in Washington are ethical. The poll also found that political corruption is an important political issue, but those Americans polled had no clear solution. Breaking down the ethical issue even further, the poll found that those Americans who defined themselves as leaning toward the Republican Party were evenly divided over the question of whether members of Congress were more ethical than used-car salesmen. As for those Americans who defined themselves as leaning toward Democratic Party, 42% said that used-car salesmen were more ethical. Only 27% of Democrats said that members of Congress were more ethical than used-car salesmen. The reason why the Rasmussen Reports compared members of Congress to used-car salesmen was not presented in the poll.

Source: Rasmussen Reports–www.rasmussenreports.com

However, if money can be described as the mother's milk of American politics, it can also be seen as the root of all evil. Whether it is campaign contributions given by "fat cats" to candidates for public office to gain access to powerful leaders or influence peddling by shady lobbyists anxious to achieve an advantage for their clients in the halls of Congress or the executive establishment, money can have a corrupting effect on the political process. Although each case of public corruption is different, there are some common denominators in the corrupting effects of money and politics. It is safe to state that the longer a political party remains in power, the greater the chances are that money will have a corrupting effect and eventually lead to damaging scandals. Furthermore, participants in money scandals usually have been individuals who have years of seniority and have risen to positions of power in which their decisions and actions can impact the direction of a particular public policy. However it is most important to note that with every act of public corruption, the level of public trust takes a hit as the fears of the American people that political decisions can be influenced by spreading money around to willing members of Congress or the executive branch are born out to be true.

Take for example the corrupting effects of money and politics on Representative Randy "Duke" Cunningham of California and Majority Leader Tom DeLay of Texas, two stalwarts of the Republican majority in Congress. In 2005 Cunningham resigned from Congress after pleading guilty to charges that he received $2 million in bribes from defense contractors in his San Diego congressional district. Government prosecutors stated that Cunningham sold his home to a defense contractor for an inflated price and that he used campaign contributions to purchase a Rolls Royce, a yacht, antiques and other valuables he used to decorate his $2.5 million mansion. After Cunningham pleaded guilty, federal prosecutor Carol Lam summed up the damage that was done to the American political system and to the faith in government officials, the bedrock of a democratic society: "The citizens who elected Cunningham assumed that he would do his best for them. Instead, he did the worst thing an elected official can do–he enriched himself through his position and violated the trust of those who put him there."[7]

An even larger-scale scandal was the so-called Abramoff scandal of 2006, which damaged the Republican leadership in the House of Representatives and most likely contributed to their loss of control in the mid-term elections that year. Jack Abramoff was what is often termed in Washington a superlobbyist. He had a long list of clients, access to the key players in government and numerous success stories of influencing the policy process for those who paid for his services. Abramoff was the chief lobbyist for the Choctaw Indians, who were seeking numerous federal permissions for their gaming and casino enterprises. He was placed under suspicion for favors he provided for members of Congress and their staff so as to benefit the legislative agenda of the Choctaw Indians.[8]

Abramoff gave members of congress and their staffs football tickets, golf trips, vacations, free meals at expensive restaurants and of course campaign contributions, all in violation of federal laws regarding lobbying. Abramoff was indicted, and in a plea agreement with the federal prosecutor he named people who benefited from his favors, including Congressman Bob Ney of Ohio, who eventually resigned. House Majority Leader Tom DeLay was also indicted on unrelated charges, but his staff members were found to have benefited from Abramoff's favors. By the time the scandal had run its course, up to sixty people, both members of Congress and staff members, including the Speaker of the House Dennis Hastert, were under a cloud of suspicion. Many of these members of Congress survived the scandal, but they often returned the campaign contributions from Abramoff and apologized to their constituents.[9]

FYI

Congress has very specific regulations regarding gifts that members and their staffs may accept. The general provisions regarding the acceptance of gifts are as follows:

- A member or employee of Congress may accept a gift only if it is unsolicited and valued at less than $50.

- Aggregate value of gifts from one source in a calendar year is less than $100, though no gifts with a value below $10 count toward the $100 annual limit.
- Gift is no cash or a cash equivalent (such as stocks and bonds). The only exceptions are gifts made by relatives and parts on an inheritance.
- Favors and benefits are not offered under circumstances that might be construed by reasonable persons as influencing the performance of their governmental duties.

It must be emphasized that there are twenty-three exceptions to these general provisions.

The numerous money-related scandals in Washington, whether the Republicans or Democrats are in power, have often stimulated discussions of moving the United States to a public financing system much like that found in Europe. For example, in Great Britain, candidates seeking seats in the House of Commons can spend only $15,000 in an election. Should they be found to have spent more than that amount, they are disqualified from running for the seat. Furthermore, each candidate is given, free of charge, the same amount of airtime on television as his or her opponent, and is permitted to send out only one free election brochure to voters in the representative district. In Canada, public financing laws are more relaxed but still severely limit expenditures. Candidates for seats in the House of Commons can spend only a set amount for the election campaign. Television and radio stations are required to provide some free airtime, and like the British campaign, the Canadian electoral process takes only weeks, not months or years. In 2004 total spending in the Canadian parliamentary elections was $212 million, considerably less than the $1.6 billion spent in the U.S. congressional elections.[10] Although the British and Canadian public financing system of elections may seem attractive and certainly inexpensive, such systems do not appear to be supported in the United States. Polling data show that the American public is in no mood to move to a public financing system. A Gallup poll in 2007 found that 56% of those polled advised candidates not to take public financing during the election campaign and to rely more on private financing.[11]

Although there are regular calls for the United States to move to a completely publicly financed system of elections at the federal level, research shows that campaign contributions and the enormous cost of elections may not be so harmful and not necessarily a breeding ground for corruption. University of Wisconsin professor John Coleman,[12] an expert on money and politics, stated in a recent study that "campaign spending makes an important contribution to key aspects of democratic life, such as knowledge and accuracy about the candidates, and does not damage the public's trust or involvement."[13] Furthermore, a study done by John Samples of the Cato Institute found that rather than sway voters with campaign contributions, politicians at all levels of government receive money from donors with the understanding that they share a common belief in a particular public policy or government initiative. Money and politics are certainly connected, and there are examples of money being the source of corruption and unethical behavior on the part of public officials. However, money and politics does not automatically create an unsavory atmosphere in the political arena that leads politicians to make policy decisions based on the amount of the contribution. Contributions in effect are used as a means of showing support and seeking that all-important opportunity to gain access to the politician to pitch an idea or advance a policy proposal through the labyrinth of the governing process.

In many respects, politicians are captives of the money machine, and as a result they grow weary of all the effort that goes into raising and spending mountains of cash. Nevertheless, they are not about to move to a European style public financing system, which might jeopardize their incumbency or completely overhaul the traditional method of using cash contributions as a means of influencing public policy. Many members of Congress and candidates for the presidency have complained openly in recent years about the amount of time they spend on the phone or at fund-raisers begging for money from deep pocket fat cats. Newly elected as a senator from Pennsylvania in 2006, Bob Casey commented on the grueling race for cash when he said, "I am sick and tired of fund-raising . . . when you sit in a room for four hours making calls, it kind of has a deadening effect on you. Anything that reduces the amount of time that you are spending fund-raising is good for the country, and it definitely is good for me."[14]

However, despite the comments of Senator Casey, when reform groups push for new campaign finance regulations or when they are publicly taken to task for receiving contributions from corporate, union or any number of special interest groups, many senators and members of the House continue to cast votes on legislation that would reduce the amount of time used for fund-raising, require free airtime to get their message to the voters or place stiff limitations on expenditures. Most members of Congress remain silent on the matter of campaign finance reform while they continue to collect contributions from wealthy contributors or the campaign-financing conduits of most lobbying organizations called Political Action Committees (PACs). When they do make a public comment, they often say they are not beholden to these contributors or they fall back on the First Amendment argument about free speech and the right of Americans to use their checkbook as a vehicle of political speech.[15]

It is probably a safe bet that comprehensive campaign finance reform and publicly financed federal elections will not become a reality in American politics. There is just too much at stake, too much money involved and too many people making a living off of the billions spent to achieve meaningful reform. The reform effort was dealt another blow in 2008 when the Supreme Court struck down the so-called millionaire's amendment, which permitted members of the House and Senate who were running against wealthy opponents to collect larger contributions to offset the financial inequity. In a 5-4 decision Justice Samuel Alito again used the First Amendment argument that the law as written by the Congress created what he termed "an unprecedented penalty" on candidates of wealth who want to spend their own money on their campaigns and exercise their rights of free political expression.[16]

The Supreme Court continued its involvement in campaign finance issues when in 2010 it overruled two previous decisions that restricted corporate contributions to support or oppose political candidates. In the ruling *Citizens United v. Federal Elections Commission* the justices by a narrow 5-4 margin stated that the government cannot ban spending by corporations in election campaigns. Again restating previous support for the First Amendment's protection of the freedom of speech, the court majority said that the government could not regulate free speech, in this case the free speech of corporate America. The justices in this case were bitterly divided as Justice John Paul Stevens, writing for the minority, stated that there is a fundamental difference between corporate speech and human speech. But Justice Anthony Kennedy, writing for the majority, stated that "If the First Amendment has any force it prohibits Congress from fining or jailing citizens, or associations of citizens, for simply engaging in political speech." President Obama denounced the decision as a major victory for "big oil, Wall Street banks, health insurance companies and other powerful interests that marshal their power every day in Washington to drown out the voices of everyday Americans." The Supreme Court decision clearly weakened the campaign finance reform effort in Congress and gave corporations a powerful tool to influence future elections with their campaign contributions.[17]

However, if campaign finance reform is not likely to come through court decisions or tough controls by Congress, it may come as a result of difficult economic times. According to data from both the Democratic and Republican parties, campaign contributions were down considerably in 2009. Long-time contributors to political parties and political campaigns were unable or unwilling to provide contributions, thus creating huge debts for the parties and individual officials. With both political parties relying on huge war chests to run campaigns, the economic downturn and its effect on contributions resulted in the formation of new strategies to fund campaigns.[18] One of those strategies is greater reliance on the Internet. Used with great effectiveness by Barack Obama in the 2008 election, candidates today are relying less on the fund-raising dinner and face-to-face asking for money and using cyberspace as the key source of gathering the millions necessary to run a competitive campaign.[19]

It is important to stress that despite the problems associated with the abuse of campaign contributions and influence peddling, the vast majority of members of Congress and candidates for office do not end up indicted by federal prosecutors or sent off to jail for their misdeeds. Most follow the rules established by the Federal Election Commission and have strict internal monitoring processes to ensure compliance with those rules. However, the real problem with the connection between money and politics in the United States is that the current system is a breeding ground for public mistrust and public cynicism. The American public's level of trust in national political leaders remains embarrassingly low as many citizens complain that rather than solve nagging national problems, politicians continue the hunt for dollars in a manner that casts doubt on whether they are voting in the national interest or satisfying a special interest.[20] However, it is important to remember that the billions spent on election campaigns in the United States is the price Americans pay for a democratic way of life. It would probably be better if the price were lower and came without the excess baggage of scandal, but this is how Americans elect leaders and this is how the bills to elect leaders are paid.

The Great Debate

Because of the controversial decision in *Buckley v. Valeo*, a debate continues over the wisdom of defining campaign contributions as a form of free expression protected under the First Amendment.

Debate Topic

Are campaign contributions a form of free speech protected by the Constitution?

Critical Thinking Questions

1. What do you see as the key reasons why European style public financing has not taken hold in the United States?
2. Politicians say that campaign contributions do not influence their votes or performance in office. Is that a credible position?
3. How should Americans reform American campaign financing and lessen the influence of money and lobbyists with money?
4. Do you agree with the Supreme Court position advanced in the *Buckley* decision that campaign contributions are a form of free speech?
5. Do you believe that political leaders make decisions independent of special interest campaign contributions?

Connections

The Federal Elections Commission is the financial watchdog of national elections. Visit its site at http://www.fec.gov

The Hoover Institution's campaign finance website is a valuable source of information on the current issues related to money and politics. See http://www.campaign-financesite.org

Common Cause is one of the most prominent public interest and reform groups active in the area of money and politics. See http://www.commoncause.org

Public Citizen has become one of the most outspoken and aggressive reform groups to seek change in the way money influences politics. See http://www.citizen.org

The Brookings Institute has a valuable site that provides up-to-date information on campaign finance reform. See http://www.brookings.edu/topics/campaign-finance.aspx

Some Books to Read

La Raja, Raymond, *Small Change: Money, Political Parties and Campaign Finance Reform* (Ann Arbor, MI: University of Michigan Press, 2008).

Samples, John, *The Fallacy of Campaign Finance Reform* (Chicago: University of Chicago Press, 2006).

Urofsky, Melvin, *Money and Free Speech: Campaign Finance Reform and the Courts* (Lawrence, KA: University of Kansas Press, 2005).

Baker, Paula, ed. *Money and Politics* (College Park, PA: Pennsylvania State University Press, 2003).

Schultz, David, *Money, Politics and Campaign Finance Reform Law in the States* (Durham, NC: Carolina Academic Press, 2002).

Notes

1. See the Center for Responsive Politics for data on election spending from 2000, 2002, 2004 and 2006 at http://www.opensecrets.org
2. The Federal Elections Commission provides a description of recent campaign financing laws and regulations. See http://www.fec.gov/info/appfour.htm
3. *Buckley v. Valeo*, 424 U.S. (1976).
4. See David Magleby and Candace Nelson, *The Money Chase: Congressional Campaign Finance Reform* (Washington, D.C.: Brookings Institution Press, 1990).
5. See Thomas Mann, Daniel Ortiz and Trevor Potter, *The New Campaign Finance Source Book* (Washington, D.C.: Brookings Institution Press, 2005).
6. Kate Zernike, "Kerry Pressing Swift Boat Case Long After Loss," *New York Times*, May 28, 2006, A1.
7. "Congressman Resigns After Bribery Plea," http://www.cnn.com/2005/POLITICS/11/28/cunningham
8. Susan Schmidt and James V. Grimaldi, "The Rise and Steep Fall of Jack Abramoff," *Washington Post*, December 29, 2005, A01.
9. Gail Russell Chaddock, "How Far Will Abramoff Scandal Reach," *Christian Science Monitor*, http://www.csmonitor.com/2006/0105/p03s03-uspo.html
10. See David Mableby, et al., "Campaign Financing in Britain and Canada," *Government by the People*, 22nd edition, 2008, p. 270.
11. "Americans Prefer Presidential Candidates Forgo Public Funding," http://www.gallup.com/poll/27394/americans-prefer-presidential-candidates-forgo-public-funding.aspx
12. John Coleman, "Comments for Public Election Funding," Conference, University of Wisconsin, January 28–29, 2006.

13. See John Samples, *The Fallacy of Campaign Finance Reform* (Chicago: University of Chicago Press, 2006).

14. David Kirkpatrick, "Senate Measures Puts Spotlight on Fund-Raising," *New York Times*, January 20, 2007, http://www.nytimes.com/2007/01/20/us/ politics/ 20ethics.html

15. The campaign reform group Public Citizen posts a Hall of Shame section on its website as part of its Clean Up Washington effort to call attention to campaign finance abuses in Congress and elsewhere. See http://www .cleanupwashington.org

16. Paul Kane, "It Pays to Be Rich," *Washington Post National Weekly Edition*, July 14–20, 2008, p. 16.

17. See Adam Liptak, "Justices, 5–4, Reject Corporate Campaign Spending Limit," *New York Times*, January 22, 2010, A1.

18. Clyde Wilcox, "Internet Fund-Raising in 2008: A New Model," *The Forum* 6, 1, http://www.bepress.com/forum/vol6/iss1/art6/

19. Paul Kane and Chris Cillizza, "Dialing for Dollars," *Washington Post National Weekly Edition*, August 6–12, 2009, p. 16.

20. Peter Nicolas and Janet Hook, "Get ready for Record Campaign Spending," *Seattle Times*, http://seattletimes.nwsource.com/html/nationworld/2008007954_ obama20.html

15 RELIGION **AND** POLITICS

Issue Focus

It is often said that people should not talk about two topics–politics and religion. However, in today's political climate politics and religion are not only becoming topics of everyday conversation, but also creating contentious national debates about the proper relationship between the two. Politics and religion have fused into a powerful mix that has had a major impact on the governing process. Supporters from many faiths seek to bring their views on moral issues into the political arena and influence policy decisions on difficult issues from abortion to gay marriage. Those who define themselves as more secular than religious seek to limit the influence of religion on politics and policy decisions. As a result, politics and religion are engaged in a difficult battle that has divided the United States.

Chapter Objectives
This issue chapter will seek to:
1. Explore the tension between those who want a strict separation of church and state and those who want to foster a closer link between religion and governing.
2. Describe the points of controversy over the role of religion in public life.
3. Discuss the current developments in church-state relations and the prospects for defusing the tensions.

SOME BACKGROUND

The United States is a nation steeped in religion and religious beliefs, a condition of national life that brings both a sense of common values and the prospect of deep political divisions. Ninety percent of Americans state a belief in God, a huge level of support for a Supreme Being, when compared with much of Europe, where only sixty percent of the French, British and Germans have such a belief. However, the strong belief in God among Americans is only part of the picture of a uniquely religious country. A recent poll from the Pew Forum on Religion and Public Life found that 72% of those Americans polled agreed with the statement "The President should have strong religious beliefs." In that same study, 51% of the respondents said, "churches should express views on political matters."[1] For many Americans organized religion and deeply held religious beliefs cannot be divorced from the arena of politics. Others however, see religion and religious beliefs as a private matter and are determined to keep government decisions free of religious influence. These opponents of religion in public life, often called secularists, view the development of public policy as requiring a neutral point of view, not influenced by one particular religious position. The clash between these two opposing views serves as the backdrop for much of the debate surrounding religion and politics in the United States.

The long history of the relationship between religion and politics in the United States began with the first immigrants, the Pilgrims who left England to escape religious persecution, thus establishing toleration of religious beliefs as one of the founding principles of the new land. Furthermore, many of the Founding Fathers and economic elites at the time of Independence and the formation of the Constitution were deeply religious individuals. For example, the opening and closing lines of the Declaration of the Independence refer to the "Creator" and "Divine Providence." The traditions of religious toleration and religious belief were joined in the First Amendment, which directed Congress to "make no law respecting the establishment of religion, or prohibiting the free exercise thereof." However, at the core of the debate over the relationship between religion and politics is the position taken by Thomas Jefferson, who advocated for a "wall of separation" between religion and the state as he feared that religious influence would be a divisive force in the formation and implementation of public policy decisions. This concern over the influence of religion on government is best shown by the fact that God is not mentioned in the Constitution. When asked at the time why references to God and religion were not included in the Constitution, Alexander Hamilton answered, "we forgot."[2]

Since those early days, religion has played an important role in many of the social and political battles for change, such as the push for women's suffrage and the civil rights movement. Moreover, Americans have seen their presidents take the oath of office ending with "So help me God" and finish their State of the Union Addresses by saying "God Bless America." Many presidents have often invoked the name of God during wartime as a means of rallying public support and providing a dose of heavenly legitimacy on a controversial policy decision. George W. Bush in his speech to Congress after 9/11, for example, stated, "Freedom and fear, justice and cruelty, have always been at war; and we know that God is not neutral between them" and after the arrest of Saddam Hussein, President Bush again invoked the name of God when he said, ". . . freedom is the Almighty God's gift to every person, every man and woman who lives in this world. That's what I believe. And the arrest of Saddam Hussein changed the equation in Iraq. Justice was being delivered to a man who defied that gift from the Almighty to the people of Iraq."[3]

Despite the fact that organized religion and belief in God have been deeply embedded in U.S. culture and U.S. governing values and systems, clarifying the exact boundaries between religion and state have been the subject of numerous constitutional challenges and legislative debates. Although the First Amendment would seem to clearly state that Congress could not establish an official religion or prohibit the free exercise of religious belief, the Supreme

Court has been called upon many times to interpret the meaning of the "establishment" clause and the "free exercise" clause as they relate to issues such as saluting the American flag, providing public financial assistance to religious schools, conscientious objection to military service, the role of religion in the workplace and the protection of religious practices.

In many of these landmark cases, the rights of minority religious groups have been the focus of the constitutional challenges as these groups advocated to practice their faith. For example, the Supreme Court found that the children of the Jehovah's Witnesses should be not be forced to salute the flag during classroom exercises, thereby upholding their view that adoring images not of their God was a violation of their faith. The Court also overturned a Wisconsin law that required children to attend school up to age sixteen, which was a violation of the Amish practice of not allowing children to attend school beyond the eighth grade. And finally, the Court permitted a small Cuban-American religious group to engage in animal sacrifice as part of their religious ceremonies, despite local health and safety rules in Florida. The decisions rendered in these cases proved that the justices in the Supreme Court viewed the free exercise clause of the First Amendment as immutable, despite the unique circumstances involved in the cases.[4]

However, there have been areas of interpretation of the First Amendment freedom of religion in which the Court has placed a wall of separation between church and state, such as with attempts by various religious organizations to allow public funding of church-related schools, curtailing the practice of erecting nativity scenes on public property during the Christmas season or prohibiting morning prayer in public schools where God was referred to in the state-sanctioned prayer. Although in the last twenty years challenges to the meaning and application of the First Amendment freedom of religion have declined significantly, this has not meant that the issue of exactly how the walls of separation between church and state should be constructed has been finalized. In fact in 2007 there was a highly publicized challenge to reciting the Pledge of Allegiance in California as an atheist father on behalf of his daughter challenged the Pledge as a violation of religious freedom and separation of church and state. He eventually lost the legal challenge, but his case reminded Americans that the tension between religion and politics continues.[5] Prayers and other religious symbols before football games, especially in the South, also created controversy. One school system in Fort Ogelthorpe, Georgia, banned high school cheerleaders from painting banners with biblical sayings on them that the players would run through at the start of each game. The decision caused such an uproar among the townspeople that parents and fans in the stands started to bring posters with biblical sayings on them in protest. However, federal courts have held that when school-supported groups or clubs promote a religious point of view, they violate the standard of separation of church and state.[6]

The connection between religion and politics is not just restricted to constitutional interpretations of the First Amendment. Religion plays an important role in the self-definition of the American people and ultimately their political affiliation. In terms of general religious categories, Protestants currently make up 51% of Americans who self-identify their religious preference. Among Protestants, Baptists are the largest denomination with their base in the South and Midwest. Increasingly, the mainline Protestant denominations such as the Methodists, Presbyterians, Congregationalists and Episcopalians are in a period of membership decline, but evangelical groups that are tied to specific churches and pastors are expanding dramatically and becoming more visible and politically active. Catholics, who make up about 25% of the nation's religious population, are found in major industrial cities in the Northeast and Midwest and in western border states where Hispanics are dominant. Jewish people, who form a small but influential religious body, are concentrated in Eastern cities such as New York and also in Florida. And Mormons, the fastest growing religious denomination in the United States, dominate the population of Utah and are spreading their influence throughout the country.

The presence of these religious groups in various locations and regions in the United States also carries over into the political arena. Baptists and other evangelical groups are solidly Republican and provide a strong base of support for the Republican Party; Catholics have historically been steadfast in their support of the Democratic Party, but their alliance with the party may be changing; Jews identify with and vote consistently for Democrats, whereas Mormons have deep ties to the Republican camp. It is important to point out that these religious affiliations and their connection to political parties are not etched in stone, but rather are tendencies that can and do change over time. For many years after the Depression of the 1930s, southern white Protestants voted consistently for the Democratic Party, only to shift allegiance to the Republican Party during the civil rights movement and after the election of Ronald Reagan. In the 2004 presidential election, many were surprised that George Bush received a majority of the Catholic vote, even though John Kerry was a practicing Catholic and Catholics had for years been major supporters of Democratic candidates. Barack Obama, however, regained the Catholic vote in the 2008 election, despite his position as a pro-choice candidate and supporter of stem cell research, two positions that are strongly opposed by the Catholic hierarchy.

Recent studies of the connection between religious affiliation and election predictability found that the extent to which voters attend church services has increasingly become a reliable predictor of voting than the more standard variables such as income, gender, age and region.[7] Republicans appear to be gaining support from churchgoers, whereas Democrats from among those described as secular (occasional churchgoers, agnostics and atheists).

Because the religious affiliation of Americans is not isolated in churches around the country but spreads out into the political arena, politicians, whether in office or seeking office, cannot ignore the evangelical vote, Catholic policy positions or Jewish views. Because there are cracks in Jefferson's walls of separation, it is impossible to examine the electoral and government processes without considering the influence that organized religions and religious believers may have on election and policy outcomes. More important, these cracks appear to be widening as churches and their members see the need to bring their beliefs into the political arena, whether by endorsing candidates for office, asking members to sign petitions or attending rallies or placing pressure on public officials to support specific policy positions that are part of their religious agenda. Churches and their members have become major players in American politics and no longer see their role as only quiet communion with their God.

On the Record

In a letter to the Danbury, Connecticut Baptist Association in 1802 Thomas Jefferson said the following:

> . . . I contemplate with sovereign reverence that act of the whole American people which declared that their legislature should 'make no law respecting an establishment of religion, or prohibiting the free exercise thereof' thus building a wall of separation between Church and State.

DEBATES, DIFFERENCES AND DIVISIONS

The contemporary tension between religion and politics arose with the *Roe v. Wade* decision supporting a woman's right to an abortion and the strong opposing response largely from the Catholic Church. Church leaders from the pope to the American bishops to the local parish priests sought to challenge the decision with a range of lobbying efforts, demonstrations and pleas to the faithful at Mass. Each year on January 22, the anniversary of the *Roe* decision, Catholic dioceses in the United States stage rallies and marches to show their unwavering opposition to abortion on demand. Right-to-life organizations with strong Catholic influence and funding have been formed throughout the country, and pastors often use the pulpit to remind their faithful of their responsibilities as members of the church to fight abortion and its supporters. Such adamancy on the abortion issue has had a political spillover effect as church leaders have begun to question the right of Catholic legislators and executives to remain in the church while publicly supporting abortion rights. In recent years, Catholic Church leaders have expanded their political agenda to include opposition to gay marriage and stem cell research. Although public opinion polls show that Catholics are not unified in their opposition to abortion, gay marriage or stem cell research, they extend sufficient support for the Church position that Democrat incumbents and candidates cannot ignore.

The intersection of religion and politics was most pronounced during the administration of George W. Bush. As a born-again Christian, President Bush developed a close alliance with the evangelical movement and relied on their support not only to win two elections but also to support various policy initiatives and value-based positions. Early in his first administration, President Bush established the Office of Faith-Based Initiatives, which was charged with encouraging churches and other religious organizations to work with government agencies to address a range of social ills and societal concerns. President Bush felt strongly that accenting the role of people of faith in responding to poverty, homelessness, hunger and family dysfunction would be more effective and successful than dealing with these problems through a large and impersonal federal bureaucracy. Critics of the initiatives stated that they feared the funneling of federal dollars into faith-based groups would be a violation of the separation of church and state doctrine and be a new way of interjecting religion into the policy sphere. The establishment of the White House Office of Faith-Based Initiatives was followed in 2004 with the formation in Congress of a "faith-based caucus" made up largely of Republicans who openly stated that their objective was to make it easier for federal money to reach church groups and other religious organizations to respond to social welfare needs.[8] Once in office, President Obama did not move as quickly as some of his secular supporters to lessen the influence of faith-based initiatives; instead the president maintained support for these organizations through a spokesman who urged "a continuation of partnerships with these organizations as long as they function in a manner that is consistent with our Constitution, laws and values."[9]

FYI

In 2004 the U.S. Conference of Catholic Bishops met in a closed retreat in Denver to discuss the issue of penalizing political leaders, particularly those in Congress, who "cooperated with evil" by supporting abortion rights. The most discussed penalty was denying communion to Catholic legislators who did not vote for the Catholic Church position on abortion. The bishops' most visible target at the time was Massachusetts Senator John Kerry, a candidate for the Democratic nomination for president and supporter of a woman's right to choose. Although conservative bishops pushed to have the conference go on record in support of the penalty (some even suggesting excommunication from the Church) more moderate voices prevailed. Cardinal Theodore McCarrick of Washington, D.C., warned the bishops that denying communion would create a "partisan political battleground. . . . It could be more difficult for faithful Catholics to serve in public life because they might be seen as not standing up for principle, but as under pressure from the hierarchy."

President Bush's strong religious beliefs and his close ties to the evangelical movement led to stinging criticism of his war policies in Iraq and his views toward the Islamic world. He was heavily criticized early on in his post-9/11 speeches when he talked about a crusade to liberate Afghanistan and those countries in the Middle East that were controlled by authoritarian governments. The use of the term *crusade* brought back images in the Middle East of the religious wars of Catholic Europe in the 8th and 9th centuries to regain the Holy Land. Also many of the president's public pronouncements were scrutinized by his liberal critics who found a pattern of religious zealotry. David Domke, writing for the *Seattle Post Intelligencer,* compiled a study of Bush statements and found that many of them were filled with religious terms such as presenting policy options as "good vs. evil" or "a calling," linking God to conceptions of freedom and liberty and numerous suggestions that God was on America's side. Moreover, liberal critics accused Bush and his religious allies, such as Attorney General John Ashcroft (who started each day with a prayer group in his office), Kansas Senator Sam Brownback (a Catholic conservative who started his campaign speeches with the call "All for Jesus, All for Jesus, All for Jesus") and former House Majority Leader Tom DeLay (who once said, "The enemies of virtue may be on the march, but they have not won, and if we put our trust in Christ, they never will."), of moving the United States to a theocratic state in which religion and religious values play a prominent role in government decision making.[10]

The growing involvement of religion in public life is in large part a response to what many evangelicals and other mainline religious leaders feel is the secularization of American society and the formation of policy decisions without concern for religious principles and traditional moral practices. Growing evidence suggests that the proportion of Americans who say that they have "no religious preference" has doubled from 7% to 14%. This increase does not reflect a turn toward atheism but rather a rejection of traditional religions, in particular the religious right. More important for the future of American politics, this spike in secularism is growing among the eighteen-to-twenty-five-year age group, in which 20% described themselves as having no religious preference. This rise in secularism has benefited the Democratic Party, which has seen its support among those who define themselves as not churchgoers, a proportion which has increased from 55% in 2002 to 67% in 2006. Democratic candidates are reluctant to stress that a solid portion of their voters' support comes from the no-preference group, because they seek to make inroads among churchgoers and attract some of the evangelical vote. However, it is clear that the secularization of American politics has benefited the Democratic Party.[11]

Conservative Republicans are constantly emphasizing that the connection between seculars and the Democratic Party is dangerous for American society and will eventually lead to a weakening of traditional values. The code term for the religious fight against secularization is the need to embrace "family values," which often translates into opposition against abortion, gay marriage and homosexuality in general, stem cell research, what is viewed as the despoiling of popular culture in movies, music, and the Internet and the behavior of celebrities. Conservative church leaders along with family-values advocates have stated openly that it is essential that religious principles and religious values become part of the political debate and that established privacy rights which run counter to those principles and values be revoked. The religious agenda thus has accented the importance of overturning the *Roe v. Wade* abortion decision, stopping any efforts to sanction gay marriage, curtailing any further experimentation related to stem cell research and limiting if not ending school curriculums that are based on evolution rather than the biblical interpretation of creation.

Although the Democrats are ambivalent about support from seculars and seek to remake their image as committed churchgoers, the evangelicals pose problems for the Republican Party. Republican Party leaders are afraid that mainstream church members and voters in general may view the support of evangelicals as a sign that the party has been captured by narrow-minded religious conservatives who advocate a policy agenda that is unattractive to the majority of the American electorate. In the 2008 Republican primaries, for example, the candidacy of former Arkansas Governor Mike Huckabee, an ordained Baptist Minister who did not believe in evolution, was popular among evangelicals. Huckabee's popularity among evangelicals was partly responsible for a series of victories in southern state primaries. However, Republican leaders quietly worried that a Huckabee candidacy would send the wrong message to the American voters and create the impression that the Republicans had become the party solely of the evangelical right.[12]

Dissension has also arisen within the Christian right movement over the topic of whether it should stick with its family-values agenda or extend its message to include issues that it heretofore has not addressed, such as global warming and efforts to reduce poverty. In 2007 the National Association of Evangelicals criticized leaders of the Christian right who had called for the firing of its Washington policy director, Reverend Richard Cizik, because of his involvement in efforts to address global warming. Two prominent leaders of the Christian right, James Dobson of the Focus on Family organization, and Tony Perkins, president of the Family Research Council, demanded Cizik's resignation for "using the global warming controversy to shift the emphasis away from the great moral issues of our time." Cizik was defended by many leaders in the National Association of Evangelicals including the Reverend Paul de Vries, the president of the New York Divinity School, who said that "I am as much against abortion as Jim Dobson, but I want that baby to live in a healthful environment, inside the womb as outside the womb."[13]

The dispute within the evangelical movement over the issue of whether holding true to the family-values agenda or expanding to an environmental and economic agenda points to the fluid nature of how religion impacts national politics. Evangelical leaders such as Cizik, de Vries and the mega church minister Rick Warren, who wrote the national bestseller, *The Purpose Driven Life* (and gave the invocation at Barack Obama's inauguration), recognize that if their movement is to increase its membership and also have an influence on public policy debates, it must not be perceived as rigid, mean-spirited and out of touch with the mainstream key issues facing most Americans.[14] This new group of evangelicals is keenly aware that young evangelicals and young people in general have shown that their priorities are not just family-values driven, but more global and economic in nature. Moreover, conservative positions on abortion, gay marriage, stem cell research and the teaching of evolution are not resonating with the American public as are issues such as global warming and the growing economic gap between the wealthy and the poor. The positions thus taken by Cizik, de Vries and Warren are being embraced by an increasing number of Republican activists and leaders who see the influence of these evangelical leaders not only expanding the base of the evangelicals but also making the evangelical movement more mainstream.

Data Bank

According to 2008 presidential election exit polls conducted by CNN, the breakdown of religious preference for Barack Obama and John McCain was as follows:

	Obama (%)	McCain (%)
Protestant	45	54
Catholic	54	45
Jewish	78	21
Other religion	73	22
No religious preference	75	23

Source: CNN, November 4, 2008

In the 2008 presidential primaries the connection between religion and politics played a major role, particularly in the campaign contests on the Republican side. The early leader Mitt Romney, the former governor of Massachusetts, was questioned repeatedly about his Mormon faith and his allegiance to the government over his faith. In a manner much like John Kennedy, who in the 1960 campaign responded to questions about his allegiance to the Vatican, Romney pledged that his personal religious beliefs would not influence his public decisions. Nevertheless, Romney had a difficult time with many evangelicals, who viewed Mormonism as not a Christian religion and therefore were suspicious of his candidacy. When Romney dropped out of the race, Mike Huckabee took up the standard of the evangelicals at the expense of a surging John McCain, who was viewed by many conservative religious Republicans as not only too moderate in terms of his policy positions but not closely tied to the religious right. When McCain eventually won the Republican nomination, he sought to mend fences with the evangelical movement.

On the Democratic side, the religious issue centered on Barack Obama's Muslim roots (his father was an African Muslim). Although Obama had for years been a member of a black Protestant Church in Chicago and defined himself as a Christian, a residue of concern remained among some voters that he was not in the mainstream of American religious life. Conservative critics such as Ann Coulter, Sean Hannity and Rush Limbaugh repeatedly mentioned that Obama's middle name was Hussein, sending a not too subtle signal that the African-American candidate for president was perhaps a closet Muslim. Obama also got caught in a major controversy when his pastor and spiritual advisor in Chicago, the Reverend Jeremiah Wright, was shown on a YouTube video damning the United States because of its racist past. Obama eventually renounced the video and separated himself from Wright, but questions were raised about how patriotic Obama was because of the influence of his pastor and whether he agreed with the position taken by the Reverend Wright.

Once elected Obama entered a maelstrom of controversy when he accepted an invitation to speak at Notre Dame University and receive an honorary degree. Conservative Catholics launched a vigorous nation-wide campaign to stop the Catholic university from giving an honorary degree to a president who was pro-choice. Obama did attend the graduation ceremony and sought to soothe the opposition by talking about finding common ground and keeping open minds and open hearts. Obama talked about the influence of the Catholic Church on his community activism and the importance of the Catholic Church in the civil rights movement.[15] However, despite the attempt at lowering the voices of opposition, the Catholic right and their bishops were energized to fight on against the pro-choice position of the president.

Despite Jefferson's belief in the importance of maintaining the wall of separation between church and state, it is now a reality of American politics that religion and religious organizations are firmly involved in national political debates and seek to influence national policy. Because the United States remains a nation of believers and churchgoers, it was inevitable that the role of religion in politics would move beyond the proclamation of "In God We Trust" on our currency to a more critical involvement in the governing process. The leadership and membership of major religious denominations in the United States are now so well organized and so politically focused that it will be difficult to go back to a time when religion was purely a private matter and when the American citizenry saw religion as having little, if any, relationship to government decision making.

balance → However, in all this discussion of the role of religion in the political realm, there seems to be an emerging consensus about how to properly balance these two powerful forces. Andrew Sullivan, one of the leading conservative thinkers in the United States and a frequent critic of the religious right, states that what is important in the political process is to move beyond religious values to what is morally correct. As he states, "The essential civic discipline in a pluralist democracy is to translate your religious convictions into moral arguments–arguments that can persuade and engage people of all faiths or none,"[16] Sullivan means that public policy should be guided by shared principles and values that are deeply held in American culture. Religion and religious organizations can help policy makers move toward shared principles and values; in fact they have a responsibility to do so. However, there is a difference between showing the way and interfering in the policy process by setting out a forceful agenda, demanding compliance with that agenda and then entering the political fray to achieve those objectives in a manner that some say places the United States on the road to becoming a theocracy. Sullivan and others like him are saying that the Constitution should guide us as we make public decisions, not the Bible or the Book of Mormon or the four gospels.

The future of American politics will be greatly affected by the extent to which religion and religious organizations strike a balance between guiding political leaders toward shared principles and values and making rigid demands, formulating narrow agendas and participating with uncompromising vigor in the political process. The American political system has always worked best when it has been based on compromise, consensus and cooperation and when policy prescriptions that were moderate, centrist and backed by the majority of public opinion were developed and approved. Breeching Jefferson's walls of separation occasionally when the national interest merits may be a positive development, but tearing down the wall to remake the country along religious lines would clearly violate the intent of the Founding Fathers and the political traditions that have guided the nation since its inception.[17]

The Great Debate

The development of a strong religious component in American politics has increasingly created a political culture that accents the importance of infusing political decisions and government policies with religious values and principles.

Debate Topic

Should there be a strict separation of church and state in the United States or should public policy be guided by religious-based values and principles?

Critical Thinking Questions

1. Do you believe that religious leaders are involving themselves too much in matters of politics and public policy and crossing over the wall of separation between church and state?
2. Do religious leaders have a moral obligation to speak out on controversial policy issues, even if that means taking partisan political positions and supporting specific candidates?

3. Some Catholic bishops believe that Catholic politicians who vote pro-choice should be excommunicated from the Church for taking an anti-Catholic position. Do you agree?
4. In today's political arena, how would you set the proper balance between church and state?
5. When political leaders face a conflict between their personal religious beliefs and a Supreme Court decision that runs against those beliefs, how should they respond?

Connections

A useful blog that presents a wide range of views on religion in American life is U.S. Religion. See http://usreligion.blogspot.com

The Pew Forum has regular studies on the role of religion in American life and politics. See http://religions.pewforum.org/

The evangelical right has a website that presents its views on the role of religion and American politics. See http://www.evangelicalright.com

The Christian Coalition, perhaps the most influential evangelical organization in the United States, provides a comprehensive examination of its positions toward political issues. See http://www.cc.org

The U.S. Conference of Bishops is the primary source of presenting Catholic Church positions on politics and public policy. Visit its site at http://www.usccb.org

Some Books to Read

Meacham, Jon, *American Gospel: God, the Founding Fathers and the Making of a Nation* (New York: Random House, 2007).

Duncan, Ann W. and Steven Jones, eds. *Church-State Issues in America Today* (Westport, CT: Praeger, 2007).

Butler, John, Grant Wacker, Randall Balmer, *Religion in American Life: A Short History* (New York: Oxford University Press, 2007).

Dionne, E.J. *What's God Got to Do with It: The American Experiment?* (Washington, D.C.: Brookings Institution Press, 1999).

Wilcox, Clyde, Carin Larson, *Onward Christian Soldiers: The Religious Right in American Politics* (Boulder, CO: Westview Press, 2006).

Notes

1. http://www.pewforum.org/religion-politics
2. See Martin Marty, "Religion and the Constitution: The Triumph of Practical Politics," http://www.religion-online.org/showarticle./asp?title=182
3. The full text of President Bush's speech to Congress can be accessed at http://www.historyplace.com/speeches/gw-bush-9-11.htm

4. For a list of key cases related to religious freedom see http://religiousfreedom .lib.virginia.edu/court/index-links.html

5. *Elk Grove Unified School District v. Newdow* 542 U.S. 1 (2004). See a debate over the Elk Grove case between Douglas Laycock, Professor of Law at the University of Texas, who filed an amicus curiae brief on behalf of 32 Christian and Jewish clergy, and Jay Alan Sekulow, Chief Counsel of the American Center for Law and Justice, National Press Club, Washington, D.C., March 19, 2004.

6. Robbie Brown, "Barred from Field, Christian Banners Find Home in Stands," *New York Times*, October 27, 2009, A12.

7. See "Religion and the Presidential Vote," Pew Research Center for the People and the Press, December 6, 2004.

8. In recent years as a result of difficult economic times, many faith-based organizations have had a difficult time finding the financial resources necessary to continue their work. See Jacqueline Salmon, "Faith-based Groups Are Hurting," *Washington Post National Weekly Edition*, March 2–8, 2009, p. 35.

9. See Carrie Johnson, "That Troublesome Bush Holdover," *Washington Post National Weekly Edition*, September 21–27, 2009, p. 15.

10. David Domke, "Bush Weds Religion, Politics to Form World View," *Seattle Post Intelligencer*, August 22, 2004, http://seattlepi.com/opinion/187081_focus-bush22.html

11. Ross Douthat, "Crisis of Faith," *Atlantic*, http://www.theatlantic.com/doc/200707/religion. See also "Brand Disloyalty," *Economist*, March 1, 2008, pp. 34–35.

12. Andrew Sullivan, "The Right and Religion," http://andrewsullivan.theatlantic.com/.m/the_daily_dish/2007/12/the-right-and-r.html

13. Laurie Goldstein, "Evangelical Group Rebuffs Critics on the Right," *New York Times*, http://www.nytimes.com/2007/03/14/us/14evangelical.html

14. Rick Warren, *The Purpose Driven Life* (Zondervan, 2002).

15. Remarks of President Barack Obama, the University of Notre Dame Commencement, May 17, 2009, Notre Dame, Indiana, Office of the Press Secretary.

16. Andrew Sullivan, op. cit. See also E.J. Dionne, "Souled Out: Reclaiming Faith and Politics After the Religious Right," *Washington Post*, January 22, 2008.

17. For a recent discussion of religion in America see E.J. Dionne and John Green, "Religion in American Politics: More Secular, More Evangelical . . . or Both?" http://www.brookings.edu/papers/2008/02_religion_green_dionne.aspx

16

SCIENCE **AND** POLITICS

Issue Focus

Just like religion, many Americans do not normally link science with politics. Yet it is clear that science and politics are connected, particularly as science influences a wide range of public policy issues such as global warming, stem cell research or evolution. Moreover, much of scientific research in the United States is supported through government appropriations. Congress funds huge scientific institutions such as the National Institutes of Health and the National Aeronautics and Space Administration, which face regular oversight by members of Congress to ensure compliance with the law. However, as with many of the issues, the fact that scientific inquiry and scientific problem solving lead to conclusions or recommendations that require political action, it is inevitable that controversy and disagreement will arise. Many in the scientific community would prefer to stay above the political fray, but their work often leads to debate, difference and division.

Chapter Objectives
This issue chapter will seek to:

1. Describe the intersection between science and politics in contemporary American governing.
2. Examine the key issues that are at the core of the public disputes involving science policy and scientific discovery.
3. Discuss the changes in the relationship between science and government from the Bush administration to the Obama administration.

SOME BACKGROUND

The terms *science* and *politics* are from two different worlds. Science is about exploring the unknown, proving hypothesis and finding answers to age-old problems. Politics, on the other hand, is about using power, making public decisions and seeking the common good. On the surface there seems to be little similarity between science and politics–one is precise and disciplined whereas the other is messy and unpredictable. Yet despite their inherent differences, the scientific and political worlds are increasingly interconnected. The scientific community seeks to advance the knowledge of the unknown and find new ways to improve people's lives. However, scientific discoveries or initiatives can at times create moral and political dilemmas that require government action.

Perhaps the best example of the tension between science and politics is the work of J. Robert Oppenheimer, one of the developers of the atomic bomb, whose participation in what came to be called the Manhattan Project remains one of the most controversial and morally charged discoveries in the history of humankind. Oppenheimer and his colleagues at the Los Alamos facility in New Mexico were deeply conflicted by their work as they recognized the enormous power of the atomic weapon, but they realized its potential to help end World War II. Years later, Oppenheimer reflected on the moral and political dilemmas associated with the Manhattan Project and the doubts that he harbored about using science for political or military purposes.[1]

Besides the potential moral dilemmas associated with scientific research, there is the fundamental linkage between the work of scientists and government support. Scientific research has a long history of reliance on governmental funding and governmental oversight. The National Science Foundation, the National Institutes of Health (NIH) and the Centers for Disease Control and Prevention, to name the most visible examples of federal government involvement in scientific and medical research, inevitably bring the political world into the work of the scientific community. This link of science to the public sector has often created tensions within the political process as specific initiatives such as using stem cells from human embryos for medical research have led to partisan disagreements and acrimonious policy debates.

Therefore the intersection of science and politics is not only unavoidable but also critically important for the common good. For example, the work or discoveries of scientists and other researchers alert the nation to a dangerous new strain of virus that requires national action, the study of climate change signals the potential impact of weather on the planet and the value of travel to outer space reminds government officials of the importance of new discoveries worthy of funding. However, despite these often-beneficial results from the scientific community, some discoveries and experiments lead to controversy and opposition as the push and pull of public opinion and interest-group activity elevate these discoveries and experiments into national issues. The scientific community relishes the independence of thought and the need to be free of intervention as it seeks the truth, but the process of scientific investigation and discovery can lead and has led to heated debates, political differences and societal divisions.[2]

In recent years there has been increased tension between the scientific community and government over a range of issues from global warming to wetlands protections. There have also been controversies related to the cloning of animals, genetically modified food, the use of animals in scientific experiments, alternative medicine and the teaching of evolution in public schools. Scientists are finding that their research and more important, their recommendations are facing either stiff opposition or worse, a refusal by some in government and the media to even acknowledge the validity of the research and the value of their recommendations. Scientists have learned a difficult lesson about how interest groups and public opinion can unite with the political establishment to block or ignore warnings from researchers who have been studying a problem for years. Part of the problem, according to Massachusetts Institute of Technology (MIT) professor Lawrence Susskind, is that complex science does not translate well into the political sphere and that scientists are often novices when it comes to working the political and governmental systems to transform their findings and warnings into public policies that will address critical environmental, biological and medical challenges.[3]

Yet despite these tensions between science and politics, the quest for scientific discoveries and advances continues. The explosion of knowledge in the contemporary era has been so dramatic that the scientific community is moving with lightening speed to address a whole host of areas, such as genetics, disease control and microbiology, that for years remained a mystery. With increasing frequency, laboratories and research institutes across the United States are engaged in cutting-edge work that will lengthen life, cure deadly illnesses, expand food production, develop new energy sources and explain not just our world but the universe. In many respects, this is the most exciting time for science; but at the same time it is also the most frustrating time as the scientific community interacts with the political community, not so much over the findings of science but over their application and implementation of these findings in American society.

DEBATES, DIFFERENCES AND DIVISIONS

It is important to first point out that the United States has long been a leader in science with many distinguished men and women making significant contributions in a wide range of fields of study. From the earliest days of the Republic with Benjamin Franklin and his experiments with electricity to James Watson's discovery of DNA, Jonas Salk's cure for polio, Werner von Braun's rocket technology and of course the unlimited brilliance of Albert Einstein's theories of space and time, Americans, either by birth or by adopted citizenship, have made medical breakthroughs that have saved countless lives, discovered new ways of understanding life, explained the universe we live in and pushed the boundaries of knowledge beyond anything ever imaginable. The excellence of Americans in the field of science has been recognized with the largest share of Nobel Prizes in science and medical research. As of 2009, 238 Americans have been awarded Nobel Prizes in medicine, physics, and chemistry, which is 47% of the awards given throughout the world in these three fields since 1901.[4]

The worldwide notoriety and leadership the U.S. scientific community achieved in the 20th and 21st centuries has thrust it into uncharted ethical and

On the Record

J. Robert Oppenheimer, after the explosion of the atomic bomb over Hiroshima, Japan in 1945, said the following:

> The atomic bomb made the prospect of future war unendurable. It has led us up those last few steps to the mountain pass; and beyond there is a different country.

Source: As quoted in Priscilla Macmillan, *The Ruin of J. Robert Oppenheimer and the Birth of the Arms Race*

moral territory. This has certainly been the case with the efforts by many scientists and medical professionals to advocate for the expansion of and federal grant support for stem cell research. Stem cells are found in most multi-cellular organisms. The two most important stem cells are embryonic and adult stem cells. Stem cells are so named because of their ability or potency to differentiate into specialized cells, which offers scientists the opportunity to transform them into muscle or nerve tissues that can then be used in medical therapies. Scientists engaged in stem cell research are convinced that they can use stem cells to achieve major breakthroughs in medicine as these cells can be targeted to treat a range of diseases such as leukemia, spinal cord injuries and Parkinson's disease.[5]

The key debate over stem cell research involves the use of embryonic cells, which are taken from a human embryo. Currently, the dominant field of research involving embryonic stem cells requires the development of and access to a line of these cells. The human embryo is destroyed in the process of using these cell lines for research. Scientists at the center of stem cell research state that the benefits of destroying the human embryo to create the lines can provide enormous breakthroughs in medicine. Opponents of embryonic stem cell research, however, vehemently disagree as they say that the destruction of the embryo is in fact destroying human life, a life that is entitled to constitutional and legal protections. Many in the pro-life movement view stem cell research as the next battleground against fetal rights and the devaluing of human life. Even those who see the benefit of stem cell research admit that it creates an ethical slippery slope, as such experiments can then lead to other controversies such as cloning of humans, much like the experiments done with sheep and cattle.[6]

The controversy over the destruction of human embryos and stem cell research entered the American governing process in 2001 when President George W. Bush stated categorically that he was opposed to this avenue of research, largely on pro-life grounds. In a compromise, Bush did support federal funding for the use of currently available lines of embryonic stem cells for research purposes but not for the creation of any new lines.

In his address to the nation in 2001 over the issue of federal funding for new stem cell lines, President Bush not only praised the scientific community for the advances it had made in combating disease and illness, but also worried about the use of embryonic stem cells, instead of so-called adult cells that are derived from the human placenta and other sources in the body. He also cautioned that stem cell research could be used for human cloning. Despite his recognition that embryonic stem cells held the potential for major advances against cancer and spinal cord injuries, he said, "I worry about a culture that devalues life, and believe as your President I have an important obligation to foster and encourage respect for life in America and throughout the world."[7] Then in 2006 and 2007 Bush, in direct opposition to Congress, vetoed the Stem Cell Research Enhancement Act, which supported additional funding for the creation of new lines of embryonic stem cells. Bush's position did not apply to privately supported funding of embryonic stem cell research.[8] Despite his impassioned position on the stem cell controversy, the president was not without his critics. Besides many prominent scientists and medical researchers who pointed to the vast potential of stem cells, Bush also had to face the pleas of former First Lady Nancy Reagan, who said on numerous occasions that stem cell research could have helped in the discovery of a cure for Alzheimer's disease, which debilitated and eventually ended the life of her husband.[9]

One of the unique characteristics of science is that it is not static, and those in the scientific community are forever moving forward with new experiments and discoveries. Already there are signs that scientists may be able to harvest stem cells from sources other than embryos with new techniques using adult skin cells, thus lessening the chances of a continuing ethical, moral and political battle. President Bush called the new techniques a "landmark achievement." These alternative methods are still in the early stages of development and may prove to be less effective than the process of extracting stem cells from human embryos. Although debates continue over the issues of differing scientific techniques used to harvest stem cells, laboratories around the world are working closely with their governments to move forward on embryonic stem cell research, which has left scientists in the United States dismayed that their own government has not allowed them to take the lead in this area of medical research.[10]

When Barack Obama took office he moved quickly to change the Bush policies toward stem cell research. In March 2009 Obama lifted the limits on federal funding for stem cell research as part of his overall commitment to support scientific research. Obama created new ammunition for his detractors by leaving open the source of the embryos that would be used in future research. Not only would human embryos be employed, but the cells created by cloning techniques could also become part of the stem cell research process. As Richard Doerflinger of the U.S. Conference of Bishops stated at the time of Obama's announcement, "If they go beyond the so-called spare embryos in fertility clinics, they are breaching an entirely new ethical line."[11]

The ethical controversy over embryonic stem cell research brings up a larger issue that has come to the fore in Washington and indeed within the most prestigious centers of scientific and medical research. The Bush administration was the target of growing complaints that funding for science did not keep pace with other countries, and as a result the United States was losing its lead as the center of scientific experimentation and discovery. In his 2008 State of the Union address President Bush stated, "To keep America competitive into the future, we must trust in the skill of our scientists and engineers and empower them to pursue the breakthroughs of tomorrow."[12] However, leading scientists who saw the government as participating in a "retardation of research" by regular cutbacks in funding immediately responded to this positive endorsement by the president. A leading particle physicist at Northeastern University in Boston bemoaned the lack of funding and the dominant position the United States has in this field. Pran Nath stated, "the Bush administration was unable to arrest this decline (in particle physics research), leaving Europe and Japan to assume the leadership role in this area."[13]

Moreover, scientists and other researchers pointed to the fact that when research funding was increased, it was often directed to defense and national security initiatives (such as missile defense), not to disease control, particle physics, biomedicine and neuroscience. The NIH has been especially hard hit during the Bush years as budgets that would fund a wide range of scientific and medical research were leveled. The Democratic Congress in 2007 approved a significant increase in the NIH budget and gained the president's approval, despite his initial decision to cut the budget by $279 million. The budget increase and the greater attention that was given by the Congress and the president, who in his last year in office began to support the work of the premier government-supported research institute, encouraged the researchers at NIH.

President Obama, taking a position quite different from his predecessor, made it clear that his administration would substantially increase scientific research and help "restore scientific integrity to government." He also promised that scientists would be "free from manipulation or coercion and that the government will listen to what they tell us, even when it's inconvenient." The Obama administration's position was quickly greeted with support from scientific and medical researchers who saw a new era of funding and public support for their work. In particular the NIH was encouraged that it would receive the funding it needed to take its research on a wide range of medical issues to a new level.[14]

FYI

The American space program has long been recognized as one of the greatest scientific achievements of humankind. Since President John F. Kennedy challenged the nation to reach the moon by 1970 (a man landed on the moon in 1969), presidential administrations have made the space program run by the National Aeronautics and Space Administration (NASA) a

(continued)

FYI   (continued)

major priority. President Bush continued this accent on the space program when in 2004 he announced plans to send astronauts back to the moon by 2020 and also later to Mars through the "Vision for Space Exploration" program. The president proposed spending $12 billion by 2009 to change the mission of NASA to one of future exploration using the moon as a launching pad. Bush's new vision was based on the completion of the international space station and the likely end of the space shuttle program, thus allowing for the United States to take a new direction in space. However, within a year of the announcement, NASA announced that it was facing a serious shortfall in its funding (estimated to be $6 billion between 2006 and 2010) because of extraordinary expenses in the shuttle program, placing the president's plans for a new vision of space exploration in jeopardy. Once Barack Obama entered office and faced huge budget deficits, he placed more emphasis on cutting back NASA's appropriations and delaying new initiatives such as manned space flight to the moon and exploratory missions to Mars. Although he was loudly criticized by members of congress with economic ties to the space program, President Obama that by 2025 there would be a new spacecraft built with the capability for longer space flights, and perhaps there would even be an attempt to land on an asteroid to gain better knowledge of how asteroids could pose a threat to the planet.

The disagreements with the Bush administration's lack of support for science have not only been limited to funding, but also surfaced in the area of presidential appointments and disputes over data. Scientists have been especially disturbed by what they consider to be numerous examples in which scientific data were suppressed or publicly criticized by Bush administration officials, Republican members of Congress or conservative allies associated with advocacy groups or think tanks. Charges were leveled at the Bush administration over findings related to harmful chemicals, climate change, evolution and sex education. Roger Launius, a former chairman of the Division of Space History at the Smithsonian Institution's National Air and Space Museum, took the lead in criticizing the Bush administration on its attack on scientific research, stating "some in industry and on the religious right have disliked the use of scientific studies by government officials as justification for actions that they viewed as counterproductive to their best interests . . . the Bush administration has been at the forefront of this effort in the first part of the 21st century."[15]

As could be expected, the issue of declining government support for science, the politicization of scientific research and the decline in world leadership in science and technology eventually entered the partisan arena. In 2003, Henry Waxman, Democratic Congressman from California, issued a scathing report criticizing what he and other minority members of the House of

Representative Committee on Government Reform viewed as serious deficiencies in the Bush administration's approach to science. In the report, Waxman identified over twenty issue areas in which the Bush administration had sought to undermine science and medicine, from abstinence education and substance abuse to global warming and missile defense. In the report, Waxman charged that the Bush administration used three major tactics to weaken the influence of scientific research—"manipulating scientific advisory committees, distorting and suppressing scientific information and interfering with scientific research and analysis." In its conclusion of the study, Waxman stated, "The Bush Administration has repeatedly suppressed, distorted, or obstructed science to suit political and ideological goals. These actions go far beyond the traditional influence that Presidents are permitted to wield at federal agencies and compromise the integrity of scientific policy making."[16]

Perhaps the most passionate battleground in science is the dispute between the scientific community and religious conservatives over the teaching of evolution in public schools. Not since the famous Scopes Trial in Tennessee in 1925 has the issue of evolution been debated with such intensity. The Scopes Trial in many respects mirrors the social and religious conditions that have made the teaching of evolution based on Charles Darwin's theory of natural selection a major national issue today. At the time of the so-called Monkey Trial, fundamentalist Christianity was on the rise in the state of Tennessee and religious leaders were exercising growing influence within the state legislature. As a result the Butler Act was passed in 1925 that prohibited the teaching of Darwin's theory and required that the Bible version of creation be at the center of the curriculum. The famous trial, which pitted William Jennings Bryan supporting the law against Clarence Darrow, who advocated on behalf of the teaching of evolution, has been fictionalized in literature and in the movie *Inherit the Wind*. In the trial, Scopes was found guilty of violating the law, but he won on appeal. But the wheels of justice moved slowly regarding the teaching of evolution in public schools. It was not until 1967 that the U.S. Supreme Court overturned a similar law in Arkansas (*Epperson v. Arkansas*) as an infringement of the First Amendment establishment clause banning public laws whose major focus was religious in nature.

Today an active and politically involved evangelical movement has advanced the theory of intelligent design, which is a more elaborate defense of creationism, as a worthy challenge to Darwin's theories and a necessary addition to existing science curriculums in public schools. Intelligent design as defined by its major advocacy group, the Discovery Institute, takes the position that "certain features of the universe and of living things are best explained by an intelligent cause, not an undirected process such as natural selection." In other words, the advocates of intelligent design believe that the complexity of all living matter could only have been designed by an intelligent creator, not by the randomness of natural selection as suggested by Darwin. Intelligent design is presented as an alternative scientific approach to creation and is supported by a small but vocal group of scientists and researchers, many of them associated with the Discovery Institute. President Bush endorsed intelligent design stating that ". . . both sides ought to be properly taught . . . so people can understand what the debate is about."[17] However, an overwhelming number of scientists and groups such as the National Center for Science Education and the National Science Teacher's Association have condemned intelligent design as pseudoscience and without merit.[18]

Data Bank

In 2004 CBS News conducted a public opinion poll to determine how the American public viewed evolution compared to creationism. By a margin of 55% to 13% Americans believed that God created humans in their present form. When asked if God guided the process of evolution rather than created humans, 27% of Americans agreed. Taking these beliefs in a God-centered creation, 65% of Americans believed that both creationism and evolution should be taught side by side in public schools and 37% responded that creationism should be taught instead of evolution.

However, despite the criticisms of mainline scientists, the theory of intelligent design and the general movement to replace the teaching of evolution with creationism (or at least have them taught side by side) developed as a national issue when school committees and boards of education in some states became dominated by conservative evangelicals who sought successfully to include the teaching of creationism in the science curriculum. In Dover, Pennsylvania, the school committee passed a policy change in the science curriculum that mandated the teaching of creationism alongside evolution. The decision immediately touched off a controversy as the scientific community realized that evolution was under attack and that the actions of the school committee in Dover could spread elsewhere. The decision of the school committee was challenged in the Pennsylvania court system and went to trial in 2005 (*Kitzmiller v. Dover Area School District*). Representatives of the intelligent design argument and the supporters of evolution took the stand and made their case not only in terms of the traditional arguments supporting each side, but also in terms of whether the actions of the school committee were in violation of the First Amendment establishment clause. In a stinging rebuke of intelligent design the judge in the case stated that intelligent design was a religious doctrine, not science, and therefore its teaching was prohibited by the First Amendment. The scientific community hailed the decision as a vindication of evolution and intelligent design as pseudoscience.[19]

The Dover trial was conducted at the same time that the Kansas Board of Education, again dominated by conservative evangelicals, voted to adopt the Discovery Institute's "Critical Analysis of Evolution" curriculum as part of the overall science curriculum for Kansas public schools. The Kansas scientific community, especially the State Board of Science Hearing

Committee, blasted the decision as including a religious doctrine in the public school curriculum. Many in Kansas were torn by the dispute between intelligent design and evolution; but at election time, six of the members of the Board of Education lost their seats, and their decision was overturned by the State Science Hearing Committee. In their reinstatement of evolution as the sole source of explaining the development of man within the curriculum, the board stated that science would once again be limited "to the search for natural explanations for what is observed in the universe."[20]

As the Data Bank survey shows, the vast majority of Americans believe in a God-centered creation and have little support for the evolutionary argument of Darwin and modern-day scientists. Although the teaching of evolution remains firmly in place in public school curriculums, the Dover and Kansas controversies (along with new controversies is Texas and other states) over intelligent design point out the work that the scientific community has before it as it seeks to convince Americans that the evolutionary explanation of human development is indeed accurate and provable. Many in the scientific community have too long been reluctant to engage in a defense of their beliefs or to become involved in public educational programs that explain their views on evolution. However, because Americans are deeply religious people and many are firm believers in the Bible story of creation, it is not surprising that the poll results would show such a significant difference between a God-centered creation and an evolutionary explanation for human development. It is difficult for many Americans to accept that their ancestors were apes and that over hundreds of thousands of years these apes evolved into modern humans. Furthermore, the randomness of natural selection as presented by Charles Darwin is difficult for most Americans to understand. It is more logical to assume that the intricacy of human life must have been the result of an intelligent designer or a powerful force or God.

During the Bush Presidency the scientific community came to understand the impact that governmental power and conservative ideology can have on a whole range of issues that in the past may not have been so politically charged. Many scientists were not prepared for the debates, differences and divisions that ensued as a result of their analyses and discoveries. Many American scientists benefit from government outlays and expect that their research and recommendations will serve as the basis of government action. However, both in terms of support and status, scientists entered a new world where government leaders and bureaucratic agencies fashioned their own policy agendas that on numerous occasions clashed with those of scientists. The result was a souring of a relationship that in the past has been cordial and cooperative.[21] With the Obama administration taking a far different approach toward science and the scientific community, scientists have hope that a new era of cooperation between science and politics will begin.

The Great Debate

The United States is a country of both extraordinary scientific and medical achievements and strong beliefs about the role of God in the creation and the evolution of humankind.

Debate Topic
What should be the proper balance between science and religion in guiding public policy?

Critical Thinking Questions

1. Do you believe that intelligent design views on creation should be taught side by side with evolution in high school?
2. Where do you stand on the stem cell debate? Does the importance of using human embryos to harvest stem cells, and according to some, killing life, overshadow the possibility of discovering a cure for many of today's diseases?
3. Many scientists have stayed on the sidelines in the debates on stem cell research and evolution, whereas religious groups have captured the headlines. Should scientists play a larger public role in defending their research findings and their views in public policy debates?
4. Do you agree with President Obama's goal of significantly increasing science research in the next few years?
5. Why is it so difficult for many Americans to support the evolutionary theories of Charles Darwin?

Connections

The National Science Teachers Association is the lead organization challenging intelligent design and other efforts to question the teaching of evolution in schools. Visit their site at http://www.nsta.org

The complicated issue of stem cell research and the political debate surrounding it is presented in a balanced discussion by the Public Broadcasting System's Nova program. See http://www.pbs.org/wgbh/nova/miracle/stemcells.html

The Coalition of Americans for Research Ethics takes positions on a range of controversial scientific and medical research, including stem cell research. See http://www.stemcellresearch.org.

The President's Council of Bioethics has presented a working paper on stem cell research. Visit the site of the council at http://bioethics.gov

The website of the American Association for the Advancement of Science is one of the most reliable sources for positions on critical scientific issues. See http://www.aaas.org/

Some Books to Read

Shermer, Michael, *Why Darwin Matters: The Case Against Intelligent Design* (New York: Times Books, 2006).

Ruse, Michael, *The Stem Cell Controversy: Debating the Issue* (New York: Prometheus Books, 2006).

Boisvert, Kate Grayson, *Religion and the Physical Sciences* (Westport, CT: Greenwood Press, 2008).

Pielke, Roger A. Jr., *The Honest Broker: Making Sense of Science in Policy and Politics* (New York: Cambridge University Press, 2007).

Roberts, Michael, *Evangelicals and Science* (Westport, CT: Greenwood Press, 2008).

Notes

1. See Priscilla MacMillan, *The Ruin of J. Robert Oppenheimer: and the Birth of the Arms Race* (New York: Penguin, 2007).
2. ABC-CLIO has developed a seven-book series *Controversies in Science* that documents some of the key scientific debates in the contemporary world. See http://www.abc-clio.com/Products/browseseries.aspx?seriesid=17
3. Alexis Madrigal, "Synthesizing Science and Politics," *Wired Science*, February 17, 2008, http://blog.wired.com/wiredscience/2008/02/synthesizing_sc.html
4. http://www.jinfo.org/US_Nobel_Prizes.html
5. For a thorough discussion of the stem cell issue, see Jospeh Panno, *Stem Cell Research: Medical Applications and Ethical Controversy* (New York: Checkmark Books, 2006).
6. Rich Weiss, "Catch-22," *Washington Post National Weekly Edition*, August 6–12, 2007, p. 34.
7. See Charles Babington, "Stem Cell Bill Gets Bush's First Veto," *Washington Post*, July 20, 2006, A4.
8. Ibid.
9. Dan Collins, "Strong Plea from a Strong Lady," *CBS News*, May 10, 2004, http://www.cbsnews.com/stories/2004/05/10/health/main616473.shtml
10. Joseph Seneca, "The Race for Stem Cell Research Dollars," *The Star Ledger*, August 13, 2006.
11. Rob Stein, "Now What Happens," *Washington Post National Weekly Edition*, March 16-22, 2009, pp. 15–16.
12. http://www.associatedcontent.com/article/569379/george_w_bush_state_of_the_union.html
13. As quoted in *Live Science*; See http://www.livescience.com/technology/080130-bush-legacy.html
14. Gardiner Harris and William Broad, "Scientists Welcome the New Administration with Joy and Hope," *New York Times*, January 22, 2009, A23.
15. Steven Salzberg, "Disappointing Science Funding," http://genome.fieldof-science.com/2007/07/disappointing-science-funding.html
16. "Politics and Science in the Bush Administration," U.S. House of Representatives Committee on Government Reform–Minority Staff, August 2003.

17. See http://www.boston.com/news/nation/Washington/articles/2005/08/02/bush_endorses_intelligent_design/

18. http://www.nsta.org/publications/evolution.aspx

19. *Tammy Kitzmiller, et al v. Dover Area School District, et al* 05 CV 2688 (2005).

20. Peter Steven, "In Kansas A Bitter Debate on Evolution," *Washington Post*, May 6, 2005, A01.

21. See Jessica Wang, *American Science in an Age of Anxiety* (Chapel Hill, NC: University of North Carolina Press, 1999).

17

THE **DRUG** WAR

Issue Focus

One of the more intractable problems facing the United States today is drug use. Whether marijuana, cocaine, heroin or so-called party drugs, illegal narcotics have become a part of American life and a huge multi-billion dollar "industry" that enriches drug barons but sadly creates enormous personal, family, and societal problems. For years governments at all levels have been seeking ways to stop drug use, especially among the young, but many of these efforts have had only mixed results. Police and drug enforcement officials have waged a constant war against drug cartels and street deals, yet their efforts have had little impact on drug use in the United States. As a result of the failure of the war on drugs, there have been calls for a relaxation of punishment for use of certain narcotics such as marijuana. These calls for a change in some of the drug laws have not quieted those who want to continue stopping the transport and sale of illegal drugs, and so the war goes on.

Chapter Objectives
This issue chapter will seek to:
1. Describe the ongoing efforts by federal, state and local authorities to stem the tide of illegal drugs entering the United States.
2. Discuss the different approaches to combating drug use in the United States and the debates that have ensued over the issue of how best to conduct the drug war.
3. Examine the growing threat from Mexican drug cartels as they increase their presence in the United States and engage in mounting violence both in the United States and in Mexico.

SOME BACKGROUND

In 1972 President Richard Nixon, in a major national pronouncement, declared a war on drugs. This was not a declaration of war in the sense that the United States would engage its military in pitched battles against another country, but rather it was a comprehensive governmental attack on both the suppliers of a range of narcotics, largely from Latin America and Asia, and their distributors, largely minorities from the inner cities. Although Nixon's war on drugs initially focused on marijuana, cocaine and heroin, his bold declaration of combat against narcotics was part of a long line of government policies dating back to the days of alcohol prohibition from 1919 to 1933.[1]

Since the declaration of a war on drugs, the United States has developed a bureaucratic-enforcement system designed to stop the supply and distribution of narcotics and allocated billions of dollars to end the illegal drug trade. President Nixon established the Drug Enforcement Agency (DEA) in 1973 to enforce drug laws and work with foreign governments to stem the tide of illegal narcotics entering the United States.[2] In 1988 President Reagan established the Office of National Control Policy as part of the Anti-Drug Abuse Act with a so-called Drug Czar as the head of the White House unit.[3] Following suit, states and localities, especially major urban centers, developed major anti-drug programs and created specialized police units for the express purpose of waging the war on drugs on the streets, in schools and in neighborhoods.

As with most wars, the war on drugs has been expensive. In 2005 a federal government report stated that $12 billion had been spent on all administrative efforts to control the drug supply, pay those involved in anti-narcotics efforts and offer rehabilitation costs. A separate study done at the same time added to these costs the amount spent on incarcerating drug offenders, which included the full range of legal adjudication and local and federal prison costs, totaling an estimated $45 billion. Not added to these figures were the personal or societal costs related to drug dealing and drug imprisonment, such as the loss of employment, the impact of violence, family hardship and health care costs.[4] Moreover, the war on drugs has led to a huge spike in the number of Americans jailed for drug possession, drug dealing and drug use. Currently, an estimated 1 million Americans are jailed each year for violating drug laws, and the majority of the prison population is individuals who have been convicted of a drug crime. Since the mid-1990s the prison population in the United States has tripled, with most of the increase due to drug convictions.[5]

The war on drugs has not been confined to the United States. Administrations since Nixon have advocated an aggressive interdiction program to stop the supply of drugs from Latin America and Asia. In particular, the U.S. DEA, the U.S. Coast Guard and U.S. Customs and Border Protection have worked with governments in Bolivia, Colombia, Mexico, Peru and many of the mini-states in the Caribbean to destroy cocaine and marijuana fields, capture drug cartel kingpins and dismantle the money-laundering apparatus that has allowed drug gangs to hide billions of dollars in ill-gotten gains. The George W. Bush administration instituted the most ambitious of such overseas drug war programs, the $5 billion Plan Colombia, to assist Colombia and neighboring countries such as Brazil, Ecuador and Panama in combating drug trafficking and guerrilla activity financed by the drug trade.[6]

The fact that Colombia is the major supplier of narcotics to the United States is the reason for the interest in expanding the drug war to such countries. According to U.S. government data, Colombia supplies between 56% and 80% of the world's cocaine and heroin, and this drug trade provides the drug cartels of Colombia with an annual income of $4 billion in non-taxed and money-laundered profits. Although Colombia is the premier source of illegal drugs entering the United States, Mexico, Bolivia and Peru are also major suppliers. The enormity of the drug trade has prompted the United States to station hundreds of drug enforcement agents in these countries and use Navy ships to patrol the waters in the Caribbean and the Pacific to seize contraband narcotics.

In recent years the Bush administration worked closely with the government of Mexican President Felipe Calderón in his expanded program to destroy the drug cartels, which have been responsible for 23,00 killings since 2006, including over 1000 police, military and other public servants.[7] An increased presence of drug enforcement agents in Mexico and greater border and sea patrols provided some of the support to control not just the increased trafficking of illegal drugs, but also the movement of weapons purchased in the United States and used by the drug smugglers. The Bush administration in 2008 developed and Congress approved Plan Merida, a security-assistance initiative, which in a three-year period will funnel over $1.3 billion in military and police assistance to Mexico and some countries in Central America. The assistance is primarily in the form of equipment such as helicopters, night-vision goggles and bullet-proof vests, because the drug gangs are well equipped with high-powered weapons, speed boats (even submarines) and aircraft to make them a formidable and violent force.[8]

The Obama administration has continued the policies of the Bush administration in supporting Plan Merida, while also sending over 450 law enforcement agents to the border and cracking down on the illegal gun trade that has allowed the drug cartels to challenge the Mexican military and police.[9] The cooperation of the Obama administration with President Calderón is also a matter of national security as over 250 cities and towns in the United States now are estimated to have a Mexican drug presence, including Atlanta, Georgia, which has become the hub of drug smuggling and drug distribution in the United States. With 80% of the methamphetamines, 90% of the cocaine and 1,110 metric tons of marijuana estimated to be entering the United States from Mexico, the Obama administration has recognized the importance of joining with Mexico in vigorously pursuing the drug war.[10]

During more than forty years in the war on drugs, the United States has achieved some notable successes in terms of drug seizures, the capture of key drug lords and the imprisonment of thousands of dealers and members of drug gangs. However, despite these successes in the war, drug use remains prevalent in the United States, especially among the young. New, more powerful and more dangerous drugs enter the marketplace with disturbing regularity, and evidence of drug abuse and drug-related deaths continues to fill the news. The resilience of the drug culture in the United States has on occasion sparked a discussion about legalizing certain drugs, especially marijuana, but such talk often leads to a stern rebuke from government officials who insist on continuing the war and punishing those who have broken the law. The reality of widespread drug use colliding with the support for the war on drugs has created a huge divide in the United States over what the next steps should be in dealing with this national and international issue.[11]

On the Record

In a meeting with Chicago's Mayor Richard Daley in 1971, President Richard Nixon said the following about drug use and its impact on America's youth:

> I was asked about marijuana because [a group is conducting] a study. Now, my position is flat-out on that. I am against legalizing marijuana. I know the arguments about (how) marijuana is no worse than whiskey. But the point is, once you cross the line, from the straight society to the drug society–marijuana, then speed, then it's LSD, then it's heroin, etc. then you're done. We've got to take a strong stand.

Source: Nixon Presidential Papers

DEBATES, DIFFERENCES AND DIVISIONS

The issue of drug use and drug enforcement in the United States is one of the most complex and difficult challenges facing public officials, and indeed the public in general. One of the key problems of drug use in America is the matter of legality. It is often heard in debates about drug policy that using legal drugs such as alcohol and cigarettes, along with certain prescription medications such as Oxycontin, can lead to addiction and other harmful physical and psychological problems, whereas possession of even small amounts of marijuana is a punishable offense, even though marijuana has been shown to have some medicinal benefits and perhaps is no more dangerous than alcohol. Punishment for possession and distribution of illegal drugs, which has been the primary cause of jail overcrowding, is also an issue. Many of those in jail, especially minorities, have been incarcerated for extended periods of time for minor drug dealing. Finally, there is the matter of whether the war on drugs is cost effective and a smart policy to continue, when by most accounts it is not making major headway and may actually be a huge failure. Most drug enforcement officials openly admit that barely 5% of the narcotics entering the United States are confiscated and that for most drugs, the supply is so plentiful that the price is affordable, if not cheap.[12]

Each of these issues of legality, incarceration and policy effectiveness stems from the prevailing position among many government officials that any loosening of the position on drug use in the United States would pose a distinct danger to social order and personal responsibility. It is alleged that decriminalization of small amounts of marijuana would open up the floodgates of drug use and lead to experimentation with more dangerous drugs. Lessening the sentences of small-time drug dealers in the inner cities is often viewed as a certain path toward deepening crime by not punishing law breakers. And admitting that a forty-year war on drug trafficking and drug use has been lost and may have been ill-advised is difficult to face, and is difficult for policy makers to admit.[13]

Data Bank

One of the primary concerns in the drug war is the early use of illegal narcotics by young Americans. States and localities have developed numerous programs to inform children, starting at the elementary school level, of the dangers of drugs and drug use. The following data from the Office of National Drug Control Policy present the use of a range of illegal drugs by eighth, tenth and twelfth graders. The data were compiled in 2006–2007.

Percentage of Students Reporting Marijuana Use

Eighth grade	2006	2007
	15.7	14.2
Tenth grade	2006	2007
	31.8	31.0
Twelfth grade	2006	2007
	42.3	41.8

Percentage of Students Reporting Cocaine Use

Eighth grade	2006	2007
	3.4	3.1
Tenth grade	2006	2007
	4.8	5.3
Twelfth grade	2006	2007
	8.5	7.8

The policy debate over the legalization or decriminalization of marijuana has perhaps led to the sharpest differences and social divisions of any of the issues related to drug use and drug enforcement. Although many in government associated with the war on drugs have consistently viewed marijuana as a gateway narcotic, suggesting that if used regularly it will lead to the use of other drugs. In 1995 the Partnership for a Drug-Free America along with White House Office of National Drug Control Policy issued a report stating that marijuana users were eighty-five times more likely to try cocaine than those who did not use marijuana.[14] However, a 2006 study done by the American Psychiatric Association found no connection between marijuana use and subsequent other drug use and as a result supported the position of marijuana defenders that the drug is not dangerous or a gateway to other drug use.[15]

Because marijuana has a level of public support and a body of evidence showing that it may not be a gateway narcotic, its possession and use has been the subject of intense lobbying to either make it completely legal or decriminalize it by mandating fines rather than arrest and possible jail time for possession or use. The debate over the legal status of marijuana has become even more complicated as the narcotic has been shown to have medicinal benefits for individuals undergoing chemotherapy and other cancer treatments for which nausea is a side effect. In fact, the debate over the medicinal value of marijuana has taken center stage in the policy arena as state officials have struggled with the issue, especially as medical professionals have validated the benefits associated with marijuana use as an anti-nausea treatment.[16]

Because of public pressure, marijuana supporters have had some success in the area of decriminalization. Since the 1970s a number of states, including Oregon, Alaska, California, Colorado, Massachusetts, New York, Nebraska, North Carolina and Ohio, have passed various forms of decriminalization legislation with most sanctions in the form of a small fine. However, in the area of legalization, marijuana supporters have faced stiff and successful opposition. In 2002 voters in Nevada rejected by a 61–39% margin a referendum initiative that would have made legal the possession of three ounces of marijuana by those over twenty-one years of age and also permitted marijuana for medical purposes. In 2004 Alaska voters rejected a proposal to end penalties for marijuana use, and in 2006 Colorado voters turned down a proposal to legalize the possession of one ounce of marijuana.

Besides the issue of whether marijuana use should be legalized or decriminalized, there is also debate surrounding the financial benefits that would be created if marijuana had the same status as alcohol and cigarettes. Studies have estimated that enforcement costs related to marijuana are over $7 billion per year and that if the government legalized marijuana use and taxed its sale over $6 billion could be raised in revenue–money that currently often ends up in the hands of either petty criminals or organized crime syndicates. Moreover, an agricultural angle to marijuana production is that it is a cash crop vital to the informal (and illegal) economy in at least twelve states. One study shows that marijuana production may add over $35 billion per year to the national economy.[17]

Numerous interest groups and public advocates are in the battle over marijuana use and enforcement. Although the White House Office of Drug National Control Policy, the DEA and private organizations such as the Partnership for a Drug-Free America and the Center on Addiction and Substance Abuse have led the opposition, there are strong advocates for marijuana legalization or decriminalization such as Law Enforcement Against Prohibition, the Drug Policy Alliance, Students for a Sensible Drug Policy and the Marijuana Policy Project. The proponents of legalization even received unexpected support in 2005, when 530 noted economists led by Nobel Prize winner Milton Friedman wrote President Bush and called for a change in federal policy, largely on economic and revenue grounds.[18] Support even came from two of the Democratic candidates for president in 2008. Both former Alaska Governor Mike Gravel and Ohio Congressman Dennis Kucinich expressed support for legalization. And in 2008 Massachusetts Congressman Barney Frank introduced legislation in the House of Representatives to legalize marijuana.[19]

Tougher enforcement procedures such as the so-called three-strikes policies of incarcerating repeat drug users and dealers for extended periods of time has contributed to a huge explosion in the national prison population that in many cases has put a significant percentage of minorities behind bars. As of 2007 over 1.5 million Americans were behind bars at the state and federal level, whereas in 1970 the number was 200,000. One of the major reasons for the dramatic increase in the prison population is drug-related incarcerations. According to the Federal Bureau of Justice Statistics 12.7% of state inmates and 12.4% of federal inmates were jailed for marijuana offenses. Furthermore, over 30% of all admissions to prisons at the state and federal level are for so-called victimless crimes, the category that includes drug possession and drug dealing.[20]

The huge increase in the U.S. prison population and its direct relationship to drug arrests and incarceration has a racial component as well. Approximately 75% of the prisoners in jail in the United States for drug offenses are individuals of color, especially African-American males. The disparity in sentencing is of greatest concern to the African-Americans in jail for drug-related offenses. According to data compiled by the Sentencing Project, African-American drug offenders have a 20% greater chance of being sentenced to prison than white drug offenders, and African-Americans receive longer prison terms for drug offenses than whites. In 2002, the average prison term of 105 months for African-Americans was 69% longer than that of 62 months for whites. The Sentencing Project also found that African Americans now serve virtually as much time in prison for drug offenses (57.2 months) as whites do for violent offenses (58.8 months).[21]

FYI

In its computerized history data system the New York State Division of Criminal Justice Services found the following arrest pattern for marijuana use in three time periods–1977–1986, 1987–1996 and 1997–2006. In the 1977–1986 period, the number of people arrested for marijuana possession was 41,000, in the 1987–1996 period it was 39,000 and in the 1997–2006 period it was 362,000. Furthermore, the study found that in the 1987–1996 period, 23,000 blacks were arrested for marijuana possession as opposed to 5,000 whites, whereas in the 1997–2006 period 196,000 blacks were arrested as opposed to 52,000 whites.

The huge number of African-Americans in jails in the United States has been most distressing to the black community. Incarceration has contributed to numerous socio-economic ills such as the break up of families, the loss of income for families of those convicted, an inability to reintegrate into the community and a deep-seated hostility toward law enforcement and public officials. As Professor Glenn Loury of Brown University stated in his testimony before the Joint Economic Committee of Congress in 2007, "For these men [who have been imprisoned for long periods of time on drug-related charges], their links to family have been disrupted; their subsequent work lives will be diminished; their voting rights are often permanently revoked. They will suffer, quite literally, a 'civic excommunication' from American democracy. It is no exaggeration to say that, given our zeal for social discipline, these men will be consigned to a permanent non-white male nether caste."[22]

In December 2007 the U.S. Supreme Court addressed the disparity in the African-American prison population because of drug-related convictions when the justices in a 7-2 ruling granted trial judges discretion to impose more lenient sentences for crack cocaine convictions, which are often the primary source of lengthy incarceration for African-American males. Justice Ruth Bader Ginsburg, writing for the majority, stated, "It would not be an abuse of discretion for a district court to conclude when sentencing a particular defendant that the crack/powder disparity yields a sentence greater than necessary." The Supreme Court decision allowing greater discretion and likely greater leniency came as a result of growing outcries by the African-American community and the Congressional Black Caucus over Congressional penalties put in place in the Reagan administration that led to the "100 to 1" sentencing disparity, under which the possession of five grams of crack cocaine incurred the same five-year prison sentence as the possession of 500 grams of powder cocaine. As a result of the Supreme Court decision, it was estimated that as many as 20,000 prisoners could petition to have their sentences reduced. The Bush administration and the two conservative judges who dissented in the case, Justices Clarence Thomas and Samuel Alito, stated that placing such discretion in the hands of the trial judges would remove Congress's right to set guidelines and leave the current sentencing guidelines without much force or meaning.[23]

One of the most hotly debated questions concerning the war on drugs is whether it has been worth it. Certainly a case can be made that an illegal industry that makes an estimated 310 billion a year and is patronized by an estimated 16 million people over the age of twelve needs to be addressed, especially because it has fostered a criminal element, led to devastating personal crises of abuse and created a national culture in which Americans have come to rely on some form of drug use, whether legal or illegal. However, increasingly, the issue of the expenditures for the drug war on the federal, state and local level combined with the dramatic expansion of the prison population has come front and center into the policy debate. Both advocates of reform and supporters of maintaining an aggressive war posture continue to engage in public debates over the question of whether a war started in 1973 should continue.

If a measure of the success of the war on drugs is the movement toward a "drug free America," then without question the effort has been a complete failure. It is unreasonable to assume that a nation of 310 million people living in an open society with standards of privacy and permissiveness would be able to establish a drug-free environment. The formation of drug-free zones around public schools, zero tolerance of drug use in schools and the business world and drug testing by many large and small businesses have not had an appreciable impact on drug use, although data from the National Institute of Drug Abuse have shown that from 1974 to 2003 both marijuana and cocaine use had declined somewhat. However although the use of these two primary illegal drugs has declined, the use of other narcotics such as heroin and methamphetamines and illegal prescription drugs such as Oxycontin has increased. If alcohol use were included in the discussion of drug usage, even though it is legal, the results would show a continued high level of Americans using drugs.[24]

One measure of the drug war that has changed significantly is the public's view of the issue as a critical priority. Many of the 1970s and 1980s surveys, which asked Americans to name the issues that required a high level of attention, found that drug use was in the top ten. But since 2001, national concerns over drugs and drug usage has virtually disappeared from survey responses and is rarely discussed in policy debates or in campaign discussions at the national level. An active discussion about drugs and drug policy continues at the state and particularly the local level, but even at the grassroots of American society the drug war is but one of many concerns facing the public and governmental officials. There has been almost a kind of grudging acceptance that drugs are part of the local landscape along with a growing realization that marijuana use may not be as dangerous as alcohol abuse, especially among the young.

For many who are critical of the war on drugs, the issue of whether war should have been waged in the first place often rises to the surface of discussion. Taking a military approach to drug use and drug enforcement, in the view of critics, placed too much emphasis on interdiction, confiscation and incarceration, rather than on promoting a whole host of preventative methods and rehabilitation. As critics point out, the war on drugs concentrated on the supply routes and dealers rather than on the reasons for drug demand and strategies to diminish that demand. Although federal, state and local budgets have allocated money for prevention and rehabilitation, and many privately funded programs have made enormous positive strides in dealing with the adverse effects of drug use and drug abuse, at the federal level in particular the accent continues to remain on a war strategy.[25]

The drug war has often been compared to the Prohibition era of 1919 to 1933, when the government, in an attempt to influence personal behavior, in this case the use of alcohol, passed a constitutional amendment and spent millions of dollars and extensive manpower to stop what became a highly lucrative underground business enterprise dealing in illegal alcohol. Americans responded to Prohibition by frequenting illegal speakeasy bars, making their own moonshine and accepting the crime and corruption that was linked to the liquor trade. In the end Prohibition was viewed as a huge public policy failure, and the nation rejoiced in 1933 when the Twenty-First Amendment negated the Eighteenth Amendment and brought the nation back to a time when alcohol was legal.

Today critics point to the failures of the war on drugs as another example of Prohibition as the government has sought to control the private behavior of American citizens with only limited success. In some respects the push to relax drug laws and drug punishments, especially for marijuana, has been driven by the admissions of major political figures. President Bill Clinton, in a highly controversial admission during his run for the White House that he smoked, but did not inhale a marijuana cigarette, became the stuff of jokes, but did awaken many Americans to the realities of drug use by a younger generation. During the 2008 campaign Democratic candidate Barack Obama admitted that he used cocaine as a teenager, and Cindy McCain, the wife of Republican candidate John McCain, did not shy away from her past drug dependency on barbiturates. President Bush admitted early in his candidacy that he was a recovered alcoholic who on at least one occasion was arrested for driving under the influence. The drug and alcohol use of key political figures in recent years has further fostered a more tolerant attitude toward illegal narcotics or the abuse of alcohol with the accent now on overcoming addiction.

As a further sign of a less aggressive policy stance toward drug enforcement, the Bush administration and its White House Office of National Drug Control Policy set more moderate goals in the war on drugs stressing the reduction of major drug usage by 10% and concentrating on working with states and localities in education programs targeted at young people. An active external component remains in the war on drugs led by the DEA, but that component has run into stiff opposition from some Latin American countries such as Ecuador, Venezuela and Bolivia where leftist leaders resent the involvement of the United States in their affairs and are opposed to some of the strategies used to break up the supply routes, such as using herbicides to kill cocaine leaves and the extradition of known drug kingpins to face charges in the United States. Colombia and Mexico continue to support the efforts of the United States in the war on drugs, but increasingly there is criticism that the efforts of these governments are halfhearted with not enough money expended on border protection and aggressive efforts to combat corruption in the ranks of the military and the police.

To say that the war on drugs is winding down would be an exaggeration, but it is safe to state that support for what was a high government priority and a near passion of past administrations has undergone a transformation in recent years. There is a growing recognition that some drugs are more dangerous than others, that legalization and decriminalization of marijuana would not create a full scale rush to harder drugs, that the incarceration of hundreds of thousands of African-American males has had a devastating effect on the black community and that the money spent on the war on drugs could be much better spent on other more pressing domestic priorities. It is impossible to predict with any certainty whether there will be significant changes in the drug laws in the Obama administration, but the new president pledged to work cooperatively and provide additional financial assistance to Mexico as it continued its bloody war with the drug cartels. With the Mexican drug wars spreading into suburban America, Obama will likely face new pressures to continue a military approach to illegal narcotics and maintain a war posture.

Even though President Obama faced enormous challenges over drug smuggling and drug violence at the border with Mexico he presented in 2010 a comprehensive drug strategy that stressed the importance of a balance between drug enforcement and reducing drug use. As he stated in a White House position paper, "By boosting community-based prevention, expanding treatment, strengthening law enforcement and working collaboratively with our global partners, we will reduce drug use and the great damage it causes in our communities."[26]

The Great Debate

The drug policies of the United States are beginning to soften, at least toward marijuana. However, government officials continue to stress the connection between drugs, addiction and violence and remain adamant about continuing the war on drugs.

Debate Topic

Should the United States continue an aggressive war on drugs or concentrate its efforts on prevention and decriminalization of drug use and rehabilitation of drug users?

Critical Thinking Questions

1. Is the drug war lost? If so, how did the United States lose it?
2. Would government be better off taxing illegal narcotics and gaining the revenue from the sale of drugs? Which drugs would you include as acceptable?
3. Do you fear that a relaxation of current drug laws will have a harmful effect on American society and lead to increased crime and addiction?
4. Should the United States continue to provide Mexico with substantial assistance to combat its war on drugs or concentrate more on border control and the illegal entry of drugs to the United States?
5. How would you advise government officials on the best way to deal with the drug issue in the United States?

Connections

The DEA is the frontline agency responsible for the war on drugs. Visit its site at
http://www.justice.gov/dea/index.htm

The White House Office of National Drug Control Policy presents the administration's point of view on drug policy. See http://www.whitehousedrugpolicy.gov

A compendium of drug data has been compiled at the "Drug Library." See http://druglibrary.org/Schaffer/LIBRARY/basicfax.htm

All facets of the war on drugs are documented at http://www.drugwarfacts.org

A critical website devoted to the negative impacts of the war on drugs is StoptheDrugWar. See http://www.stopthedrugwar.org

Some Books to Read

Fish, Jefferson M. *Drugs and Society: U.S. Public Policy* (Lanham, MD: Rowan & Littlefield Publishers, 2005).

Caulkins, Jonathan, *How Goes the War on Drugs: An Assessment of U.S. Drug Problems and Policy?* (Santa Barbara, CA: Rand Corporation, 2005).

Youngers, Coletta, A. *Drugs and Democracy in Latin America: The Impact of U.S. Policy* (Boulder, CO: Lynne Reiner Publishers, 2004).

Carpenter, Ted Galen, *Bad Neighbor Policy: Washington's Futile War on Drugs in Latin America* (New York: Palgrave Macmillan, 2003).

Robinson, Matthew, Renee Scherlen, *Lies, Damned Lies and Drug War Statistics: A Critical Analysis of Claims Made by the Office of National Drug Control Policy* (Albany, NY: State University of New York Press, 2007).

Notes

1. For background on U.S. policy toward drugs and drug use see Erich Goode, *Drugs in American Society*, 6th edition (New York: McGraw Hill, 2004), Chapter 4.
2. http://www.justice.gov/dea/history.htm
3. For a chronology of U.S. drug policy, See Jefferson M. Fish, *Drugs and Society: U.S. Public Policy* (Lanham, MD: Rowan & Littlefield, 2005).
4. See 2005 National Survey on Drug Use and Health: National Findings, http://www.oas.samhsa.gov/NSDUH/2k5NSDUH/2k5results.htm
5. See data from the National Organization for Reform of Marijuana Laws and its article "Decriminalizing Pot Will Reduce Prison Population," November 21, 2007, http://www.norml.org/index.cfm?Group=ID=7431
6. See Michael Brown, "Counternarcotics Strategies in Latin American," Testimony Before the House Committee on International Relations, Sub-Committee on Hemispheric Affairs, March 3, 2006. Also see Joanne Kawell, "Drug Economies of the Americas,"*NACLA Report on the Americas*, September/October, 2002, pp. 8–17.
7. Bert Wilkinson, "An Unappetizing menu," *The Economist*, May 22, 2010, p. 42.
8. "Buying Weapons in the U.S. Gun Smugglers Supply Mexican Drug Cartels," *New York Times*, April 15, 2009, A1.
9. Randall Archibald, "Drug Cartel Violence Spills Over From Mexico Alarming U.S.," *New York Times*, March 23, 2009, A1.

10. See Sam Enriquez, "Mexican Leader Joins War on Drugs as U.S. Turns Its Back," *Baltimore Sun*, February 4, 2007.
11. Ethan Nadelman, "Drugs," *Foreign Policy*, September/October, 2007, pp. 24–30.
12. Moises Naim, *Illicit: How Smugglers, Traffickers, and Copycats are Hijacking the Global Economy* (New York: Doubleday, 2005).
13. Office of National Drug Control Policy website, op.cit.
14. See Partnership for a Drug-Fee America Reports on Teens' and Parents' Attitudes About Drugs, April 1996, http://www.ndsn.org/APRIL96/PDFA.html
15. As reported in http://www.scienceblog.com/cms/study-says-marijuana-no-gateway-drug-12116.html
16. See Jesse McKinley, "Push to Legalize Marijuana Gains Ground in California," *New York Times*, October 28, 2009, A17.
17. http://www.prohibitioncosts.org/endorsers.html
18. This letter is presented at http://economics.about.com/od/incometaxestax-cuts/a/legalize_pot.htm
19. "Rep. Frank says He'll File Bill to Legalize Marijuana," http://www.boston.com/news/local/massachusetts/articles/2008/03/22/rep_frank_says_hell_file_bill_to_legalize_marijuana
20. http://www.ojp.usdoj.gov/bjs/drugs/htm
21. The Sentencing Project, "The Federal Prison Population: A Statistical Analysis," http://sentencingproject.org. There is recent evidence that black prison populations related to drug offenses is in decline. See Solomon Moore, "Decline in Blacks Imprisoned of Drug Offenses," *New York Times*, April 15, 2009, A11.
22. Glenn Lowry, Testimony before Joint Economic Committee of the U.S. Congress, October 4, 2007.
23. Michael Doyle, "Supreme Court Permits Flexible Sentencing," http://www.mcclatchydc.com/2007/12/10/22896/supreme-court-permits-flexible.html
24. See data and analysis from the National Institutes of Health at http://www.nida.NIH.gov/infofacts/hsyouthtrends.html
25. Jonathan P. Caulkins, Peter Reuter, Morton Y. Iguchi, "How Goes the War on Drugs: An Assessment of U.S. Drug Problems and Policy," Rand Public Research Center, 2003. See also "El Paso's Small Step," *Economist*, September 26, 2009, p. 40.
26. See National Strategy to Reduce Drug Use and its Consequences, White House, Office of Press Secretary, May 11, 2010.

18

ENERGY USE AND ENERGY CONSERVATION

Issue Focus

Energy sources and economic development are so closely intertwined that should the supply of energy be cut off or depleted, the United States and indeed the entire industrialized world would experience serious challenges. Because the link between energy and growth is so critical, the issues of how best to develop new energy sources, how to protect existing sources of energy and deciding how to properly prioritize the use of a range of energy sources have prompted major debates in the political arena and among the American people. At the same time that the debate over energy sources is causing division in the nation, another area of debate is occurring over conservation measures and their impact on economic growth. We now live in a "green era" in which many Americans are stressing the importance of moving from oil, gas, coal and nuclear power to solar, wind, geothermal and biofuel power and are joining these new "green" sources of energy with strict conservation measures. Not surprisingly, the advocates of green alternatives are clashing with the proponents of traditional sources of energy, and in the process creating a deep divide in Washington and throughout the country.

Chapter Objectives
This issue chapter will seek to:
1. Explain the challenges the United States faces in this age of diminishing natural resources, dependency on foreign sources of energy and the emergence of alternative energy sources.
2. Discuss the differences that exist over energy use and energy conservation as they relate to the impact on the national economy and the environment.
3. Explore the public policy options that are currently being discussed to address energy use and energy conservation.

SOME BACKGROUND

The United States is the largest user of energy in the world consuming about 26% of the energy resources available. The major source of this energy use is fossil fuels, in particular petroleum, which provides approximately 40% of the total followed by coal (23%) and natural gas (another 23%); the remaining 14% is made up of a mix of nuclear and hydroelectric power and other renewable sources.[1] As the United States moved from a rural and agricultural society in which wood and later coal were the energy mainstays to an urban and industrial society in which petroleum was king, the level of energy consumption increased significantly. The rise of an ever-growing consumer society with the accent on the acquisition of more and more petroleum-based products, especially the automobile, added to this demographic and economic shift.

At present, the primary consumer of energy in the United States is the industrial sector with transportation secondary. Residential users and commercial enterprises make up the remainder of the energy sectors. American economic development over the years has been fueled by heavy usage of available energy sources as the manufacturing sector or smokestack industries relied heavily on oil and coal. Besides the industrial sector, the critical source of energy use, mainly gasoline products, has been in transportation. Americans love their cars, especially big cars, and show only a passing interest in mass transit or small compact vehicles. In the United States taking the train or subway to work is not popular, whereas the Europeans take pride in their extensive and heavily used train system and their fuel-efficient automobiles. The combination of a vibrant industrial sector and a nation in love with the automobile has created heavy energy use and an unquenchable reliance on petroleum products. The United States is an energy giant, not in terms of producing energy, but in terms of using it.[2]

Translating this reliance on petroleum products into numbers, U.S. oil consumption is about 21 million barrels per day, 50% of which is in the form of gasoline. Increasingly, the oil the United States uses is imported. In 1970 the United States imported about 10% of its oil, but by 2004 the level of importation had risen to 65%. Some estimates place the level of oil importation in the next ten years at 75%, unless conservation or alternative energy measures are taken to lessen dependence.[3] The cost of U.S. oil usage is approximately $700 billion a year (on a daily basis that is about $1.4 billion; hourly that is about $41 million).

The major benefactors of U.S. oil use and the rising cost of oil are largely but not exclusively Middle Eastern countries. Fifty-five percent of the oil Americans use comes from foreign sources, especially Saudi Arabia, the world's largest producer of oil. Venezuela, Nigeria and other nations are also members of the oil cartel known as OPEC, the Organization of Petroleum Exporting Countries. Although the United States has been successful at times convincing the Saudis and other nations to increase production and therefore bringing the price down somewhat, the OPEC producers have in the main sought to control supply and drive the price up, thereby amassing huge fortunes by feeding the oil habit of the United States. Unfortunately, the United States has only about 3% of the world's known oil reserves, although there are fairly substantial untapped reserves in the Southwest, the Gulf of Mexico and Alaska.[4]

During the years when oil products such as gasoline and home heating oil were inexpensive, Americans paid little attention to energy and showed little interest in energy conservation. In 1973 Americans got a hint of the impact that foreign oil production and price controls can have as OPEC staged an embargo on the sale of oil to the United States in retaliation for U.S. foreign policy support of Israel. For months the oil embargo created long lines at gas stations and short tempers as Americans waited to fill up their cars with expensive gas. (I have vivid memories of sitting in a gas line to get my three-gallon allotment from the gas station manager who stood with the gas pump in one hand and a tire iron in the other for protection.) Since the 1973 oil embargo, OPEC and other oil-producing nations not affiliated with OPEC have been more concerned with profit rather than politics. Fortunately for the United States, these oil-producing countries kept production high and prices low to cash in on America's love affair with cars.

With the cost of gas relatively cheap, Americans bought big SUVs and trucks, drove seventy to eighty miles an hour and took long automobile or recreation-vehicle vacations. The automobile industry did little to dissuade Americans from buying big cars and trucks and even fostered the driving culture that created the huge Hummer SUVs with fuel consumption of less than twelve miles per gallon. Besides the push for bigger gas-guzzlers, there was little concern about moving away from oil as a source of home heating and no compunction to develop new sources of energy such as solar or even to make homes more energy efficient. Americans often could not bring themselves to place huge solar panels on their roofs, and efforts to create wind farms in some areas of the country faced the Not In My Backyard (NIMBY) syndrome.

However, big oil price increases that started in 2007 and carried over into 2008 began to push the American people and government officials to take action as the cost of a gallon of gas rose to $4.00 in some regions. Inflation began to rear its ugly head, and workers, desperate to make ends meet in the new energy environment, struggled to find ways to cut back on gasoline. Within a matter of months during 2008 the subway and the train quickly became options as Americans left their cars at home. Although the Great Recession of late 2008 and 2009 caused a precipitous drop in the price of oil and thus gasoline, the energy cost crunch is expected to rear its ugly head again. With countries such as China and India along with other developing nations becoming major users of petroleum products, demand for oil has increased further. This new level of demand has affected not just the price of gasoline and heating products, but all sorts of food and commercial products that rely on oil in some form during production. Americans have reluctantly come to the realization that not only has the price of gasoline changed but the world demand has as well. It has begun to sink in that Americans are no longer going to be the privileged minority that will benefit from cheap energy. Americans might continue to use energy more than other countries, but they will now have to pay for that energy at levels never anticipated.

DEBATES, DIFFERENCE AND DIVISIONS

Americans see every day the cost of gasoline and home heating oil as they fill up their cars or heat their homes. They know quite well that countries in the Middle East are amassing huge national currency reserves (mostly in dollars) as a result of the United States' reliance on foreign oil. Americans also know that those big SUVs or pick-up trucks they drive are not fuel efficient, although they are roomy and fun to drive. When debates, differences and divisions do occur, whether among the general public or in the halls of government, those points of conflict are usually over how best to bring down the price of energy, how to become less reliant on foreign oil sources and how to establish conservation measures that will save not only energy but also dollars and cents for the cash-strapped consumer. As with many of the issues discussed so far, there are no agreed-upon national solutions to the energy crisis facing the United States, only the recognition that something must be done to deal with a real energy crisis.[5]

Outside the corridors of power in Washington, average Americans have begun to adopt a wide range of home- and car-based measures to lessen their energy use and the one-way transfer of national wealth to OPEC. Following in large part the models of energy conservation used during the Arab oil embargo of the 1970s, the American consumer has harkened back to tried and true conservation measures, such as trading in their SUVs and trucks for hybrid cars that increase miles per gallon, winterizing their homes, purchasing more efficient light bulbs and appliances and driving less or taking public transportation. Also some environmentalists have called for a return to the fifty-five miles per hour highway driving option that was popular during the 1973 oil embargo and pushed by then President Jimmy Carter.[6] According to the U.S. Environmental Protection Agency, reducing the speed to fifty-five miles per hour can save as much as 20% in fuel use and drop yearly fuel costs by over $1,000. These conservation measures are supported by polling data. Surveys indicate that Americans support the move to change their lifestyle and move toward conservation. A Gallup poll in 2008 found that more than 50% of Americans placed a higher priority on conservation than on increasing the supply of oil.[7] Furthermore, although many Americans believe that ultimately technological advances will ease the energy crisis, they have little confidence that a magic solution to the energy crisis will come anytime soon and are resigned to taking whatever small measures they can to bring down fuel costs.

However, while Americans are seeking to deal with the impact of high energy costs on their household budgets, the federal government is locked in a fierce fight over just how best to set national energy policy. As can be expected, those from the conservative side are convinced that the answer lies with tax incentives to develop alternative energy sources, a lessening of regulations to drill for oil in regions that have a protected status and a renewed emphasis on nuclear power and more environmentally sound coal (often times called *clean coal*). Those of the liberal persuasion stress that government must take a more active role in requiring high mileage standards for American-made automobiles, moving quickly to simpler energy sources such as solar panels and wind turbines and creating a carbon emission tax on industry. Because the conservative model is largely based on market-based incentives and the liberal view relies on government initiatives and regulation, both sides in this debate over energy policy have become embroiled in a familiar push and pull over how best to solve a national problem.

On the Record

As early as 1999, leading figures in the oil industry were predicting significant changes in energy sources and energy usage. Mike Bowlin, chairman and CEO of oil conglomerate ARCO and chairman at that time of the American Petroleum Institute, said the following:

> We've embarked on the beginning of the Last Days of the Age of Oil. Nations of the world that are striving to modernize will make choices different from the ones we have made. They will have to. And even today's industrial powers will shift energy use patterns. . . . The market share for carbon-rich fuels will diminish, as the demand for other forms of energy grows. And energy companies have a choice: to embrace the future and recognize the growing demand for a wide array of fuels; or ignore reality, and slowly–but surely–be left behind.

Source: Winning the Oil Endgame, http://www.oilendgame.com/

In President Bush's last State of the Union address in 2008 he stated that his administration was committed to aggressively pursuing measures that will make the United States energy independent.[8] Later at the International Renewable Energy Conference he stated that his administration had spent $12 billion on research to develop alternative energy sources and was working with the private sector to encourage, through tax incentives, further research on alternative energy sources. Biodiesel and ethanol were at the top of the president's list of alternative energy sources. Biodiesel fuel has grown dramatically in the last few years, and there are now over 650 biodiesel fueling stations in the United States. However, the president was most excited about ethanol as a key answer to energy independence. The United States is the world's largest producer of ethanol (which is derived from corn), and the president pledged to expand the ethanol program. The Energy Department had already spent over $1 billion in research to make the cost of the fuel more cost efficient and cost competitive. Finally, at the conference the president accented the need to renew America's national commitment to nuclear power. Because of citizen and environment concerns over nuclear power, especially nuclear waste and nuclear accidents, the United States has not built a new nuclear plant in decades. The president was committed to changing that situation and ease regulatory limits to help permit new nuclear power plant construction. The Bush administration viewed all these alternatives as creating new industries, new technologies and most of all new jobs. Many in energy conservation circles are convinced that the next generation of job growth will be in the environmental and energy fields as the American entrepreneurial spirit directs its innovation toward a green revolution and with that revolution a new sector of the economy and employment.[9]

Although President Bush was touting the enormous possibilities of new technologies and new sources of energy, he was not willing to support any policy initiatives that placed immediate and strict controls on carbon dioxide emissions in the form of a carbon tax on automobiles and industries and other tax measures that would in his view be "anti-economic growth." As the president said on numerous occasions, he did not support the Kyoto Accord, which recommended a carbon tax and target dates for a reduction in emissions. The president remained adamant that agreeing to the positions in the Kyoto Accord would have a detrimental impact on the national economy as American industrial and automotive sectors would become less competitive and less profitable.[10]

Instead of supporting the Kyoto Accord and any proposals from Democrats that would affect economic development and corporate viability, Bush praised the essential elements of the Energy Independence and Security Act of 2007 that supports research on alternative energy sources and requires modest gas mileage targets to increase energy efficiency. Bush, however, was not content to just advocate for changes in Americans' use of oil and the need to move to new energy sources. He also continued his support for drilling at the Arctic National Wildlife Refuge, which environmentalists and liberal Democrats in Congress have opposed, and for a relaxation of regulations on further drilling in the Gulf of Mexico, off the coast of California and in the Southwest. Bush and the oil-and-gas industry take the position that these areas contain perhaps as much as 25–30 billion barrels of oil and 80 trillion cubic feet of natural gas. Currently, the United States has proven reserves of about 30 billion barrels of oil and 200 trillion cubic feet of natural gas.[11] Critics remain concerned that drilling in these areas poses a major threat to the environment both in terms of animal and fish life, and in the prospects of oil leaks and other threats associated with drilling. President Obama angered environmentalists when in 2010 he announced that he would support offshore drilling in the Gulf of Mexico, in Alaska and off the east coast as one part of his overall energy policy. Republicans praised the change of policy, although it was likely that the president was using the renewed drilling position only as a bargaining chip for Republican support on a broader energy bill.[12]

Obama's support for offshore drilling took a turn when in April 2010 an oil-drilling platform in the Gulf of Mexico caught fire and eventually collapsed, killing eleven men. At first British Petroleum (BP), which leased the platform, downplayed the environmental impact from the escaping oil, but within a few days the assessment of the expanse of the oil spill created by the platform fire increased significantly. An oil spill the size of Connecticut affected the coastline from Louisiana to Florida and endangered animal and plant life throughout the region, along with some of the nation's most plentiful shrimp fishing grounds. As the oil spill spread and BP was initially unable to stop the leak, critics began to describe the environmental disaster (the worst in U.S. history) as "Obama's Katrina" as it accused the government of not acting quickly enough and with a level of bureaucratic coordination necessary to deal with the oil spill. Environmentalists, on the other hand, reminded Americans and the proponents of offshore drilling that this catastrophe proved their point not only about the dangers of such resource extraction so close to American shores, but also about the need to move away from dependence on foreign oil.

Data Bank

The soaring price of oil in 2008 prompted a national frenzy over the profits that American and other international oil companies were making. In April 2008 British Petroleum reported a 63% increase in first quarter profits to $7.6 billion, Royal Dutch Shell a 25% increase to $9.1 billion and Chevron, the second largest American oil firm, a 10% increase to $5.17 billion, its biggest first-quarter profit ever. And ExxonMobil, the largest American-based oil company, led the profit makers with a 17% increase in profits to 10.9 billion, the second biggest quarterly profit in the history of the United States. By 2009, however, as a result of decreasing demand associated with the recession, ExxonMobil's profits dropped by 50%. Other major oil companies also experienced sharp declines in profits.

Source: ABC News

Offshore drilling has moved front and center in the debate over energy and energy conservation, but when Barack Obama entered the White House he listed his goals for energy policy as "support for the next generation of biofuels, setting America on a path to oil independence, and improve energy efficiency by 50% by 2030." Democratic leaders have targeted the oil companies for their excess profits and in particular for their staunch defense of government subsidies that reached $18 billion in 2008. The oil company executives were brought regularly to House and Senate hearings to face angry Democrats who wanted to know why the subsidies were necessary and of course why gas prices were so high. The executives defended the subsidies as a way of assisting them in the very expensive process of finding new oil fields and in developing new refining capacity. They defended the price of gasoline as the result of heightened worldwide demand and regular supply dislocations as instability in some oil-producing countries such as Nigeria posed serious problems that elevated the cost of oil per barrel.[13]

Democrats also took on the SUV and the pick-up truck, which benefited from less stringent fuel efficiency standards. They also criticized the Bush administration for what they felt was too slow a push to achieve high fuel efficiency goals. The Democrats berated Bush for making 2020 the target date for enhanced fuel efficiency standards, stating that this was a concession to the automotive industry, which many members of Congress felt was dragging its feet on making American-made cars attain higher levels of fuel efficiency. The Democratic position on energy that emerged in 2007 and 2008 was to pressure Detroit car makers to move quickly to produce energy-efficient cars. As Barack Obama stated to an audience in Detroit as far back as 2007, "I went to Detroit, I stood in front of a group of automakers, and I told them that when I am president, there will be no more excuses—we will help them retool their factories, but they will have to make cars that use less oil."[14]

Also the Democrats have on numerous occasions lambasted the Bush Administration for failing to dip into the U.S. Strategic Petroleum Reserve, an oil depository system of 640–700 billions of gallons of oil the United States keeps in reserve for crisis periods or shortages (the Reserve would likely provide about fifty days of oil should an emergency arise). In 2008 the Democrats wanted the Bush Administration to open up the Reserve and pump billions of gallons of gas into the consumer system as a way of lessening the impact of price increases. The Bush Administration refused this request. However, Congress persisted in trying to loosen up the administration's reluctance to make changes in the status of the Strategic Petroleum Reserve. The Democrats in Congress passed legislation in 2008 demanding that the Energy Department discontinue purchasing oil to place in the Reserve. The Energy Department did comply and ended contracts with OPEC that placed 70,000 barrels of oil a day in the Reserve. Most experts saw the end of the purchase orders as a symbolic gesture that would have little impact on the daily price of oil.[15]

There has also been a growing debate among the scientific community about the drawbacks to ethanol use, an alternative energy source supported by the Democrats. Critics of ethanol use state that such gas may actually heighten carbon dioxide emissions, thereby fostering even more global warming. Furthermore, the use of corn in the process of making ethanol is creating a shortage of this key grain as a basic food source. Because ethanol was first targeted as an alternative to foreign oil, many American farmers have switched from selling corn as a food product to selling corn as a source of ethanol and they have also planted less of other grains in an attempt to cash in on this new source of energy. In 2008 there were severe shortages of food in many poor countries as one result of the switch over to corn-based ethanol and also steep price increases for many foodstuffs throughout the world, including the United States.[16]

FYI

Energy usage varies widely in the United States by region and urban center. Dallas, Texas, has one of the highest average annual residential electricity usages in the country with 16,116 Kilowatt hours per customer followed by Houston, Texas, with 14,542 Kilowatt hours of average annual

(continued)

FYI (continued)

residential electricity usage. New York has one of the lowest average annual residential electricity usages with 4,696 Kilowatt hours per customer. The high usage of the two Texas cities is likely the result of long hot summers compared to those in New York. The same can be said for region as the Pacific coast region, which has about a 35% less energy use compared to the North Central (with cold winters) and South Central (with warm summers) parts of the country.

Source: New York City Mayor's Office of Sustainability

Although clear differences exist in Washington decision-making centers about the most effective approach to energy conservation and energy independence, states have begun to take action to deal with the crisis. One of the most promising areas of energy development is wind power. Texas has taken the lead in wind power, followed by California. Both states have developed wind farms with the Horse Hollow Wind Energy Center in Texas, now the nation's largest wind farm.[17] Also solar energy is moving forward again, after an initial start in the 1970s followed by a steep drop-off in support. States such as Nevada have built major solar power centers as part of its solar energy generating systems. Nine solar plants have been constructed in the desolate Mojave Desert, making the entire system the largest solar plant in the world. Currently, the United States leads the world in geothermal energy, with seventy-five projects either completed or under way. However, support for alternative energy sources such as wind power is not always welcomed. Massachusetts has been involved in a long debate over placing a wind farm off the coast in the Nantucket Sound. Residents in the area expressed extensive opposition as they claim a negative impact on the ocean and on marine and bird life.[18] In 2010, however, Obama administration Secretary of the Interior Ken Salazar gave final approval for the wind farm, the first offshore installation in the country.

With the arrival of the Obama administration, energy policy entered a new era as the president vowed to push forward with measures to reduce Americans' dependence on foreign oil, provide government support and financing to help foster the development of green technologies and perhaps most important, pressure Detroit automakers to produce cars with high mileage ratings and low carbon emissions. By bringing new appointees into the Environmental Protection Agency and the Department of Energy, Obama moved quickly to reverse Bush-era policies that placed the United States in opposition to international agreements such as the Kyoto Accord, placed new emissions regulations on the coal and electric power industries and included billions of dollars in his first budget to promote energy-saving projects along with tax credits for working families to bring greater energy efficiency to their homes.

One of the more contentious debates over Obama energy policy was what came to be called a cap-and-trade proposal designed to curb carbon emissions from industrial plants and thereby contribute to a lessening of global warming. The cap-and-trade system consisted of credits that could be traded between companies allowing them to emit carbon dioxide. Those companies that had leftover credits (because they were energy efficient) could sell them to other companies. This process of cap and trade was designed as a means of encouraging industries to conserve energy and not pollute the environment. Democrats and environmentalists hailed the system as a way to get industries to cap their emissions, whereas many business groups, particularly in the Midwest, stated that this cap-and-trade system was a tax on fossil fuels that would prove disastrous to their profits.[19] However, as the debate over energy and environmental policy progressed in the Congress, the cap-and-trade proposal began to lose support as not only too complex, but likely to lead to higher energy costs to the consumer. Eventually President Obama did not mention cap and trade as a priority for his energy plan.[20]

Although cap and trade remained in the forefront of energy policy, a more comprehensive bipartisan bill authored by Senators John Kerry of Massachusetts (D) and Lindsey Graham of South Carolina (R) stressed target dates for reducing carbon emissions, offering incentives to the coal industry to develop clean coal alternatives and financial incentives to the nuclear power industry, allowing states to prohibit oil and gas exploration within thirty-five miles of their coastline, and perhaps most important mandating that proceeds from the auction of cap-and-trade arrangements would be returned to the consumer.[21] The accent on returning profits to consumers from the cap-and-trade process was a response to an alternative bill proposed by Republican Senator Susan Collins of Maine and Democrat Senator Maria Cantwell of Washington. They proposed what they termed a cap-and-dividend process, which would use the profits that would come from major oil and gas companies trading these energy credits and return them to consumers via a yearly check.[22] As with most comprehensive legislation, the energy/environment bill in Congress was entangled in partisan politics and was the subject of intense lobbying by both energy providers and environmental groups.

Although cap and trade often received the primary share of media attention, President Obama's most ambitious energy policy initiative was the announcement in May 2009 of new uniform federal standards to regulate both fuel economy and greenhouse gas emissions. Cars made in the United States from 2012 to 2016 would be required to have an average fuel economy standard of 35.5 miles per gallon by 2016. The standards, according to the government experts, would reduce oil consumption by 1.8 billion barrels over the four-year period of the program and reduce gas emissions by approximately 900 million metric tons. Detroit automakers, in part because the government owned a share of both GM and Chrysler, supported the standards as a way of lowering consumer costs on gasoline, cleaning up the environment and responding to a shift in consumer choice toward more fuel-efficient cars. Moreover, the Detroit automakers went along with the Obama energy standards because they mandated uniform rules about gas mileage standards and lowered compliance costs to meet differing requirements in different states.[23]

The Obama administration has set a series of ambitious goals to deal with the energy crisis in the United States and indeed elsewhere in the world.

The president has promised that the United States will end its dependence on foreign oil and replace that oil with a string of new green technologies. Meanwhile the accent will be placed on tough measures to change U.S. industrial policies and practices and incentives to everyday Americans to think about conservation and live green. In many respects, the energy debate going on in Washington and throughout the country is the most important of all the contentious issues, because it deals with the future environmental health of the United States and indeed the planet.

It must be emphasized though that although the key phrase in the energy debate is "energy independence," many experts believe that the United States not only will never become energy independent, but that market forces, rather than government programs, remain the most effective way to provide Americans with the oil they need. Despite all the promise shown by alternative technologies and the rise of ethanol and biofuels, the use of these sources of energy will not be sufficient to provide the United States with that $1.4 billion a day craving for oil. Justin Fox, the editor-at-large of the business magazine *Fortune*, advocated for market forces and a continued flow of oil from the Middle East when he stated, "right now it costs less to pump oil from the sands of the Arabian peninsula than from pretty much anywhere else on earth. Why would we want to punish ourselves by cutting ourselves off from the cheapest oil?"[24] Although Fox's position may not resonate with Americans paying ever-rising prices for gas at the pump, the argument made by Fox is that "going green" will not automatically make the United States energy independent, at least not in the next thirty to forty years. Despite the promises of politicians, Americans will likely remain energy dependent and must accept the harsh reality of a long-term process of change and sacrifice that might bring the United States closer to energy independence. Fox's position is echoed by highly respected energy expert Daniel Yergin, who stated in *Foreign Policy* that "global energy use will increase almost 50% from 2006–2030–and that oil will continue to provide 30% or more of the world's energy in 2030."[25]

Many Americans are convinced that there are solutions to our energy dependence, especially in the auto industry, that have languished for years without action being taken, while oil and gas companies have been making windfall profits without care and concern for the impact on the American consumer and the American economy. Americans will demand action of their national political leaders and will hold them accountable if significant changes in their energy system are not forthcoming. However, the key to the energy crisis will be the way in which the American consumer reacts to the current price of gasoline and home heating oil. Will Americans cut back on driving, will they drive fifty-five miles per hour, will they spend the money to insulate their homes, will they trade in their SUVs for hybrids and will they take the commuter train or subway to work rather than ride alone on the freeway? These are ultimately questions of lifestyle and consumerism that were never raised during the good old days of cheap energy. There are signs that Americans are beginning to change their old habits (albeit reluctantly) as they think twice about driving short distances, buying roomier and powerful cars, ignoring that winter window draft and driving alone to work. However, years of habits do not die easily, and many Americans continue to blame the oil companies for price gouging (which is a constant refrain both at gas stations and in the corridors of Congress) rather than look at the manner in which they use oil products.

What is often ignored, however, in this energy debate is what has been said before with respect to other issues–the world is changing and the United States is not the only major economic power. The demand for oil will only increase, not just from China and India, but from scores of other countries that have become more economically advanced in the last twenty years and as a result are creating heightened demands for petroleum products. It is safe to state that the days of cheap oil and low gasoline prices are gone forever. We now live at a time when everyone in the world (except those countries such as Saudi Arabia where gasoline is fifty cents a gallon) will have to face the reality that a key natural resource, a resource that is critical to economic advancement, is going to be expensive.

The Great Debate

The key to the U.S. energy crisis is the ending or at least lessening of the dependence on foreign oil, although this will require significant changes in the way Americans live and work.

Debate Topic

Can the United States significantly diminish its dependence on foreign oil or is the American lifestyle such that the country will remain tied to oil as the major source of energy?

Critical Thinking Questions

1. Will Detroit carmakers be able to produce fuel-efficient cars by 2016 as mandated by the Obama administration?
2. Do you believe that the American people and American business can make the adjustments and sacrifices necessary to bring an end to the energy crisis?
3. Are wind, solar and ethanol the answers to our energy crisis?
4. Do you agree with the Bush policy of offshore drilling in California and in the Gulf of Mexico and also in Alaska's Arctic Reserve, even though there may be environmental dangers?
5. What suggestions would you make to deal with the energy crisis in the United States?

Connections

The U.S. Department of Energy is responsible in large part for U.S. energy policy. Visit its site at http://www.doe.gov

View the White House position on energy at http://www.whitehouse.gov/infocus/energy

The American Physics Society has a helpful website on energy policy for the 21st century. See http://www.aps.org/policy/statements/00_3.cfm

The Environmental Working Group is one of the key sites for a discussion of alternative energy sources. See http://www.ewg.org

A key organization advancing the cause of environmentalism, conservation and reduction in greenhouse gases is Conservation. Visit its website at www.conservation.org

Some Books to Read

Kline, Benjamin, *First Along the River: A Brief History of the U.S. Environmental Movement* (Lanham, MD: Rowan & Littlefield, 2007).

Makhijani, Arjun, *Carbon Free and Nuclear Free: A Roadmap for U.S. Energy Policy* (Takoma Park, MD: Institute for Energy and Environmental Research Press, 2007).

Black, Brian and Donna Lybecker, *Great Debates in American Environmental History* (Westport, CT: Greenwood Press, 2008).

Komjathy, Thomas, *The Modern Patriot: A Voter's Guide to U.S. Energy Policy* (New York: AuthorHouse, 2006).

Parra, Francisco, *Oil Politics: A Modern History of Petroleum* (London: I.B. Tauris, 2004).

Notes

1. U.S. Department of Energy, Annual Energy Report, July 2008.
2. For background discussion of U.S. energy politics and policy see Walter A. Rosenbaum, *Environmental Politics and Policy*, 6th edition (Washington, D.C.: Congressional Quarterly Press, 2004).
3. The data are from the Department of Energy. See http://www.eia.doe.gov/pub/international/iealf/tablee1.xls
4. See Energy Information Administration, World Consumption of Primary Energy Type and Selected Country Group–1980–2004, July 31, 2006.
5. Steven Mufson, "The Energy Revolution," *Washington Post National Weekly Edition*, April 13–19, 2008, p. 27.
6. See United States Environment Protection Agency, Department of Transportation and Air Quality, "Reducing Highway Speed," http://www.epa.gov/smartway
7. http://www.gallup.com/poll/15820/public-priorities-environment-vs-economic-growth.aspx
8. http://www.c-span/executive/stateoftheunion.ASP
9. Ibid.
10. "Bush: Kyoto Treaty Would Have Hurt Economy," *MSNBC*, June 30, 2005, http://www.msnbc.msn.com/id/8422343/
11. See "Refuge Has Long Been a Major Environmental Battleground," *Los Angeles Times*, March 17, 2005.

12. See "Florida Critics Blast President's Offshore Drilling Plan," http://www.cnn.com/2010/POLITICS/03/31/energy/environmentalists/index.html
13. See the Democratic Party position at http://www.democrats.org/a/national/clean_environment/energy/. See also "Pelosi Stands Firm Against Offshore Drilling," *International Herald Tribune*, July 17, 2007, http://www.nytimes.com/2008/07/17/world/americas/17iht-pelosi.1.14566464.html.
14. Nick Bunkley and Michelene Magrod, "Obama Criticizes Automakers on Fuel Economy," *New York Times*, May 7, 2007, http://www.nytimes.com/2007/05/07/us/politics/07cnd-obama.html
15. "House Proposal to Tap Strategic Oil Reserves Fails," http://www.msnbc.com/id/25839620
16. Steven Mafson, "Ethanol Industry Gets Boost from Bush," *Washington Post*, January 25, 2007, D01.
17. "Turbine Time," *Economist*, July 19, 2008, pp. 41–42.
18. See CBS News for "Storm Over Mass Wind Mill Plan," http://www.cbsnews.com/stories/2003/06/26/sunday/main560595.shtml
19. "Sins of Emission," *Economist*, March 14, 2009, pp. 26–27.
20. John M. Broder, " 'Cap and Trade' Loses Its Standing as Energy Policy of Choice," *New York Times*, March 26, 2010, A13.
21. See the highlights of the energy/climate bill in *Boston Globe*, April 25, 2010, A11.
22. See Bill McKibben, "Bringing the Heat," *New Republic*, April 29, 2010, pp. 16–17.
23. "Obama Administration's National Fuel Efficiency Policy: Good for Customers, Good for the Economy and Good for the Country," White House Office of the Press Secretary, May 19, 2009.
24. Justin Fox, "Energy Independence is a Disaster in the Making," http://www.money.com/2006/02/28/news/economy/pluggedin_fortune/index.htm
25. Daniel Yergin, "It's Still the One," *Foreign Policy*, September/October, 2009.

19 POVERTY AND SOCIAL WELFARE

Issue Focus

One of the functions of the U.S. government that has expanded over time is responding to the needs of those Americans who are poor and require some level of assistance. Since the Depression of the 1930s and during the recent Great Recession, government has become increasingly involved in developing policies and programs that seek to alleviate poverty and provide opportunities for those who are poor to move out of poverty. Despite the growth in government's social welfare responsibility, there has been widespread opposition from those who believe that the expenditures related to poverty reduction are excessive and not properly monitored. Moreover, an additional criticism is that governmental leaders, especially under Democratic Party rule, have not been vigorous in demanding that those in poverty help themselves and not become dependent on assistance programs. As a result of these criticisms, there have been significant changes made in social welfare policy in the United States, but those changes have only heated up the debate over how much the government should support those in need.

Chapter Objectives

This issue chapter will seek to:

1. Present the policy evolution of public-supported welfare in the United States, with particular emphasis on the welfare reform achieved during the Clinton administration.

2. Examine the points of division both in the United States and in policy-making circles over whether governments at all levels should provide assistance to those in need or should instead rely more on private support and accent personal responsibility.

3. Describe the current challenges faced by those in poverty or those facing other economic, health or personal problems and the role of government in dealing with those challenges.

SOME BACKGROUND

Despite the enormous wealth in the United States there are approximately 47 million Americans or nearly 16% of the population who are defined by the government as poor. In a country of 310 million people that means one in eight Americans lives in poverty and almost 13 million children grow up in poverty. When compared with other advanced industrial democracies, the United States has not been successful, despite numerous programs, at reducing poverty and moving the poor into the mainstream of American economic life. As Isabel Sawhill, a noted poverty expert at the Brookings Institution has stated, "Despite our wealth . . . poverty is more prevalent in the United States than in most of the rest of the industrialized world. It is also more prevalent now than it was in the early seventies, when the incidence of poverty of America reached a post-war low."[1]

The profile of a poor person in the United States is an individual (or for funding analysis usually a family) who falls below a government-established poverty line, an income level that is used to determine who is eligible for the various programs designed to assist the poor. In 2009 that poverty line was set at an annual income of $22,050 for a family of four. In many cases that family of four is headed by a young, single female who is likely to be African-American or Hispanic and lives in a rural area (one in seven residents) or urban center (one in nine residents). Whites make up approximately 11% of the poor in the United States, whereas other racial groupings have far higher levels of poverty–African-Americans, 24%, Hispanics, 22%, Asians, 12% and American Indians, 24%. As to the geographic region with the largest percentage of poor people, the South, according to census data compiled in 2003, had 14% of its population defined as poor and the Midwest had the lowest percentage of poverty with 10.7% defined as poor.[2]

The key demographic relative to poverty in America is young single women. Much has been written about the feminization of poverty in the United States as young women who have children out of wedlock or whose husbands or boyfriends have divorced or abandoned them make up a large percentage of the poor.[3] Divorce, in particular, creates serious financial challenges for women. Studies have shown that when a woman is divorced with young children, her standard of living decreases by 73%, whereas the standard of living for a man experiencing divorce increases by 42%. With little education, young children, irregular child support payments and few marketable skills, these young women make up the bulk of those Americans on welfare. According to U.S. Census data from 2005, the poverty rate among single male heads of households was 17.6%, whereas that among single female heads of households was a staggering 36.9%.[4]

Although there has been much emphasis on the feminization of poverty in the United States, poverty can touch just about anyone and can be found just around the corner. The loss of a job or some sort of disability can easily contribute to a person or family falling below the government standard. Even those Americans who are working can often qualify for government assistance, as minimum wage jobs ($6.75 in 2008) do not provide enough income to lift a working family above the poverty line. The government estimates that about 10% of those families that qualify for assistance are employed full-time. Growing evidence suggests that America is now a country that has millions of working homeless people as high rents and energy costs combined with low wages make it difficult for the working poor to maintain residences, forcing them into shelters or some type of congregate housing.[5] There is also mounting evidence that the United States has a high incidence of income inequality as the gap between the rich and the poor grows and the Americans in the middle class are struggling to maintain a modicum of income stability.[6]

To respond to the presence of poverty in America, federal and state governments have developed a wide range of public assistance or welfare programs designed to address the many causes and challenges faced by those who are poor. It is often said that the United States has a two-tiered social welfare system. The top tier of social insurance is for members of the middle class who benefit from programs such as Social Security, Medicare and unemployment compensation. In each of these programs the employee or the employer or both make contributions through a payroll deduction toward the payment of the insurance and then receive the benefit upon retirement or if hospitalized or unemployed. These social insurance programs are popular among Americans because they help fund retirements, hospital stays and periods of unemployment.

The second or lower tier of the social welfare system is designed to address the economic problems brought on by poverty or disability. At the core of the second-tier social welfare system are programs well known to Americans such as food stamps (subsidies to purchase food), Medicaid (medical care for the poor), Supplementary Security Income (SSI; to assist seniors with additional income), the Job Opportunity and Basic Skills (JOBS) program and Temporary Assistance for Needy Families (TANF), which in 1996 replaced the Aid to Families with Dependent Children (AFDC) program. Such programs usually provide direct payments to single parents with children, food stamps, housing subsidies, job training and free or reduced medical care. These programs are in large part based on a means test, which requires those seeking assistance to prove that they fall below the government poverty standards and are indeed eligible for assistance. The government has also developed a tax credit program called the Earned Income Tax Credit (EITC), which provides rebates for poor Americans who file their income tax and show a level of income that merits a tax rebate through the EITC program.

The second-tier programs, which provide a safety net for those who are less fortunate or need some temporary assistance to get them through a tough period, have become the target of government belt-tightening, partisan bickering and public criticism. A series of polls by CBS and the *New York Times* taken in the mid-1990s (before substantial welfare reform was initiated) showed overwhelmingly negative views toward those on welfare. One poll revealed that a majority of Americans believed "people are so dependent on welfare that they will never get off," and a subsequent poll found that a similar majority of respondents believed that welfare recipients should enter work programs and "should stop receiving welfare benefits."[7]

Poverty, disability and growing income inequality in America have been the driving forces behind numerous social welfare programs developed by the government dating as far back as the so-called mother's pensions in the 1920s that were given to single mothers who had no means of support and had a number of children to care for. These public assistance programs were expanded significantly during the Great Depression era in the 1930s when President Franklin Delano Roosevelt introduced the New Deal with its alphabet soup of lettered programs (such as the Civilian Conservation Corp [CCC] and the Works Progress Administration [WPA]). These programs were designed to put unemployed Americans to work on public projects. After World War II and certainly during the heyday of liberal Democratic control of the presidency and the Congress, welfare programs expanded, specifically during the Johnson administration's Great Society, with initiatives such as the food stamp program, Head Start program (pre-kindergarten opportunities for poor children) and public housing projects.

It was not until the onset of the Reagan administration in 1981 that direct public assistance and the entire welfare system came under greater scrutiny as the emphasis of government shifted toward personal responsibility, church and community assistance and job training. Although the welfare programs that were in place since the New Deal and the Great Society continued to receive government support, budget increases were more modest and eligibility requirements were tightened. Moreover, greater reliance was placed on state solutions for those on welfare rather than large-scale federal government programs. The key transition in the fight to change welfare policy in the United States came in 1994 when the Republicans took control of the House and Senate and pushed the Clinton administration to support new approaches to poverty reduction. After decades of liberal democratic solutions to poverty that accented heavy government involvement and huge outlays of federal funds, the conservative revolution started by Ronald Reagan placed its mark on the welfare system.[8]

DEBATES, DIFFERENCES AND DIVISIONS

It is often said that Americans are the most generous and caring people on earth, but that designation has not stopped them from engaging in spirited public policy debates over the extent to which government should come to the assistance of the poor and the needy. Many Americans continue to hold true to the deep-seated traditions of a strong work ethic, self reliance and the principle of individual responsibility as the keys to economic success, not government programs. Large government outlays for welfare and a redistributive policy of moving assistance from taxpayers to the poor are viewed as paternalistic, fostering dependency and creating a huge "nanny state" in which government spends huge portions of the national budget on taking care of the poor. Because of widespread support for this anti-welfare position, frequent efforts have been made in the political arena to cut back many of the second-tier programs discussed earlier, make eligibility more difficult or move those eligible into work or training programs. Conservatives in policy-making circles have often targeted income-transfer programs to the poor such as public assistance, food stamps and Medicaid as creating a cycle of dependency and as a result the poor feel no pressure to remove themselves from the welfare rolls.

Supporters of government intervention in poverty reduction, however, stress the humanitarian nature of government poverty reduction programs and the obligation of government to provide a safety net of support for those most vulnerable. These supporters of government activism cite the failures of the market system to address poverty, the income inequality growing in the United States and the inability of religious, community and charitable organizations to fully respond to the growing level of poverty. Moreover, the supporters of government poverty reduction programs show that many welfare programs have had a positive impact on the poor such as the Head Start program that gives young children an early educational experience. Also many government-sponsored job training programs have helped to lift the poor out of poverty by providing them with the skills necessary to become financially independent.

In recent years, the trend in policy circles has been to move away from income transfer programs and begin experiments with what has come to be called workfare, programs that set limits on the time an individual can receive welfare benefits and require recipients to find work or be trained for work to eventually move out of the public assistance system. As a result of a waiver from the Reagan administration regarding rules associated with the AFDC program, the state of Wisconsin, under the leadership of Republican Governor Tommy Thompson, developed its own workfare-like program that eventually became a model for other states and stimulated efforts at the federal level to take measures that completely revamped the long-running AFDC program. AFDC had been heavily criticized as fostering the culture of dependency and not providing sufficient incentives for poor people to get off the welfare rolls. In a ten-year period ending in 1997, the AFDC caseload statewide in Wisconsin dropped by 50%, and in inner cities such as Milwaukee, the drop was 25%. The success achieved in Wisconsin in reducing the number of AFDC recipients spread to a whole host of states as governors took the lead in forming policies that accented work and set time limits for participation in AFDC programs.[9]

The welfare reform movement that started in Wisconsin eventually led to a national debate over federal involvement in poverty reduction. This debate centered on the landmark legislation formally called the Personal Responsibility and Work Opportunity Reconciliation Act, which came to be called the Welfare Reform Act of 1996. After two versions of the bill were vetoed by President Clinton because of his concern that Republicans were merely seeking to end welfare without proper safeguards for work training and work opportunities, the president signed a third version of the bill. Republicans reminded the president that in his 1992 election campaign he promised to "end welfare as we know it."[10] Clinton paid a heavy price for his agreement to sign the legislation as liberals felt he caved in to Republican pressure and left the poor more vulnerable to the scourge of poverty.[11]

On the Record

In a radio address following the signing of the Personal Responsibility and Work Opportunity Reconciliation Act of 1996 President Bill Clinton said the following:

> What we are trying to do today is to overcome the flaws of the welfare system for the people who are trapped on it. We all know that the typical family on welfare today is very different from the one that welfare was designed to deal with 60 years ago. We all know that there are a lot of good people on welfare who just get off of it in the ordinary course of business but that a significant number of people are trapped on welfare for a very long time, exiling them from the entire community or work that gives structure to our lives. . . . From now on, our Nation's answer to this great social challenge will no longer be a never-ending cycle of welfare; it will be the dignity, the power, and the ethic of work. Today we are taking an historic chance to make welfare what it was meant to be: a second chance, not a way of life.

The Welfare Reform Act had at its core the concepts of welfare to work and time limits for receiving benefits. The legislation required that after a set period, usually two years, at least 50% of those on the state welfare rolls would be required to work. If those targets were not met, federal funding would be reduced. The key to the welfare reform initiative was state control through block grants–large appropriations of federal money that would be used to fund the new programs and provide job training and other assistance to those seeking to get off welfare. The legislation dismantled AFDC and replaced it with a scaled-down federal program called TANF. Most important, the legislation allowed each of the fifty states to set rules for how long welfare recipients could remain on the assistance rolls while they sought work or trained for work. Once the time period for finding or training for work was over the welfare recipients would be denied public assistance. The Welfare Reform Act of 1996 thus made poverty reduction and government programs a largely state responsibility and stressed the importance of self-help.

The most controversial parts of the Welfare Reform Act were the steep cuts in the food stamp program and the decision to refuse welfare benefits to legal immigrants. The food stamp program had been a regular target of Republicans who viewed it as filled with fraud and abuse. Supporters of the program feared that the cuts from 80 cents per person per meal to 66 cents would place an undue economic burden on the poor. This cut would translate into a reduction for a family of four of $435 over a two-year period with some of the poorest families losing over $600 in food stamp subsidies.[12] The other decision to deny benefits to legal immigrants was also controversial and contested because over 600,000 legal immigrants would lose Medicaid benefits and over 1 million food stamp subsidies. The position of those supporting the cuts to legal immigrants claimed that the benefits were a magnet to family members of immigrants who were already in the United States. Opponents of the cuts claimed that these legal immigrants paid taxes, held jobs and were law-abiding residents of the United States who would be seriously impacted by the changes. Because of the shift to state control of welfare reform, some governors pledged that they would provide assistance to legal immigrants despite the intent of the law.[13]

The Welfare Reform Act immediately set off a chain reaction of state welfare programs designed to meet the federal legislation and to implement rules and regulations on time in assistance programs, job training requirements and benefit levels. Almost immediately it became apparent that some states with more resources would be able to offer more training and benefit alternatives. Vermont, for example, was viewed as a state that would be able to invest more generously in welfare reform programs, whereas Texas and many southern states would not have the capability to provide a range of alternative employment options. Wisconsin, the initial leader in welfare reform, offered four employment options–regular employment, trial jobs with state subsidies, community service jobs and transitional skill development for those with few marketable skills.

However, it became clear in the days after the law was passed that there would be extensive state experimentation in implementing the new law and a range of uses for the federal block grants designed to speed the movement from welfare to work. Some states such as Arkansas decided to provide incentives that would offer bonuses to welfare recipients who found jobs, whereas New York developed large public works programs much like the New Deal alphabet programs. The states, however, did have a common approach to the new law by agreeing that welfare officials would help recipients train and find work and more important, realize that the welfare system had indeed changed and was accenting work, with public assistance only a temporary solution.

In February 2006 Congress reauthorized the TANF program and mandated that states increase the amount of work participation among those receiving welfare benefits. Currently 50% of welfare recipients must work at least thirty hours per week, but there are differences among the states as to what qualifies as work, how to calculate the level of state work participation and the manner in which states will be credited for caseload reductions. However, despite these areas of disagreement over the rules, nine states have already toughened the work requirements, with Iowa, Michigan, Tennessee and Wisconsin demanding that welfare recipients work forty hours a week. There is agreement among state and federal officials that those states that have not strengthened their work requirements will have to do so in the coming years.[14]

Data Bank

The block grant program to the states called TANF that replaced the federal AFDC created a system of significant disparity among the states. Nine states, namely, New York, Vermont, Connecticut, Massachusetts, Rhode Island, Delaware, Washington, California and Hawaii, provided allocations per child of over $1,500, whereas seven states, namely, South Carolina, Alabama, Mississippi, Louisiana, Arkansas, Texas and Idaho, provided allocations of less than $500. Such disparity of allocation was one of the early concerns that certain states would become magnets of welfare reform as recipients "followed the money."

Source: Center for Law and Society and U.S. Census data

During the heady days of economic prosperity in Clinton's second term, the Welfare Reform Act achieved significant success, at least in terms of substantial reductions of those receiving governmental assistance. From 1994 to 2002, there was a 57% reduction in the welfare caseload in the United States, as those on assistance moved into the world of work. In many states, government officials pressed hard to get people off the welfare rolls, although single mothers, for example, had difficulty with day-care needs and transportation and men often could not find work that paid a sufficient salary to move them and their families above the poverty line. Although many political leaders praised the Welfare Reform Act and its implementation by the states, there was another side to this success story.

The substantial drop in the welfare rolls benefited from a strong economy, low unemployment and states with the capacity to provide worker training programs. Conservatives touted the success rate in the new welfare environment as not only reducing the number of people receiving government assistance, but fostering a new culture of work and responsibility. Michael Tanner of the libertarian Cato Institute, citing a study done by the Manpower Demonstration Research Corporation, stated that "the majority of former welfare recipients believe that their lives will be better in one to five years. Many of these recipients actually praise welfare reform for encouraging them to look for work, for giving them a fresh start and for giving them a chance to make things better for themselves and their children."[15]

However, as the country entered more difficult economic times in 2008 and 2009 the number of people seeking welfare assistance increased dramatically and political leaders, particularly Democrats who initially supported the legislation, began to have second thoughts. Peter Edelman, a former assistant secretary in the Department of Health and Human Services during the Clinton administration and critic of the Welfare Reform Act, stated in 2008 "if there is no national controversy about welfare reform, we paid an awfully high price."[16] Edelman and many other liberals and social welfare activists blasted the legislation as an attack on the poor, particularly on single mothers, and an unrealistic experiment in moving people from poverty into work. According to the Congressional Research Service, the number of poor single mothers, neither working nor receiving cash assistance, increased from less than 20% before the welfare reform to more than 30%, with the number of children in poverty increasing from 11.6 million to 12.8 million.[17]

FYI

According to Philip Mangano, President Bush's chief advisor on homelessness, about 2 million Americans are homeless on any given night. However, of that 2 million about 10% are chronically homeless, meaning that they suffer some serious mental deficiency, drug or alcohol addiction or disability. Many of these chronic homeless individuals, usually males, are not only the saddest members of American society, but their personal and health problems are often a drain on emergency rooms, jails and shelters. In major cities throughout the country a chronically homeless individual can cost as much as $150,000 annually to care for. To deal with the chronically homeless, Mangano and his Interagency Council on Homelessness have developed a revolutionary plan called Housing First, which is simple in its objective: to provide a home for these individuals along with the services necessary to get them back on their feet. The Housing First program has swept the nation and has achieved remarkable results, not only in reducing the costs of taking care of the chronically homeless but in providing a simple solution to homelessness, a home.

Source: The U.S. Interagency Council on Homelessness

The Welfare Reform Act of 1996 fostered numerous analytical studies to determine just how successful the legislation was and whether improvements in poverty reduction have indeed been achieved. In 2006 the Urban Institute undertook a major study of poverty and welfare reform called the National Survey of America's Families. The researchers found that in the ten-year period since the legislation there was "an improving picture for families on welfare, a relatively stagnant situation for those who left welfare, and deteriorating circumstances for families with no welfare experience." One of the most encouraging findings of the study was that the percentage of welfare recipients employed increased significantly between 1997 and 2002, but declined among former recipients and those avoiding welfare.[18]

However, the study also found that the impact of welfare reform measures was not without serious consequences. The researchers at the Urban Institute verified the problems associated with work programs in a weak economy and the growing levels of poverty as poor people were unable to find work. The study concluded that "the entire package of reforms had little effect on income and poverty" but that "certain policies–including more lenient eligibility requirements for welfare recipients and more generous financial incentives to work–do seem to make a difference." Of greatest concern for the researchers was the continued high level of child poverty in the United States and the problems associated with insufficient funding of child-care subsidies and health care coverage for children. Childhood poverty continues to be a disturbing condition in the United States, and the weakened national economy combined with declining support at the federal and state level has done little to address the growing numbers of young people who are poor.[19]

Since the signing of the Welfare Reform Act of 1996 there is no doubt that the concepts of welfare to work, time limits for receiving benefits, block grants from the federal government to the states and state control of welfare requirements are now firmly in place in the United States. Proponents of the changes will tout the declining caseloads and the thousands of success stories of former welfare recipients now leading independent and successful lives. Critics of the new system, while acknowledging the decline in caseloads and evidence of successful transitions from welfare to work, point out that much of the positive results came during strong economic times and that as a result of the a softer economy since 2007 there are new signs that those in poverty are growing in numbers and the demands for a deeper safety net are increasing. If the national economy continues to remain weak while federal and state support for those in need remains inadequate, the gains achieved in welfare reform since 1996 will be nullified and the policy prescriptions placed into question.[20]

However because the welfare system in the United States moved from a government spending–income transfer approach to a welfare to work model, American poverty reduction programs are now part of a larger ideological debate between liberals and conservatives. Liberals remain convinced that support for key programs such as food stamps, Medicaid, health insurance for children, day-care subsidies and housing support is insufficient to meet the needs of the poor, whereas conservatives hold true to their belief that poverty will not be reduced by large government programs but rather by individual responsibility, job training and work. As can be expected, when two differing ideologies ram heads, there are elements of truth and effectiveness in both approaches. If poverty reduction were an easy policy challenge, then moving poor people toward a more prosperous life would have been solved decades ago. If there is an answer with some degree of certainty, it is that a government safety net that does not foster lifelong dependency combined with solid incentives and opportunities to move off of welfare into the world of work and independence is the pathway to poverty reduction and welfare reform. One thing is certain about poverty reduction in the United States—a strong economy is often the critical ingredient for moving people from welfare to financial independence.[21]

The Great Debate

Because poverty remains a serious problem in the United States, there continue to be differences in policy approaches for dealing with poverty, with liberals accenting government intervention and assistance and conservatives stressing work and personal responsibility.

Debate Topic

What model of poverty reduction is best in dealing with poverty, the government-supported safety net approach or the work and personal responsibility approach?

Critical Thinking Questions

1. Why do you believe there are over 47 million Americans officially classified as poor?
2. The United States has one of the highest levels of income inequality between the rich and the poor? Why do such inequalities exist in one of the richest countries in the world?
3. Some critics of the American welfare system contend that the United States has developed a culture of dependency that has led to continued reliance on government assistance. Do you agree?
4. Should the United States follow the example of the Scandinavian countries, which have a generous social welfare system and a wide safety net (and higher taxes)?
5. What are Americans' obligations as U.S. citizens to help those who are poor?

Connections

The Welfare Rights Organizing Coalition is one of the more prominent advocates for those on welfare. See http://wroc.org

The National Center for Children in Poverty is the foremost advocate for children at or below the poverty level. See http://www.nccp.org/

The Heritage Foundation has been a vocal critic of welfare policy in the United States. View its position on welfare reform at http://www.heritage.org/research/welfare/tst071906a.cfm

The U.S. Interagency Council on Homelessness is the federal government's advocate for the homeless. Visit its site at http://www.ich.gov

For a more complete explanation of the TANF program see http://www.in.gov/fssa/dfr/4068.htm

Some Books to Read

Howard, Christopher, *The Welfare State Nobody Knows: Debunking Myths About U.S. Social Policy* (Princeton, NJ: Princeton University Press, 2006).

Ward, Deborah, *The White Welfare State: The Racialization of U.S. Welfare Policy* (Ann Arbor, MI: University of Michigan Press, 2005).

Mink, Gwendolyn, Solinger, Rickie, Piven, Frances Fox, *Welfare: A Documentary History of U.S. Policy and Politics* (New York: NYU Press, 2003).

Katz, Michael, *In the Shadow of the Poorhouse: A Social History of Welfare in America* (New York: Basic Books, 1986).

Blau, Joel, Abramovitz, Mimi, *The Dynamics of Social Welfare Policy* (New York: Oxford University Press, 2003).

Notes

1. See Isabel Sawhill, "Poverty in the United States," *The Concise Encyclopedia of Economics,* http://www.econlib.org/library/Enc/PovertyinAmerica.html
2. Ibid.
3. See Gertrude Schaffner Goldberg and Elinor Kremen, eds. *The Feminization of Poverty* (Westport, CT: Greenwood Press, 1990).
4. See "People and Families in Poverty: Selected Characteristics," U.S. Bureau of the Census, http://www.infoplease.com/finance/economy/people-poverty-characteristics.html
5. Julia Vitello-Martin, "Homeless in America," *Wall Street Journal,* January 18, 2007, A17.
6. Uri Berliner, "Haves and Have Nots; Income Inequality in America," http://www.npr.org/templates/story/story.php?storyId=7180618
7. As reported in the *Journal of Sociology and Social Work,* January 94/April 95.
8. See a discussion of the Reagan policy toward social welfare policy in D. Lee Baldwin, *The Social Contract Revisited: Aims and Outcomes of President Reagan's Social Welfare Policy* (New York: Urban Institute, 1984).
9. Robert Rector, "Wisconsin's Welfare Miracle," Hoover Institution, March and April, 1997, http://www.hoover.org/publications/policyreview/3573807.html
10. See Remarks on Signing of Act, Bill Clinton Transcripts, http://www.milestone-documents.com/documents/view/bill-clintons-radio-address-on-the-welfare-reform-act/
11. Dan Froomkin, "Welfare's Changing Face," *Washington Post,* July 23, 1998, http://washingtonpost.com/wp-srv/politics/special/welfare/welfare.htm
12. Chris Jenkins, "Food Stamps Must Stretch Even Further," *Washington Post National Weekly Edition,* June 28, 2008, p. 33.
13. "Welfare Reform Ten Years Later," Urban Institute, http://www.urban.org/toolkit/issues/welfarereform.cfm?renderforprint=1
14. See The Family and Social Services website for an explanation of the TANF program, http:www.in.gov/fssa/dfr/4068.htm
15. Michael Tanner, "The Critics Were Wrong: Welfare Reform Turns 10," http://www.cato.org/pub_display.php?pub_id=6629

16. Peter Edelman, "The True Purpose of Welfare Reform," *New York Times*, May 29, 2002, A21.

17. See Allison Stevens, "Single Mom's Poverty Spikes After Welfare Overhaul," http://www.womensenews.org/story/080703/single-moms-poverty-spikes-after-welfare-overhaul

18. As reported by the Urban League, http://www.urban.org/center/anf/nsaf.cfm

19. See the congressional testimony of John Podesta, "Poverty in America: Bad and Getting Worse," and Robert Rector, "Poverty in America: Not Bad, and Getting Better," Testimony during hearings on "Economic Opportunity and Poverty in America" before the U.S. House of Representatives, Committee on Ways and Means, Subcommittee on Income Security and Family Support, April 26, 2007.

20. "Welfare Reform 10 Years Later," op.cit.

21. See Isabel Sawhill, R. Kent Weaver, Ron Haskins and Andrea Kane, eds. *Welfare Reform and Beyond: The Future of the Safety Net* (Washington, D.C.: Brookings Institution Press, 2002).

20 NATIONAL DEFENSE

Issue Focus

Defending the United States from attack and protecting its interests abroad is not only the highest priority of the American government but it is also big business. Thousands of companies are tied into the defense establishment, making billions of dollars in profits and employing hundreds of thousands of workers. Because of its importance to the nation, defense spending is one of the key stimulants of the American economy. However, defending the United States, despite its high priority, is not without its detractors and competitors for scarce government resources. Although the defense establishment has historically been adept at convincing Congress and the American people of the need for increased spending, the contentious issue of the proper balance between national security spending and domestic programs remains. This competition for the attention of government and the resources decisions made by government has created a lively debate over national priorities.

Chapter Objectives
This issue chapter will seek to:
1. Explain the influence of what President Eisenhower called the military-industrial complex on defense spending and federal budget priorities.
2. Discuss the issues and concerns surrounding weapons procurement and defense contracting and the impact of defense spending on the national economy.
3. Describe the Obama approach to defense spending in light of the phased withdrawal from Iraq and the changing priorities of the government.

SOME BACKGROUND

The generally accepted policy position in the United States is that the primary purpose of the government is to protect the nation and its people from attack or the threat of attack. The Preamble to the U.S. Constitution validates this purpose when it states that one of the chief responsibilities of the new government is to "Provide for the Common Defense." Since the inception of the United States as a nation, the U.S. government formed a military and provided it with weapons, equipment, training and support necessary to complete its stated mission. Over time, the U.S. military has grown not just in numbers and weapons, but in its role both as defender of the nation and as peacemaker, liberator and occupying force in foreign theaters of operation. Ronald Reagan, who was most responsible as president for a major build-up in national defense, best summed up the importance of maintaining a strong defense when he gave a memorable national security speech in 1983 and said the following:

Since the dawn of the atomic age, we've sought to reduce the risk of war by maintaining a strong deterrent and by seeking genuine arms control.

"Deterrence" means simply this: making sure any adversary who thinks about attacking the United States, or our allies, or our vital interests, concludes that the risks to him outweigh any potential gains. Once he understands that, he won't attack. We maintain the peace through our strength; weakness only invites aggression.[1]

The U.S. military has indeed come a long way from the early days of the war of independence. From Washington's valiant efforts to keep his army intact during those dark days at Valley Forge to the current Department of Defense headquartered in one of the world's largest buildings, the armed forces of the United States have historically been a major, if not leading, institution within American government. Today the U.S. Department of Defense, by far the nation's biggest bureaucracy, is made up of almost 3 million people: 1.4 million in uniform, 800,000 civilians and 700,000 reserves.

The cost of running this large bureaucracy is staggering. In 2008 the budget for the Pentagon, including special supplements to fund the war in Iraq and the cost of nuclear weapons, was $750 billion. At that spending level, the United States allocates 3.7% of its gross domestic product (GDP) to the military, which is relatively low compared to its spending during World War II (37% of GDP) and the Vietnam War (9.4% of GDP in 1968). It is also important to point out that the U.S. military spending is larger than that of 168 other nation-states and is approximately 47% of the world's total military spending.[2] To bring some perspective to the defense budget of $750 billion, the cost of running the U.S. Department of State, the diplomatic bureaucracy, was $26 billion in 2007, and there are more members of military marching and concert bands than there are Foreign Service Officers. Finally, the Defense Department spends the most on operations, which include wars, military personnel and research and development of new weapons systems and equipment. Currently, the Defense Department budget makes up about 19% of the entire federal budget and is half of all discretionary spending (spending that is not mandated payments to individuals such as Social Security and Medicare).[3]

With so many employees and such a significant budget, the Defense Department dominates the public policy scene in Washington. Presidents have often won the highest office because of their unqualified support for the Defense Department and their willingness to use military force to protect national security interests. Congress has also played a key role in enhancing the power potential of the Pentagon as members regularly jockey to win support for new weapons systems in their home districts as well as protecting military bases that are situated in their states. And, the American public can almost always be counted on to show their patriotic spirit by supporting the men and women in uniform.

The sheer size and cost of the military establishment in the United States and its influence within the corridors of power in Washington often raises these key questions: how much military spending is enough and what about other competing national priorities? As many critics of defense spending and Pentagon influence often remind the president and members of Congress, the Constitution also mandates that the government should "Establish Justice, Ensure Domestic Tranquility and Promote the General Welfare." President Eisenhower in a memorable speech upon leaving the presidency in 1960 warned the nation about the power of what he termed the *military-industrial complex*. In Eisenhower's view, the military and its partners in industry, who were vying for lucrative weapons, equipment and supply contracts, had such influence on the policy process and setting national priorities that combined they posed a threat to a fair and balanced budget and indeed the national interest. Eisenhower's admonition to the American people to be wary of the military-industrial complex has not diminished in intensity as there are constant debates in policy circles about the costs of maintaining our military establishment and how those costs impact other social and domestic programs.[4]

Besides the issue of the budget and spending power of the military and the political influence of its allies in the industrial and technological sectors of the national economy, there is also the more critical concern about the capability and readiness of the modern U.S. military. Since the Vietnam War, when the Johnson administration imposed a military draft, the armed forces have been completely volunteer in nature, both in the regular service components of the Army, Navy, Air Force and Marines and in the state national guards and reserves. However in recent years, as a result of the commitments of ground troops in Afghanistan and Iraq, major questions have been raised about whether the military is suffering from overstretch because troops serving in the Middle East and other theaters of operation have been forced to endure long periods of duty and they are also brought back into service despite returning to the reserves. There has been much talk by military commanders and critics of the Bush policy in Afghanistan and Iraq about whether the military has been severely weakened and its war-fighting capacity compromised. As a result of these issues of capability and readiness, there have been calls for new efforts of recruitment, the creation of whole new battalions and even some legislative efforts to return to the military draft.

Because the U.S. military occupies such a prominent and essential position in the government and American society, it has enjoyed a high level of national trust and respect. However, when examined from the perspectives of its competition for scarce budgetary resources, its role in an ever-changing and demanding international arena and its ability to serve the national security interests of the United States, the military has in recent years faced increasing scrutiny and criticism. There is no doubt that the Iraq war has cast a light on the military and its leadership and forced a review of spending, mission and readiness. The outcome of this review in the coming years will play an important role in defining the future of the military and may lead to a transformation of the armed forces.

On the Record

Upon leaving office in 1961, Dwight Eisenhower gave what is now considered his most famous speech on the dangers of the military-industrial complex. The key sections of that speech are as follows:

> This conjunction of an immense military establishment and a large arms industry is new in the American experience. The total influence–economic, political, even spiritual–is felt in every city, every state house, every office of the federal government. We recognize the imperative need for this development. Yet we must not fail to comprehend its grave implications. Our toil, resources and livelihood are all involved; so is the very structure of our society. In the councils of government, we must guard against the acquisition of unwarranted influence, whether sought or unsought, by the military-industrial complex. The potential for the disastrous rise of misplaced power exists and will persist.

DEBATES, DIFFERENCES AND DIVISIONS

Because of the responsibility of the U.S. Military for national security and its high standing among the American public, debates, differences and divisions involving the defense establishment have for decades centered not on the importance of the military or personnel issues, but rather on issues such as the cost of weapons systems, the cozy relationship of military with business interests providing those weapons systems and the value and effectiveness of modernizing the armed forces. In recent years, the Defense Department has placed increased emphasis on more sophisticated and ultimately more expensive weapons systems to match new war strategies.

For example, the F-22A fighter program, the Air Force's most advanced combat aircraft, has a price tag of $65.3 billion. The cost of the F-22A exploded to the point where the Air Force had to reduce the number of aircraft purchases from 648 to 243. However, even with that reduction in number and cost, one F-22A will cost the American taxpayer $355 million.[5] The cost of the F-22A has been the focus of discussions within the Obama administration as it seeks to trim defense costs, and questions arise as to whether the supersonic jet fighter fits into future defense strategies. Proponents of the F-22A often cite the economic benefits of the fighter jet. However, as Daniel Wheeler of the Center for Defense Information, a Pentagon watchdog group, stated about the F-22A debate, "It's the first test of whether President Obama is going to go along with business as usual or instead will bring much needed change to the Pentagon."[6] In 2009 the democratically controlled Senate voted to stop buying the F-22A fighter jets, thus handing the Obama administration a key victory as it sought to rein in weapons appropriation costs. However, political leaders in states who were impacted by the decision criticized it, because building the jet employed an estimated 25,000 people in forty-six states.[7]

Besides decisions about moving forward with specific weapons systems, the cost overruns and the outright waste and fraud have regularly embarrassed the Pentagon and fed the critics of military spending with new ammunition. In 2008, the Government Accountability Office did a study of weapons systems purchased by the Pentagon and found cost overruns in seventy-two of these purchases costing a total of $1.6 trillion. One particular program, the Army's Future Combat System, the next generation of computer-driven weaponry for the battlefield, cost $200 billion, which was $40 billion over the initial 2003 estimate. Despite these examples of huge cost overruns, the problem has not abated. In 2010 the Pentagon admitted that the cost of the F-35 Joint Strike Fighter Program had doubled to $113 million per plane since 2001.[8] These cost overruns are joined by numerous examples of corrupt practices, especially in Iraq and Afghanistan. Senator Bernie Sanders of Vermont, a long-time critic of the Pentagon and defense spending, documented a long list of waste and fraud, such as the Air Force paying a private contractor $32 million to construct an air base in Iraq that was never built and a $300 million contract to the Afghan military in which old and defective ammunition was sold through the Army Sustainment Command. Even more troublesome was the fact that the faulty ammunition was shipped through China, which was a violation of U.S. statutes. As Sanders stated in his criticism of defense-related waste, "At a time when this country has a $9.3 trillion national debt, a declining economy, and enormous unmet needs, the time is long overdue for Congress to stop rubber-stamping White House requests for military spending and to address the Pentagon's needs within the context of our overall national priorities."[9]

Data Bank

The procurement allocations, money for weapons systems, are at the heart of the Defense Department budget. A sampling of the procurement requests of the Defense Department for key weapons systems is presented here for the 2008 budget:

> Missile defense–$8.8 billion
> F-35 Joint Strike Fighter–$6.1 billion
> Carrier replacement program–$3.1 billion
> DDG 1000 Destroyer–$3.5 billion
> Virginia class submarine–$2.7 billion
> C-130 tanker aircraft–$1.6 billion
> San Antonio class amphibious transport dock–$1.4 billion
> Littoral combat ship–$1.2 billion
> Space-based Infrared System–$1.1 billion

In total the 2008 proposed Defense Department procurement budget was $84.1 billion.

The enormous costs of these weapons systems have in recent years led the Defense Department to keep a closer eye on expenditures and take action against contractors that have either delayed in finishing a project or engaged in questionable billing and construction practices. In 2007, Navy Secretary Donald Winter canceled the construction of the second littoral combat ship with Lockheed Martin. The cancellation was based on Lockheed Martin's decision to increase the cost of the littoral combat ship from $220 million to $410 million. The littoral combat ship was supposed to be the next generation of the Navy's fleet and eventually make up one sixth of the 313-ship U.S. fleet, but cost overruns and disputes between the Pentagon and Lockheed Martin placed the entire program on hold.[10] Lockheed Martin is but one of scores of major defense contractors who vie for lucrative government contracts. Lockheed Martin tops the list of contractors (with $36 billion in defense revenue) followed by Boeing ($30 billion), Northrop Grumman ($23 billion), Raytheon ($19.5 billion), General Dynamics ($18.7 billion) and L-3 Communications ($9.9 billion). Most of the top government contractors are manufacturers of sophisticated aircraft, Navy ships and cutting-edge radar and guidance technologies.[11]

Another side to the military-industrial complex is the foreign military sales program that has been aggressively pursued by the Defense Department and the various major defense contractors. Between 2005 and 2006, $21 billion of contracts for U.S.-made weapons and weapons systems were sold abroad. The Bush administration increased its foreign military sales as a means of currying favor with its allies and making new friends, particularly in the new post-9/11 world of anti-terror initiatives. Countries that were previously banned from receiving U.S. arms sales such as Pakistan, India and Indonesia were allowed to purchase weapons. Pakistan, a key ally in the war on terrorism, purchased $5 billion in sophisticated F-16 fighter jets in 2005 from Lockheed Martin Corporation, and Saudi Arabia placed an order worth $3 billion for Black Hawk helicopters and Bradley armored land vehicles. Even smaller countries such as the tiny sheikdom of Bahrain purchased $1 billion in military equipment from 2001 to 2006. For defense contractors, foreign military sales are a hedge against cuts in regular military procurement and of course are enormously profitable. Critics of this arms trade emphasize that the United States is the number one supplier of weapons to countries around the world, contributing to an ever-growing arsenal of deadly weapons that shift resources in many countries away from domestic needs to national defense.[12] Once Obama entered office there was little change in the emphasis on foreign military sales, in fact there was a sharp expansion of weapons transfers to India and Pakistan with cargo planes ($2 billion) and long-range reconnaissance planes ($ 2.1 billion) sold to India and F-16 fighter jets ($3 billion) sold to Pakistan.[13]

It is also important to mention that defense contractors impact state and local economies as manufacturing and research and development facilities are job generators that contribute significantly to economic development. During the Vietnam War and then the Reagan era it was estimated that one out of ten working Americans was employed either directly in a defense-related industry or in an industry that received some government contracts. This ratio diminished during the Clinton and also Bush years, but it does point out the importance that defense contractors bring to state and local economies. So too with military bases, which house thousands of soldiers and their families. In places with major military installations such as Ft. Hood (Texas), Ft. Campbell (Kentucky), Ft. Benning (Georgia), Newport News Naval Base (Virginia), 29 Palms Marine Base (California) and Offutt Air Force Base (Nebraska), surrounding towns benefit from the presence of the military personnel in terms of off-base housing, retail stores, banking and numerous small businesses.

Since 1989 the Department of Defense and Congress initiated a series of base closures and realignments that were hotly contested in communities and states which recognized the economic impact of such actions. In four rounds of closures–1989, 1991, 1993 and 1999–over 350 military bases and installations were closed by the Base Realignment and Closure Commission (BRAC). The largest number of closings occurred during the Clinton administration, which did not have a good relationship with the military community. Because of this tension the Clinton administration faced a huge outcry of criticism by local officials and state and national representatives who knew that the closings would create near ghost towns that were once booming communities. However, the Clinton administration accepted the BRAC recommendations and went ahead with the closures and realignments. The closings continued into the Bush administration. A fifth round of closures in 2005 was part of then Secretary of Defense Donald Rumsfeld's effort to streamline the military and make it more mobile and ready for quick responses to threats around the world.[14]

FYI

The federal budget is in simple terms a list of priorities: where best to spend the American taxpayers' money. Although budget decisions are rarely made in terms of either/or options, there is validity in seeing how spending on the military may impact various social programs or domestic needs. The following list provides some specific examples of the choices involving military versus domestic spending.

> One bunker buster guided bomb ($145, 600) or associate degree training for twenty-five registered nurses
> 1,000 M-16 rifles ($586,000) or rent subsidies for 1,000 families
> One hour of the war in Iraq ($46 million) or repair, improve or modernize twenty schools
> Seven unmanned Predator spy drones ($130 million) or nutrition programs for 200,000 families
> Three tests of the missile defense system ($275 million) or eradicate polio worldwide

(continued)

FYI   (continued)

Amphibious Warfare Landing Ship Program ($413 million) or child-care for 68,000 children

One Stealth bomber ($2.1 billion) or annual salary and benefits for 38,000 elementary teachers

One year of nuclear weapons program ($16 billion) or health care coverage for 7 million children

Source: War Resisters League

There are some signs that the American public is beginning to recognize the fiscal impact of military spending on the overall federal budget and on critical national priorities. A Gallup poll in 2008 found that 44% of those Americans polled said that the government was spending too much on defense, whereas 22% said that the government was spending too little.[15] Part of this negative view of defense spending is that Americans are growing more conscious of the costs associated with the Iraq war. Although estimates vary and there are ideological biases in the calculations of the costs of the war, it is likely that the United States has spent nearly $1 trillion on the war and war-related costs (such as caring for the wounded and paying death benefits). Some analysts such as the Nobel Prize winning economist Joseph Stiglitz claim that the Iraq war has cost the United States as much as $3 trillion. Although there was a dispute about Stiglitz's contention on the cost of the war, the fact that the bill to the taxpayers was at least $1 trillion was not lost on the American people.[16]

Besides the cost of defending the United States and paying for military operations such as the wars in Iraq and Afghanistan, another critical issue that has fostered extensive debate and division, especially in the ranks of the armed forces, concerns the battle readiness of the various military branches. The issue of combat readiness goes back to the Clinton administration when the end of the Soviet Union provided an opportunity to cut back on the defense budget that had grown during the Reagan and George H.W. Bush years. Clinton talked proudly about the "peace dividend," although he did not shy away from deploying troops for peacekeeping missions in Bosnia, Haiti and Kosovo. During this period Defense Department officials began to complain that the military was beginning to experience a readiness issue, and concerns rose within the Pentagon about whether the United States could fight a two-front war in the future. Also during the Clinton years, as a result of a red-hot economy and plentiful jobs, the volunteer army did not attract personnel as in past years, thus further creating a problem of declining enlistments and thinning ranks. Clinton faced increased criticism from Republicans for decreasing defense spending and creating a problem with declining enlistments and general military readiness.

The issue of readiness surfaced again during the 2000 presidential campaign when George W. Bush said in his nomination speech "if called on by the commander-in chief today, two entire divisions of the Army would have to report . . . Not ready for duty, sir."[17] Bush was referring to reports from the military that two divisions were not properly equipped and supported in order to be combat ready. Although Pentagon officials criticized the allegation, the fact that the Republican candidate for president took a position about combat readiness in a prominent speech alerted the nation to a pending problem. Although after 9/11 the military had no difficulty recruiting Americans to join the armed forces, the ongoing war in Iraq made the issue of combat readiness a critical issue in the armed forces.[18] As the war dragged on, soldiers were often forced to extend their tours of duty or were called on for additional tours. These tour extensions intensified the opposition to the war at home among military families and also contributed to growing personal problems in military families, such as divorce and strained relationships.

In 2003 the Army War College presented a study that the American military was near the breaking point as a result of unrealistic logistical demands, shortages of spare parts and reserves and National Guard units that were unprepared to fight the kind of urban warfare that was occurring in Iraq.[19] Many governors with National Guard units in Iraq complained to the Bush administration that their capability to deal with natural disasters at home was severely compromised by the deployment of units to Iraq and the failure of the government to adequately upgrade the equipment used for domestic disaster relief. When President Bush announced the surge strategy and asked for an additional 30,000–40,000 troops, the issue of military overstretch surfaced again as more of the top military commanders questioned whether the United States had the capacity to put sufficient "boots on the ground." Moreover, Democrats in Congress (and families of soldiers in the field) constantly complained that the Bush administration was not providing its men and women on the ground in Iraq with adequate equipment, from steel-reinforced Humvees to bulletproof vests to spare parts for helicopters. As a result there were calls for the creation of whole new divisions, a rebuilding of the reserves and National Guard and for shifting budget dollars from future procurements to essential battlefield equipment.[20]

Democrats in Congress also jumped on the readiness issue by using the problems of the military as a new approach to arguing for a withdrawal from Iraq. Building upon influential House Democrat John Murtha's controversial statement in 2005 that the "army is broken," Speaker of the House Nancy Pelosi and key members of the House Armed Services Committee such as Congressmen Neil Abercrombie of Hawaii and Solomon Ortiz of Texas pushed for a readiness resolution that would demand that the Bush administration provide more money for ground troops in Iraq and develop a strategy to deal with what many generals in the Pentagon described as a military overstretch. Sentiment among Democrats regarding the readiness resolution was best represented by Democratic Congressman Joe Sestak of Pennsylvania who framed the argument as essential for U.S. national defense. Sestak stated, "This (the readiness resolution) is about America's security. We have an army that can't deploy anywhere else in the world." Republicans were quick to respond to the Democrats and their readiness resolution. House Minority Leader John Boehner of Ohio said, "House Democrats' Iraqi policy is like a broken Magic 8 Ball, no matter what question you ask, the answer is always Retreat."[21]

One of the key challenges of the Obama administration in the coming years is its commitment to develop a new fighting strategy for the military, which will include major cuts in programs such as missile defense, ship building and the aforementioned F-22A. However, more importantly the Obama administration is seeking to push the Pentagon to formulate new approaches to the kinds of war the United States will fight in the future. The president and his Secretary of Defense Robert Gates are seeking to transform the military from its conventional war fighting mode so prominent during the Cold War to a the kind of insurgency and anti-terrorist battles that are currently waged in Iraq and Afghanistan. Such a shift would place greater emphasis on intelligence gathering, the use of unmanned drones and developing elite special forces units.

The ongoing national debate over how much military spending is enough and whether budget resources should be shifted elsewhere is not new to American politics and will certainly continue. Even with a reduction in the U.S. presence in Iraq, there are not only new threats in the world from Iran and North Korea, but, as discussed earlier, there are significant readiness problems for the regular armed forces, the National Guard and the Reserves due to the wars in Afghanistan and Iraq. Members of both parties in Congress can be expected to support a rebuilding of the American military at what will likely require huge budgetary resources that will again compete with domestic needs. Unlike the fall of the Soviet Union, which allowed the Clinton administration to benefit from the peace dividend as it cut military spending, the post-9/11 world has numerous threats or potential threats to U.S. security interests. The complexity of the threats in this new world of multiple security challenges will do little to diminish the power and influence of the military-industrial complex.

In 1953, at the onset of his first administration, President Dwight Eisenhower provided a glimpse of his concern over military spending when he stated, "Every gun that is made, every warship launched, every rocket fired signifies, in the final sense, a theft from those who hunger and are not fed those who are cold and not clothed. This world in arms is not spending money alone. It is spending the sweat of its laborers, the genius of its scientists, the hopes of its children."[22] It may be surprising to many that an American president whose whole career before he entered the White House was in the military would be so worried about the military-industrial complex and the impact of military spending on domestic programs and domestic needs. However, because Eisenhower was a military man he understood the power of the military and its allies in industry to dominate the budget process and drive national priority setting. Eisenhower was not soft on the use of military force, but he did recognize that valuable and essential programs that deal with education, health and welfare can be marginalized if not eliminated in the race to defend the United States or extend its influence abroad by military means. Eisenhower likely sought a proper balance between military spending and domestic spending and a commitment on the part of future presidents to ensure that the United States not only provide for the common defense but also promote the general welfare.

The Great Debate

How much military spending is necessary to ensure the protection of the United States and U.S. interests and assets abroad has long been the key question related to the defense budget.

Debate Topic

Should the United States continue to spend at its current levels on the military, or should spending shift to other domestic needs?

Critical Thinking Questions

1. What is more important, building a new generation of fighter jets and other expensive weapons systems and thus maintaining jobs and profitability for major defense contractors or saving hundreds of billions of dollars in defense costs?
2. What is your impression of President Eisenhower's warning about the undue influence of the military-industrial complex?
3. Does the United States need to formulate a new fighting strategy to deal with the changing threats in the world?
4. If indeed the U.S. military is broken as some allege, how does it reform, regroup and revitalize?
5. Do you agree that the U.S. military should be the primary peacekeeping force in the world, placing our soldiers at risk and costing billions of dollars?

Connections

The first stop in gaining a better understanding of U.S. military policy is the Defense Department website. See http://www.defense.gov/

The Senate Armed Services Committee has a valuable website on military policy and programs. See http://armed-services.senate.gov

For a compendium of recent defense-related news and trends see the Defense News site at http://www.defensenews.com

The Rand Corporation, a think tank that does extensive work on military matters, has a valuable website. See http://www.rand.org

A critic of defense policy, the Project on Defense Alternatives, is an important website to visit. See http://www.comw.org

Some Books to Read

Eland, Ivan, *Putting "Defense" Back into U.S. Defense Policy: Rethinking U.S. Security in the Post-Cold War World* (Westport, CT: Praeger Publishers, 2001).

Powell, Colin, et al., *U.S. Defense Policy* (New York: Council on Foreign Relations, 2001).

Hossein-zadeh, Ismael, *Political Economy of U.S. Militarism* (New York: Palgrave Macmillan, 2006).

Turse, Nick, *The Complex: How the Military Invades Our Everyday Lives* (New York: Metropolitan Books, 2008).

Robert Gates and Department of Defense, *National Defense Strategy* (Kissimmee, FL: Signalman Press, 2009).

Notes

1. http://www.famousquotes.me.uk/speeches/Ronald_Reagan/3.htm
2. For comparative data on military expenditures, see *Stockholm International Peace Institute Yearbook*, 2007.
3. Office of Management and Budget, "Historical Tables: Budget of the United States Government," http://www.whitehouse.gov/omb/budget/fy2008/pdf/hist.pdf
4. Public Papers of President Dwight D. Eisenhower, 1960, pp. 1035–1040.
5. http://topics.nytimes.com/topics/reference/timestopics/subjects/m/military_aircraft/f22_airplane/index.html
6. Christopher Drew, "A Fighter Jet's Fate Poses a Quandary for Obama," *New York Times*, December 10, 2008, B1
7. Ann Gerhart and Perry Bacon Jr., "The Attack That Killed the F-22," *Washington Post National Weekly Edition*, August 3–9, 2009, p. 13. See also Christopher Drew, "Victory for Obama Over Military Lobby," *New York Times*, October 29, 2009, B2.
8. Ann Flaherty and Pauline Jelinek, "Fighter Jet Cost Doubles Since 2001: $ 113m Each," *Boston Globe*, Marcy 11, 2010, A10.
9. Bernie Sanders, An Expanding Military Budget Taxpayers Can't Afford," *Boston Globe*, May 20, 2008.
10. Noah Schahtman, "Navy Chief Smacks Lockheed, Cancels LCS," http://blog.wired.com/defense/2007/04/last_week_when_.html
11. Peter Bauer, "Business Booming for U.S. Defense Contractors," http://www.defensenews.com/index.php?S=07
12. Leslie Wayne, "Foreign Sales by U.S. Arms Makers Doubles in a Year," http://www.commondreams.org/headlines06/1111-02.htm
13. Yochi J. Dreazen and Amol Sharma, "U.S. Expands Arms-Sales to Rivals," *Wall Street Journal–Asia Edition*, February 26–28, 2010, p. 5.
14. Defense Base Closure and Realignment Commission, 1993 Report to the President (PDF), U.S. Department of Defense (1993-07-01).
15. Gallup Poll, February 11–14, 2008.
16. Joseph Stiglitz and Linda Bilmes, The Three Trillion Dollar War: The True Costs of the Iraq Conflict (New York: W.W. Norton, 2008).
17. http://Transcripts.cnn.com/TRANSCRIPTS/0011/03/se.04.html

18. See "America's Post-911 Military: Can Congress Reform Our Shrinking, Aging, Less Ready, More Expensive Forces?" http://www.proteusfund.org/files/pdfs/Post%209-11%20Military.pdf

19. Conrad Crane and W. Andrew Terrell, "Reconstructing Iraq: Insights, Challenges and Missions for Military Forces in a Post-Conflict Scenario," Strategic Studies of the U.S. Army War College, 2003.

20. "President Bush's War Has Cost Our Country Dearly," *Democratic Caucus's Senate Journal*, February 28, 2008.

21. Roxanna Tiron, "Members Warn of National Crisis in Military Readiness," *The Hill*, November 25, 2007, http://www.thehill.com/leading-thenews/members_warn_of_national_crisis_in_military_readiness_2007-11-25.html

22. Public Papers of President Dwight D. Eisenhower, op.cit.

21 IRAQ **AND** AFGHANISTAN

Issue Focus

In the 1960s and 1970s the United States was embroiled in an unpopular war in Vietnam to stop the communist Vietcong from controlling the southern part of Vietnam and creating what at that time was called a "domino effect"–spreading communist influence through Southeast Asia. Since 2003 the United States has been embroiled in conflicts in Iraq and Afghanistan, this time to crush the terrorist threat, whether in the form of what was thought to be weapons of mass destruction in the hands of the dictator Saddam Hussein in Iraq and the growing military strength of the radical Taliban insurgents in Afghanistan. While in Iraq the United States made a major commitment of soldiers and resources to bring stability and ultimately a form of democracy to a country that had only known cruel authoritarianism. Now the United States is moving out of Iraq confident that relative stability and democracy are in place. In Afghanistan, however, the United States has renewed its involvement after years of attention on Iraq. The Obama administration has made a major commitment, similar to George Bush's commitment in Iraq, to bring stability and a form of democracy to Afghanistan. As history has shown, both of these interventions have caused years of contentious debate and deep divisions in the United States over decisions to reshape the internal political and security situation in these two nations. These debates and divisions will likely remain at the forefront of foreign policy analysis and national security assessment for years to come.

Chapter Objectives
This issue chapter will seek to:

1. Examine the current political and military situation in Iraq and the challenges for the Obama administration as it begins a phased withdrawal.

2. Present the disagreements among Washington policy makers about the current status and the future direction of U.S. presence in Iraq and Afghanistan.

3. Describe the challenges faced by the Iraqi and Afghan governments and the United States in the coming years.

SOME BACKGROUND

When President Bush spoke to the American people on March 19, 2003, announcing that the United States had begun the attack on Iraq to remove the dictator Saddam Hussein from power and then proudly stood before the

"Mission Accomplished" banner aboard the USS *Abraham Lincoln* on May 1, 2003, few Americans (and certainly few in the Bush administration) anticipated that the United States would for the next seven years be engulfed in a sectarian civil war that would claim the lives of over 4400 American soldiers, injure over 30,000 and cost by most estimates at least $1 trillion. What had started out as a bold move to secure weapons of mass destruction, replace an authoritarian government with democracy and change the political and governing climate of the Middle East had become one of the most divisive and controversial foreign policy actions in modern American history.[1]

The war in Iraq has been the central political issue in the United States and the focus of intense debate between the Bush administration and its critics. President Bush paid a high price for his defense of U.S. policy in Iraq as his approval rating for most of 2008 sunk below 30%. The president's decision to initiate a surge strategy by increasing the number of U.S. troops in Iraq and securing Baghdad and other regions from anti-American insurgents and religious militias did provide him with a temporary jump in his popularity and support from stalwarts within his party and in the conservative movement. However, as the 2008 presidential campaign heated up, Democratic candidates were relentless in their criticism of the war and called for various timetables for withdrawal from Iraq.[2]

As the war dragged on, critics of the Bush administration's policy pointed out that a military solution could not replace a political solution unless the two prominent religious sects, the Shi'ites and the Sunnis, agreed to resolve a number of key differences involving the distribution of oil revenue, regional control and national leadership. The president, however, was adamant in his refusal to change course in Iraq and took solace in the fact that the level of violence in Iraq diminished significantly in 2008 and as a degree of normality settled in.[3] Old animosities among the religious and tribal groups in Iraq, however, made it difficult to bring a political solution that would unify the country and begin to address numerous everyday challenges such as regular electricity, water supply and most important security.

As the Iraq war moved to the post-surge phase during the Obama administration, the debate over the U.S. presence in Iraq shifted from war fighting and counter-insurgency to what strategy to follow as the United States sought a prudent and effective means of drawing down its military commitment to Iraq. The term *exit strategy* became more prominent in policy-making circles and on the campaign trail. The question of how and when should the United States withdraw from Iraq became the focus of discussion. Since those heady days in 2003 when President Bush pronounced Mission Accomplished, the government and the people of the United States have engaged in a dialogue about how to end U.S. involvement, retain American influence in the Middle East and ensure that the decision to war did lead to some positive developments.

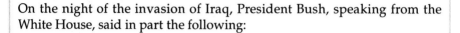

On the Record

On the night of the invasion of Iraq, President Bush, speaking from the White House, said in part the following:

> Our nation enters this conflict reluctantly–yet, our purpose is sure. The people of the United States and our friends and allies will not live at the mercy of an outlaw regime that threatens the peace with weapons of mass murder. We will meet that threat now with our Army, Air Force, Navy, Coast Guard and Marines, so that we do not have to meet it later with armies of fire fighters and police and doctors on the streets of our cities.

Less than two months later on the deck of the USS *Abraham Lincoln* and before the banner "Mission Accomplished," President Bush said in part the following:

> In the images of celebrating Iraqis we have also seen the ageless appeal of human freedom. Decades of lies and intimidation could not make the Iraqi people love their oppressors or desire their own enslavement. . . . Everywhere that freedom arrives, humanity rejoices; and everywhere that freedom stirs, let tyrants fear. We have difficult work to do in Iraq. . . . We are helping to rebuild Iraq where the dictator built palaces for himself instead of hospitals and schools. And we will stand with the new leaders of Iraq as they establish a government of, by, and for the Iraqi people. The transition from dictatorship to democracy will take time, but it is worth every effort. Our coalition will stay until our work is done and then we will leave and will leave behind a free Iraq.

DEBATES, DIFFERENCES AND DIVISIONS

The Obama administration and legislative leaders from both parties in Congress are now focusing on what a withdrawal from Iraq would look like. Yet while attention is on the future, vigorous debates continue between liberals and conservatives over the wisdom of invading Iraq and how history will judge the occupation and nation-building actions of the United States.[4] From the perspective of the Bush administration and its supporters, removing a dictator who gave the impression that he was hiding weapons of mass destruction and then establishing a democratic-like state in the midst of Middle Eastern authoritarianism and radical Islamism were in the best national security interests of the United States and indeed did send a strong signal to both dictators and terrorists that this country was willing to use military force to face them.

Because President Bush was ending his time in office and the future of Iraq would be in the hands of his successor, the key issues surrounding the U.S.

presence in Iraq and the future of our commitment there were debated during the 2008 presidential campaign. Republican candidate for president, Senator John McCain, at one point in the campaign stated that the United States might have to stay 100 years in Iraq as a stabilizing force. This comment elicited intense negative public opinion response prompting McCain to back away and promise that if elected he would achieve internal peace, effective governance and national security within Iraq in the four years of his administration. McCain, however, was not willing to remove U.S. troops from the region, as he suggested that the United States would likely have to keep forces in the region (perhaps in neighboring Kuwait, the Kurdish region of Iraq or a sizeable Navy presence offshore) for an indefinite time. McCain often made the comparison to the U.S. commitment to South Korea, where over 35,000 soldiers remain stationed and to Europe after World War II, where hundreds of thousands of troops stayed for years facing the Soviets and their communist allies.[5]

The position of McCain and other conservatives was based on the belief that any quick and massive U.S. withdrawal from Iraq would send the wrong signal to Iran, the major supporter of radical Shi'ite groups, Palestinian militants and terrorist insurgents in Iraq. From this perspective, the United States would be viewed as weak and unwilling to influence the direction of government and security interests in the Middle East. Without a sizeable American military presence, McCain and others believed that Iran would quickly fill the power vacuum in the region, turn Iraq into an Islamist state and push toward its ultimate objective of destroying Israel. The United States could not just cut and run after removing Saddam Hussein and building a new government system, but rather must remain active and present in the region to continue to protect itself from Islamist extremists and continue to change the political environment in the Middle East. To do otherwise, in this view, would only embolden the enemies of the United States and, in the words of Senator McCain, "allow the terrorists to follow us home."[6]

From the perspective of the Democratic Party and its candidates for president, McCain and the conservatives were only following a failed policy and keeping U.S. troops in the middle of a sectarian civil war. Their primary objective was to develop a speedier timetable for withdrawal, while sending clear signals to the Iraqi leadership that they need to move quickly to develop a reliable military and police and take aggressive steps to solve a range of political issues that have divided Shi'ites and Sunnis. Democratic candidate Barack Obama stressed during the presidential campaign that the answer to the Iraq imbroglio was not a long-term military commitment but a political solution built upon effective governance. Obama accused the Iraqis of becoming dependent on the U.S. presence and unwilling to make tough political compromises because of their view that the American military would remain in large numbers for years to come. By setting a firm timetable for withdrawal of a large segment of the 140,000 troops in Iraq and leaving behind a greatly reduced force that would remain in most instances within military bases, the United States would send a clear signal to the Iraqi government that the occupation was over and that Iraq had to meet its own security challenges.[7]

Furthermore, Democratic leaders like Obama complained that the U.S. invasion and occupation only worsened its influence and reputation in the Middle East, emboldened the terrorists and expanded their ranks and actually strengthened the radical government in Iran and the authoritarian dictatorship in Syria. A phased withdrawal on a much quicker timetable with the option of keeping some military force in the region would enhance U.S. interests and weaken the rationale of the terrorists to fight the Americans in a holy jihad.[8]

Data Bank

Americans have been regularly polled on their views about the Iraq war, but in 2008 many of the polls concentrated on their views about withdrawing from Iraq and ending the U.S. military presence. A Rasmussen poll conducted in May 2008 found that 62% of Americans polled wanted the troops brought home from Iraq within a year, whereas 24% wanted the troops to leave immediately. The percentage of Americans who wanted the troops to stay until the mission is accomplished was 34%.

Source: Rasmussen Reports, May 6, 2008

In the last few years there has been an almost endless supply of expert opinions on the ramifications of various withdrawal options from Washington insiders, academic scholars and those in the Middle East, especially the Iraqis, who would obviously be affected by any policy change implemented by the Obama administration. The following is a series of these opinions and recommendations:

- The Iraq Study Group, a bipartisan group of respected American leaders headed by former Indiana Congressman Lee Hamilton and former Secretary of State James Baker, in December 2006 released its report and recommended a phased withdrawal of U.S. combat troops from Iraq, a dialogue with Syria and Iran on the future of Iraq and the Middle East and a quicker transfer of responsibility to the Iraqis for national security.[9]
- A National Intelligence Estimate, which reflected the views of the various segments of the intelligence community, stated in January 2007 that American forces were "an essential stabilizing element in Iraq" and warned that "Iraqi security forces would be hard-pressed to assume significantly expanded responsibilities in the next 12–18 months."[10]
- A war-games scenario conducted by the U.S. military and made public in July 2007 found that if the U.S. combat troops withdrew from Iraq the majority Shi'ites would drive the minority Sunnis out of their base in Anbar Province, Southern Iraq would become engulfed in a civil war and the Kurds in the North would invite U.S. troops to establish a base there. The result would be the partition of Iraq into three regions.[11]

- Peter Bergen, terrorism expert and CNN analyst, stated in May 2007 that a withdrawal of U.S. combat troops would damage America's reputation in the Middle East and hand "al Qaeda and other terror groups a propaganda victory that the United States is only a 'paper tiger.' " A withdrawal by the United States, according to Bergen, would "play into their [al Qaeda's] strategy, which is to create a mini-state somewhere in the Middle East where they can reorganize along the line of what they did in Afghanistan in the late 90s."[12]
- A poll conducted in 2007 among residents of Baghdad and reported by the State Department found that 64% of Baghdad residents were concerned about a sudden withdrawal of American troops and wanted the troops to stay until security was firmly established. Only 34% of the Baghdad residents said that the United States should leave immediately.[13]
- Abu Fayad, an aide to a Shi'ite member of Parliament, stated in 2007, "Without a strong and visible American presence, the government would collapse. Of course there will be many different wars, Basra, Diwaniya, Baghdad. Everyone will try to control Iraq's fortune. The Americans failed, but they should stay."[14]

FYI

As the Bush Administration struggled over the future of Iraq and the U.S. involvement in that country there were the inevitable comparisons with the Vietnam War and the U.S. exit from Vietnam in 1975, with the now-famous picture of Vietnamese loyal to the United States desperately trying to get on helicopters on the roof of the U.S. Embassy in Saigon, some making it to safety and others left behind to certain imprisonment and death. President Bush in 2007 warned those who advocated a withdrawal from Iraq using the Vietnam comparison. Bush stated, "Whatever your position in that debate [about withdrawal from Iraq], one unmistakable legacy of Vietnam is that the price of America's withdrawal was paid by millions of innocent citizens, whose agonies would add to our vocabulary new terms like 'boat people,' 'reeducation camps' and 'killing fields.' " It is important to point out that thirty years after the end of the Vietnam War, the United States had developed ever-growing economic ties with Vietnam and President Bush traveled to that country for trade talks.

Source: White House Press Release

As can be seen from these few snapshot observations regarding future policy options regarding Iraq, there are some common themes and observations. There is no doubt that in the minds of many experts and Iraqis a withdrawal of U.S. combat troops, especially if that withdrawal were to be over a short period of time and involve considerable personnel, would likely lead to heightened sectarian violence between Shi'ites and Sunnis and perhaps lead to a de facto partition of the country with the Kurds in the North, the Sunnis in some areas in the middle of the country and the Shi'ites controlling the south. There could also be a revival of al Qaeda activity in the country, because a withdrawal could lead to greater influence of Iran in the Iraqi affairs.

As the withdrawal scenario plays out in Washington and Baghdad, a number of political and military considerations must be taken into account by President Obama, the Pentagon and the government of Iraq that hold the key to any shift in current policy. First, the Iraqi political leaders, in particular Prime Minister Nouri al-Maliki, have relied too heavily on their perception that the United States will remain in Iraq with high levels of combat troops for an extended period of time. As a result al-Maliki and his government ministers were slow to meet President Bush's series of critical benchmarks that signify progress on national security, oil revenue, provincial elections, power-sharing formulas and infrastructure development. Many of those benchmarks remained unmet or only partially attained during the early days of the Obama administration.[15]

As critics of the open-ended commitment of the Bush administration have often pointed out, the United States lost a good deal of leverage with the al-Maliki government with its pledge to remain in the country until "victory is achieved." This commitment created an atmosphere of laxity among Iraqi leaders in meeting benchmark goals and resolving past sectarian grievances. Those in opposition to the Bush administration's refusal to consider a timetable for withdrawal have often stated that the Iraqis would become vigorous in pursuing these benchmarks and dealing with divisive ethnic and religious issues only if they were faced with the reality of an imminent U.S. withdrawal.[16] This accent on forcing the Iraqis to take action on the benchmarks is at the center of the Obama position about the need for a specific timetable for withdrawal.

Second, the United States, if it is to move forward with a withdrawal policy, will have to consider how best to deal with radical Shi'ite leaders such as Moqtada al Sadr whose militia controls much of southern Iraq. Al Sadr and his militia have waged an on-and-off war with the United States and the British, creating periods of tentative stability alongside times of open warfare. The future stability of Iraq depends in large part on bringing al Sadr and other Shi'ite religious leaders into the mainstream of national politics rather than as a force for revenge against the Sunnis or as allied with Iran. When Democrats talk about the importance of a political solution in Iraq, their remarks often refer to the need to integrate al Sadr and his militias into a Iraqi nation state that takes orders from the government in Baghdad rather than the government in Tehran.[17]

Finally, what may be the key to a successful withdrawal is the importance of building on the advances made in Iraq since the initiation of the surge strategy. The surge did achieve a promising level of stability and security in Baghdad, and the cooperation of Sunni leaders in Anbar Province and other areas helped to dismantle the insurgent movement. However, these advances can only be viewed as tentative. Both General David Petraeus, the commander of U.S. forces in Iraq, and Ambassador Ryan Crocker testified before Congress in 2008 that what success has been achieved in establishing security zones in Iraq cannot be considered firm or lasting. There are still serious concerns about the fighting capability of the Iraqi military and police, and the positive relations with Sunni groups such as the "Sons of Iraq" militia are not set in stone and are based on a U.S. withdrawal. These surge-related successes also must be linked with much more aggressive infrastructure progress as many Iraqis continue to experience long electrical blackout periods, unsafe water, dismal trash and sewer services and cynical views about the honesty of their own government officials. Iraq today is in many respects a more secure nation than it was two years ago, but so much of that security could collapse at any moment.[18]

The future of U.S. involvement in Iraq and the future of Iraq thus remain unclear and tentative. Some progress has been made, but enormous challenges of reconciliation, national security and economic development will continue to face the Iraqi government and the Iraqi people. The security agreement between the two countries is critical to the future of U.S. involvement in Iraq and Iraqi stability. The United States had been pressing the Iraqis to sign a long-term security agreement, which would allow American troops to remain in Iraq. President Bush and Iraqi Prime Minister al-Maliki signed a preliminary agreement in December 2007 that promised a finalized agreement in 2008. Many in Iraq were suspicious of the agreement, believing that it will lead to permanent U.S. military bases in Iraq and the ability to intervene from those bases to other countries in the region. Shi'ites associated with al Sadr and his Mahdi Army were especially aggressive in staging protests against the security agreement.[19] However in November 2008 the Iraqi cabinet approved the agreement called the Status of Forces Agreement, committing the United States to leave urban areas on June 30, 2009, and the country no later than December 31, 2011.[20]

The future of Iraq and U.S. policy toward Iraq depend in large part on how successful this experiment in democratic nation building in the Middle East becomes in the years ahead. The Bush administration expressed supreme confidence in the early days of the invasion of Iraq that it would be able to transform the dictatorship of Saddam Hussein into a thriving democracy with popular elections, effective governing institutions, the rule of law and guarantees of human rights. After several years of war, Iraq remains a "work in progress." Although there have been elections, a constitution and democratic institutions, much of the democratic nation building is only in its infancy and what is more, the concept of a nation is far from being realized. The vision that the Bush administration initially presented to the American people of a speedy and complete transformation of Iraq is still just that, a vision.

As for President Obama, he has maintained his commitment to a withdrawal but is open to changing the timetable based on the level of internal security in the country. In the early days of his administration Obama did push back his administration's target date for withdrawal of all combat troops by August 10 because of advice from his commanders on the ground (all troops would be withdrawn by the agreed-upon date of December 31, 2011). The emphasis now for the United States is to remove its troops and equipment from Iraq, while assisting the Iraqi military only when asked. The removal process is a logistical nightmare as over the years the United States turned Iraq into a huge military base with 140,000 troops and hundreds of billions in equipment and support services.[21] However, the commitment that began in 2003 with the invasion of Iraq to end the regime of Saddam Hussein has reached the exit point, but it is an exit point with an uncertain future. The current policy position of the United States is that the Iraqis are stable and strong enough to fend off the militants and function as a struggling but effective democracy that no longer needs a huge American military presence.[22]

Success in the future will thus be defined in long-range terms and incremental steps. As U.S. Ambassador to Iraq Ryan Crocker stated in 2008 in his testimony before the Senate Foreign Relations Committee:

> as monumental as the events of the last five years have been in Iraq, Iraqis, Americans and the world ultimately will judge us far more on the basis of what will happen than what has happened. In the end, how we leave and what we leave behind will be more important than how we came. Our current course is hard, but it is working. Progress is real although still fragile. We need to stay with it.[23]

However, no matter what happens in terms of internal security and stability in Iraq after the withdrawal of U.S. troops, the definition of success in that country will depend not on what Washington policy makers do, but on what Iraqi leaders do and how the Iraqi people react to the decisions and actions of their leaders. It is sometimes lost in the news reports of dead and injured American soldiers, but the Iraqi people have suffered tragic losses of life, perhaps well over 100,000 people since the beginning of the war, with an estimated 2 million people displaced to other parts of the country or as refugees in neighboring countries. There is no doubt that Iraqis also yearn for a return to stability, security and what passes for normality in a country that has been ravaged and transformed by the U.S. invasion.

Although the Obama administration remains committed to assisting the Iraqis with substantial aid assistance, attention has shifted to neighboring Afghanistan where the president, in the face of deep disappointment by his supporters has taken the position that the United States must defeat the Taliban terrorists. As Obama often mentioned during the presidential campaign, while the Bush administration was placing its emphasis on defeating the insurgency in Iraq, the Taliban in Afghanistan were regrouping and becoming a serious threat to the government of Hamid Karzai, the pro-U.S. president of Afghanistan. Once Obama entered office he ordered a complete review of U.S. presence in Afghanistan to determine what direction the United States should follow in that troubled country.

After weeks of internal discussions between Obama, his national security team and the Pentagon, the President ordered an Iraqi-style surge of an additional 30,000 troops, which would increase the total United States military presence to nearly 100,000. Obama did qualify the commitment of the new troops to eighteen months, as he presented the new commitment as not open ended, but rather designed to force the Afghan government to build a national army and the institutional structures necessary for stability and sustainability. As the president stated in announcing the new strategy for Afghanistan:[24]

> Many people in the United States–and many in partner countries that have sacrificed so much–have a simple question: What is our purpose in Afghanistan? After so many years, they ask, why do our men and women still fight and die there? And they deserve a straightforward answer. . . . So I want the American people to understand that we have a clear and focused goal: to disrupt, dismantle and defeat al Qaeda in Pakistan and Afghanistan, and to prevent their return to either country in the future. That's the goal that must be achieved. That is a cause that could not be more just.

Obama's decision on Afghanistan faced intense criticism from liberals in Congress and among his supporters who felt he was following the same route of George Bush and getting the United States entangled in a war that could last for years. Concerns have been raised over the mounting cost of the war—over 1000 soldiers dead, growing budget commitments (the 2010 budget request was over $70 billion), the weakness of the Afghan army, the unpopularity of the government, and the skepticism of the American people about a long-term presence in Afghanistan.[25] The President, however, was convinced that the United States and its allies fighting in Afghanistan could not afford to let the Karzai government fall to the Taliban. A Taliban victory would in the President's view only embolden the terrorists and provide al Qaeda with a new site for its terrorist operations. Obama was also convinced that his military leaders on the ground in Afghanistan, especially General Stanley McChrystal, had a counter-insurgency plan that would win over the Afghan people, whose support was critical to defeating the Taliban.[26]

Obama's decision to support a surge and to not leave Afghanistan without defeating the Taliban is a work in progress. While the surge has helped secure some areas of the country under the control of the Taliban and a number of key Taliban leaders have been killed in drone strikes along the border with Pakistan, there remain serious problems of governance and corruption. President Karzai won reelection in 2009 in what was viewed by most independent observers as a fraudulent process. Moreover, Karzai and his government remain weak and rife with corruption, mostly associated with the opium trade. The institutions of government are in shambles and the economy is dependent on illicit drugs and foreign assistance. The prospects that the United States may remain longer in Afghanistan than promised by President Obama are real and as a result the debate over whether the United States should cut its losses and leave the country as it did in Iraq will continue unabated.[27]

The Great Debate

The decision by President George W. Bush to invade Iraq will for generations be debated as to whether this military intervention was warranted and whether it enhanced U.S. security interests.

Debate Topic

Was the United States correct in invading Saddam Hussein's Iraq, and was the intervention a success?

Critical Thinking Questions

1. Should the Obama administration be flexible with its timetable for withdrawal, or should it abide by the agreement with the Iraqis?
2. Do you believe that the United States should maintain a long-term presence in the Middle East?
3. Is President Obama correct in following a Bush-like surge strategy in Afghanistan?
4. Do you believe that the deaths and injuries of thousands of American soldiers in Iraq have been in vain or a valuable contribution to freedom and democracy in the Middle East?
5. How will history judge the U.S. decision to go to war with Saddam Hussein's Iraq?

Connections

The position of the United States toward the Iraq war is best viewed at the White House website, especially President Obama's speech to the troops during a visit to Iraq. See http://www.whitehouse.gov/blog/09/04/07/The-President-Speaks-to-the-Troops/

The Iraq Study Group has a website that presents its analysis of U.S. policy in Iraq. See http://www.usip.org/isg/index.html

The Saban Center for Middle East Policy at the Brookings Institution is a valuable resource for understanding Iraq and the Iraq war. See http://www.brookings.edu/saban/iraq-index.aspx

Dahr Jamail has one of the most respected websites providing a Middle Eastern view of the war in Iraq, Afghanistan? and indeed the entire Middle East. See http:// dahrjamailiraq.com/gallery

The Middle East Research and Information Project is another key source of policy analysis on Iraq, Afghanistan and the Middle East. See http://www.merip.org

Some Books to Read

Allawi, Ali A., *The Occupation of Iraq: Winning the War, Losing the Peace* (New Haven: Yale University Press, 2008).

Thomas Ricks, *Fiasco: The American Military Adventure in Iraq, 2003 to 2005* (New York: Penquin, 2007).

Engel, Richard, *War Journal: My Five Years in Iraq* (New York: Simon & Schuster, 2008).

Jones, Seth, *In the Graveyard of Empires: America's War in Afghanistan* (New York: W. W. Norton, 2010).

Woodward, Bob, *State of Denial: Bush at War, Part III* (New York: Simon & Schuster, 2007).

Notes

1. See Meredith Buel, "Middle East Analysts Skeptical About New Iraq War Strategy," *Voice of America News*, January 12, 2007, http://www1.voanews .com/english/news/a-13-2007-01-12-voa65-66690332.html?rss=war
2. Juan Cole, "Five Years of Iraq Lies," http://www.salon.com/news/opinion/ feature/2008/03/19/iraq_five
3. See, for example, Elisabeth Bumiller, "Bush Strengthens Defense of Iraq Policy in Latest Speech," http://www.nytimes.com/2005/08/24/international/ middleeast/24cnd-prexy.html
4. See Douglas Feith, *War and Decision: Inside the Pentagon at the Dawn of the War on Terrorism* (New York: HarperCollins, 2008).
5. See the John McCain and other Republican presidential candidate's position on the Iraq war at http://www.associatedcontent.com /article/295075/The_republican_ presidential_candidates_html?cat=75
6. See a critical discussion of McCain's position on "cutting and run" at http://www .huffingtonpost.com/paul-abrams/McCain_cut-and-run-from-a_b_129755.html
7. See Barack Obama's position on Iraq during the presidential campaign at http://content.usatoday.com/news/politics/election2008/issues.aspx?1&c=12
8. For a discussion of the withdrawal option, See Michael O'Hanlon, "Reality and the Iraq War," Brookings Institution, http://www.brookings.edu/opinions/ 2008/0311_iraq_ohanlon.aspx
9. http://www.usip.org/isg/iraq_study_group_report/report/1206/index.html
10. "Prospects for Iraq's Stability: Some Security Progress but Political Reorientation Elusive," *National Intelligence Estimate*, August 2007.
11. Jeffrey Goldberg, "After Iraq," *Atlantic*, January/February, 2008, pp. 69–77.

12. Peter Bergen, "What Osama Wants," *New York Times*, October 26, 2006, http://nytimes.com/2006/10/26/opinion/26bergen.html

13. See "Most Iraqis Favor Immediate Pullout Polls Show," *Washington Post*, September 27, 2006, A22.

14. Michael Gordon and Alissa Ruki, "Strife Forseen in Iraq Exit, but Experts Split on Degree," http://www.nytimes.com/2007/05/27/world/middleeast/27withdraw.html

15. Thom Shanker and Steven Lee Myers, "General's Advice to Suspend Cuts Reflects Bleak Assessment of Iraq Military," *New York Times*, April 10, 2008, A10.

16. See "Bush: Iraq Benchmarks Report Cause for Optimism," http://www.cnn.com/2007/POLITICS/07/12/us.iraq/index.html

17. "Links with Militia Render Many Iraqi Units Useless," *Washington Post National Weekly Edition*, September 10–16, 2007, p. 9.

18. See full text of General Petraeus's testimony at http://www.politico.com/news/stories/0907/5735.html

19. U.S. Senate Committee on Foreign Relations, "Iraq After the Surge: What Next?" April 8, 2008.

20. Campbell Robertson and Stephen Farrell, "Pact Approved in Iraq, Sets Time for U.S. Pullout," *New York Times*, November 17, 2008, A1. See also "U.S. Security Agreement and Iraq," Council on Foreign Relations, http://www.cfr.org/publication/16448

21. Bryan Bender, "Iraq Exit Poses Daunting Logistics," *Boston Globe*, July 28, 2009, A1.

22. Greg Jaffe, "It's Iraq's War Now," *Washington Post National Weekly Edition*, August 10–16, 2009, p. 25.

23. http://www.politico.com/news/stories/0907/5735.html

24. See the president's remarks at the White House website, http://whitehouse.gov/blog/09/03/27/A-New-Strategy-for-Afghanistan-and-Pakistan/

25. "Reinforcing failure?" *Economist*, September 26, 2009, p. 35.

26. Bob Woodward, "The Case for Afghanistan," *Washington Post National Weekly Edition*, September 28–October 4, 2009, pp. 6–7.

27. Dexter Filkins, "The American Awakening," *New Republic*, March 11, 2010, pp. 23–28.

22 IRAN

Issue Focus

Through much of the Cold War era, the United States and the Soviet Union competed in a nuclear arms race in which both countries increased their arsenals of nuclear weapons and delivery systems. Since the Reagan administration, the United States and the Soviet Union (now Russia) signed a series of agreements to cut back these nuclear arsenals. However, while the tensions between these two superpowers waned, other countries sought to build nuclear weapons and missile systems. Iran is one of those countries. For the last decade, despite objections from the United States and the international community and stiff economic sanctions, Iran has moved forward with the development of nuclear weapons and missiles. The radical Islamic government in Tehran is determined to use nuclear weapons as a means of national power and regional dominance. Attempts to open up Iran's nuclear facilities have been rejected as have attempts to reach a diplomatic compromise. Meantime, Iran is in the throes of an internal political struggle between moderates and extremists over the direction of their country. In the United States the threat from Iran has become an issue of national security with differences of opinion on how best to deal with a dangerous rogue state.

Chapter Objectives
This issue chapter will seek to:

1. Describe the emergence of Iran as a potential nuclear threat and dominant strategic force in the Middle East.

2. Explain the different approaches to dealing with a radicalized Iran by Washington policy makers in the Bush and Obama administrations.

3. Examine the "threat scenarios" should Iran develop a nuclear weapon.

SOME BACKGROUND

In 1979 the Shah of Iran, Mohammed Reza Pahlavi, was ousted from power after the administration of President Jimmy Carter weakened its support for the authoritarian monarch. This shift in U.S. policy toward the Shah allowed radical elements within the country led by exiled cleric Ayatollah Khomeini to take over the leadership of Iran. Within weeks of his return to power, Khomeini revealed his hatred for the United States calling it the "Great Satan" and began mobilizing his supporters to destroy any vestiges of Western influence such as movie theaters and the sale of alcohol. However, when the Carter administration reluctantly allowed the Shah into the United States for cancer treatment, the Ayatollah intensified his anti-American campaign and permitted a group of extremist students to take over the American Embassy in Tehran and hold fifty-two diplomats and other personnel hostage for 444 days. Despite a failed military rescue attempt approved by President Carter, the breaking of diplomatic relations and the freezing of over $12 billion in Iranian assets in the United States, the Khomeini regime refused to budge on the hostage release. On the day when Ronald Reagan took the oath of office on January 20, 1981, the Iranians freed the hostages, a final gesture of defiance against the Carter government.[1]

The Iranian hostage crisis was but one event in a long history of U.S. involvement in Iran dating back to the 1950s when the Central Intelligence Agency worked to remove nationalist Prime Minister Mohammed Mossadeq from power, thus leading the way for the Shah to become Iran's leader and form a long diplomatic and economic relationship with Washington. Iran became the center of American influence in the Middle East and a key provider of oil for the U.S. economy.[2] However, U.S. ties with Iran were for many nationalists, intellectuals and radical Islamists another example of imperialism and oil-based foreign policy that had to be removed from the Middle East. With Khomeini and other radical clerics in power and the deeply anti-American regime immensely popular with many in the country, Iran set about using its oil wealth and growing ties to radical groups in the region to attack U.S. interests. In 1983 the Lebanese militant group Hezbollah, which was funded by Iran, attacked the U.S. Marine barracks in Beirut, killing 241 Marines. In 1996 the Khobar Towers in Saudi Arabia, a U.S. military housing complex, was bombed, killing scores of Americans. A U.S. court, relying on intelligence gathering from numerous agencies of the government, stated that the Ayatollah Khomeini had approved the bombing.

During the Clinton administration, despite the history of intense anti-Americanism and terrorist attacks, there were some brief signs of a thawing of relations with Iran. A new Iranian president, the Ayatollah Khatami, called for a dialogue with the West. There were some minor signs of a new era of relations, but key issues such as U.S. ties to Israel made any real change in relations impossible. All the while Iran was becoming a major force in the Middle East as it continued to fund terrorists groups and began developing a nuclear energy program that many in the United States saw as a front for the construction of weapons of mass destruction. In the years following 9/11, Iran evolved into an extremist rogue state that incited instability in the region, while pursuing the capability to be a military force and dominate the Persian Gulf region and indeed the entire Middle East.

The ascent of George W. Bush to the presidency in 2001 did little to close the divide between the United States and Iran. In 2002, in his State of the Union address, President Bush gave his famous "Axis of Evil" speech in which he singled out Iraq, North Korea and Iran as the three major threats to the world and implied that the United States might be required to take action against these states. The president voiced concern about the growing capacity of these three countries to develop nuclear weapons and delivery systems that would threaten the United States and the world. The speech angered the Iranian government and ended any hope of moving toward some level of diplomatic discourse or compromise on issues such as support for terrorism and the nuclear program.

Relations between the United States and Iran became even more difficult when in 2005 the Iranians elected Mahmoud Ahmadinejad as president. Ahmadinejad was a hard-line extremist who, like the Ayatollah Khomeini, talked about destroying Israel. Ahmadinejad even went so far as to say that the Holocaust never occurred. The Iranian leader had no interest in negotiating with the United States and saw the U.S. invasion of Iraq as the first step in what would eventually become an attack on his country. More important, Ahmadinejad moved quickly and openly to advance Iran's nuclear program. Despite public claims that the program was designed only to enhance Iran's energy output, the Bush administration, other western countries and the United Nation's International Atomic Energy Agency (IAEA) all viewed the nuclear program as a bold attempt to develop weapons of mass destruction. Despite warnings from the Bush Administration and the European Union and regular inspections and complaints by the IAEA that Iran was in non-compliance with the Nuclear Non-Proliferation Treaty, Ahmadinejad continued to press forward with the nuclear program, while denying that his country had anything but a peaceful use for nuclear power.[3]

The intransigence of the Iranian government under President Ahmadinejad intensified the Bush administration's efforts to isolate Iran both diplomatically and with economic sanctions. However, as the war in Iraq dragged on, Bush also feared that because of the close ties of the Shi'ite groups in Iraq with Iran, a withdrawal of U.S. troops from Iraq would lead to an Iraqi government that was a puppet state of Tehran and an extension of radical Islamism in the region. The huge divide between the Bush administration and the radical regime of Ahmadinejad left many in Washington and throughout the United States with the feeling that the country was heading toward an inevitable confrontation with Iran, or worse yet a nuclear-armed Iran ready to attack Israel.

On the Record

At a conference in Tehran in October 2005 Iranian President Mahmoud Ahmadinejad made his most controversial speech in which he expressed doubt about the Jewish Holocaust. The speech caused a firestorm of controversy and validated the view among many that Iran was becoming a radical nation and a threat to stability in the world. The key elements of the speech are provided here:

They (the Jews) have invented a myth that the Jews were massacred and place this above God, religions and the prophets. The West has

(continued)

On the Record   (continued)

given more significance to the myth of genocide of the Jews even more significant than God, religion and the prophets. . . . If you have burned the Jews, why don't you give a piece of Europe, the United States, Canada or Alaska to Israel? Our question is, if you have committed this huge crime, why should the innocent nation of Palestine pay for this crime?

Source: Translation by CNN

DEBATES, DIFFERENCES AND DIVISIONS

The emergence of Iran as both a radical Islamist state and a potential nuclear power has created clear differences in political and governing circles on what steps need to be taken to respond to this new threat. The differences over Iran range from how real and imminent the nuclear threat is to whether diplomatic overtures to the Ahmadinejad government would be proper rather than military containment, and perhaps even military intervention. The Bush administration made it clear as Iran became more belligerent toward international inspections and sanctions that the United States would not tolerate a nuclear power on Iraq's border with ambitions to dominate the region. There were even reports that the United States was developing plans for an air strike against the Iranian nuclear complex. The highly respected investigative reporter Seymour Hersh, writing in the *New Yorker* magazine in 2007, stated that such contingency plans for an attack on Iran were in the works on the instructions of Vice-President Cheney and were supported by the Israeli government, which viewed the Iranian government as determined to use its nuclear arsenal in some future attack. President Bush also hinted at the possibility of such an attack. When asked in 2006 about U.S. options in dealing with Iran, Bush stated that "All options are on the table."[4]

The investigative reports and vague references of a possible military attack on Iran were met with intense criticism by those opposed to Bush policy in the Middle East. Opponents viewed a military response to the Iranian nuclear program and its support for terrorists as ill-conceived, certain to create further instability in the region and guaranteed to foster even more intense hatred of the United States. Democrats in Congress and presidential candidate Barack Obama accented the need to engage the Ahmadinejad government in diplomatic negotiations. Obama expressed interest in meeting with the Iranians and stated that the past policies of the Bush administration that pushed for a military strategy in dealing with U.S. adversaries were ill-advised. Moreover, Obama pointed out that the Bush administration had met with the North Koreans over their nuclear weapons program and developed a six-nation framework for their compliance with international non-proliferation agreements.[5] According to Obama, the same strategy should be pursued with the Iranians. The North Korean model for dealing with nuclear proliferation by so-called rogue regimes, however, became controversial when in 2009 the government of Kim Jong Il, detonated an underground nuclear test and pledged to continue testing its ballistic missiles that could carry nuclear warheads as far as Alaska.

The tough policy of the Bush administration toward Iran created a fissure in its relations with the European countries, which were involved in seeking a negotiated settlement with the Ahmadinejad government that would accent a reduction in the economic sanctions and provide a series of trade-and-aid incentives. These benefits would be implemented when there was clear evidence that Iran was complying with the Non-Proliferation Treaty and abiding by the inspection demands of the IAEA. Since 2003 when the Europeans began talks with the Iranians, the Bush administration was a reluctant partner and often objected to portions of the incentive package, especially guarantees of security for Iran and a respected role in the Gulf region. The Bush administration refused to sign on to any agreement that in effect legitimized the Ahmadinejad regime and gave Iran the potential for a free rein in the Gulf. As for the Europeans, they were convinced that the Bush administration missed an opportunity to negotiate with the Iranians and achieve a "grand bargain" that would lessen if not eliminate the potential nuclear threat from Iran and provide it with assurances that the United States would not engage in a military strike in the future.[6]

The controversy over what to do about Iran got even more complicated when in November 2007 a National Intelligence Estimate found that Iran had stopped its nuclear weapons program in 2003. Although the estimate did state that Iran at one time was working on a nuclear weapons program and still had the major component parts necessary should it decide to renew its program, the analysis in effect weakened the arguments made by the Bush administration. The National Intelligence Estimate caused a huge uproar in Washington and especially in the Bush administration, which had been claiming all along that Iran posed a nuclear weapons threat that needed to be addressed.[7]

The administration slammed the report, but senior intelligence officials who were involved with the 140-page analysis stated that "We got new information that we judged to be credible that changed a judgment on a key point."[8]

President Bush stressed that Iran still had the capability to restart the program and downgraded the relevancy of the National Intelligence Estimate. As the president stated, "Iran's decision to halt its nuclear weapons programs suggests it is less determined to develop nuclear weapons than we have been judging since 2005 . . . I believe they want a weapon and I believe that they're trying to gain the know-how as to how to make a weapon under the guise of a civilian nuclear program." There is no doubt that the National Intelligence Estimate diminished the ability of the Bush administration to push for a more aggressive policy toward Iran and gave the Iran government a public relations victory.[9]

However, the National Intelligence Estimate also had a downside for the Iranian government, which lost its main argument that there needed to be a united front in the country against possible American aggression. With the military option of the Bush administration weakened, President Ahmadinejad was left with no impending outside threat and was required to concentrate on dismal economic and social conditions in his country such as food and power shortages, inflation, unemployment and rising social unrest. Critics of the Bush policy saw the impact of the National Intelligence Estimate as a new opportunity to weaken the Ahmadinejad government and build up support for a change in government. There were also signs that the National Intelligence Estimate might spur other nations in the region such as Saudi Arabia to play a larger role in containing Iran, now that Ahmadinejad had lost a key piece of his anti-American strategy.[10]

As a result of the changed strategic atmosphere that followed the National Intelligence Estimate, many Middle Eastern countries began to recognize that a resurgent Iran was a threat to stability in the region and that some cooperative containment effort was required. The Arab countries, however, were wary of the United States as they believed that the Bush administration was still holding to its belief that Iran would move forward with its nuclear weapons program and that some form of military containment was essential. Middle East expert Vali Nasr of the Fletcher School of Law and Diplomacy at Tufts University commented on the regional response to the National Intelligence Estimate challenge of the Bush policy: "The Arab governments around the Persian Gulf have been very worried about the rise of Iranian power, but what worries them more is that they don't believe the U.S. can execute an effective policy. Anytime an administration is undermined by its own intelligence agencies and its policy looks like its collapsing, Arab governments become nervous."[11]

Data Bank

At the heart of the issue of Iran's disputed nuclear weapons program is the 1968 Nuclear Non-Proliferation Treaty. The treaty became effective in 1970 with its ratification by the United States, the United Kingdom, the Soviet Union and forty other signatories. In total 189 nation-states, including Iran, have signed the treaty. In 1995 the parties to the treaty decided to extend the treaty indefinitely; only India, Pakistan, Israel and North Korea have not signed the treaty. At issue with Iran's program is the claim by the IAEA that the Iranian government violated Article IV of the treaty when it secretly sought to enrich its stockpile of uranium, a key step in the process of creating nuclear weapons.

The publication of and subsequent controversy surrounding the National Intelligence Estimate on Iran's nuclear weapons program did not diminish the tensions between the Bush administration and the regime of Mahoud Ahmadinejad. The Bush administration turned its attention from Iran's nuclear weapons threat to its smuggling of conventional weapons into

Iraq. In 2007 President Bush accused Iran of providing weapons, money and other means of support to the Iraqi insurgency that resulted in the death of at least 170 American military personnel. The Iranian government vigorously denied the charges, but the United States provided evidence from the markings on weapons and explosive devices that linked them to Iran. A further step in escalating the tensions between the United States and Iran was the discussion within the Bush administration to designate the Iranian Revolutionary Guard Corps (IRGC) and its elite Quds Force as terrorist organizations because of their involvement in training and supporting the Iraqi insurgency. Although there was considerable support for taking such action, it was the first time that a nation-state declared an armed unit of a sovereign country a terrorist organization. As this internal White House discussion on declaring the IRGC and the Quds Force as terrorist organizations progressed, the Iranians shot back with a parliamentary resolution that declared the Central Intelligence Agency and the U.S. Army as terrorist organizations.[12]

The Bush administration's discussions over the IRGC and the Quds Force spurred partisan debate within the Senate. Some senators worried that the designation would heighten the tensions between the United States and Iran and perhaps be perceived as a signal of impending military action. The Senate in September 2007 passed a non-binding resolution (76-22) declaring the IRGC and the Quds Force as terrorist organizations and advised the White House to impose further economic sanctions on Iran. The resolution ran into considerable Democratic opposition as senators such as Majority Leader Harry Reid and Senate Foreign Relations Chairman Joseph Biden were wary of taking this position, seeing it as the first step toward a military engagement with Iran. As a result, a separate resolution sponsored by Biden passed (75–23) that sought greater diplomatic efforts (including direct talks with Iran) to bring a political solution to the Iraqi war. Biden and others in the Senate were convinced that any future resolution toward the conflict in Iraq would have to include Iran and that the declaration naming the IRGC and its elite Quds Force as terrorist organizations would only hamper efforts to achieve a diplomatic breakthrough.[13]

After considerable debate within the White House, the Bush administration decided in October to declare the IRGC as responsible for nuclear proliferation and the Quds Force as a terrorist organization responsible for providing roadside bombs, rockets and other explosives to the Shi'ite militias and the Afghan Taliban fighters. Both of these actions triggered further economic sanctions against Iran. President Bush, using his authority under Executive Order 13224 to "identify individuals, businesses, charities and extremist organizations engaged in terrorist activities," implemented a policy that allowed the United States to freeze the assets of terrorist groups linked to the Iranian government and make it more difficult for foreign businesses to function in trade and other relations with Iran. Because the terrorist declaration was tied to heightened economic sanctions and the disruption of foreign businesses dealing with Iran, Democrats and other critics of the Bush policy toward Iran saw the decision as weakening the prospect of enhancing diplomacy and a negotiated settlement of the disputes with the Ahmadinejad government in Tehran.

The declaration of the IRGC as the key link in the acquisition of nuclear materials and thus the source of the violations of the 1968 Non-Proliferation Treaty was viewed by many experts as a major step in shining an international light on the danger posed by this military organization. As Ray Takeyh of the Council on Foreign Relations stated at the time, "They (the Revolutionary Guards) are heavily involved in everything from pharmaceuticals to telecommunications and pipelines. . . . Many of the front companies engaged in procuring nuclear technology are owned and run by the Revolutionary Guards."[14] As part of the Bush decision regarding the IRGC, the U.S. government promised to list many of the IRGC's business and financial operations as the first step in the sanction process, thereby sending a signal to foreign companies that the United States would closely monitor any deals with the growing business enterprises of the IRGC and contracts or other arrangements would suffer economic retaliation from the United States. As one high-level U.S. official stated, "Anyone doing business with these people will have to reevaluate their actions immediately. . . . It increases the risks of people who have until now ignored the growing list of sanctions against the Iranians."[15]

FYI

The IAEA has been the ongoing watchdog of the nuclear program in Iran as it sought to determine whether the government was in compliance with the 1968 Non-Proliferation Treaty. Originally established in 1957 as the "Atoms for Peace" organization, the IAEA, which is headquartered in Vienna, Austria, has grown into a 2,200-member staff of technical experts and other professionals charged with ensuring compliance with international agreements. Because it has been monitoring the Iranian nuclear program, the IAEA has complained about issues of access to information, transparency and the ability to interview key members of the Iranian nuclear program. Always moderate and diplomatic in its operations, the IEAE in 2008 criticized the Iranian government for its failure to answer key questions about lingering doubts concerning the militarization of its nuclear program. The Director General Mohamed ElBaradei has become a vocal critic of the Iranian government and raised questions about the true objective of the nuclear program in Iran.

Source: IAEA website and the *Boston Globe*, May 28, 2008.

The Bush administration did not step back from its position that the Iranian government was a terrorist threat, and as a result it took aggressive action. In 2007 U.S. military units entered the Iranian consulate in Erbil, Iraq (in the Kurdistan region) and arrested five members of the staff who were viewed by U.S. intelligence agents as security threats. The action was condemned by the international community as a violation of the Vienna Convention on Consular Relations, and also by Democrats such as Senator Joseph Biden who said the president did not have the authority to take such military action against the diplomats of a foreign government. The Iraqi government also criticized the raid as an impediment to the advancement of positive relations with Iran. Later in 2007 the United States released two of the five diplomats and seven other Iranians who were not viewed as security threats.[16]

The Iranian government has shown a stiff resolve when faced with U.S. policies designed to isolate it in the international community and intimidate it with threatening actions. In 2008 Iranian speedboats engaged American warships in what U.S. Navy commanders described as provocative actions as they moved close to American warships in the Strait of Hormuz. The Iranians denied that their boats were acting in a threatening manner, but the United States provided the international media with audio and video clips that supported their version of the Iranian action. The 2008 incident followed upon a 2007 incident in which fifteen British sailors were captured on the high seas by the Iranians and detained for allegedly invading Iranian territorial waters. The British government and navy denied the allegations, and after a week the sailors were released unharmed. Both incidents confirmed the Bush administration's position that the Iranian government was continuing to act outside the bounds of international law and remained a threat to regional security and stability.[17]

As for the Obama administration it has accented the importance of finding common ground, but the response from Tehran has been cool as the government and the clerics responded that they wanted clear evidence that the United States was following a new path. In particular, they wanted a reduction in the economic sanctions and a renewal of trade. There was no talk of ending their nuclear program, which they continued to say was for peaceful energy purposes, not military action. Moreover, there were increasing signs that the Iranians had all the components necessary for the building of multiple nuclear weapons and were indeed moving forward with the program.[18]

The Obama initiative to restart talks with Iran received a setback in May 2009 when the Ahmadinejad government launched a missile with the capacity to reach Israel, U.S. bases in the region and indeed the entire Middle East.[19] Although the Obama administration still maintained its posture of a diplomatic solution to the Iranian threat and hoping that Ahmadinejad would lose out in a critical national election later in 2009, critics of this approach pointed out that the Iranian government under Ahmadinejad was incapable of finding a diplomatic solution. Charles Vick of a security think tank in Virginia echoed this position when he stated, "What it says (the missile launch) is 'Yeah, Mr. Obama, we will talk with you, but we are not changing our direction.'"[20]

Although Iran continued to take a belligerent position toward the United States and the missile launching reminded Washington policy makers that the nuclear threat from the Ahmadinejad government was real, public opinion polls showed a lack of support among the American public for any aggressive action, including war, against Iran. A poll conducted by CBS in 2006 found that 55% of Americans preferred that the Bush administration follow a path of diplomacy in dealing with Iran. Only 21% said that they supported military action, whereas 19% said that Iran posed no threat to the United States.[21] These poll responses have not changed dramatically since 2006, especially since the National Intelligence Estimate that questioned the Iranians' nuclear capability. Many Americans and certainly critics of the Bush approach to Iran believe that some sort of military intervention, such as a bombing of the nuclear facilities (by the Israelis in particular), would further engulf the United States in a strategic quagmire in the Middle East and further damage U.S. relations with the governments in the region.[22]

There is no question that Iran has become a major force in the Middle East and is currently led by a radical, unpredictable and anti-American government. In June 2009 the Iranian people went to the polls to elect a president with Ahmadinejad running against three other candidates, including a popular reformer Mir Hossein Moussavi. In what appeared to be a fraudulent election count, Ahmadinejad was declared the winner and received the important endorsement from the ruling religious leaders in the Guardian Council. The news of Ahmadinejad's victory touched off days of street demonstrations and violence as the more youthful, educated and urban Iranians fought the government and sought to have the election thrown out. The turmoil in Iran raised questions in the United States as to how the Obama administration should respond–with a strong denunciation of the radical government or a muted critique of a questionable democratic process. Obama, who had advocated for more open ties to Iran and a dialogue with the government, chose the later strategy to see how the reform uprising would play out. However with Ahmadinejad in control of the police, the militia and the military and backed up by the clerics, the reform movement was contained (at least for the time being). With the Ahmadinejad government remaining in power and holding fast to its anti-American and pro-nuclear policies, it will be very difficult for President Obama to find common ground through a diplomatic effort.[23]

There is thus a deadlock on Iranian policy, and an ominous feeling concerning nuclear proliferation by rogue regimes. Besides the intransigence of the Ahmadinejad government to deal with the IAEA and the international community and reach some sort of grand bargain on nuclear weapons, the dangerous and unstable government in North Korea has also refused to abide by international agreements and continues its threatening policies of developing nuclear weapons and even targeting them against the United States. The combination of a nuclearized Iran and North Korea is a matter of enormous seriousness for the world. It will be up to the Obama administration to fashion a strategy that seeks ways to contain or diminish the threat from both of these countries. However, because Iran sits at the center of an always-volatile Middle East and has been a champion of radical terrorists groups, the prospect of the regime in Tehran pushing forward with its nuclear weapons program has the potential to de-stabilize the entire region and embolden the terrorists.[24]

The Great Debate

Critical to the policy discussions over Iran is Obama's position of seeking a diplomatic solution to the nuclear threat as opposed to the isolation and containment measures of the Bush administration.

Debate Topic

Should the United States seek out the Iranian government and initiate diplomatic talks to resolve the crisis or maintain a posture of containment and isolation?

Critical Thinking Questions

1. Should the United States engage in a preemptive strike against the Iranian nuclear facilities to delay or destroy their capacity to build a nuclear weapon?
2. Is it foolhardy and ill-advised for the Obama administration to deal with a radical Islamist government in Iran?
3. Should the United States engage in covert operations to destabilize or help remove the current extremist government in Iran?
4. As the United States leaves Iraq and the Iranians fill the void, what should be the response by the Obama administration?
5. Is the grand bargain as proposed by the Europeans as a solution to the Iran problem possible?

Connections

View the National Intelligence Estimate on Iran's nuclear capability at http://www .dni.gov/press_releases/20071203_release.pdf

The State Department has a comprehensive presentation of U.S. policy toward Iran. See http://www.uspolicy.be/issues/iran/iran.asp

The House of Representatives Committee on Foreign Affairs conducted hearings in 2008 on U.S. policy in Iran. See the full text of the hearing at http://www .internationalrelations.house.gov/hearing_notice.asp?id=1016

The Council on Foreign Relations produced a Task Force Report on Iran. It can be viewed at http://www.cfr.org/publication/7194

For the Republican position on the United States-Iran relations, see http://www .washingtonprism.org/Blog/index.cfm/dopost/yes/id/34

Some Books to Read

Takeyh, Ray, *Hidden Iran: Paradox and Power in the Islamic Republic* (New York: Holt, 2007).

Evans, Michael D., *Showdown with Nuclear Iran: Radical Islam's Messianic Mission to Destroy Israel and Cripple the United States* (New York: Thomas Nelson, 2006).

Axworthy, Michael, *A History of Iran: Empire of the Mind* (New York: Basic Books, 2008).

Gonzalez, Nathana, *Engaging Iran* (Westport, CT: Praeger, 2007).

Ansari, Ali, *Confronting Iran: The Failure of American Foreign Policy and the Next Great Crisis in the Middle East* (New York: Basic Books, 2007).

Notes

1. For background on Iran and U.S policy see Babak Gonji, *Politics of Confrontation: The Foreign Policy of the USA and Revolutionary Iran* (London: Tauris Academic Studies, 2006).
2. See Stephen Kinser, *All the Shah's Men: An American Coup and the Roots of Middle East Terror* (New York: John Wiley, 2003).
3. "Spinning Out Nuclear Talks," *Economist*, April 19, 2008, p. 60.
4. Seymour Hersh, "Shifting Targets: The Administration Plan for Iran," *New Yorker*, October 8, 2007.
5. Michael Gordon and Jeffrey Zeleny, "Obama Envisions New Iran Approach," *New York Times*, November 2, 2007, http://www.nytimes.com/2007/11/02/us/politics/02obama.html
6. "Reigning in Iran," *Boston Globe*, May 28, 2008.
7. "Iran: Nuclear Intention and Capabilities," *National Intelligence Estimate*, November 2007.
8. Tom Gjelten, "Iran NIE Reopens Intelligence Debate," http://www.npr.org/templates/story/story.php?storyId=18177103
9. "Bush: Nuke-less Iran Remains Dangerous," http://edition.cnn.com/2007/POLITICS/12/04/iran.nuclear/index.html
10. Tom Gjelten, "Intelligence Estimates on Iran Cuts both Ways," http://www.npr.org/templates/story/story.php?storyId=18128448&ft=&f5370436
11. Ibid.
12. Robin Wright, "Iranian Unit to Be Labeled Terrorist Group," *Washington Post*, August 15, 2007, A01.
13. David Hersenhorn, "Senate Urges Bush to Declare Iran Guard a Terrorist Group," *New York Times*, September 27, 2007, http://www.nytimes.com/2007/09/27/washington/27cong.html
14. Iranian Unit to Be Labeled Terrorist Group, op.cit.

15. Senate Urges Bush to Declare Iran Guard a Terrorist Group, op.cit.
16. http://www.npr.org/Templates/story/story.php?storyId=6806038
17. http://www.timesonline.co.uk/tol/news/politics/article3761058.ece
18. Joby Warrick, "Iran's Nuclear Know-How," *Washington Post National Weekly Edition*, December 21, 2009–January 3, 2010, p. 17. See also "Conservative or Conservative," *Economist*, March 22, 2008, p. 13.
19. Alan Cowell and Nazila Fathi, "Iran Test-Fires Missile That Put Israel in Range," *New York Times*, September 29, 2009, A15.
20. Farah Stockman, "Iran Fires Missile, Tests U.S.," *Boston Globe*, May 21, 2009, A1.
21. See http://www.publicdiplomacy.org/75.htm
22. "Israel and Iran: Coming to a City Near You?" *Economist*, July 12, 2008, pp. 58–59.
23. Farah Stockman, "Iran Cool to Suspending Nuclear Agenda," *Boston Globe*, May 31, 2008, A3.
24. See James M. Lindsay and Ray Takeyh, "After Iran Gets the Bomb," *Foreign Affairs*, March/April 2010, Volume 89, Number 2, pp. 33–49.

23 CHINA

Issue Focus

When conversations among international affairs experts turn to the issue of power projection and global influence in the 21st century, China is often the first nation discussed. China, today, is clearly an emerging power, an economic juggernaut that is growing each year by leaps and bounds. It has become the factory to the world, exporting its goods and reaping the wealth associated with its export sector. China's growth has contributed to an expanding middle class anxious for consumer goods and a political and military class that seeks to play a wider role in Asia, and long–term, in the world. In the next twenty years China will be a country that cannot be ignored, but its growing power has concerned many in the West, particularly the United States, especially since China holds a significant portion of the debt obligations of the United States and is developing a military that could pose a threat to its neighbors and U.S. interests. Some believe that China's economic development will eventually lead to democratic development, but currently the Chinese Communist leadership is refusing to open up the country's political system. China's economic power, its military expansion and its refusal to develop a democratic system have led to serious debates in the United States over just how the U.S. government should deal with China.

Chapter Objectives
This issue chapter will seek to:
1. Describe the enormous economic growth of modern-day China and its impact on trade and other ties to the United States.
2. Explain the points of disagreement between China and the United States such as human rights, product safety issues and military expansion.
3. Present the future challenges for the United States as it interacts with China, an economic powerhouse and potential military competitor.

SOME BACKGROUND

In 1949 the People's Republic of China was established. The Communists led by Mao Zedong defeated the forces of Chiang Kai-shek's Kuomintang Party and set China on a path toward Marxist-Leninist rule. Under Mao's stern and dogmatic control China became a model of revolutionary Communism pledged to ideological purity and unbending support for the principles of socialist economics, communal living, mobilization of the rural masses and centralized control of political power. With Mao at the center of government, China moved through a number of distinct periods: the failed One Hundred Flowers era, a brief effort to open Chinese society; the Great Leap Forward, a sweeping program to remake China into an industrial power and the highly controversial Cultural Revolution, during which millions of the middle class and intellectuals were relocated by fanatical Red Guard youths into reeducation camps or imprisoned for challenging the existing doctrine of the Communist Party elite. Mao's China became one gigantic experiment in orthodox Communism and a cruel totalitarian state.[1]

When Mao died in 1976 China entered a two-year period of struggle as moderates in the Communist Party sought to strip the ideologues of power (in particular the so-called Gang of Four, which included Mao's wife). By 1978 the old guard was pushed out, and a new group led by Deng Xiaoping took power. Under the leadership of Deng, China shed its ideological orthodoxy and put in place an economic system that opened the country to western investment and trade. Many of the Cultural Revolution's restrictions were also relaxed, which allowed the country's leading minds and experienced administrators to return to their previous occupations. China by the 1980s began to show signs of an economic boom as its low wages, absence of environmental and labor safety controls and openness to the West fostered yearly gross domestic product (GDP) growth rates in the 8–10% range. The drabness of the Mao era was replaced by westernization and the presence of a thriving and consumer-oriented middle class. However, despite economic liberalization, there was little toleration of political liberties. In 1989 students and workers in Beijing staged a massive protest in Tiananmen Square that glorified western democracy and criticized the political restrictions of their government. Deng and his supporters in the party sent in the People's Liberation Army to crush the demonstration and jail or execute thousands of the protesters. The clear signal to the West and to the Chinese people was that Deng and his communist party supporters would tolerate economic openings but would not allow any political liberalization.[2]

Since the crackdown at Tiananmen Square, the Chinese leadership has continued the melding of economic liberalization with authoritarian rule. However, China's dismal human rights record and its refusal to open up the political system have not diminished its continuing "off the charts" economic development. Since the 1980s China has maintained its yearly growth rates of 8–10%, widened its huge trade surplus with western countries, especially the United States, and amassed trillions of dollars in foreign reserves. Chinese goods now flood the market of most western countries, making it the unquestioned "factory to the world." As a sign of its enormous economic transformation and growing influence, China hosted the 2008 Summer Olympics in Beijing, which was viewed by governmental officials and the everyday citizen as its introduction to the modern world.[3] There were numerous protests surrounding the opening of the Olympics, particularly the cruel domination of Tibet, but the Chinese authorities were able to maintain social and political control as the country basked in the glow of international legitimacy.

In many ways China remains a developing country with significant poverty in the rural areas and major challenges in key areas such as education, health care, infrastructure and housing. The per capita income in China for 2009 was $6,600 (est.) compared to $46,400 in the United States. Outside many of the urban areas are dirt poor farming communes where schools and hospitals are in short supply. Because these rural areas have little resemblance to the key centers of the economy, China remains a developing country. However, despite these deep pockets of poverty, there is no doubt that after thirty years of huge national growth, China is experiencing a white-hot domestic economy, an ever-widening industrial base and the development of modern cities such as Beijing, Shanghai and Hong Kong (returned to Chinese rule in 1999 by the United Kingdom).

The status of China as both an emerging economic power and a nation with long-term strategic designs has been viewed by the United States as both an opportunity and a potential threat. There is a huge American investment presence in China, with most of the familiar brands readily visible in the major cities. In 2006 U.S. investment in China was over $3 billion.[4] However, although the American investment presence is considerable and growing, so too is the reliance on trade with China. In 1997 the percentage of U.S. imports from China was 7% of the total, but by 2007 the percentage of imports had risen to 16%. This Chinese trade increase has created a U.S. trade deficit of $256 billion in 2007. Increasingly, Americans are grumbling about seeing *Made in China* labels on an ever-growing list of goods they purchase and the loss of manufacturing jobs in the United States as a direct result of China becoming the factory to the world. There is even a direct link to higher gasoline prices experienced in the United States, as the Chinese, to fuel their growing economy, have heightened international demand, resulting in higher prices at the pump.[5]

As China continues its transformation from Communist orthodoxy to a major economic force in the world, there is more and more concern in governing circles in this country that the next challenge to American economic and military dominance in the world may come from the Chinese. Besides its economic development, China has shown signs that it seeks to expand its military and play a larger regional role in Asia. Most China experts do not see such a challenge in the short term, but admit that with over 1 billion hardworking and politically compliant people, a vibrant and highly successful economy and visions of power and grandeur, China must be viewed as a nation on the move. How to deal with China's economic power now and its potential military and international power in the future are questions that are likely to be debated in the United States for many years to come.

On the Record

Ben Bernanke, the chairman of the Board of Governors of the Federal Reserve System, spoke at a meeting of the Chinese Academy of Social Sciences in Beijing in 2006. In his remarks Bernanke commented on the progress and challenges facing the Chinese economy and U.S. economic relations with China. A portion of his remarks are presented here:

China's development and its opening up to the global economy have also benefited the United States in many ways. China is now the second-largest source of U.S. imports; these imports boost U.S. real income by allowing U.S. households to purchase consumption goods and U.S. firms to purchase intermediate inputs at lower cost. China is also a growing market for investment and exports by U.S. firms. Since joining the World Trade Organization U.S. exports to China have more than doubled. . . . The economic relationship between China and the United States is of extraordinary importance, and both countries have much to gain from interactions with each other. Serious challenges exist as well requiring both countries to address areas such as energy, the environment, intellectual property right and global imbalances.

Source: The Federal Reserve, December 15, 2006

DEBATES, DIFFERENCES AND DIVISIONS

Although the United States and China have developed a close economic relationship and the American consumer has come to depend on inexpensive Chinese goods, there are some serious areas of tension between the two countries and significant challenges for the United States in the coming years. From a general perspective, there are now signs that in the coming years the Chinese economy will surpass that of the United States, not in terms of individual income and standard of living, but in terms of macroeconomic indices such as national GDP. Stated simply, China will become the world's largest economy by 2025 and will grow to 130% the size of the United States economy by 2050.[6] It must be emphasized that China has three times more people than the United States and its export economy has been driven by an undervalued currency (the yuan) that enhances its trade advantage. Nevertheless, there is a growing concern in Washington and among economic analysts that this economic rise of China poses a direct threat to the American economy. This likely future push past the United States into first place in the world's economy has stimulated nationalist bravado in the United States over the impact of a dominant China on the stature and reputation of the American economy. Secretary of the Treasury Hank Paulson during the waning days of the Bush administration in 2007 argued that the Chinese economy cannot expect to dominate international trade without facing challenges. As Secretary Paulson commented on China's position as the world's top trader, "I put the U.S. economy up against any in the world in terms of competitiveness–that's a fact."[7]

FYI

China's economic growth has had a wide-ranging impact on the income and standard of living of many of its people. Some examples of how China has developed into a consumer society are given here:

According to the U.S. Commerce Department, China's middle class (defined as per capita income over $8,000) currently totals 200 million people.

Merrill Lynch estimated in 2004 that China had 300,000 millionaires.

China currently has the world's largest mobile phone network with 432 million users as of 2006. In 2000 China had 87 million users.

In 2002 China replaced Japan as the world's second largest personal computer market, and in 2006 China became the world's second largest Internet user (after the United States).

World Bank data show that from 1981 to 2001, 400 million Chinese people moved out of extreme poverty.

Source: "China: A Threat to the U.S. Economy," Congressional Research Report, January 23, 2007

Paulson's confidence in U.S. export growth and its impact on Chinese trade dominance is also supported by growing domestic and international dissatisfaction with China's failure to adjust its currency rates. A bipartisan group of senators led by Democratic Senator Charles Schumer of New York and Republic Lindsey Graham of South Carolina warned China that failure to adjust the yuan would lead to Congressional action to place a 27% tariff on Chinese imports. Members of Congress also sought to publicly humiliate the Chinese over the currency issue by branding the country as a "currency manipulator." But Paulson's predecessor at Treasury, John Snow, was able to persuade Congress not to take the action, but rather to rely on quiet diplomatic efforts among the major industrial powers to persuade China to change its currency policies. With this kind of pressure, the Chinese did revalue the yuan by 2% against the dollar in 2005, but many in Congress were dissatisfied with this action saying that it was far too little and only a token gesture.[8] Later, in 2009 the Obama administration faced a more aggressive China over currency values. The Chinese castigated the United States for its role in the world economic meltdown and pushed for a new foundation currency to replace the dollar, which it saw as weak and without financial legitimacy. The Chinese, who hold hundreds of billions of dollars in U.S. debt obligations, have used their position as "lender of first resort" as a bargaining chip as they resist pressure to change their currency policies.[9]

Despite the threats from legislators in the United States and the aggressive position of the Chinese toward the dollar, Chinese officials have been unwilling to make wholesale changes on the value of yuan, in large part because its current inflexibility has been the primary reason for trade dominance and the growth in foreign reserves. To date there has been little change in the value of yuan and the response from Congress and other western nations has also been muted, because demand for cheaper Chinese goods remains high and countries are reluctant to antagonize one of their key trading and investment partners. Moreover, many economists and financial experts are not convinced that a revaluation of the yuan would have that much of a favorable impact on U.S. imports from China or its overall trade deficit. Economist Joseph Stiglitz pointed out that the U.S. trade deficit is nine times China's trade surplus and as a result, "even larger reevaluations are not likely to do much to the global imbalances."[10]

Problems with the trading relationship between China and the United States shifted from the complexities of international currency to the everyday concerns of the American consumer. In 2007 there were a series of product problems with goods made in China as tests showed high levels of lead paint in toys, contaminated dog food, and toothpaste and cough syrup that contained chemicals used in anti-freeze. Numerous deaths were reported both in the United States and around the world, along with hundreds of cases of illness as young children came in contact with the lead-contaminated toys. The Consumer Product Safety Commission, which monitors non-food goods, stated that in recent years 60% of all its recalls were related to Chinese-produced items. The main source of the problem is that China has lax regulatory and environmental rules and high levels of corruption in its factories and bureaucratic ministries (the head of the Chinese bureaucracy responsible for food safety was executed for corruption in 2007). U.S. companies that contracted with Chinese firms to manufacture these consumer products were also criticized for lax oversight, and the Food and Drug Administration (FDA) was taken to task by Congress for not being aggressive enough in monitoring Chinese food products entering the United States.[11]

As a result of the contaminations and recalls, many U.S. companies such as General Mills, Kellogg's and Toys"R"Us promised to be more vigilant in monitoring the production of goods made in China, and federal agencies such as the Food and Drug Administration (FDA) and the Consumer Product Safety Commission announced that they would be sending more inspectors to factories in China to oversee the manufacturing of Chinese consumer goods. However, critics in Congress placed some of the blame on U.S. corporations, which were viewed as unwilling to alert the public to the potential dangers of Chinese goods, especially food products. Senator Sherrod Brown, a Democrat from Ohio, castigated the food companies by stating, "Food companies have been among the most resistant to informing the public about their ingredients. Now that's more worrisome because these ingredients are coming from an unregulated environment."[12]

Data Bank

China has one of the world's fastest growing economies as is evident from the following data on the average annual real GDP growth rates from 1960 to 2009:

Time period	Average annual growth rate (%)
1960–1978–pre-reform	5.3
1979–2005–post-reform	9.7
1992	14.2
1994	13.1
1996	10.0
1998	7.8
2000	8.4
2002	9.1
2004	10.1
2006	10.5
2007	11.4
2008	9.6
2009 (est.)	8.7

Source: Official Chinese Government data

Disputes between the United States and China are not just associated with economic concerns; a number of key foreign and military policy disputes have caused serious differences and have the potential to create a troubling division between these two trading partners. Differences between China and the United States have risen in the last few years over Chinese control of Tibet, military threats to Taiwan (the breakaway country that China seeks to regain control of), and the support China has given to the repressive and genocidal regime in Sudan as it searches for new sources of oil. These foreign and military problems occur against the backdrop of China's desire to play a larger and more respected role in the international community.

Since 1959 Tibet has been under the control of the Chinese government. In 1959 an uprising of the Tibetan people triggered an intervention by the People's Liberation Army and stripped the nation of its independence. The leader of the Tibetan opposition is the Dalai Lama, a religious monk who went into exile in 1959 and has worked since then to reestablish independence for his country and its people. After taking control of Tibet, the Chinese crushed dissent, imprisoned opposition leaders and refused to consider any type of autonomy for what was once an independent nation. In recent years, the

Chinese have built a railroad to the capital city of Lhasa, which has allowed the migration of the Han ethnic group (the dominant Chinese ethnic group) into Tibet as a means of extending China's control. The Chinese have also kept in hiding the successor to the Dalai Lama, a young man who holds the title of the Panchen Lama. Over the years the Chinese have not hesitated to put down uprisings against their rule by using deadly force against protestors.[13]

In 2002, the Dalai Lama began talks with the Chinese government. The beginning of discussions between the Chinese and the Dalai Lama were encouraged by the Bush administration, although the official U.S. policy is that Tibet is a part of the People's Republic of China. President Bush used a 2005 meeting with the president and premier of China to stress the importance of religious freedom and human rights in Tibet. Paula Dobriansky, under-secretary of state for democracy and global affairs and special coordinator for Tibetan issues, told a congressional committee in 2007 that the United States was "greatly encouraged by the promise of discussions," but that these discussions have not produced positive results and were marked by "negative rhetoric" from the Chinese government. Dobriansky hoped that China would become "a responsible stakeholder in the global system and find that a more enlightened policy toward Tibet would be an important step toward enhancing and complimenting the respect it has earned from economic transformation."[14]

With the onset of the 2008 Olympics, the Chinese accused the Dalai Lama of fomenting uprisings in Tibet as a means of pressuring the government to relax its controls. But as the Dalai Lama stated in an address before the New York think tank, the Council of Foreign Affairs in 2008, "For nearly six decades, Tibetans in the whole of Tibet . . . have had to live in a state of constant fear, intimidation and suspicion under Chinese repression. Nevertheless in addition to maintaining their religious faith, a sense of nationalism and their unique culture, the Tibetan people have been able to keep alive their basis aspiration for freedom."[15]

With extensive worldwide support for his cause, the Dalai Lama has remained hopeful that he can convince U.S. officials to place renewed pressure on the Chinese government and to engage in meaningful talks that bring an end to the occupation of his country and the repression of his people. Although the Dalai Lama has sought to stay away from publicly criticizing United States-China relations, it is clear that his supporters want the United States to take a much more aggressive stance toward China and to use its diplomatic and economic leverage to push China to change its policy toward Tibet. The demonstrations in 2008 are likely to be but a prelude to more intensive challenges to the Chinese government and to force the United States to reevaluate its commitment to freedom and human rights with its key trading partner. The tension between China and the United States intensified in 2010 when President Obama met with the Dalai Lama despite the strenuous objections of the Chinese leadership. Obama was intent on sending a message to China about its human rights violations in Tibet and its policies of control of that territory.[16]

Although Tibet has captured the headlines in recent years, the ongoing dispute between China and Taiwan has been the focus of U.S. foreign policy in the Asian region. After the communist revolution of 1949 over 2 million Chinese aligned with the Kuomintang Party of Chiang Kai-shek left mainland China and established a government on the island of Taiwan. Since that time Taiwan has been a point of tension in mainland China as the Chinese government has sought to regain control of the island and establish what has been called a "One-China Policy." On numerous occasions there been military confrontations between the Chinese and the Taiwanese as both nations have developed large weapons arsenals and used tough, uncompromising rhetoric to heighten tensions.

Up until 1979 the United States recognized Taiwan as the country that it chose to engage diplomatically, but then switched its recognition to the Beijing government "as the sole legal government of China." Washington policy makers through a series of presidential administrations maintained close but informal ties with Taiwan under the auspices of the Taiwan Relations Act, but ended its Mutual Defense Treaty, which provided that the United States would come to the assistance of Taiwan if it is attacked by China. The United States has continued to provide Taiwan with defensive military equipment and more importantly has strong trade and investment ties with the island nation. The Taiwanese were disappointed at the decision of the United States regarding recognition and the resulting loss of influence in Washington, but that change in status has not had a major impact on trade relations. The United States is now Taiwan's third largest trading partner and Taiwan is the United States' ninth largest trading partner.[17]

In recent years tensions between China and Taiwan have decreased as there has been a spike in trade and more movement of people from island to mainland and back. There have been numerous talks between the two governments and a diplomatic framework for a solution to the dispute called the "Cross-Strait Framework for Peace and Stability" has been established. The United States has officially welcomed the reductions in tensions and the accent on a diplomatic solution to the One-China issue. Chinese leaders, however, remain adamant that they want Taiwan to become a province of the People's Republic of China and not a breakaway nation. As a result, the United States, serving as a broker between the two countries, remains cautious that hostilities between China and Taiwan could erupt at any time and that both nations might engage in a war that would damage two of the major economic powers in the region. One of the chief strategic responsibilities of the U.S. Pacific fleet is to monitor the potential for hostilities between China and Taiwan and be ready to serve as a "show of force" to limit war between two adversaries.[18] President Obama continued his posture of challenging the Chinese when in 2010 he increased military assistance to Taiwan, a move that further strained relations with the Chinese leadership and, in the view of many, weakened future efforts to deal with other issues such as trade and currency.[19]

Much of U.S. foreign policy toward China is to convince Chinese leadership to become a more responsible member of the international community and change the manner in which it operates both domestically and externally. China continues to have the reputation as a "difficult state" that holds to its authoritarian ways and engages in policies that are outside the bounds of traditional international norms of behavior. The most recent evidence of this is China's relations with Sudan, which is oil-rich and a new trading partner with the Beijing government. Sudan has been viewed by the international community as responsible for the genocide of hundreds of thousands of people in the Darfur region of the country. China, which could influence the government of Sudan through its oil-trade policies, has been reluctant to take an active role in forcing the Sudanese government to end its genocide.

In 2006 the United States and other western nations made a public declaration accusing the Chinese of failing to use its oil-trade relations with Sudan to end the killing in Darfur. China has in the past refused to speak against the government of the Sudan in the United Nations and has blocked attempts by the Security Council by using its veto power in that body to stop any sanctions against the Sudanese. Observers of China's position in Sudan cite concern in Beijing that cooperating with the United Nations and other western powers over human rights abuses and genocide in Sudan would put its own practices under closer scrutiny. As Chinese scholar Ming Wan of George Mason University states, "In effect it [China] doesn't want the U.N. to have any sanctions on countries for human rights reasons. It itself is vulnerable."[20]

The United States continues to work behind the scenes trying to convince the Chinese to soften their ties to Sudan and to work diplomatically to end the genocide in Darfur. Washington officials such as Bush administration Deputy Secretary of State Robert Zoellick tried to convince the Chinese that if they seek to be taken seriously in the international community and play an active role in solving problems, they need to show it by pressuring the Sudanese government to end genocide and place human rights above oil policy. There was some evidence in 2008 that China was working quietly with the Sudanese to stop its policies toward the people in Darfur, but these efforts were seen as modest and no real break from its continued effort to accent trade ties based on its energy needs rather than considering those policies within the context of international human rights policies.[21]

If there is a distinct common theme in China-United States relations, it is convincing the Chinese leadership to follow policies and take actions that accent human rights, support for democracy and respect for international standards regarding freedom of movement, access to information and the rule of law. Despite China's close trade and investment ties to the United States and its expanding middle-class consumer society yearning for western goods, the government remains firmly authoritarian. There are some small signs of nascent democratic movements, particularly at the village level, and a general national desire to be like western nations, but too often the communist party leadership clamps down on dissidents, blocks Internet access, supports rogue regimes for economic gain and drags its feet on seeking diplomatic solutions to difficult national and international problems.

The United States has been on the record seeking to push China into the mainstream of western democratic practice and international standards of behavior. Most of these efforts to change China can be categorized as "quiet diplomacy," as Washington officials have not sought to pressure China or engage in public denouncements of its regime and the manner in which it operates. Naturally, the significant trade and investment ties with China are part of the reluctance to pressure its governing leaders in ways that jeopardize American economic and financial interests.[22] The Obama administration has not taken steps that are different from the policies of President Bush, but many supporters of human rights in China are counting on President Obama to be much more forceful with the Chinese over their handling of public protest groups and the general climate of authoritarian control.

For now the United States appears to be willing to allow the forces of capitalism to push the country away from its authoritarian roots and begin the formation of democratic values and practices. However, in the future should China seek to move beyond becoming more than an international powerhouse in trade and investment and playing a military and strategic role in Asia or using its enormous foreign reserves to gain ever larger control of United States corporate or financial interests, then quiet diplomacy and bilateral cooperation could easily lead to public displays of tension and perhaps even confrontation.[23]

The Great Debate

Since the emergence of China as a major economic powerhouse, there has been a lingering concern in many U.S. circles that not enough emphasis was placed on forcing China to open up its society and move toward democracy, but rather the United States stuck to its policy of trade and investment without political strings attached.

Debate Topic

Should the United States tie human rights changes in China to its trade and investment policies or remain uninvolved with the internal political matters of the Chinese people and their government?

Critical Thinking Questions

1. Do you believe that a prominent U.S. trade and investment presence in China can have an influence on liberalizing the Chinese authoritarian regime?
2. Has the United States become too dependent on Chinese consumer goods just like it has become too dependent on Middle Eastern oil? If so, what should the United States do about this dependency?
3. Is China destined to become the next military threat to the United States?
4. What can the United States learn from the Chinese economic miracle?
5. Should the U.S. government become more aggressive in supporting the Tibetan people in their struggle against Chinese domination?

Connections

The United States-China Economic and Security Review Commission is one of the U.S. government's key agencies with specific responsibility for monitoring U.S. relationship with China. Visit its site at http://www.uscc.gov

The U.S.-China Business Council is a trade organization that seeks to advance economic and financial ties with China. Seehttp://www.uschina.org

The Department of State provides a thorough presentation of all aspects of China and the Chinese people. See http://www.state.gov/r/pa/ei/bgn/18902.htm

The University of Southern California has one of the foremost institutes devoted to China. See http://china.usc.edu/

The Chinese Embassy in the United States is a valuable source for examining the latest in U.S.-China relations. See http://www.china-embassy.org/eng

Some Books to Read

Sutter, Robert, *China's Rise: Implications for U.S. Leadership in Asia* (Washington, D.C.: East-West Center, 2006).

Fisher, Richard D., *China's Military Modernization* (Westport, CT: Praeger, 2008).

Goh, Evelyn, *Meeting the China Challenge: The U.S. in Southeast Asian Regional Security Strategies* (Washington, D.C.: East-West Center, 2005).

Kenny, Henry, J. *Shadow of the Dragon: Vietnam, China and the Implications for U.S. Foreign Policy* (Washington, D.C.: Potomac Books, Inc., 2002).

Gifford, Rob, *China Road: A Journey into the Future of a Rising Power* (New York: Random House Trade Paperbacks, 2008).

Notes

1. For background on these early periods in Chinese history see John Fairbanks and Merle Goodman, *China: A New History* (New York: Belknap Press, 2006).
2. The Deng modernization period is documented by Orville Schell and David Shombaugh in *The China Reader: The Reform Era* (New York: Vintage, 1998).
3. The economic development of modern China is the focus of Gary Hamilton's *Commerce and Capitalism in China* (Lanhan, MD: Routledge, 2006).
4. The social and economic changes in modern China are discussed in Doug Guthrie, *Dragon in A 3 Piece Suit: The Emergence of Capitalism in China* (Princeton, NJ: Princeton University Press, 2001).
5. Philip Bouring, "U.S. and China on a Collision Course," *International Herald Tribune*, http://www.iht.com/articles/2005/04/26/news/edbowring.php
6. "China to Be World's Largest Economy in 2025," *China Daily*, See http://www.chinadaily.com.cn/china/2008-03/05/content_6510506.htm
7. Ambrose Evans-Pritchard, "US Will Retake Economic Superpower Crown," http://www.telegraph.co.uk/finance/comment/ambroseevans_pritchard/2819359/US-will-retake-economic-superpower-crown.html

8. Chan, John, "China's Yuan Revaluation a Response to US Pressure," *World Socialist Web Site*, http://www.wsws.org/articles/2005/jul2005/yuan-j29.shtml

9. Wayne M. Morrison and Marc Labonte, "China's Holdings of U.S. Securities: Implications for the U.S. Economy," Congressional Research Service Report for Congress, January 9, 2008.

10. China's Yuan Revaluation a Response to US Pressure, op.cit.

11. Laura Smith-Spark, "Chinese Product Scares Prompt US Fears," http://news .bbc.co.uk/2/hi/americas/6275758.stm

12. Nelson Swartz, "Companies in US Increase Testing of Chinese Goods," *New York Times*, July 1, 2007, http://www.nytimes.com/2007/07/01/business/ 01 imports.html

13. Howard French, "Growing Gulf Divides China and Old Foe," *New York Times*, March 3, 2008, http://www.nytimes.com/2008/03/29/world/asia/29china .html

14. "The US on Tibet," http://www.voanews.com/uspolicy/2007-03-22-voa4.cfm

15. See www.cnn.com/2010/POLITICS/02/18/obama.dalailama/index.html

16. "Dalai Lama's Speech on the 49th Anniversary of Tibetan National Uprising Day," March 10, 2008. See http://www.cfr.org/publication/15986/dalai_lamas_ speech_on_the_49th_anniversary_

17. Nick Amies, "Washington's Arms Deal With Taiwan Threatens US-China Relations," http://www.globalresearch.ca/index.php?context=va&aid=17347

18. See Background Notes: Taiwan, United States Department of State, http://www .state.gov/r/pa/er/bgn/35855.htm

19. Jeremy Derfner, "What Is the One-China Policy?" *Slate*, May 24, 2000, http://www .slate.com/id/1005379

20. "China-Sudan Trade Relations Complicate Darfur Crisis," http://www.pbs .org/newshour/updates/China-Darfur_04-25-06.html

21. Ibid.

22. "The Chinese Economy: Progress and Challenges," Speech by Federal Reserve Chairman, Ben Bernanke, Beijing, China, December 15, 2006, http://www .federalreserve.gov/newsevents/speech/bernanke20061215a.htm

23. See the discussion of U.S.-China relations after the Great Recession in James Fallows, "Interesting Times," *Atlantic*, May 2009, pp. 54–63. See also Robert Kaplan, "The Geography of Chinese Power," *Foreign Affairs*, May/June 2010, Volume 89, Number 3, pp. 22–41.

24 ISRAEL **AND** PALESTINE

Issue Focus

Probably the most intractable foreign policy problem facing the United States since the end of World War II has been the Israeli-Palestine dispute. A clash over religion, land, economic justice and security, the Israelis and the Palestinians have been locked in constant conflict, with little progress made toward the resolution of their differences. Since 1948 when Israel became a state, the Palestinians and their allies in the Middle East have refused to acknowledge Israel's right to exist and have waged war and regular terrorist attacks on Israel. Israel has responded with its superior military force and has expanded its territory and invaded Palestinian safe havens such as the Gaza Strip and the West Bank of the Jordan River. These two enemies show little sign of coming to an agreement soon on what many in the West, including the United States, see as the solution–a Palestinian state and the recognition of Israel's right to exist. After numerous failed efforts at a diplomatic agreement, Israel and Palestine continue their fight.

Chapter Objectives
This issue chapter will seek to:
1. Present the history of U.S.-Israel relations and the reasons for the continued diplomatic, economic and military support of the Israelis.
2. Explain the emerging debate over the extent to which the United States should take a more balanced position toward all the participants in the Middle East and not hold to an exclusive relationship with Israel.
3. Discuss the various plans and proposals for bringing to an end the long-standing Israeli-Palestinian dispute.

SOME BACKGROUND

In May 2008 the nation of Israel celebrated its sixtieth birthday with parades, speeches and fireworks. The recognition of sixty years of nationhood was both a time of enormous national pride and lingering anxiety–pride that the Israeli people had built a nation in the midst of the Arab world and anxiety that for sixty years Israel had not been able to establish lasting security with their neighbors in the Arab world. Since declaring independence on May 14, 1948, Israel has fought a series of wars–the Arab-Israeli war of 1948 against Egypt, Syria, Jordan, Lebanon and Iraq, the Six-Day war of 1967 against Egypt, Syria and Jordan and the Yom Kippur War of 1973 against Egypt and Syria. In each instance the Israelis were successful in defeating their enemies and in the case of the Six-Day War annexed the West Bank of the Jordan River from Jordan, the Gaza Strip and the Sinai Peninsula from Egypt and the Golan Heights from Syria.[1] Also since declaring nationhood the Israelis have been locked in a constant confrontation with the Palestinian people, who lay claim to the land controlled by Israel, and the Hezbollah fighters in Lebanon (a militant group aligned with the Palestinians), who have on numerous occasions been engaged in battle with Israel on the border between the two countries.

While Israel has maintained constant vigilance against its Arab neighbors and developed the premier military force in the Middle East, it has also sought to achieve diplomatic solutions that would provide for national security. In 1979 Israeli Prime Minister Menachem Begin and Egyptian President Anwar Sadat met in the United States and under the careful guidance of President Jimmy Carter achieved a historic breakthrough as both countries signed a peace agreement in which the Israelis gave back the Sinai Peninsula to Egypt in exchange for diplomatic recognition and a pledge by the Egyptian government not to engage in any further attempts to invade Israel. In 1994 Jordan signed a similar peace agreement with Israel normalizing relations. However, although the Israel-Egypt Peace Accord and the Jordanian agreement were significant diplomatic breakthroughs, the most intractable problem has been the Palestinian homeland and the ongoing intifada (uprising) of the Palestinian people led by the Palestinian Liberation Organization (PLO) and its successor groups in the Gaza Strip (Hamas) and on the West Bank of the Jordan River (Fatah). Despite countless international diplomatic efforts involving U.S. presidents and international organizations such as the United Nations, the Israeli-Palestinian conflict continues with periods of calm broken by periods of terrorist attacks in major Israeli cities followed by Israeli retaliation against a new generation of fighters such as the Hamas and Hezbollah organizations.[2]

In recent years, the Israeli government has cautiously sought to establish a framework for peace with the Palestinians. Under the auspices of President Bill Clinton there were negotiations in 2000 that sought to establish a Palestinian state, but those negotiations broke down as Chairman Yasir Arafat, the leader of the PLO, refused to agree to a permanent settlement of hostilities. In 2001 the new Israeli Prime Minister Ariel Sharon withdrew his military forces from the Gaza Strip, again as a means of restarting peace negotiations. After Arafat's death in 2004, there was hope that an agreement could be reached, but the continued building of Jewish settlements on the West Bank and the construction of a huge concrete barrier between Israeli and Palestinian areas on the West Bank made negotiations impossible. By 2006 the terrorist group Hezbollah, which was supported by Iran, launched one of the most serious rocket attacks on Israeli cities in years. The Israelis responded with an invasion of Southern Lebanon and fierce bombing of Hezbollah outposts. Israeli military failed to dislodge or debilitate the

Hezbollah fighters, in what many observers considered to be a stunning defeat for Israel's armed forces. The engagement ended with a cease-fire agreement, but virtually no progress toward a diplomatic solution to the Israeli-Palestine impasse.[3]

Throughout Israel's sixty years as an independent and sovereign nation, the United States has maintained close diplomatic and military relations with it. Israel is the closest ally of the United States in the Middle East and the largest recipient of both American economic and military assistance. American presidents have pledged to defend Israel against attacks and have pursued numerous avenues of negotiations to bring peace to the region and end the Palestinian problem. Issues related to Israel and its security have consistently been at the forefront of American foreign policy and will likely remain at the forefront for the immediate future. Israel's foreign and military policy has also meshed with U.S. objectives in the region. For example, Israel has been a force against extremists and terrorists in the region–it has kept in check the authoritarian state of Syria, which has long been viewed as a supporter of terrorists groups, and its military, particularly its air force, has dominated the the Middle East. Furthermore, Israel's hidden nuclear arsenal of perhaps as many as 150 nuclear warheads and missile delivery systems provides a wall of security and a threat to its adversaries. Perhaps most importantly, United States and Israeli intelligence agencies work closely together to gather and share information about threats in the region, and the leaders of both nations inform each other regularly about military actions that might be necessary to ensure the security of both Israel and the United States.[4]

Because of the importance placed on Israel and its security, lobbyists and the Jewish-American public have constantly pressured the American political system. The so-called Jewish lobby has been a powerful force for ensuring that the U.S. policy continues to support the state of Israel and that U.S. political leadership does not negotiate with its adversaries in ways that compromise the legitimacy and sovereignty of the Jewish state. Jewish business and social leaders in the United States are major contributors to both major political parties, members of Congress and presidential aspirants. Moreover, Jewish fund-raising organizations have contributed billions of dollars for the state of Israel since 1948 to ensure that the Jewish state would have the resources necessary for economic and social growth. This support for Israel, either from various government sources or from a generous and committed Jewish philanthropic community, has combined to make Israel a modern and dynamic state with a strong economy, an educated workforce and substantial social institutions that rival any country in the world.

However despite the successes Israel has achieved after sixty years as a nation, there remains that lingering anxiety and uncertainty associated with constant threats by adversaries in the region and unyielding positions by terrorist groups. Israel has engaged in preemptive strikes against targets in neighboring countries such as Iran and Syria that were deemed potentially threatening to its security. Israel also remains at war with terrorists groups such as Hamas and Hezbollah, who have shown little interest in solving long-festering problems through diplomatic negotiations. As a result, Israel and its society are always on guard against attack: underground air-raid shelters are commonplace, military service is mandatory and spending on military weapons and equipment takes huge chunks out of the national budget. Israel, despite the normalcy that is often seen in its major cities and many of its settlements, remains a nation under siege with regular threats from those in the region who hold to the view that the Jewish state has no legitimacy and Israelis must be pushed out of the Arab world.

On the Record

American presidents have consistently shown support for Israel's right to exist and pledged American assistance when Israel has been threatened. Here is a sampling of presidential statements of that support:

Gerald Ford–The United States . . . has been proud of its association with the State of Israel. We shall continue to stand with Israel. We are committed to Israel's survival.

Jimmy Carter–We have a special relationship with Israel. It's absolutely crucial that no one in our country or around the world ever doubt that our number one commitment in the Middle East is to protect the right of Israel to exist.

Ronald Reagan–Israel exists; it has a right to exist in peace behind secure and defensible borders; and it has the right to demand of its neighbors that they recognize those facts.

George H.W. Bush–We were with Israel at the beginning. We are with Israel today. And we will be with Israel in the future. No one should doubt this basic commitment.

Bill Clinton–America and Israel share a special bond. Our relations are unique among all nations. Like America, Israel is a strong democracy, as a symbol of freedom, and oasis of liberty, a home to the oppressed and persecuted.

George W. Bush–Israel is our ally and in that we've made a very strong commitment to support Israel, we will support Israel, if her security is threatened.

Barack Obama–Israel is a stalwart ally of the United States. We have historical ties, emotional ties. As the only true democracy of the Middle East it is a source of admiration and inspiration for the American people. . . . It is in U.S. national security interests to assure that Israel's security as an independent Jewish state is maintained.

DEBATES, DIFFERENCES AND DIVISIONS

Although the United States is Israel's staunchest ally and according to President George W. Bush "America's Best Friend," that does not mean that there are no areas of disagreement between these two friends, or that the United States has not taken policy positions that have caused tensions with government leaders in Tel Aviv.[5] At the top of the list of these areas of tension is the longstanding criticism of the Israeli construction of settlements on the West Bank, often termed by the Jews as the biblical area of Judea and Samaria. The Palestinians see these settlements as proof that Israel is an expansionist nation and unwilling to negotiate a homeland for the Palestinian people. U.S. presidents in recent years have gone on record in opposition to the settlements and the frequent removal of Palestinians and other Arab people who occupy the land where the settlements are being built. President Clinton had public disagreements with then Prime Minister Benjamin Netanyahu over Israel's expansion of the settlements at the time of sensitive negotiations with the PLO's Yasir Arafat. George W. Bush continued the U.S. position against the settlements but did agree with Prime Minister Elud Olmert that in future negotiations "realities on the ground" (the settlements) cannot be ignored and should not be an impediment to a future peace agreement with the Palestinians.[6]

The United States has also been uneasy about Israel's human rights policies regarding the Palestinians and its less than stellar international reputation as an abuser of Palestinian rights, particularly the killing of innocent civilians when it has retaliated against Hamas or Hezbollah leaders or terrorist targets. Many international human rights organizations such as Amnesty International have castigated the Israelis for their harsh measures against the Palestinians.[7] U.S. officials have openly criticized the Israelis for their policy of responding to violence with violence and their justification for attacking civilian sites that they see as often harboring terrorists. Recently, the issue that has caused growing concern in Washington is the huge concrete security wall that is being built across large sections of the West Bank as a means of shutting out potential terrorists from entering Israel. U.S. officials were unwilling to take a firm stand against building the wall, in part because the Bush administration was building its own wall along the border with Mexico to limit access of illegal immigrants.

Washington and Tel Aviv have also clashed over a range of policies dealing with relations with Syria, arms sales to China and the status of Jerusalem. The Bush administration was adamant in pressing Israel not to engage in talks with the Syrians that could lead to a return of the Golan Heights in exchange for a peace agreement. The United States is opposed to the talks because it sees Syria as an agent of terrorist support in Iraq. In the area of arms sales, Israel is one of the leading weapons suppliers to the world and has been providing China with what the United States views as sensitive security equipment that could compromise American forces in Asia. Israel has continued with its China contacts, causing tensions with Pentagon officials who are concerned about China gaining valuable information from the Israelis. Finally, the question of the status of Jerusalem as the capital of Israel has been debated for years. Israel holds to the position that Jerusalem is the rightful capital of Israel, and the United States has in principle accepted that view. However, there has been intense criticism of such a move by the Palestinians and much of the Arab world. The U.S. Congress at one time mandated that the U.S. embassy be moved from Tel Aviv to Jerusalem, but a series of presidents have resisted, thus angering the Israelis. The status of Jerusalem has not surfaced as a critical issue in recent years, but it will always remain an unresolved problem.[8]

Data Bank

The Bush administration announced in August 2007 that it was making a long-term commitment to Israel's national defense by providing $30 billion in assistance. In FY 2008 the United States provided Israel with $2.4 billion in Foreign Military Financing (FMF), with annual increases of approximately $3.1 billion through 2018. The ten-year military assistance program will allow Israel to purchase some of the most advanced weaponry in the U.S. arsenal, such as the F-35 Joint Striker Fighter jet. At the announcement Nicolas Burns, under-secretary of state for political affairs stated, "We consider this $30 billion in assistance to Israel to be an investment in peace–in long-term peace. Peace will not be made without strength. Peace will not be made without Israel being strong in the future."

Source: "U.S. Foreign Aid t o Israel," CRS Report to Congress, January 2, 2008

Although U.S.-Israeli relations are largely a foreign policy issue, a contentious debate has developed in domestic political circles over the influence of the Jewish lobby. In 2006 two political scientists, John Mearsheimer and Stephen Walt, published a book (originally a "talking paper" on the Internet) entitled *The Israel Lobby and U.S. Foreign Policy*. This book caused an immediate controversy as its central thesis was that lobbying groups who advocate for pro-Israel positions within U.S. government have such influence among political leaders and policy makers that those in the White House and Congress place regional security interests of the United States in jeopardy to ensure the security of Israel. Mearsheimer and Walt contend that Israel holds a special place in the U.S. foreign policy system in terms of foreign military aid received, diplomatic support in multilateral organizations such as the United Nations and public statements of support in the Middle East.[9] Such support, argue the authors, makes it difficult, if not impossible, for U.S. policy makers to take positions that may be beneficial in achieving peace-making goals that include the entire Middle East.

For example, according to Mearsheimer and Walt, when U.S. officials seek to advance talks about a Palestinian state, criticize the settlement policy of the Israeli government or seek to initiate closer ties to Middle Eastern states, they immediately are faced with stern rebukes from lobbying groups such as the American-Israel Public Affairs Committee (AIPAC) and the Conference of Presidents of Major Jewish Organizations, which take the lead as the primary lobbying groups active in the American political arena. The authors further allege that AIPAC membership is made up of hard-line American Jews who are linked to the conservative Likud Party in Israel and are rigidly opposed to policies of the U.S. government that are viewed as endangering the Jewish state or making accommodations with states or groups in the Middle East that could lead to a more balanced foreign policy approach.[10]

Mearsheimer and Walt allege that the power of the Jewish lobby is most pronounced in Congress where it has a long record of success in convincing representatives and senators to vote a strict "Israeli line," despite the fact that voting in such a manner might have consequences that limit U.S. options in the Middle East or compromise diplomatic efforts. As the authors state about the power of AIPAC in the Congress:

> AIPAC itself . . . forms that core of the Lobby's influence in Congress. Its success is due to its ability to reward legislators and congressional candidates who support its agenda, and to punish those who challenge it. Money is critical to US elections . . . and AIPAC makes sure that its friends get strong financial support from the many pro-Israel political action committees. Anyone who is seen as hostile to Israel can be sure that AIPAC will direct campaign contributions to his or her political opponents. AIPAC also organizes letter-writing campaigns and encourages newspaper editors to endorse pro-Israel candidates.[11]

Reaction from AIPAC, other Jewish lobbying groups and a large segment of the Jewish-American community in the United States was swift and strong. Mearsheimer and Walt were taken to task on a number of fronts, especially the suggestion that the Jewish lobby has waged a campaign of intimidation against members of Congress and the White House using campaign contributions and votes to get their way in the formation and execution of U.S. policies in the Middle East. The authors also faced criticism for their contention that the power of the Jewish lobby extends to Europe as actions taken by governments and institutions in countries such as Great Britain, France and Germany were presented in the book as excessive and bordered on anti-Semitism. Many Jewish leaders in Europe were highly critical of the Church of England when it divested its stock portfolio in Caterpillar Inc. because that company makes bulldozers that Israelis use to destroy Palestinian homes. Leaders of the Jewish lobby charged that a "new anti-Semitism" is at work in the United States and Europe that must end if Israel is to survive the onslaught not just from its enemies in the region but from its enemies in the West.[12]

There was some support for the position of Mearsheimer and Walt, such as the endorsement of President Jimmy Carter's National Security Advisor

Zbigniew Brzezinski who agreed that U.S. policy in the Middle East was limited because of the fierce opposition and the influence of the Jewish lobby.[13] However, overall there were numerous newspaper and blog criticisms of the Mearsheimer and Walt position on the Jewish lobby, in particular to their suggestion that an informal network of Jewish leaders both in and out of government advocate policies that are viewed as appeasing terrorist groups or are openly critical of Israeli human rights policies toward the Palestinians.[14] These suggestions of Mearsheimer and Walt that a conspiracy or a cabal of economic and financial interests that controls the levers of power in the United States caused outrage in the Jewish community. Harvard Law Professor Alan Dershowitz was one of the many critics of the Mearsheimer and Walt book who not only pointed out factual errors in the book, but also the suggestion by the authors that a Jewish cabal was at work to skew U.S. policy in Israel's favor and against U.S. security interests. As Dershowitz stated in a *Huffington Post* blog, "Jews should not be ashamed to stand up for themselves and decry the sort of people who would blame all their own problems or all of America's problems on Jewish 'power', 'influence' and 'manipulation'. Those attitudes are indisputably anti-Semitic."[15]

FYI

Since the historic 1979 peace agreement between Israel and Egypt, there have been numerous other diplomatic attempts to bring peace to the region and guarantee Israel's right to exist free of attacks and a Palestinian state. A list of the peace efforts in the last fifteen years is given here:

1993–Israeli Prime Minister Yitzhak Rabin and PLO leader Yasir Arafat agreed to the Oslo accords for limited Palestinian self-rule on the West Bank and Gaza Strip.

1994–King Hussein of Jordon and Rabin signed peace treaty ending 46 years of war.

2000–Summit meeting at Camp David initiated by President Clinton and including Israeli Prime Minister Ehud Barak and Yasir Arafat ended without resolution.

2001–Prime Minister Barak started talks with Yasir Arafat in Egypt in another attempt to achieve a peace agreement. The talks ended in failure.

2003–So-called Road Map to peace in the Middle East was presented by the United States, the European Union, the United Nations and Russia.

2005–Prime Minister Ariel Sharon and Palestinian President Mahmoud Abbas declared ceasefire and Israel pulled troops out of Gaza Strip.

2007–Israel and Palestine entered into talks over settlement issue on the West Bank.

2008–Israeli Prime Minister Olmert and Abbas agreed to new talks over settlements and security issues, but little progress was achieved.

2010–Barack Obama brings together Israeli Prime Minister Benjamin Netanyahu and Palestinian President Mahmoud Abbas for a new round of peace talks.

Despite the vociferous debate within the Jewish community and academia over the influence of lobbying pressure in support for Israel and the charges and countercharges about anti-Semitism, the article by Mearsheimer and Walt did cast light on the relationship between the United States and Israel and forced some candid analysis of what unwavering support for Israel may have on foreign policies related to other states and issue dilemmas in the Middle East. As Mearsheimer and Walt stated at the conclusion of their original paper on the Jewish lobby:

> What is needed is a candid discussion of the Lobby's influence and a more open debate about U.S. interests in this vital region. Israel's well-being is one of those interests, but its continued occupation of the West Bank and its broader regional agenda are not. Open debate will expose the limits of the strategic and moral case for one-sided US support and could move the US to a position more consistent with its own national interest, with the interest of the other states in the region, and with Israel's long-term interests as well.[16]

Mearsheimer and Walt may have opened up a contentious controversy regarding the Jewish lobby, but nationally public opinion polls have consistently pointed to broad support for U.S. policies toward Israel and great admiration for the way in which Israel has persevered in the face of constant threats. Regular polling of American attitudes about U.S.-Israel relations show that nearly 50% of the respondents believe that support for Israel is correct, although a growing percentage of respondents believe that the United States provides too much assistance to Israel. However, when asked to name the country that Americans feel favorably toward and see as a close ally, Israel is at the top of the list. In Israel, polls show a similar positive view of the United States and a belief that the U.S. national security and anti-terrorism policy is the right one. Israelis are grateful for U.S. military and economic assistance and hold to the view that cooperation with the United States has forced its enemies to think twice about taking aggressive action toward Israel.[17]

A relatively recent development within the United States has bolstered the close relationship with Israel. The Christian Right has articulated strong support for Israel based in large part on biblical writings, especially what is often called messianic theology: the view that Christ will make his second coming in the Holy Land of Israel and that the current battle between the Jews and the Palestinians is similar to the ancient battles between the

Israelites and the Philistines, with God taking the side of the Israelites. Many of the evangelical television ministers such as Pat Robertson have publicly stated the importance of support for Israel as it faces the terrorist threat from Hamas and Hezbollah. Robertson, in particular, has pleaded with listeners to send cash donations to organizations with ties to Israel and write their elected representatives about the importance of continuing support for the Jewish state. The backing of the evangelical movement has been a welcome surprise to the Jewish community both in the United States and in Israel, as the political clout of the Christian Right continues to be a powerful electoral and governing force in American politics.[18]

American politics is often described as interest-group driven. There is no doubt that whether in the electoral arena or in the policy process, Jewish Americans, either individually or through a number of advocacy organizations, have had significant success in ensuring that U.S. policy makers hold true to the historic relationship that has developed between the United States and Israel. Jewish campaign contributions are sought after by candidates running for public office, and the Jewish vote is often a key factor in state and national elections. The combination of powerful interest organizations, campaign financing support and solid bloc voting has made Jewish Americans a powerful force in American politics. Although Jews make up only about 3% of the voting population, they have a high turnout rate and usually cast their vote for liberals or Democrats or both by upwards of 80%.[19] This political power has been the foundation upon which solid and long-lasting support for the state of Israel has been built. Jewish advocacy organizations such as AIPAC make no excuses for their aggressive lobbying efforts and their success in convincing governmental leaders that the cause of Israel is just and its actions to protect its people, its land and its sovereignty is right.

Although some Americans are concerned about the extent to which this country assists Israel and supports its policies, and there is a growing discussion about whether the United States should follow a more balanced foreign policy in the Middle East, there is little doubt that the Jewish community will continue to have the ear of American presidents and other leading governmental officials in the United States. In a region where the United States is often viewed with suspicion, if not disdain, and where there is little in the way of functioning democratic practice, Israel is an oasis of support and governing that the United States cannot reject. No presidential administration or Congress would do anything to jeopardize sixty years of friendship and alliance, especially now that the Middle East is even more of a tinderbox with multiple sources of threats. The Jewish lobby may be, as Mearsheimer and Walt suggest, too powerful in the corridors of power in Washington, but that power is not going to diminish anytime soon.[20]

However, with the United States so vested in remaking the Middle East, there is bound to be growing points of dispute between two old friends and allies. For example, any hope of achieving peace with the Palestinians must be based on the issue of the Jewish settlements, the security wall and a contiguous and unified state. Each of these issues that are critical to the Palestinians poses problems for the Israelis. Therefore, when any presidential administration engages in Middle East negotiations over the issue of Palestine, the success of such negotiations is in immediate jeopardy. U.S. officials can quietly chide the Israelis to be more flexible and accept a compromise, but the response from the Jews is usually couched in terms of national security and the history of terrorism and broken promises from the Palestinians.

Such was the case in 2010 when Israeli commandos boarded a small armada of ships seeking to break through a blockade set up by Israel to stop goods and perhaps weapons into Gaza. The raid on the ships in international waters caused an immediate international outcry, especially in Turkey where the ships began their journey. Again the United States was caught in the middle, this time with Turkey a key ally and its long time friend, Israel.

For the Obama administration the solution to the Palestinian imbroglio that has moved front and center is the creation of two states that would make up sovereign Palestine. Although the the two-state solution–establishing and recognizing the sovereignty of a Palestinian state in the Gaza Strip and the West Bank of the Jordan River–is not a new proposal, the Obama administration is pressing hard with the new Prime Minister Benjamin Netanyahu to embrace this policy initiative and once and for all achieve a modicum of peace in the region. In 2010 the Obama administration became more outspoken in its criticism of Israel's continued expansion of settlements in Jerusalem, to the point where relations between the two countries soured with both sides hardening their positions.[21] Of course, resolution of the long-standing dispute such as the two-state solution is but one of many initiatives tried over the years to end the conflict between Israel and Palestine, but the United States, no matter what administration is in office, has not wavered from what it views as the importance of bringing peace between these two adversaries.

No matter what happens with the two-state solution process or any other peace initiative, U.S.-Israel relations will remain as they have for decades–friendly, supportive and based on the position that the Jewish state has the right to exist free from external threats, whether conventional, terror-based or perhaps in the future, nuclear. The United States will likely pay a price for its close ties to Israel, but Israel is a reliable ally and in an area of the world where there is little certainty and constant flux, a reliable ally is critical and essential.

The Great Debate

The Mearsheimer and Walt contention that U.S. officials have consistently caved into pressure from the Jewish lobby to the detriment of a more balanced Middle Eastern policy provides a perfect theme for a debate.

Debate Topic

Should the United States institute a more balanced approach to its Middle East policy by lessening its longstanding support of Israel and reaching out to other nations and groups in the region, even radical groups, in the hopes of advancing other interests and perhaps solving the Israel-Palestine conflict?

Critical Thinking Questions

1. Is the Jewish Lobby too powerful in American politics?
2. Should the United States demand that Israel make significant diplomatic efforts and land concessions to solve the Palestinian problem?
3. Do you agree with the current U.S. position that the United States is pledged to come to the military assistance of Israel if its sovereignty and very existence is threatened?
4. What is holding back a lasting peace between Israel and Palestine?
5. Are Hamas and Hezbollah terrorist organizations as defined by the U.S. government, or simply independence fighters seeking to establish an independent Palestinian state?

Connections

The U.S. Embassy in Israel provides a good overview of the relationship between the two countries. See http://usembassy-israel.org.il

The Almanac of Policy Issues provides a thorough guide of past policies of the United States toward Israel. See http://www.policyalmanac.org/world/archive/crs_israeli-us_relations.shtml

Shmuel Rosner is one of the most influential journalists and bloggers in Israel. View his blog at www.haaretz.com/rosner

The MidEastWeb provides a wealth of information and analysis on U.S.-Israeli relations. See http://www.mideastweb.org

The U.S. Department of State's background notes on Israel are a valuable source of information. See http://www.state.gov/p/nea/ci/is/

Some Books to Read

Mearsheimer, John J. and Stephen M. Walt, *The Israel Lobby and U.S. Foreign Policy* (New York: Farrar, Straus, and Giroux, 2008).

Laqueur, Walter and Barry Rubin, ed. *The Israel-Arab Reader* (New York: Penguin, 2007).

Kurtzer, Daniel C. and Scott B. Lasensky, *Negotiating Arab-Israeli Peace* (Washington, D.C.: United State Institute of Peace, 2008).

Druks, Herbert, *The Uncertain Alliance: The U.S. and Israel from Kennedy to the Peace Process* (Westport, CT: Greenwood Press, 2001).

Honig-Parnass, Tivka, *Between the Lines: Israel, the Palestinians, and the U.S. War on Terror* (Chicago, IL: Haymarket Books, 2007).

Notes

1. For background see Howard M. Sachar, *A History of Israel from the Rise of Zionism to Our Time* (New York: Alfred Knopf, 2007).
2. See James Galvin, *The Israel-Palestine Conflict: One Hundred Years of War* (New York: Cambridge University Press, 2007).

3. See Amos Harel and Avi Issacharoff, *34 Days: Israel, Hezbollah and the War in Lebanon* (New York: Palgrave MacMillan, 2008).
4. For a discussion of the current issues facing Israel, see Gershom Gorenberg, "Israel," *Foreign Policy*, May/June, 2008.
5. For a discussion of presidential administration's relations with Israel see Herbert Druks, *The Uncertain Alliance: The U.S. and Israel from Kennedy to the Peace Process* (Westport, CT: Greenwood Press, 2001).
6. See Tim McGirk, "Bush in Israel: The West Bank Problem," *Time*, Jan 9, 2008, http://www.time.com/world/article/0,8599,1701826,00.html
7. Amnesty International's position against the settlements can be found at their website. See http://www.amnesty.org/en/news-and-updates/Israel-urged-to-stop-settlement-expansion-east-jerusalem-2010-03-10
8. U.S. Presidents positions on Israel are found at http://www.jewishvirtuallibrary.org/jsource/US-Israel/presquote.html
9. John Mearsheimer and Stephen Walt, *The Israel Lobby and U.S. Foreign Policy* (New York: Farrar, Straus and Giroux, 2007).
10. See the AIPAC website at http://www.AIPAC.org. For an analysis of the Jewish Lobby see Robert C. Liberman, "The 'Israel Lobby' and American Politics," *Perspectives on Politics*, June 2009, Vol. 7, No. 2, pp. 235–258.
11. A condensed version of the Mearsheimer and Walt book gleaned from the original online presentation of the work was published by the London Review of Books. See http://lrb.co.uk/v28/n06/print/mears01.html
12. See Stephen Zunes, "Why the U.S. Supports Israel," *Foreign Policy in Focus*, May 2002.
13. See Brzezinski's view in "A Dangerous Exemption," *Foreign Policy*, July/August 2006, pp. 63–64.
14. For more in-depth discussion of the controversy over the Jewish Lobby, see James Kirchick, "Street Creed? Who Does the New Israel Lobby Really Represent," *New Republic*, May 28, 2008, pp. 14–16.
15. Alan Dershowitz, "The Lobby, Jews and Anti-Semites," http://huffingtonpost.com/alan_dershowitz/the_lobby_jews_and_anti_b_18998.html
16. London Review of Books, op.cit. p. 33.
17. Mitchell Bond, "Public Opinion Toward Israel," http://www.jewishvirtuallibrary.org/jsource/US-Israel/American_attitudes_toward_Israel.html
18. Why the U.S. Supports Israel, op.cit.
19. Steven Windmueller, "Are American Jews Becoming Republicans: Insights into Jewish Political Behavior," *Jerusalem Viewpoints*, December 15, 2003, http://www.jcpa.org/jl/vp509.htm
20. Jim Vandehei, "Congress Giving Israel Vote of Confidence," *Washington Post*, July 19, 2006, A05.
21. See the remarks of Vice-President Joe Biden on U.S.-Israeli relations in a press briefing related to talks with Prime Minister Benjamin Netanyahu, www.whitehouse.gov/The-press-office/remarks-vice-president-biden-and-prime-minister-netanyahu-a-joint-statement-press

25 GLOBALIZATION

Issue Focus

The world is no longer made up of isolated countries and separate regions with limited contacts. Today the operative term to describe the new world situation is globalization. In the globalized world, countries and regions are increasingly linked in ways never imagined just thirty years ago. Expanded trade in goods and services, the movement of people from one country to another, the exchange of ideas and cultural mores and the electronic interconnection of banking, currency and stock market positions and policies are now commonplace and drive this relentless push to create a global system. The Internet and mass communication have contributed to the advance of globalization as the new world order becomes just a mouse click away or the redirection of a satellite dish. Globalization offers countries and people new opportunities to grow and prosper, but there are downsides to this new phenomenon, especially for those without the education, the skills and the competitive entrepreneurial spirit to ride the wave of change. There are thus winners and losers in the globalized environment, which creates the basis for debates, differences and divisions.

Chapter Objectives
This issue chapter will seek to:
1. Explain the new global economic system and the involvement of the United States in it.
2. Discuss the policy disagreements that have arisen over how the United States can best compete in the global economy, with particular emphasis job loss in this country.
3. Describe the challenges the United States faces as globalization places new pressures on the American economy and American life.

SOME BACKGROUND

If you have ever been to any of the Disney theme parks, there is a popular ride called "It's a Small World." As happy parents and wide-eyed kids ride in small boats to the sounds of the song "It's a Small World," they see life-like children dressed up in the costumes of their homelands and holding flags of their countries. The object of the ride is to drive home the message that although our planet is large, with people from many different cultures, speaking many different languages and believing in many different religions, an interconnectedness of people and places makes a diverse world really a small world. Today a more formal word for that interconnectedness is *globalization*. We live in a time in which advances in communication, transportation, and information transmission have made the world smaller and in the process billions and billions of new connections are created every day, from the movement of capital and people, the trading of goods and services, the expansion of Internet contacts along with the introduction of new ideas, new products, new lifestyles and new values throughout the world. It is not an exaggeration to state that globalization has revolutionized the way we live, bringing both enormous change and significant challenges as nations and people seek to adjust to a smaller and smaller world.[1]

This enormous expansion of worldwide contacts that has come to be called globalization is most pronounced and influential in the economic and financial sectors of most countries. We now live in a global economy in which exports and imports play a prominent role in the shape and growth of nations. Governmental leaders are championing the benefits of more open trade, foreign investment, relaxed corporate regulations, tax incentives for businesses and the benefits of the capitalist market system as the keys to making globalization a success. The United States has been one of the major proponents of globalization, and since the 1980s, during the Reagan administration, it has advocated within governing and business circles both domestically and internationally for a reformulation of the rules of economic development and financial expansion. Often called the Washington Consensus, political leaders, corporate heads, economists, bankers and other advocates of a more liberalized approach to national growth and international integration pushed for the acceptance of a series of changes in the manner in which economies and governments work, which can be summed up as follows:

Establishment of the private sector as the source of economic growth

Elimination of tariffs on imported goods (free trade)

Expansion of exports and a de-emphasis on traditional sectors of production

Openness to foreign investment and an end to the nationalization of key economic assets

The movement of work and the production of goods to foreign sites (outsourcing)

Privatization of state enterprises

Deregulation of bureaucratic controls on businesses

Maintenance of a low rate of inflation

Elimination of corrupt practices in public and private sectors

Reduction in the number of government workers.[2]

At its core the Washington Consensus was the triumph of the capitalist ethic over the statist system that was not only used in the former communist countries, but also served as the basis of national development in many less-developed countries. With the fall of communism and many less-developed countries desperate for new ways to stimulate their economies, the prospect of moving to a global system with new rules quickly became attractive. Some nations such as China, South Korea, Singapore and Taiwan became known as the Asian Tigers as their economies moved forward with huge spurts of growth and development.[3] Later other countries in Latin America such as Mexico, Chile and Brazil followed suit as they opened their countries to free trade, foreign investment and the market system. Many other countries in the former Soviet Union, Eastern Europe and other Asian countries such as India, Vietnam and Thailand accepted the global rules and began to enjoy significant upswings in their economies. By the new millennium, globalization had become firmly established and was enhancing economic development in those countries that embraced the Washington Consensus.[4]

However, although the principles of globalization were being implemented, the downside of this new form of economic and financial interconnectedness was beginning to be experienced in the same countries that were enjoying enhanced growth and personal wealth. Signs that a globalized economy could create deep divisions between those who benefited from it and those who saw little change in their lives began to surface in a number of countries, particularly in the less-developed world.[5] Charges of huge job shifts from wealthy countries to poorer countries where labor was cheaper angered workers who became unemployed, data that pointed to rising levels of income inequality showed that globalization had some winners but many losers, and frequent examples of workers who were treated unfairly as they toiled for low wages in modern-day sweatshops owned by multinational companies spurred demonstrations and violent protests by a rising chorus of anti-globalization activists. The message delivered by these anti-globalists was that the new rules of the international economy were stacked against the poor, the unskilled and those who worked in the old-line manufacturing jobs. More troubling, too often governments and multi-national corporations ignored many of the human problems and class separations that accompanied this modern-day form of doing business and enhancing national growth. Globalization thus became a cause for economic optimism, yet a serious threat to income and job security.[6]

On the Record

Thomas Friedman, the Pulitzer Prize journalist from the *New York Times*, has written widely about globalization and its impact on the modern world. In his seminal work on how the world is changing as a result of globalization, Friedman remarked that with the end of the Cold War and the decline of communism a new system took shape and replaced the tensions that dominated international politics for over fifty years. In his book

The Lexus and the Olive Tree, Friedman said the following about the new globalization system with its positive economic contributions and pitfalls:

> The globalization system, unlike the Cold War system, is not static, but a dynamic ongoing process: globalization involves the inexorable integration of markets, nation-states and technologies to a degree never witnessed before–in a way that is enabling individuals, corporations and nation-states to reach around the world farther, faster, deeper and cheaper than ever before, and in a way that is also producing a powerful backlash from those brutalized or left behind by this new system.

Source: Thomas Friedman, *The Lexus and The Olive Tree*, pp. 7–8

DEBATES, DIFFERENCES AND DIVISIONS

Although the globalization paradigm was heavily influenced by the Washington Consensus and promoted by U.S. leaders, its implementation in the American economy has caused extensive controversy and negative reaction. Perhaps the best place to begin the discussion of the debates, differences and divisions surrounding globalization and its effect on the U.S. economy is the passage of the North American Free Trade Agreement (NAFTA). Signed by President George H.W. Bush, Prime Minister Brian Mulroney of Canada and President Carlos Salinas of Mexico in 1992, NAFTA was seen as the beginning of what was envisioned as a region-wide free trade zone stretching from Alaska to Argentina that would allow goods, services and capital to move without the imposition of tariffs or other controls. Such a liberalized economic system envisioned heightened economic growth for the three countries, creation of new jobs and the spread of prosperity to a broader spectrum of the population. On the signing of the NAFTA agreement President Bush stated that the three nations were embarking, "on an extraordinary enterprise [that would create] . . . the largest, richest and most productive market in the entire world; a $6 trillion market of 360 million people that stretches 5,000 miles from Alaska to the Yukon to the Yucatan Peninsula."[7]

The agreement was presented to the American people as a huge economic benefit as it would create hundreds of thousands of new export jobs, grant greater access to the Canadian and Mexican markets, allow cheaper Mexican goods to enter the United States and enhance the profits of both large-scale multi-nationals and small- and medium-size businesses who would enjoy enhanced opportunities for growth. However, the NAFTA agreement was not without its problems, which organized labor, environmentalists and those political leaders who advocated for a more protectionist trade policy rather than fostering unfettered trade and investment quickly pointed out. In the 1992 presidential campaign between George H.W. Bush and Bill Clinton, a third-party candidate, H. Ross Perot took a strong stance against

NAFTA stating that it would create a "giant sucking sound" from jobs leaving the United States and heading south to Mexico where wages were less, unions were weak and labor and environmental rights were negligible.[8]

Although Bill Clinton, an advocate of NAFTA, won the election, the Democratic-controlled Congress was wary of the agreement in large part because of the concerns expressed by Perot, and it threatened to dismantle or at least severely weaken the agreement. Michigan Democratic Congressman David Bonior spoke for many of those in opposition to NAFTA when he stated, "The working people who stand against this treaty don't have degrees from Harvard. . . . And most of them have never heard of Adam Smith. But they know when the deck is stacked against them. They know it's not fair to ask American workers to compete against Mexican workers who earn $1 an hour." However, despite the opposition of Bonior and other Democrats, Clinton was able to forge a coalition of supporters (that included many pro-business Republicans) to pass the NAFTA agreement and launch the United States into the new era of free trade and a global economy.[9]

Since the passage of the NAFTA agreement in 1994 both Presidents Clinton and George W. Bush have sought to expand trade agreements in the western hemisphere, with President Bush successfully negotiating the Dominican Republic–Central American Free Trade Agreement (DR – CAFTA) and the Congress approving it in 2005. Clinton and Bush both stressed the economic successes they attributed to the new free trade environment as they pointed to significant growth in exports, foreign direct investment and job creation. Business supporters of NAFTA pointed to a jump in U.S. employment from 110 million jobs in 1993 to 137 million in 2006, with manufacturing output increasing by 63% between 1993 and 2006. Although critics of NAFTA claim that the job and output benefits achieved during these years cannot be solely attributed to NAFTA, there is no doubt that the new globalist approach to economic development had a favorable impact in the United States.[10]

Although free trade and enhanced foreign investment were strongly supported by the Bush administration and its allies in the business community, there was growing opposition from the same sources that were active during the NAFTA legislative debate in 1994, only this time there was ten years of data and experience with NAFTA that gave labor unions, environmentalists and protectionists ammunition to convince Congress to end its unqualified support for the key foundations of globalization. Critics of NAFTA, CAFTA and other bilateral free trade agreements stated that since 1993 over 900,000 jobs, many in the manufacturing sector in the United States, had "gone south, outsourced to countries that paid much lower wages and offered little or no benefits."[11] Although supporters of free trade agreements declared that millions of new jobs had been created in the export sector as the United States expanded trade, unions and other opponents of these agreements were not swayed by the claims of employment benefits. The liberal Economic Policy Institute stated, "If the United States exports 1,000 cars to Mexico, then American workers are employed in their production. If, however, the United States imports 1,000 cars from Mexico rather than building them domestically, then a similar number of Americans who otherwise would have been employed in the auto industry will have to find other work."[12]

Environmentalists were also active in criticizing the free trade system put in place since NAFTA. They pointed to lax environmental standards as U.S. and other foreign companies working in the maquiladoras (free-trade-zone industrial parks) in Mexico or elsewhere in the hemisphere polluted rivers, dumped toxic wastes and failed to implement clean air standards. The result was growing environmental decay in the poor countries of the region that posed a health hazard to the workers and those living near the factories. Although the DR–CAFTA agreement did have more rigid environmental safeguards, there was general skepticism that these safeguards would be enforced. Environmentalists also feared that ultimately an environmental or human disaster would occur in these loosely regulated industrial free zones.

Data Bank

The rank order of U.S.-based non-financial multi-national corporations in Latin America by sales in the year 2004 is as follows:

General Motors Corporation
Wal-Mart Stores
Bunge
Ford Motor Company
Delphi Automotive Systems Corporation
AES
Exxon Mobil Corporation
Cargill, Inc.
Hewlett-Packard
General Electric
Lear Corporation
ChevronTexaco

Source: Economic Commission for Latin America and the Caribbean, 2005

Although much of the criticism associated with globalization has emphasized job loss, weak labor standards and environmental degradation, those who tout the benefits of globalization claim that the free trade or free market regime at the heart of the new global economy has had a significant impact on poverty, life expectancy, literacy and infrastructure formation. The argument made by these advocates of globalization is that those countries that have implemented the system have seen across the board socio-economic growth and prosperity; in short, globalization "lifts all boats." Critics of globalization continue to accent the high levels of income inequality in the less-developed world over the last twenty-five years, yet there is evidence that improvements in poverty levels and other education and health indices have occurred.

Using data from the World Bank and other sources, the pro-globalists point to the decline in the number of people in the world who are living on $1 or $2 a day, often the measure used to define the extent of poverty in the less-developed countries. World Bank data published in 2002 (which measured poverty in the less-developed world since 1981) show that the number of people living on $1 and $2 a day in East Asia declined by 80.7% and 52%, respectively. In Latin America the declines were less dramatic with 8% and 29% declines in those living on $1 and $2 a day, respectively. Only in Sub-Saharan Africa was there no positive effect; those living on $1 or $2 a day actually increased.[13] Data compiled in 2005 by Global Research, which was not broken down into regions, found that nearly 50% of the world's people–3 billion–were living on $2.50 a day.[14] It must be emphasized, however, that there are deep disagreements among globalization experts about the connection between the new global system and poverty reduction. Many experts show that countries such as China and India, which are often viewed as the best examples of the benefits of globalization in lessening poverty, have advanced not only because of free trade and free market but also because of public policy reforms such as land reform, education, population control, strong leadership and political stability.[15]

The Bush administration regularly accented the advances made in poverty reduction and tied those advances to globalization. When Bush pushed for new trade agreements with Colombia and Panama in 2008 he often made the connection between the free trade or free market model of globalization and poverty reduction. Speaking in 2008, during a time when there was Congressional opposition to the free trade agreement with Colombia, Bush presented his arguments in favor of the globalization regime. He stated, "These agreements will level the playing fields for business, workers and farmers here in the United States. These agreements will help our friends in neighborhoods (in Latin America) and help them lift themselves out of poverty. These agreements will counter the false populism promoted by some nations in the hemisphere. These agreements will strengthen the forces of freedom and democracy throughout the Americas."[16]

FYI

Globalization has also transformed sleepy little islands and heretofore low-profile states in the Caribbean into prosperous tax havens and financial centers where corporations and individuals from the United States and other countries transfer their profits and wealth to avoid hefty tax bills from the Internal Revenue Service (IRS). The Cayman Islands, for example, is the fifth largest banking center in the world with $1.4 billion in assets, and Bermuda, a British protectorate is now the richest "country" in the world with a per capita income of nearly $70,000. The increasing prosperity of offshore financial centers is the source of intense debate within the United States as it is claimed that the IRS loses up to $70 billion in revenue each year from corporate and private transfers of profits and wealth offshore. Although it is legal for corporations and individuals to transfer their money offshore, U.S. companies such as Stanley Works, Tyco and Ingersoll-Rand have faced criticism as being unpatriotic and not shouldering their fair share of the nation's tax burden.

Source: Michael Kryzanek, United States-Latin American Relations, 4th edition, p. 286

Despite President Bush's cheerleading for globalization and his push for the expansion of free trade agreements, he and his supporters faced stiff opposition from those who were less concerned with the possible impact of free trade and expanded foreign investment on growth in developing countries and more focused on what they view as the detrimental impact of a new global economy on the American economy. Media critics such as Pat Buchanan of MSNBC and Lou Dobbs of CNN waged a relentless television campaign against free trade agreements and concentrated instead on job loss, spiraling trade deficits, the declining value of the dollar and the growing financial power of countries such as China and India. Dobbs (who had a special section of his news program entitled "Exporting America") along with a growing number of members of Congress called for a halt to free trade agreements and closer scrutiny of the impact that new emerging nations such as China and India had on the U.S. economy.[17] After some twenty-five years of little opposition to the globalization model, except from organized labor and some Democrats in Congress with a large base of workers affected by the loss of jobs offshore, there is now in the United States increasing concern from a wide spectrum of Americans over the downsides of this new economic system and even calls for protectionist legislation that would ensure job security, protect American assets and return to the days of "Made in the USA."[18]

The suspicions of the American people toward globalization were evident during the presidential primary campaign of 2008 when voters in heavily industrialized states, such as Ohio, Michigan and Pennsylvania, expressed their misgivings, if not outrage, over lost jobs to countries such as Mexico and China. Both Democratic candidates Barack Obama and Hillary Clinton pledged that if elected they would review the NAFTA agreement and renegotiate the terms of the trade relationship so as to benefit the United States. Senator John McCain, the Republican nominee, expressed confidence in NAFTA and other free trade agreements, but opponents of globalization criticized him for not recognizing the impact the agreement has had on American jobs. The pressure to revise the free trade rules and revisit NAFTA and other such agreements may be a popular political position, but the possibility of such a renegotiation is problematic and support for such changes would certainly be opposed by Mexico and Canada, both of which have experienced varying degrees of economic success under NAFTA.[19]

Besides jobs, another issue related to globalization has also become a political flashpoint in both the United States and the less-developed world. Agricultural subsidies, which are designed to support the domestic agricultural sector, have angered many poor countries. The Congress has consistently passed pro-agricultural legislation that includes billions (nearly $4 billion in recent fiscal years) in subsidies to make American farm products cheaper to sell abroad. These subsidies make it extremely difficult for less-developed countries to compete with American farm products, and they raise the price of imported goods from the United States on essential commodities. Numerous international meetings (the so-called Doha Round of trade negotiations) have been held under the auspices of the World Trade Organization (WTO) to solve the subsidy issue and bring some trade relief to the less-developed countries, but the agricultural lobby in the United States (and also in Europe and Japan) is so powerful that there has been little movement to reduce the subsidies. As foreign critics of U.S. agricultural policy point out, the United States is for free and open trade except when it comes to protectionist subsidies that benefit a key economic sector.[20]

After an initial positive response to free trade and free trade agreements such as NAFTA and expanded investment in countries such as China and Mexico, American public opinion has begun to sour on the new global economy. In a poll conducted by World Public Opinion in 2006, Americans were evenly divided on globalization with only 24% responding positively to the new rules of internal economics and 24% stating a negative view (the remainder of the responses were either "don't know" or opinions that reflected a view that globalization was neither good or bad). In the poll Americans also showed concern over foreign investment in the United States with 44% stating that such investment was "dangerous" and 36% viewing foreign investment as "necessary and positive."[21] Increasingly, Americans are seeing foreign countries such as China and the oil sheikdoms of the Middle East use sovereign wealth funds (state-managed investment capital generated from successful trade or oil revenue) to invest in or purchase outright U.S. corporations, banks and investment houses or gain substantial stock control in those entities. This foreign investment influence has begun to hit a nationalist nerve in the United States with fears that foreign countries may in the future have undue influence on the American economy.

The current negativity in the United States toward globalization is not likely to diminish in the short term, but then neither is the new global economy going to collapse and be replaced by a new paradigm. Globalization, despite its deficiencies, is firmly in place and being embraced by more and more countries.[22] American political leaders are aware that the voting public has seen enough of "Made in China," jobs going south and foreign countries buying U.S. assets. In the coming years protectionist legislation is certain to be debated in the Congress and placed high on the agenda of the president as pressure builds to redesign globalization so as to ensure that the American manufacturing sector has the ability to survive and perhaps even be reborn.

However, to many who have studied the globalization model and seen how it benefits the corporate bottom line, the redesign of the new global economy will be a difficult task. There remain in this country and in the world powerful economic and financial interests that continue to insist that globalization is the key to prosperity and general national development. Some adjustments may be made to the globalization regime, such as more job training programs, protection of certain industries and demands that nations trade not just freely but fairly. However even if these reforms do occur, the foundation of free trade and free market upon which globalization was built is secure and lasting.

While the debate over the future of globalization and the American economy ensues, people in the United States will continually be reminded that the world has changed and the new global economy is a reality. They will still get Indian customer service personnel when they call for advice on their computers or cell phones, notice "Made in China" on most of the goods they buy, see a flood of foreign tourists coming to the United States to buy goods because of a weak dollar and find that the world has indeed become smaller or as Thomas Friedman calls it, "flat," as more and more countries compete with, and in some cases surpass, the United States. Globalization has indeed changed the world, and strangely an idea and system of economic rules that started in the United States and was promoted by the U.S. government and business community has now come back to challenge the economic supremacy of the United States.

The Great Debate

Despite its clear benefits to the world economy profit margins, there is no doubt that the globalization regime has its downsides, especially when it comes to job security, environmental protection and worker pay. This clear separation of benefits and drawbacks can be the basis for a debate.

Debate Topic

Should the United States rewrite the rules of the globalization system regarding worker rights and environmental protection, even if such actions have a detrimental effect on corporate competition in the world economy?

Critical Thinking Questions

1. Do you support the rules of the new global economy as outlined in the Washington Consensus?
2. Should the United States renegotiate trade agreements such as NAFTA to protect domestic manufacturing jobs?
3. Supporters of the new global economy have said that globalization will "lift all boats" and eventually bring prosperity to an ever wider group of workers both

in the United States and in the less-developed world. Do you agree with this analysis?

4. Globalization has created powerful multi-national corporations with significant economic international influence. Is this a positive development?

5. Should the global agricultural rules change to allow less-developed countries to compete more effectively with the rich countries, even if such rule changes have a negative impact on U.S. agriculture?

Connections

Globalization 101 is a website that provides basic information on recent trends and issues related to the new global economy. See http://www.globalization.org

The World Bank has numerous studies of globalization that can be accessed from its website. See http://www.worldbank.org

The Federal Reserve Bank of Dallas has a series of working papers devoted to globalization. See http://www.dallasfed.org/research/staff/2008/staff0801.cfm

The World Growth Institute provides balanced analysis of globalization. See http://www.worldgrowth.org

The Economic Policy Institute is one of the more respected critics of globalization. See http://epinet.org

Some Books to Read

Stiglitz, Joseph, *Making Globalization Work* (New York: W.W. Norton, 2007).

Baylis, John, Smith, Steve, Owens, Patricia, eds. *The Globalization of World Politics* (New York: Oxford University Press, 2008).

Bhagwati, Jagdish, *In Defense of Globalization* (New York: Oxford University Press, 2007).

Lechner, Frank J., John Boll, eds. *The Globalization Reader* (New York: Wiley-Blackwell, 2007).

Held, David, Anthony McGrew, *Globalization/Anti-Globalization* (Cambridge, UK: Polity, 2007).

Notes

1. For background see Manfred Steger, *Globalization: A Very Short Introduction* (New York: Oxford University Press, 2003).

2. For a discussion of the Washington *Consensus* see Maggie Black, *The No-Nonesense Guide to International Development* (London: Verso UK, 2002), pp. 50–70.

3. The most widely read and influential book on the new global economy is Thomas Friedman, *The World is Flat* (New York: Farrar, Straus, and Giroux, 2007).

4. Each year *Foreign Policy* rates the level of globalization in the countries of the world. See "Globalization Index," *Foreign Policy*, November/December 2008, pp. 68–76.

5. See Gary Burtless, Ribert J. Laurence, Robert Litan, and Robert Shapiro, *Globalphobia: Confronting Fears About Open Trade* (Washington, D.C.: Brookings Institution Press, 1988).

6. Robert E. Scott, "The High Price of Free Trade," Economic Policy Institute, November 17, 2003, http://www.epi.org/publications/entry/briefingpapers_bp147

7. See this discussion of NAFTA in Michael Kryzanek, *U.S.-Latin American Relations*, 4th ed. (Westport, CT: Praeger, 2008), pp. 284–286.

8. "Perot Gores His Own Ox in Debate," *Congressional Quarterly*, November 13, 1993, p. 1305.

9. *Foreign Policy Bulletin*, November/December, 1992, pp. 35–36.

10. Robert Pastor, "The Future of North America," *Foreign Affairs*, July/August, 2008.

11. Jyoti Thottam, "Is Your Job Going Abroad," *Time*, March 1, 2004, pp. 26–30.

12. The High Price of Free Trade, op.cit. See also "Debating the Central American Free Trade Act," http://www.pbs.org/now/politics/caftadebate.html

13. See "Poverty Drops Below 1 Billion, Says World Bank," World Bank Press Release, April 15, 2007-2007/159/DEC.

14. See "Poverty Facts and Stats," http://www.globalissues.org/article/26/poverty-facts-and-stats

15. Paul Collier, "The New Third World," *Washington Post National Weekly Edition*, October 29-November 4.

16. George W. Bush, Remarks on the Colombia Free Trade Agreement, Washington, D.C. April 7, 2008, http://www.presidentialrhetoric.com/speeches/04.07.08.html

17. "Lou Dobbs Testifies Before Congress on Free Trade," http://www.cnn.com/2007/us/03/28/dobbs/testimony/index.html

18. See the critique of globalization in Kenneth Sharpe and Matthew Slaughter, "A New Deal for Globalization," *Foreign Affairs*, July/August, 2007. See also "The Ten Year Track Record of NAFTA: U.S. Workers' Jobs, Wages and Economic Security," *Public Citizen*, http://www.citizen.org/documents/NAFTA_10_jobs.pdf.

19. Jake Tapper, "McCain: Obama Misleading Voters on NAFTA," *ABC News*, February 28, 2008. http://www.abcnews.go.com/politics/vote2008/story?id=4360446. See also Elizabeth Malkin, "NAFTA's Promise, Unfulfilled," *New York Times*, March 24, 2009, B3.

20. Bruce Stokes, "Doha's Winners and Losers," *National Journal*, March 17, 2006, http://nationaljournal.com/scripts/printpage/cgi?/about/njweekly/stories/2006/0317nj2.htm

21. http://www.americans-world.org/digest/global_issues/globalization/general.cfm

22. For a critique of globalization see Robert Skidelsky, "Gloomy About Globalization," *New York Review of Books*, April 17, 2008, pp. 60–63.

THE GREAT RECESSION

Issue Focus

The United States has faced no greater economic and financial challenge in modern times than what has come to be the Great Recession. Unlike the Great Depression of the late 1920s and the 1930s, the Great Recession that started during the waning days of the George W. Bush administration did not reach the depths of what economists view as the key indicators of a complete collapse of the national economy—long periods of negative economic growth, massive unemployment (20% and above on a national scale) and a serious decline in living standards that extends to the vast majority of Americans. Nevertheless, the Great Recession created a significant decline in the national economy as Americans saw their retirement savings depleted or wiped out, housing foreclosures and personal bankruptcies skyrocket to unprecedented levels and unemployment rates hover around 10% with some regions, particularly the so-called Rust Belt in the Midwest, experiencing job-loss rates around 15%. The Great Recession has been the most difficult challenge of the Obama administration. Upon taking office the president instituted a range of policy responses designed to get the national economy back on track, such as bank bailouts, stimulus spending for job creation and government takeover of failed companies and financial institutions. These measures, which placed the federal government in the forefront of the attempt to end the recession, led to extensive partisan debate and ideological division over the extent that the government rather than the free market system should manage the economy and recovery. Even though the country is moving out of the Great Recession, these debates over the role of the government in the national economy continue.

Chapter Objectives

This issue chapter will seek to:
1. Explain the evolution of the economic meltdown experienced by the United States.
2. Describe the steps taken by both the Bush and Obama administrations to deal with the economic crisis.
3. Discuss the short-term and long-term impacts of the government's policies to deal with the economic crisis.

SOME BACKGROUND

In the fall of 2008 the United States experienced its most serious economic and financial crisis since the Great Depression of the 1930s. In a matter of a few months starting in September 2008, the Stock Market lost 37% of its value, major investment houses either went out of business or were forced to merge with others, millions of Americans saw their retirement incomes (401ks) that were tied to the stock market or mutual funds significantly reduced and housing foreclosures and personal bankruptcies skyrocketed as workers who lost their jobs (2.6 million jobs were lost from September to December 2008) were unable to make mortgage or credit card payments. The speed with which this economic meltdown occurred stunned both Wall Street and Main Street as Americans saw their wealth, their retirement income and their jobs disappear. After over two decades of enormous economic growth and wealth accumulation, the United States was on the brink of financial collapse.[1]

Although no economic crisis can be traced to a single source, experts often linked the economic meltdown of 2008 to the sub-prime mortgage market. During the heady days of rising housing prices when many homes increased in value by double digits, banks, lending institutions and mortgage brokers fashioned a process, called the sub-prime market, in which potential homeowners with little or no credit history, few assets and incomes that could not sustain a mortgage payment over time were convinced that buying a home was within their means, especially since housing prices would continue to increase, thus providing the new homeowners with greater equity and the potential to sell the property for a profit. These sub-prime mortgages were packaged by the thousands and sold to banks and investment houses, which then resold them to investors who were promised a healthy profit as the housing market continued to advance.[2]

When it became clear that these sub-prime mortgages were over-valued and not insured, and when millions of these first-time home buyers could not meet their payments, the financial house of cards began crashing down. First the quasi-government corporations Freddie Mac and Fannie Mae that held major portions of the sub-prime market announced that they were in trouble. Then venerable investment houses such as Bear Stearns, Lehman Brothers and American International Group (AIG) acknowledged that they were hemorrhaging billions of dollars. Then major banks such as Bank of America, Citigroup and Wachovia admitted that they too were in serious financial distress. The United States for a time was close to a financial collapse.[3]

These announcements sent shockwaves throughout the country as the American public was stunned over the extent of the meltdown and increasingly angry over how Wall Street had brought the nation's economy to its knees with risky ventures and pure greed. Each day brought bad news about how the sub-prime mortgage process had destroyed the American financial system and how unscrupulous investors with little government regulation or oversight had created a complex system of money management and wealth generation that in the end was untenable. No one was safe from the ravages of the economic meltdown as billionaires and average Americans lost huge chunks of their wealth or savings. Within this climate of anger and fear, the Bush administration took drastic measures to get the major players in this sub-prime debacle back on their feet and protect the U.S. economy from disaster.

President Bush and his Secretary of the Treasury Henry Paulson quickly moved to push through Congress a $710 billion bailout plan, the Troubled Asset Relief Program (TARP), that would be administered by a new agency. The bailouts were designed to inject money into those institutions that were on the brink of collapse and unable to function as a mortgage creditor, a source of loans or a provider of investment capital. The Bush administration intervened in the financial sector in an unprecedented manner because it realized that the American economy was basically at a standstill with money drying up, jobs disappearing, homes being boarded up and the confidence level of the American people hitting an all-time low. Despite the gloomy outlook for the economy, President Bush stated on September 24 in a major address to the American people, "Our economy is facing a moment of great challenge, but we've overcome tough challenges before and we will overcome this one."[4]

As the United States headed through the presidential election and into 2009, the economic news did not get any better, in fact it got worse. More banks and investment houses announced that they were deep in trouble, millions of Americans lost their homes to foreclosure and the level of unemployment doubled to 9% as the economic meltdown turned into the Great Recession. More seriously, the economic meltdown had become global as other industrial countries experienced the same challenges as the United States. By the time Barack Obama took the oath of office on January 20, the United States was experiencing negative economic growth, widespread corporate downsizing and signs everywhere that getting out of this crisis would not be quick and would require extraordinary measures.

FYI

A brief chronology of the key events of the fall 2008 as the Bush Administration sought to cope with the ever-growing economic meltdown is given here:

> August 9–Fannie Mae posted $2.9 billion loss in second quarter.
> August 27–Fannie Mae and Freddie Mac executives were forced to resign over sub-prime mortgage problem.
> September 15–Record 1.2 million homes hit by foreclosure.
> September 15–Lehman Brothers filed for bankruptcy.
> September 17–Government took over Fannie Mae and Freddie Mac in $200 billion bailout.
> September 17–Government took over AIG in $85 billion bailout.
> September 21–Secretary of the Treasury Henry Paulson proposed $700 billion bailout of banks and financial institutions.

October 1–USA/Gallup poll found that financial meltdown has harmed 56% of Americans.

October 2–Jobless claims hit seven-year high.

October 3–Wachovia Bank merged with Wells Fargo Bank.

October 10–Dow Jones stock average dropped below 8,000.

October 17–Factory production dropped by largest amount in 34 years.

October 27–Big Three automakers announced that they were running out of cash.

October 30–Federal Reserve Bank cut interest rate to 1%.

November 6–Labor Department announced that layoffs were up by 79% from October 2007.

November 21– Dow Jones averages dropped 450 points, the eighth double digit drop in twelve days.

November 24–Democrats in House pushed for massive stimulus bill.

December 18–Chrysler closed for one month.

December 19–President Bush approved $17 billion auto bailout.

January 14, 2009–Retail sales plunged in December.

January 20–Barack Obama in his inaugural addresses promised to get the American economy moving again.

DEBATES, DIFFERENCES AND DIVISIONS

In a manner similar to Franklin Delano Roosevelt, who entered office at the height of the Great Depression and immediately laid out a series of proposals to get the American economy moving again, Barack Obama acted quickly and forcefully to use federal spending and federal control to deal with the Great Recession. Just four days into his presidency Obama pushed Congress to adopt an $825 billion recovery package that included stimulus funds designed to put Americans back to work on a full range of public projects and tax cuts aimed primarily at the working and middle classes to provide a jolt to the flagging economy. Although there was criticism from Congressional Republicans who charged that the stimulus money would lead to wasteful spending and the tax cuts were meager (in most cases $13.00 a week less in federal withholding taxes), there was no doubt that the president, backed by a Democratic Congress, would get his way.

President Obama followed up his stimulus and tax initiatives with an ambitious bailout plan that was far bigger than the one instituted by President Bush. Obama's Treasury Secretary Timothy Geitner announced on February 11 that the administration was going to propose a $2.5 trillion rescue plan that combined bailout money, private investment capital and the decision of the Federal Reserve Bank to print money. Geitner's proposal was based on the administration's analysis that the financial situation was far worse than previously known and that bold measures had to be taken to ensure that financial institutions were on solid ground. At the heart of the proposal was the creation of so-called bad banks program that would use taxpayer revenue and private capital to purchase the bad assets of failing banks. Also the plan called for using as much as $1 trillion to expand lending in the country, which had dried up since the fall meltdown. Finally, Geitner made it clear that banks, which received federal bailout money, would be subject to government oversight and regulation, with greater emphasis on transparency of bank holdings and limits on executive compensation.[5]

The Obama proposals on the stimulus package, the tax cuts to the working and middle classes and the expansion of credit were based on Keynesian economic theories (named after the British economist John Maynard Keynes) that stressed the importance of government spending and lending as the keys to recovery from a slumping economy. In Keynes view, and that of President Obama, if consumer spending and bank lending has dried up, the government must step in and act as the spender and lender of last resort. Republicans in Congress and conservatives in general were outraged by the Obama economic proposals because little emphasis was placed on major tax cuts, especially to business, while the stimulus package and the lending expansion created huge deficits and eventually a national debt that would create an enormous financial burden on future generations of Americans. Moreover, Republicans began talking about the impact that all the governmental intervention in the economy would have on the capitalist model, which was the foundation of the American system.[6] Claims that the Obama administration was taking the country down the road to nationalization of private enterprise and eventually socialism, filled the air.

The complaints of the Republicans in Congress about the direction that the Obama administration was taking the country had little impact on the legislative process. On February 17 President Obama signed the American Recovery and Reinvestment Act, a $787 billion stimulus package (the Republicans and some Democrats were able to chip away some of the original $825 billion proposed by the administration) that the president said would "set our economy on a firmer foundation." Obama admitted in his remarks before he signed the bill that, "today does mark the beginning of the end, the beginning of what we need to do to create jobs for American scrambling in the way of layoffs." Obama also signaled that this stimulus bill might not be the end of his effort to use deficit spending as a means of jump starting the economy.[7] He hinted that a second stimulus bill might be needed down the road, if the $787 billion was not sufficient to get Americans back to work and move the country out of recession. Despite the passage of the stimulus package in the House (along strict party lines), the president was able to convince only three Republican senators to support the bill, evidence that the spirit of bipartisanship was sorely lacking as the administration moved forward with its economic recovery plans.

One day after signing the American Recovery and Reinvestment Act, Obama moved from stimulus, taxes and lending to the home mortgage foreclosure crisis, which many viewed as the source of the economic meltdown. The president presented a plan designed to help 9 million American homeowners to refinance their mortgages and in the process save them from losing their homes. This government program was estimated to cost $475 billion, of which $75 billion would go directly to hard-pressed homeowners and the rest to further strengthen the now-government-controlled mortgage lenders, Fannie Mae and Freddie Mac. With one in ten home mortgages either delinquent or in foreclosure, the Obama proposal was welcome news to many Americans and essential in the president's view, to stop "unraveling homeownership . . . and the American dream itself."[8]

On the Record

On February 24, 2009, President Obama addressed a Joint Session of Congress and spoke about his vision for rebuilding the shattered American economy.

> The weight of this crisis will not determine the destiny of this nation. The answers to our problems don't lie beyond our reach. They exist in our laboratories, and our universities, in our fields and our factories; in the imaginations of our entrepreneurs and the pride of the hardest-working people on Earth. Those qualities that have made America the greatest force of progress and prosperity in human history we still possess in ample measure. What is required now is for this country to pull together, confront boldly the challenges we face, and take responsibility for our future once more.

Source: The White House, Office of the Press Secretary

As the Obama administration moved forward with its economic plans for dealing with the Great Recession, two areas of its policy initiatives became the most contentious and controversial, the budget, and the bailouts of Chrysler and General Motors (GM). In March 2009, President Obama presented to Congress a $3.6 trillion budget for fiscal year 2010, which highlighted the president's commitment to invest in health care, education, global warming reduction and alternative energy production. In his budget statement the president stressed that the expenditures were necessary to make, "long overdue investments in education so every child can compete in the global economy, undertaking healthcare reform so that we can control costs while boosting coverage and quality, and investing in renewable sources of energy so that we can reduce our dependence on foreign oil."[9]

Although Obama promised that the deficits created by this spending plan would decrease through reductions in defense appropriations, the ending of support for agribusiness subsidies and tax increases on the wealthy, the Republican minority in Congress was in no mood to accept this budget without a fight. Republicans quickly countered that the deficits created by the president's budget would be four times larger than any since the end of World War II, and by the end of his first term in 2013 the national debt held by the public since 2003 would rise from 58.7% to 67.2% of GDP.[10] Although George W. Bush's budgets during his eight years in office were out of balance by over trillions of dollars, the Republicans saw the Obama budget for 2010 and for subsequent years as irresponsible and leading to tax increases and unacceptable national debt obligations. The Republicans accented the importance of restraining government spending, particularly on Obama's health care reform, and stressed the importance of avoiding tax increases on the wealthy. The approach advocated by the Republicans, in short, cut spending and cut taxes.[11]

Just as contentious and controversial were the Obama administration's efforts to save Chrysler and GM from going out of business. After the Obama administration approved an initial bailout of $30 billion that was designed to prop up the two major automakers while they restructured, it was clear that both Chrysler and GM were on the verge of bankruptcy and unable to make the necessary changes required by the government to take their companies into a profitable mode. As a result the Obama administration and the two autogiants engaged in a period of negotiation to come to an agreement about how to keep them viable and avoid liquidation, which would mean the loss of hundreds of thousands of jobs and the demise of automaking in the United States. Ford Motors was never part of the government's bailout plans or near bankruptcy. Despite facing downward sales, Ford remained the most viable of the Big Three.

Although Chrysler filed for bankruptcy and eventually merged with Fiat, an Italian car manufacturer, General Motors, the largest of the Detroit automakers, was the focus of the Obama administration's efforts to restructure. In late May the government struck a deal with GM that gave the federal government 60% ownership of the company in return for an additional $30 billion in assistance. Although GM also entered Chapter 11 bankruptcy with the support and encouragement of the Obama administration, the $30 billion restructuring plan approved by the government gave hope to many employees and car dealers that the company would soon be on the road to recovery. The plan was a difficult one as the United Autoworkers Union (UAW) was forced to make major concessions on pay, pensions and health benefits, and GM management was encouraged by the government to take the company in a new direction accenting smaller, more fuel-efficient cars. Nevertheless, the bankruptcy and restructuring process led to the layoff of up to 21,000 workers and the closing of hundreds of dealers nationwide.[12]

The GM restructuring agreement that followed the intervention in the banking industry prompted conservative critics to claim that indeed the Obama administration was taking the country down the road to socialism. Many in the business community took the position that GM should have been allowed to fail and that the government had no business interfering with market forces and becoming a majority shareholder in a private enterprise.

Michael Steele, the chairman of the Republican Party, best articulated the position of those who criticized the GM restructuring plan when he said on June 2, 2009, "No matter how much the president spins GM's bankruptcy as good for the economy, it is nothing more than another government grab of a private company and another handout to the union cronies who helped bankroll his presidential campaign."[13]

Despite the partisan rancor over the Obama administration's use of government intervention to respond to the challenges of the Great Recession, by June 2009 the economy showed some faint signs of recovery. Speaking to Congress at this time, Federal Reserve Chairman Ben Bernanke reported that the recession could be over by the end of 2010, based on preliminary reports of increased lending by banks, modest but consistent growth in the stock market, a slight increase in factory orders and home building and more positive news of consumer confidence. These faint signs, however, were balanced by continued weak retail sales, unemployment figures that inched upward and little sign of relief in the areas of personal bankruptcies and home foreclosures. Washington, Wall Street and Main Street were looking for any sign of hope that the economy was starting to rebound from the worst downturn since the Great Depression and were finding only a mixed bag of trends.

Increasingly, however, more and more economists and financial experts were predicting that by 2010 the United States would show signs that the recession had run its course. Nevertheless those economists were also saying that the next stage of recovery would be weak with growth rates reaching at best 3% increases in gross domestic product (GDP) in 2010 and perhaps as well in 2011. By mid-2010 there were more positive signs of a stronger-than-expected recovery, especially in retail sales, consumer confidence and corporate earnings. However, what worried the Obama administration (not only from an economic but political viewpoint, because mid-term Congressional elections were slated for November 2010) was that unemployment data showed that despite increases in new jobs added the

Data Bank

Together the Bush administration and especially the Obama administration spent about $7.8 trillion in late 2008 and in 2009 to address the economic meltdown and the ongoing Great Recession. A breakdown of the expenditures is given here:

Stimulus plan–$575 billion
Tax cuts–$212 billion
Federal Reserve–short-term lending to business, mortgage and credit markets, Bear Stearns and AIG bailouts–$3.8 trillion

(continued)

Data Bank (continued)

> Federal Deposit Insurance Corporation–bank debt, guarantees and deposit insurance–$1.2 trillion
>
> S. Treasury–bank investments, foreclosure relief, auto bailout, AIG rescue and TARP programs–$771 billion
>
> Joint Programs–Guarantees to Citigroup and Bank of America–$411 billion
>
> Other–Freddie Mac and Fannie Mae–$1.6 trillion

Sources: Federal Reserve, Bureau of Economic Analysis

rate of unemployment remained near 10% with over 15 million workers without jobs. Although the stimulus package was designed to get millions back into gainful employment, only a more vibrant private economy would be able to put the nation on the road to full employment, and that goal appeared to be years away.

Whenever the United States comes out of the Great Recession and begins a robust recovery, the focus of attention of the country and indeed the world will not only be on GDP growth data and employment numbers, but more importantly on the Obama administration's bold and comprehensive use of government intervention, government spending and government regulation as the tools for dealing with the economic crisis. As discussed earlier, not since the days of Franklin Delano Roosevelt has an American president used the full power of government to get the nation back on track. However, just as Roosevelt had his detractors who feared the dismantling of the capitalist system and the introduction of state-directed economic policies, Obama faces partisan skeptics who are concerned that the American economy will be burdened by higher taxes, higher deficits, higher debt and extensive regulation as the government dominates the private sector and guides the country toward a new model of national development. Evidence of the Obama administration's continued commitment to use government to deal with the Great Recession was its support for a comprehensive financial overhaul of Wall Street that accented a consumer protection agency with the power to monitor and regulate the activity of banks and investment houses and avoid future meltdowns.[14]

Although Obama and his economic and financial advisors are confident that their policies were the right ones to deal with the economic meltdown and the Great Recession that followed, they nevertheless were dealing with an unprecedented crisis of global proportions without a guidebook on how to get the United States into a recovery mode. In the next few years the American people will have a better opportunity to judge the Obama economic and financial policies and determine whether the guidebook used by the government had the correct remedies or, as critics are quick to point out, was a prescription for long-term disaster.[15]

The Great Debate

In dealing with the Great Recession, the Obama administration stressed the importance of quick infusions of government money, either in economic stimulus plans or in bailouts of key institutions.

Debate Topic

Did the Obama administration follow the correct policy course of action by using government spending to move the country from recession to recovery?

Critical Thinking Questions

1. Is the government or the private sector the best source of stimulus for economic recovery?
2. How concerned are you about the trillions of dollars of debt that the Obama administration has created in its efforts to jump start the U.S. economy?
3. Republican critics of the Obama administration state that the key to the economic recovery was massive tax cuts on individuals and businesses, not massive government spending and debt accumulation. Do you agree with this economic recovery strategy?
4. Should the Obama administration have allowed GM and Chrysler to fail rather than prop them up with bailouts and eventual government ownership?
5. It has been said that the bailouts of the banks were a huge transfer of national income from the American taxpayers to the banks, who were in part responsible for the economic meltdown. Was the government's support of the big banks and investment houses a wise move considering that the taxpayers footed the bill?

Connections

The Federal Reserve Bank and its chairman, Ben Bernanke, are a key source of economic and financial data relative to the current state of the American economy. Its website is at www.federalreserve.gov/

The White House Council of Economic Advisors are President Obama's top aides who are responsible for charting the steps that need to be taken to address the Great Recession. The White House site for the Council can be found at www.whitehouse.gov/administration/eop/cea/

Nouriel Roubini, a New York University economic professor, is often viewed as correctly predicting the economic meltdown and as a result has become a major advisor and commentator on the current state of the American economy. See his blog at www.stern.nyu.edu/~nroubini

The Republican Party and its members of Congress differ sharply with the Obama plan for the recovery. See their positions on various aspects of the American economy at http://www.ontheissues.org/republican_party.htm

Paul Krugman, a leading liberal economic commentator and Noble Prize recipient, has supported and criticized Obama's economic policies. See his comments at www .krugman.blogs.nytimes.com/

Some Books to Read

Read, Colin, *Global Financial Meltdown: How We Can Avoid the Next Economic Crisis* (New York: Palgrave Macmillan, 2009).

Talbott, John, R. *Obamaeconomics: How Bottom-up Economic Prosperity Will Replace Trickle-down Economics* (New York: Seven Stories Press, 2008).

Shiller, Robert, *The Sub-Prime Solution: How Today's Global Financial Crisis Happened and What to Do About It* (Princeton, NJ: Princeton University Press, 2008).

Posner, Richard, *A Failure of Capitalism: The Crisis of 08 and the Decent into Depression* (Cambridge, MA: Harvard University Press, 2009).

Kuttner, Robert, *Obama's Challenge: America's Economic Crisis and the Power of a Transformative Presidency* (New York: Chelsea Green Press, 2008).

Notes

1. David Lightman, "Congressional Budget Office Compares Downturn to Great Depression," *McClatchy Washington Bureau*, January 27, 2009.
2. "From the Sub-Prime to the Terrigenous: Recession Begins at Home," *Land Values Research Group*, June 2, 2009.
3. Chris Isidore, "It's Official: Recession Since December 07," *CNN Money*, http:// money.cnn.com/2008/12/01/news/economy/recession/index.htm
4. See http://www.foxnews.com/wires/2008Oct17/0,4670,MeltdownBushQuotes, 00.html
5. Gullapalli, Diya and Anand Shefali, "Bailout Money Funds Seem to Stanch Outflow," *Wall Street Journal*, September 20, 2008.
6. "Fed's Spending Is Risky Business," http://marketplace.publicradio.org/ display/web/2008/12/22/pm_shadow_bailout/
7. Sasha Issenberg, "$787 Billion Stimulus Bill Approved," *Boston Globe*, February 14, 2009, A1.
8. Remarks of President Barack Obama on the Home Mortgage Crisis, White Office of the Press Secretary, February 18, 2009.
9. Address by President Barack Obama to Joint Session of Congress, White House Office of the Press Secretary, February 24, 2009.
10. Matthew Benjamin, "Cost of U.S. Crisis Action Grows, Along with the Debt," *Bloomberg News,* October 10, 2008.
11. Helene Cooper and Carl Hulse, "Obama Defends Budget Proposal," *New York Times*, March 18, 2009, A1.

12. Fact Sheet: Obama Administration Restructuring Initiative for General Motors, Office of the Press Secretary, May 31, 2009.

13. See http://www.mlive.com/auto/index.ssf/2009/06/pocdast_rnc_chairman_michael_s.html

14. Matt Viser, "Debates Stalls on Wall Street Overhaul," *Boston Globe*, April 27, 2010, A1.

15. For a more dismal view of the prospects for a sustained recovery from the Great Recession see Peter Boone and Simon Johnson, "The Next Financial Crisis," *The New Republic*, September 23, 2009, pp. 24–26.

INDEX

A

Abercrombie, Neil, 279
Abortion, 142–154
  conscience clause on, 151
  income and, 149
  partial birth, 145, 148
  public funding of, 70
  race and, 149
  religion and, 209, 210, 211–212
  stem cell research and, 221–222
Abramoff, Jack, 198
Abu Ghraib scandal, 33–35
Activists, 10
Advisory Commission on Consumer
  Protection and Quality in the Health
  Care Industry, 64
Affirmative action, 120–122, 124–125
Afghanistan war, 38, 284, 292–294
  cost of, 95
  hate groups and, 20
  national defense and, 273
  under Obama, 41
  surge in, 33
  Taliban in, 32
AFL-CIO, 6
African Americans. *See* Race
Aging, 3
  health care costs and, 61
  Social Security/Medicare and,
    104–105, 107
Agostini v. Felton, 133
Agricultural subsidies, 344, 353
Ahmadinejad, Mahmoud, 299–300,
  301–303, 305–306
Aid to Families with Dependent
  Children (AFDC), 260, 262
Airport security, 17, 20–21, 27
Alito, Samuel, 147–148, 150, 200, 238
Alliance for Marriage, 174
Al-Maliki, Nouri, 290, 291
Al Qaeda, 290
  retaliation against, 31–33
  supporters in the U.S., 26
  threat of, 40–41
Al Sadr, Moqtada, 290

Alternative energy sources, 54–55,
  247–249, 251, 252, 254
American Association of Retired Persons
  (AARP), 6, 107, 112
American Civil Liberties Union (ACLU),
  123, 181, 186
American-Israel Public Affairs
  Committee (AIPAC), 329
American Medical Association, 151, 160
American Recovery and Reinvestment
  Act, 352–353
American Values, 143, 174
Amnesty International, 186
Anthony, Susan B., 143
Anti-Drug Abuse Act, 232
Arafat, Yasir, 324, 327
Aravolis, John, 176
Arms trade, 276, 327–328
Army's Future Combat System, 275
Ashcroft, John, 211
Asian Americans. *See* Race
Assimilation, 83–84
Astrue, Michael, 107
Asymmetrical warfare, 31

B

Baby boomers, 61, 104–105, 107
Bader Ginsburg, Ruth, 238
Baker, James, 288
Balanced Budget Amendment, 99
Barletta, Lou, 82
Base Realignment and Closure
  Commission (BRAC), 277
Bauer, Gary, 143, 174
Baybee, Jay, 39
Baze v. Rees, 187
Begin, Menachem, 324
Bergen, Peter, 289
Bernanke, Ben, 313, 355
Biden, Joseph, 303, 305
Bin Laden, Osama, 31, 37
Bipartisan Campaign Reform Act
  (BCRA), 194
Black box of decision making, 11
Blackmun, Harry, 145–146

Blair, Tony, 33, 52
Bloomberg, Michael, 52, 137, 138
Boehner, John, 280
Bonior, David, 340
Border Protection, Anti-Terrorism and
    Illegal Immigration Control Act, 80–81
Bork, Robert, 147
Boumediennne v. Bush, 35
Bowers v. Hardwick, 170
Bowlin, Mike, 248
Boy Scouts of America, 170
Brady, Jim, 157, 159
Brady Act, 157
Brady Campaign to Prevent Gun
    Violence, 158, 159
Brady Center to Prevent Gun Violence,
    162, 164
Breyer, Stephen, 164
Bridge to Nowhere, 99
British Petroleum (BP), 249–250
Broad, Eli, 138
Brookings Institution, 94
Brown, Michael, 18
Brown, Sherrod, 315
Brownback, Sam, 211
*Brown v. Board of Education of Topeka
    Kansas*, 117, 125
Bryce, James, 9
Brzezinski, Zbigniew, 329–330
Buchanan, Patrick, 84, 343
Buckley v. Valeo, 193–194
Bureaucracy, 11, 97
Bureau of Alcohol, Tobacco, Firearms
    and Explosives, 160
Burns, Nicolas, 328
Bush, George H. W.
    on civil rights, 119
    environmental policies of, 49–50
    on Israel, 326
    on NAFTA, 339
    national defense under, 278
    on taxation, 92
Bush, George W., 240
    on abortion, 145, 151
    on China, 317
    drug war under, 232–233
    on education reform, 130, 135
    energy policies of, 248–249, 250–251
    federal deficit under, 354
    on gay rights, 170, 171, 173
    on globalization, 342
    on global warming, 49, 51–53
    Great Recession under, 349–351
    on gun rights, 162
    on health care, 66–67, 69
    homeland security under, 15–16
    on illegal immigration, 75, 78–80
    on intelligent design, 225–226
    on Iran, 298–305
    Iraq war under, 36–38, 41, 284–287,
        289–291
    on Israel, 326, 327, 328
    on Medicare, 112
    national defense under, 273, 276, 277,
        278–280
    policies of on terrorists, 31–33
    presidential power expanded by, 26–27
    on race and civil rights, 122
    on religion, 206, 208, 209–211
    science policies of, 221–225, 227
    on Social Security, 109–110
    on stem cell research, 221–222
    Supreme Court appointments by,
        147–148
    taxation and spending under, 93–95,
        97, 99
    terrorist detainees under, 33–35, 39
    trade agreements under, 340
    USA Patriot Act and, 21–23
    war on drugs under, 238
Business
    campaign donations by, 196–197
    in China, 312, 313
    energy use and, 245
    globalization and, 338
    health care costs and, 60
    military-industrial complex and, 273,
        274
    oil company profits, 250
    taxation of, 96–97

C

Campaign finance, 192–204
    corporate donors in, 196–197
    corruption linked to, 197–199
    free speech and, 193, 194, 200–201
    gifts and, 198–199
    interest groups in, 194, 195–196
    public financing for, 199–200
    soft money in, 194

Cantwell, Maria, 253
Capitalism, globalization and, 337–345
Capital punishment, 180–191
  cost of, 184–185
  as cruel and unusual, 180–181
  deterrent value of, 184–185
  by lethal injection, 187–188
  public opinion on, 182
  race and, 183, 186
  wrongful death in, 183–184
Carbon dioxide emissions, 249, 253
Carey, Rea, 173
Carnegie Endowment for International
  Peace, 40
Carter, Jimmy, 247, 297–298, 324, 326
Casey, Bob, 200
Casey-Kirschling, Kathleen, 104, 110
Cato Institute, 48, 199
Cayman Islands tax havens, 342–343
Center for American Progress, 40
Center for Reproductive Rights, 151
Center for Responsive Politics, 159,
  195, 196
Center of Immigration Studies, 77
Centers for Disease Control and
  Prevention, 19, 142, 160, 219
Central Intelligence Agency (CIA), 39, 303
"Changing Demographic Profile of the
  United States, The," 2–3
Charter schools, 130, 135–136
Cheney, Dick, 24, 32, 39, 42, 300
Chertoff, Michael, 19, 21
Chiang Kai-shek, 318
China, 255, 310–322
  currency rates in, 313–315
  economic development in, 311–312,
    316, 338
  globalization and, 342, 343
  human rights in, 311, 317, 319, 320
  in international community, 318–320
  Israel arms trade with, 327–328
  product safety in, 315
  Taiwan and, 316, 318
  Tibet and, 316–317
  trade deficit with, 314–316
Cho, Seung Hui, 161
Chrysler bailout, 353, 354
Citizenship, 78–79, 117
*Citizens United v. Federal Elections
  Commission*, 201

Civil Rights Act, 118, 119
Civil rights movement, 117–119, 177
Civil War, 89, 117
Cizik, Richard, 212, 213
Clean Air Act, 49–50
Clear Skies Initiative, 51
Climate Action Report, 51
Climate change, 45–58
Clinton, Bill, 240
  on education reform, 135
  environmental policies of, 50–51
  on gay rights, 169–170
  on gun rights, 157
  on health care, 61–66, 69
  on Iran, 298
  on Israel, 326
  on Israel and Palestine, 324
  on NAFTA, 339–340
  national defense under, 277, 280
  policies of on terrorists, 31–33
  taxation and spending under, 92–93, 95
  welfare under, 261, 262–267
Clinton, Hillary Rodham, 54, 62,
  65–66, 343
Cloning, 222
CNN, 4, 25
Coalition to Stop Gun Violence, 156
Coast Guard, 16, 17, 232
Coburn, Tom, 99
Coleman, John, 199
Collins, Susan, 253
Colorado Alliance for Immigration
  Reform, 76–77
Columbine High School shootings, 158
Compromise, 1
Congressional Black Caucus, 238
Congressional Budget Office, 98, 99
Congressional committees, 10
Congressional Research Service, 2–3
Connerly, Ward, 122
Consensus, 1, 2
Conservation. *See* Energy use and
  conservation; Environmental issues
Conservatives, 4, 41, 96, 149, 150
Constitution
  Balanced Budget Amendment, 99
  Bill of Rights, 155–156
  Eighth Amendment, 180–181
  Fifteenth Amendment, 117
  First Amendment, 193, 194, 226

Constitution (*Continued*)
  Fourteenth Amendment, 117, 121
  Marriage Protection Amendment,
    173, 174
  on national defense, 271, 273
  original intent of, 147
  Second Amendment, 155–167
  Thirteenth Amendment, 117
Constitutional rights
  abortion, 142–154
  capital punishment and, 187–188
  as cultural value, 10
  gay rights, 168–179
  gun ownership, 155–167
  homeland security and, 17
  Patriot Act and, 21–23
  privacy, 144–145, 146–147
  race and, 116–128
  torture policies and, 33–36, 38–40
Container Security Initiative (CSI), 16
Cooney, Philip, 52
Copenhagen climate summit, 47, 54
Corzine, Jon, 188
Coulter, Ann, 214
Council of Foreign Affairs, 317
Creationism, 225–227
Credit Enhancement for Charter Schools
    Facilities Program, 121
Crocker, Ryan, 291, 292

D

Dalai Lama, 316, 317
Daley, Richard, 234
Daniel, Matt, 174
Death penalty, 180–191
Defense Department, 97
Defense of Marriage Act (DOMA), 170
DeLay, Tom, 198, 211
Demographics, 2–3, 75, 104–105, 258
Deng Xiaoping, 311
Department of Health and Human
    Services, 78, 97
Department of Homeland Security, 15–21
  Advisory System, 17–18
  airport security efforts, 17, 20–21
  criticisms of, 17–21
  First Responders program, 16–17
  formation of, 15–16
  illegal immigration and, 85
  size of, 17

Dershowitz, Alan, 330
Detainee Treatment Act, 34
De Tocqueville Alexis, 1
De Vries, Paul, 212, 213
Diallo, Amadou, 123
Dionne, E. J., 68
Dirksen, Everett, 112
Disability, 260
Discovery Institute, 225, 226
District of Columbia v. Heller, 163
DNA testing, 180, 184
Dobbs, Lou, 84, 343
Dobriansky, Paula, 317
Dobson, James, 174, 212
Doerflinger, Richard, 222
Dominican Republic–Central
    American Free Trade
    Agreement (DR–CAFTA), 340
Domke, David, 211
Donohue, John, III, 185
"Don't Ask, Don't Tell" policy,
    169–170, 176
Douglas, William O., 146
Drug Enforcement Agency (DEA), 232
Drug war, 231–243
Duncan, Arne, 139
Dunningham, Randy "Duke," 198

E

Earmarking, 99
Earned Income Tax Credit (EITC), 260
Earth Summit (1992), 50
Economic and Tax Reconciliation Act of
    2001, 93–94
Economic Policy Institute, 340–341
Economy
  in China, 311–312, 313–315
  globalization and, 336–347
  Great Recession, 348–359
  health care costs and, 60
  illegal immigrants in, 75, 76–77, 81
  national defense and, 276–278
  public opinion on, 5
  Reaganomics on, 91
  welfare and, 265–266
Edelman, Peter, 265–266
Education
  accountability in, 130, 138
  Centers of Excellence, 17
  charter schools in, 130, 135–136

cost of, 134
funding for, 137
gun rights and, 160
high-stakes testing in, 130, 131–132
homeschooling, 136–137
international comparisons of, 132
race in, 117, 121–122, 123, 124–125
reforming, 129–141
religion and, 207, 212
school choice in, 133–136
teaching evolution in, 225–227
voucher systems in, 133–136
Einstein, Albert, 220
Eisenhower, Dwight, 273, 274, 280–281
Elites, 10
Employment Non-Discrimination Act
    (ENDA), 173
Energy Independence and Security
    Act, 249
Energy use and conservation, 244–257
    alternative energy and, 54–55,
        247–249, 252, 254
    in China, 319
    foreign energy sources and, 245,
        246–247
    fuel economy standards and, 54, 245,
        246, 247, 250–251, 253
    nuclear power, 247
    oil supplies and, 248, 249–250
    regional differences in, 251–252
    U.S. rates of, 244–245
Environmental issues
    Arctic oil drilling, 249
    energy use and conservation,
        244–257
    free trade, 341
    global warming, 45–58
    interest groups on, 7
Environmental Protection Agency (EPA),
    51, 247, 252
Equal protection, 121
Ervin, Clark Kent, 18
Ethanol, 248, 251
Evangelical Christians
    family values agenda of, 211–213
    gay rights and, 174–175
    homeschooling and, 136
    on Israel, 331–332
    political participation by, 209–211
    political party affiliation of, 208

Evolution, 225–227
ExxonMobil, 250

F

Fair and Legal Employment Act
    (Arizona), 82
Falbus, Orval, 119
Falwell, Jerry, 174
Families USA, 60
Family Research Council, 174
Family values, 211–213
Fannie Lou Hamer, Rosa Parks and
    Coretta Scott King Voting Rights Act
    Reauthorization and Amendments
    Act, 122
Fayad, Abu, 289
Federal Bureau of Investigation (FBI), 21,
    37, 157
Federal deficit
    China and, 314
    under Obama, 353–354
    Social Security/Medicare and, 112
    taxation and, 91, 93–94–95, 97–98
Federal Election Campaign Act of 1972,
    193–194
Federal Elections Commission, 192, 193,
    195
Federal Emergency Management Agency
    (FEMA), 16, 18–19
Federalist, The, 6–7
Federalist Party, 89
Federal Reserve Bank, 112, 313, 351
Feingold, Russ, 194
FEMA. *See* Federal Emergency
    Management Agency (FEMA)
First Responders program, 16–17
527 Organization, 194
Flake, Jeff, 99
Flax, Marilyn, 188
Focus on the Family, 174
Food and Drug Administration (FDA),
    169, 315
Ford, Gerald, 326
Ford Motors, 354
Foreign Intelligence Surveillance Act
    (FISA), 22, 23
Foreign Intelligence Surveillance Court,
    21–23
Founding Fathers, 206
Fox, Justin, 254

Frank, Barney, 236
Franklin, Benjamin, 220
Franks, Tommie, 32
Freedom, 10
Friedman, Milton, 236
Friedman, Thomas, 338–339, 344
Ft. Dix attack, 24–26
Fuel economy standards, 54, 245, 246, 247, 250–251, 253
Fuller, Ida, 103
Fullilove v. Klutznick, 121
Furman v. Georgia, 181, 182

G

Gates, Bill, 138
Gates, Robert, 38, 176, 280
Gay rights, 168–179
  "Don't Ask, Don't Tell" policy, 169–170, 176
  hate crimes and, 173, 175
  marriage, 168, 170–176
  religion and, 211–212
Geitner, Timothy, 351–352
General Electric (GE), 53
General Motors bailout, 353, 354–355
Geneva Convention, 35, 36
Global Climate Coalition, 52
Globalization, 336–347
  agricultural subsidies and, 344
  China in, 313
  definition of, 336–337
  illegal immigration and, 76, 85
  NAFTA and, 339–341
Global Research, 342
Global warming, 45–58
  causes of, 46, 47, 51, 53
  emission controls and, 50–51
  religious agenda and, 212
  scientific community on, 47–48, 54–55
  skepticism about, 48
  state actions on, 52–53
Gonzales v. Carhart, 145
Goodridge v. Department of Public Health, 171–172
Gore, Al, 45–46, 50
Government
  2011 budget breakdown, 95–96
  balance in, 26
  campaign finance and, 192–204

federal budget, 277–278
  health care costs and, 60–61
  spending, 88–102
Government Accountability Office, 275
Gradison, Bill, 65
Graham, Franklin, 175
Graham, Lindsey, 253, 314
Gratz v. Bollinger, 121
Gravel, Mike, 236
Great American Boycott, 81
Great Depression, 89–90, 106, 261, 351
Great Recession, 348–359, 349–350
Great Society, 105, 261
Greenhouse effect, 46
Gregg, Judd, 107
Gregg v. Georgia, 181
Griswold v. Connecticut, 146
Guantánamo Camp Delta, 24, 34–35, 38–40, 42
Gun Control Act, 157
Gun Owners Protection Act, 157
Gun rights, 155–167
  background checks and, 160–161
  child safety and, 160
  gun-show purchases, 160–161
  international comparison of, 161–162
  personal security and, 157, 158, 159
  Second Amendment on, 155–156

H

H1N1 virus, 19
Hamdan v. Rumsfeld, 35
Hamilton, Alexander, 206
Hamilton, Lee, 288
Hannity, Sean, 214
Hansen, James, 52
Hastert, Dennis, 198
Hate crimes, 124, 173, 175
Hate groups, 41
Head Start, 262
Health care, 59–73. *See also* Medicaid; Medicare
  abortion and, 142–154
  in Canada, 63
  costs of U.S., 60, 64–65
  deficiencies in, 61
  in emergency rooms, 60–61
  illegal immigrants and, 77
  managed care in, 62, 63–65
  Medicare reform and, 111

Patients' Bill of Rights and, 64
public opinion on, 5
public option in, 68–70
single-payer systems, 61, 63
stem cell research and, 212, 219
Health Insurance Association of America,
  62, 65
Health Security Act, 62
Hemenway, David, 159
Henigan, Dennis, 158
Hersh, Seymour, 300
Hezbollah, 298, 324–325
Hispanics. *See* Race
HIV/AIDS, 169
Hoffman, Bruce, 40
Holder, Eric, 35
Holocaust, 299–300
Holt, John, 136
Homeland security, 15–30
  department of, 15–21
  national defense and, 271–283
  Patriot Act and, 21–23
  Protect America Act and, 23–24
  public opinion on, 24–26
Homeland Security Advanced Research
  Projects Agency (HSARPA), 17
Homelessness, 266
Homeschooling, 136–137
Homicide rates, 162, 184
Hospital Insurance Fund, 108
Housing, 123, 124, 266–267
Huckabee, Mike, 212, 213
Human rights
  in China, 311, 317, 319, 320
  in Israel, 327
  torture and, 33–36, 38–40, 42
Human Rights Campaign, 173
Huntington, Samuel, 84
Hurricane Katrina, 18–19, 46
Hussein, Saddam, 32–33, 206
Hyde, Henry, 144

I

Illegal Immigration Relief Act
  (Pennsylvania), 82–84
Immelt, Jeffrey, 53
Immigration
  aging population and, 110
  assimilation and, 83–84
  demonstrations over, 81

guest worker programs and, 78, 80
  illegal, 74–87, 110
  national security and, 16, 17
  welfare reform and, 263–264
Immigration and Customs Enforcement
  Agency, 75
Immigration and Nationality Act, 85
Income
  abortion rights and, 149
  in China, 312
  globalization and, 341–342
  inequality in, 259–260
  race and, 120–121, 124
  race in, 123
Inconvenient Truth, An, 45–46, 50
India, 255, 342, 343
Individualism, 10
Intelligent design, 225–227
Interagency Council on Homelessness,
  266
Interest groups, 5–8
  on abortion, 143
  in campaign finance, 194, 195–196, 200
  on capital punishment, 181, 186
  on education reform, 132
  on gay rights, 172–175
  on global warming, 52
  on gun rights, 156, 158–159
  in health care, 62, 67
  on illegal immigration, 81, 83
  on Israel, 325, 328–332
  on marijuana legalization, 236
  most influential, 7–8
  on science, 220
  on Social Security, 107
  on taxation and spending, 90
  umbrella, 6–7
Intergovernmental Panel on Climate
  Change, 47, 48, 55
Internal Revenue Service (IRS), 89, 108,
  342–343
Internet, 336
  in campaign finance, 201
Iran, 41, 287, 297–309
  hostage crisis, 297–298
  in terrorism, 298–305
Iraq Study Group, 288
Iraq war, 31–33, 32–33, 284–296
  Abu Ghraib scandal, 33–35
  alienation of Middle East in, 41

Iraq war (*Continued*)
anti-terrorism *vs.* nation building in, 36–38
under Bush, 210–211
cost of, 95, 278, 285
exit strategy in, 285, 288–289
hate groups and, 20
national defense and, 273, 279–280
National Guard in, 279
nation building and, 291
public opinion on, 5
Islam, 210–211, 214
Israel, 323–335
Iran on, 299, 305
peace efforts in, 330–331
U.S. ties with, 325
Israel-Egypt Peace Accord, 324
Israel Lobby and U.S. Foreign Policy (Mearsheimer & Walt), 328–331
Issue overload, 8

J

Jackson, Andrew, 193
Jackson, Jesse, 118
Jefferson, Thomas, 206, 209, 214
Jim Crow laws, 117
Job Opportunity and Basic Skills (JOBS), 260
Jobs
affirmative action and, 120–122, 124–125
aging employees in, 110
gay rights and, 173
globalization and, 338, 340–341
in the Great Recession, 355–356
illegal immigrants and, 78, 80, 81–83
poverty and, 259–260
public opinion on, 5
Johnson, Lyndon, 93, 105, 120, 261, 273

K

Kaine, Timothy, 160
Kanka, Richard, 188
Karzai, Hamid, 32, 292–294
Kellerman, Arthur, 159–160
Kennedy, Anthony, 150, 201
Kennedy, Edward, 61, 64, 80–81, 130
Kennedy, John F., 156–157, 213, 223
Kennedy, Robert, 157
Kerry, John, 194, 210
Keynes, John Maynard, 352
Khatami, Ayatolah, 298

Khomeini, Ayatollah, 297–298
Kim Jon Il, 300–301
King, Martin Luther, Jr., 117, 118, 119, 157
Kleck, Gary, 159
Klein, Joel, 137
Krugman, Paul, 94
Kucinich, Dennis, 236
Kyoto Accord, 50–51, 53
Kyoto Protocol, 249, 252

L

Lam, Carol, 198
Launius, Roger, 224
Lawrence v. Texas, 170
League of United Latin American Citizens (LULAC), 7
Lisa McCalmont, 187
Legal Defense Fund, 181
Lexus and the Olive Tree, The (Friedman), 338–339
Liberals, 4, 96, 150
Life expectancy, 64, 341
Limbaugh, Rush, 214
Literacy, 341, 342
Lobbyists, 10. *See also* Interest groups
Local Law Enforcement Hate Crimes Prevention Act, 173
Lomborg, Bjorn, 55
Loury, Glenn, 237–238

M

Madison, James, 6–7, 12
Malcolm X, 119
Mangano, Philip, 266
Manhattan Project, 219
Mann, Horace, 130, 131
Manpower Demonstration Research Corporation, 265
Mao Zedong, 310–311
Marijuana legalization, 233, 234, 235–236. *See also* War on drugs
Marriage, gay rights to, 168, 170–176
Marriage Protection Amendment, 173, 174
Marshall, John, 89
Marshall, Margaret, 171–172
Marshall, Thurgood, 117
Martini, John, 188
Mayors Against Illegal Guns Coalition, 162
McCain, Cindy, 240

McCain, John
on Afghanistan, 38
on campaign finance, 194
exit polls on, 4–5
on globalization, 343–344
on health care, 64
on illegal immigration, 80–81
on Iraq, 36, 287
religion and, 213
on taxation, 96
McCarrick, Theodore, 210
McChrystal, Stanley, 293
McCleskey v. Kemp, 186
McCulloch v. Maryland, 89
McDonald v. Chicago, 163–164
McVeigh, Timothy, 41
Mearsheimer, John, 328–331, 332
Medicaid, 260
illegal immigrants and, 77
Medical savings accounts, 69
Medicare, 66–68, 105–115, 260
cost of, 105, 109
coverage of, 105
fiscal crisis in, 110–113
Hospital Insurance Fund, 108
means test for, 112
reimbursements by, 112
Medicare Prescription Drug,
Improvement and Modernization
Act, 67
Megan's Law, 188
Metaska, Tanya, 157, 158
Mexico, 233, 240, 339–341
Michelman, Kate, 143
Military-industrial complex, 273, 274
Miller, George, 130
Ming Wan, 319
Minorities. *See* Race
Moderates, 4
Mohammed, Khalid Sheikh, 35, 39
Monge, Luis, 181
Moore, Dorothy, 136
Moore, Raymond, 136
Moral values, 5
Mossadeq, Mohammed, 298
Moussavi, Mir Hossein, 306
Mullen, Mike, 176
Mulroney, Brian, 339
Multi-national corporations, 341
Murtha, John, 279

N
Napolitano, Janet, 20–21
Nasr, Vali, 302
Nath, Pran, 223
National Abortion Rights Action league
(NARAL), 143
National Aeronautics and Space
Administration (NASA), 223–224
National Association of Colored People
(NAACP), 7, 117, 123, 181
National Association of Evangelicals, 212
National Center for Science Education, 226
National Commission on Retirement
Policy, 108
National defense, 271–283. *See also*
Afghanistan war; Iraq war
battle readiness and, 278–280
cost of, 272
deterrence in, 272
economic development and, 276–278
military-industrial complex and,
273, 274
weapons systems in, 274–276
National Education Association
(NEA), 132
National Firearm Act, 156
National Gay and Lesbian Task
Force, 173
National Guard, 279, 280
National Home Education Research
Institute, 136–137
National Infrastructure Protection Plan
(NIPP), 16
National Institute of Drug Abuse, 239
National Institutes of Health (NIH),
219, 223
National Intelligence Estimate, 288,
301–302, 306
National Response Plan, 20
National Rifle Association (NRA), 7, 156,
157, 158–159, 161, 163–164, 164–165
National Science Foundation, 219
National Science Teacher's
Association, 226
National Security Agency (NSA),
22–23
National Survey of America's Families,
266–267
"Nation at Risk, A," 129–130, 131
Native Americans, 116–117, 198

Natural disasters
  homeland security and, 19–20
Netanyahu, Benjamin, 327, 333
New Deal, 89–90, 91, 103, 105–106, 261,
  351
New York Times, 53
Ney, Bob, 198
9/11 terrorist attacks, 15–16
Nixon, Richard, 193, 231, 232, 234
Nobel Prizes, 220
No Child Left Behind Act, 6, 130, 139
North American Free Trade Agreement
  (NAFTA), 339–341, 343
Nuclear Non-Proliferation Treaty, 299,
  301, 302, 304
Nuclear power, 247, 248
Nuclear weapons
  in Iran, 299, 300–302, 304, 305–307
  in Israel, 325
  in North Korea, 300–301, 306–307

O

Obama, Barack, 240
  on abortion, 150–151
  on Afghanistan, 33, 38, 292–294
  campaign finance by, 201
  on China, 314, 317, 320
  drug war under, 233
  economic recovery policies of, 97–98,
    350, 351–356
  on education reform, 135, 139
  energy policies of, 249–250, 252–254
  exit polls on, 4–5
  on gay rights, 173, 176
  on globalization, 343
  on global warming, 53–54
  on gun rights, 164
  on health care, 61, 62, 66, 68–71
  homeland security under, 19, 24
  on illegal immigration, 84–85
  on Iran, 300, 305–307
  on Iraq, 37, 284, 287–288, 290, 291–292
  on Israel, 326, 333
  Middle East policies of, 41
  national defense under, 274–275, 280
  policies of on terrorists, 38–40
  race relations and, 125
  religion and, 208, 210, 213, 214
  science policies of, 222, 223, 224, 227
  on Social Security/Medicare, 111

  taxation and spending under, 93, 96–98
  on terrorist detainees, 35–36
  on torture, 42
  war on drugs under, 240
O'Connor, Sandra Day, 147, 150
Office of Faith-Based Initiatives, 210
Office of Management and Budget
  (OMB), 95–96, 98, 99
Oklahoma City bombing, 41
Old Age, Survivors and Disability
  Insurance (OASDI). *See* Social
  Security
Olmert, Elud, 327
Omnibus Budget Reconciliation Act, 93
OPEC, 246, 247, 251
Opinion Research Corporation Poll, 25
Oppenheimer, J. Robert, 219, 221
O'Reilly, Bill, 84
Organization of Economic Cooperation
  and Development (OECD), 132
Ortiz, Solomon, 279
Oswald, Lee Harvey, 156–157

P

Palestine, 323–335
Palestine Liberation Organization
  (PLO), 324
Parker v. District of Columbia, 163
Parks, Rosa, 117, 119
Partial Birth Abortion Ban Act, 145, 148
Partisanship, 1–2, 48–49
Partnership for a Drug-Free America, 235
Partnership to Fight Chronic Disease, 61
Patients' Bill of Rights, 64
Patrick, Deval, 125
Paulson, Hank, 313–314
Paulson, Henry, 350
Pelosi, Nancy, 250, 279
Perkins, Tony, 174, 212
Perot, H. Ross, 339–340
Personal responsibility, 108–109,
  261–262
Personal Responsibility and Work
  Opportunity Reconciliation Act,
  262–267
Petraeus, David, 291
Pew Forum on Religion and Public
  Life, 205
Pew Research Center for the People &
  the Press, 25–26, 48

Pharmaceutical Research and Manufacturers of America, 67
Plan Merida, 233
Planned Parenthood, 144
Planned Parenthood v. Casey, 144
Plan of Attack (Woodward), 33
Pledge of Allegiance, 207
Political Action Committees (PACs), 200
Political participation, 10
   race and, 116–119, 125
   religion and, 207–208, 209–211, 214–215
Politics
   American approach to, 1
   corruption in, 197–199
   money and, 192–204
   religion and, 205–217
   science and, 218–230
Pollution, states producing most, 46
Population, 3
   China, 313
Poverty, 258–270. *See also* Welfare programs
   abortion rights and, 149
   childhood, 267
   in China, 312
   feminization of, 259, 266
   globalization and, 341–343
   international comparison of, 258–259
   race and, 120, 123
   religious agenda and, 212
Powell, Colin, 32, 125
Printz v. United States, 157
Private Guns, Public Health (Hemenway), 159
Program for International Student Assessment, 132
Prohibition, 239–240
Project Safe Neighborhoods, 162
Protect America Act, 23–24
Public opinion, 2
   on abortion, 148–149
   on campaign finance, 197
   on capital punishment, 182, 188
   on education, 130–131, 137, 138–139
   on energy use, 247, 254–255
   on evolution and creationism, 226, 227
   on gay rights, 172
   on globalization, 344–345
   on global warming, 48, 54–55
   on gun rights, 164–165
   on health care, 70
   on homeland security, 24–26
   on Iran, 306
   on Iraq war, 288
   on Israel, 331
   on national defense, 278
   on race relations, 125
   on religion, 205
   on science, 220
   on Social Security/Medicare, 110–111, 113
   on taxation, 89, 90, 96
   on taxation and spending, 90
   on threat of terrorism, 40
   on trust in politicians, 201–202
   on welfare programs, 260
Public policy
   implementation of, 11
   interest group influence on, 5–8
   model of, 9
   process of creating, 8–11
Purpose Driven Life, The (Warren), 212

Q

Quadrango, Jill, 63

R

Race and race relations, 116–128
   abortion rights and, 149
   affirmative action and, 120–122, 124–125
   capital punishment and, 183–184, 186
   demographics of, 3
   gay rights and, 175, 177
   illegal immigration and, 75–87
   income and, 120–121
   interest groups on, 7
   poverty and, 259
   racial profiling, 123–124
   segregation and, 117–118
   war on drugs and, 237–238
Racial profiling, 123–124
Rasmussen Reports, 197
Rasul v. Bush, 35
Reagan, Nancy, 222
Reagan, Ronald, 147, 222
   economic policies of, 91–92
   on education reform, 129
   globalization under, 337
   on gun rights, 157

Reagan, Ronald (*Continued*)
Iran hostages and, 298
national defense under, 272, 276–277, 278
religion and, 208
Social Security under, 104, 106
taxation and spending under, 90, 91–92
in war on drugs, 232, 238
welfare under, 261
Reaganomics, 91–92
Regents of the University of California v. Bakke, 121
Religion, 205–217
abortion rights and, 142–154
on evolution, 225–227
family values and, 211–213
gay rights and, 174–175
homeschooling and, 136
Islam, 210–211, 214
Israel and, 331–332
secularization and, 211–212
separation of state and, 206, 207, 210, 214
stem cell research and, 212
Reverse discrimination, 120–121
Rhee, Michelle, 137
Rice, Condoleezza, 32, 125
Ridge, Tom, 16, 18
Rights. *See* Constitutional rights
Rizzo, John, 40
Roberts, John, 148, 150
Robertson, Pat, 175, 332
Roe v. Wade, 142, 143, 144–148, 150, 209. *See also* Abortion
Romney, Mitt, 66, 213
Roosevelt, Franklin Delano, 89–90, 91, 103, 105–106, 261, 351, 356
Royal Dutch Shell, 250
Rumsfeld, Donald, 32
Ryan, George, 182

S

Sadat, Anwar, 324
Sageman, Mark, 40
Salazar, Ken, 252
Salinas, Carlos, 339
Salk, Jonas, 220
Samples, John, 199
Sanders, Bernie, 275
Sawhill, Isabel, 259

Scalia, Antonin, 164
School choice, 133–136
Schwarzenegger, Arnold, 52
Science, 218–230
ethics and, 220–221
evolution and, 225–227
on global warming, 47–48, 54–55
government funding of, 219, 222–224
stem cell research, 212, 219, 221–222
Scopes Trial, 225
Searches and seizures, 21–23
Secret Service, 16
Secularization, 211–212
Secure Border Initiative (SBI), 75
Secure Fence Act, 75, 78
Selden, David, 82
Sensenbrenner, James, 80
Sentencing Project, 237
Sestak, Joe, 279
Sharon, Ariel, 324
Sharpton, Al, 118
Shay's Rebellion, 89
Shepard, Matthew, 173
"Silver tsunami," 104–105
Slavery, 116, 117
Snow, John, 314
Social Security, 103–115, 260
cost of, 105, 109
cost-of-living adjustments to, 104
funding of, 109–110
privatization of, 108–109
retirement age and, 110
"Social Security and Medicare: The Impending Fiscal Challenge," 112
Social Security Trust Fund, 104–105, 108
Social welfare. *See* Welfare programs
Solar energy, 252
Space program, 223–224
Special interest groups. *See* Interest groups
Spitzer, Eliot, 83
Spoils system, 193
Stamp Act, 89
Stanton, Elizabeth Cady, 143
State Children's Health Insurance Program (SCHIP), 67–68
State of Emergency (Buchanan), 84
States
on abortion, 143, 145
on affirmative action, 121–122

on capital punishment, 181–182, 185, 188
on education reform, 133–136, 137–138, 139
energy policies in, 252
environmental policies of, 52–53, 54
on gay rights, 170–171
on gun rights, 160–161
health care policies in, 65
on illegal immigration, 81–83
marijuana legalization in, 236
Status of Forces Agreement, 291
Steele, Michael, 354–355
Stem cell research, 212, 219, 221–222
Stem Cell Research Enhancement Act, 222
Stevens, John Paul, 201
Stewart, John, 195
Stiglitz, Joseph, 278, 315
Strategic Petroleum Reserve, 251
Sub-prime mortgages, 349–350
Sudan, 316, 319
Suicide, 160
Sullivan, Andrew, 214–215
Supplementary Security Income (SSI), 260
Supply-side economics, 91–92
Supreme Court
on abortion, 142, 144–148
on campaign finance, 193–194, 200–201
on capital punishment, 181–182, 186, 187, 188
fighting words doctrine, 124
on gay rights, 170
on gun rights, 156, 157, 162–164
on race and civil rights, 117, 119, 121, 124–125
on religion, 206–207
on school choice, 133
on sentencing inequality, 238
on taxation, 89
on teaching evolution, 225
on terrorist detainees, 35
Surveillance
Patriot Act and, 21–23
Protect America Act and, 23–24
Susskind, Lawrence, 220
Swift Boat Veterans, 194
Swine flue, 19
Syria, 325, 327

T

Taiwan, 316, 318
Takeyh, Ray, 304
Taliban, 32, 38, 41, 284, 292–294
Tanner, Michael, 265
Task Force on National Health Care Reform, 61–62
Tauzin, Bill, 67
Taxation, 88–102
capital gains tax, 94
earmarking and, 99
estate tax, 94
fairness in, 90, 100
federal deficit and, 91, 93, 94–95, 97–98
globalization and tax havens, 342–343
Great Recession bailouts and, 356
illegal immigrants and, 77
income tax, 89
reform proposals, 100
Social Security and, 107, 109–110
Tax freedom day, 93
Tax Reform Act (1986), 91
Taylor, Jerry, 48
Temporary Assistance for Needy Families (TANF), 260, 263, 264, 265
Temporary Worker Program, 79
Tenet, George, 32
Terrorism
cyber attacks, 27
dealing with terrorists, 31–44
homeland security and, 15–30
Iran and, 298–305
in Israel and Palestine, 324, 325–326, 327
public opinion on, 5
racial profiling and, 123–124
torture policies and, 33–36, 38–40
Think tanks, 10
Thomas, Clarence, 125, 238
Thompson, Tommy, 262
Thorpe, Kenneth, 61
Tiananmen Square, 311
Tibet, 316–317
Torture, 33–36, 38–40
Townsend Act, 89
Transportation Security Agency (TSA), 17
Trickle down economics, 91–92
Troubled Asset Relief Program (TARP), 350

U

Umbrella groups, 6–7
Unemployment compensation, 260
United Autoworkers Union, 354
United Nations
  Intergovernmental Panel on Climate
    Change, 47, 48, 55
  International Atomic Energy Agency,
    299, 301, 304
  Kyoto conference, 50
United States v. Miller, 156
Universal Declaration of Human
  Rights, 36
University of California at Los Angeles
  Center for American Integration and
  Development, 77
Urban Institute, 94, 184, 266–267
Urrea, Luis Alberto, 76
USA Patriot Act, 21–23
U.S. Border Patrol, 76, 78, 79
U.S. Census Bureau, 3, 120, 259
U.S. Chamber of Commerce, 6
U.S. Customs and Border Protection
  (CBP), 17, 232
  in homeland security, 16
U.S. Department of Defense, 272, 275, 276
U.S. Department of Education, 135,
  136, 139
U.S. Department of Transportation, 54

V

Values
  capital punishment and, 183–184
  family, 211–213
  political, 9–10
  public opinion on, 5, 10
Van Cleave, Philip, 161
Veterans Administration, 67
Vick, Charles, 306
Vietnam War, 284, 289
Virginia Tech University massacre,
  158, 161
Von Braun, Werner, 220
Voting Rights Act, 118, 119, 122
Voucher programs, 133–136

W

Wagoner, G. Richard, Jr., 60
Wallace, George, 117
Wall Street reforms, 356
Walt, Stephen, 328–331, 332

War on drugs, 231–243
  cost of, 232, 238
  effectiveness of, 234, 238–240
  jail overcrowding from, 234, 236–238
  marijuana legalization and, 233, 234,
    235–236
War on terror, 32–44
Warren, Rick, 212, 213
War Resisters League, 277–278
Washington Consensus, 337–338
Washington Post, 54
Watergate scandal, 193
Watson, James, 220
Waxman, Henry, 224–225
Welfare programs, 258–270. *See also*
    Medicare; Social Security
  block grants in, 264, 265, 267
  government spending on, 97
  illegal immigrants and, 77
  individual responsibility and, 261–262
  Obama on, 98
  public opinion on, 260
  reform of, 262–267
  welfare to work model in, 263–267
Welfare Reform Act, 262–267
"What If Roe Fell? The State by State
    Consequences," 151
Wheeler, Daniel, 274–275
White House Office of National Drug
    Control Policy, 232, 235, 240
*Who Are We? The Challenge to America's
    Identity* (Huntington), 84
Wind farms, 252
Winkler, Adam, 163
Winter, Donald, 276
Woodward, Bob, 33
World Bank, 342
World Public Opinion, 344
World Trade, 344
World Trade Organization, 313
World War II, 90

Y

Yergin, Daniel, 254
Yoo, John, 39

Z

Zelman v. Simmons-Harris, 133
Zoellick, Robert, 319
Zubaydah, Abu, 39
Z visas, 80, 81

CPSIA information can be obtained at www.ICGtesting.com
Printed in the USA
LVOW10s0747210216

476039LV00020B/500/P